THE TITANIC

Wyn Craig Wade is a clinical psychologist, associated with Michigan State University, who has done special work in the field of disaster behavior. He is a member of the Titanic Historical Society.

THE TITANIC

End of a Dream

Wyn Craig Wade

FUTURA PUBLICATIONS
LIMITED

A Futura Book

First published in Great Britain by
George Weidenfeld & Nicholson Limited 1980

First Futura Publications edition in 1980

Copyright © Wyn Craig Wade 1979

ISBN: 0 7088 1864 1

Printed in the United States of America

Futura Publications Limited,
110 Warner Road,
Camberwell, London SE5

In memory of my father,

WYNDEL C. WADE

1921–1976

Contents

Acknowledgments

I would like to express my gratitude first and foremost to the Titanic Historical Society, Inc. (Box 53, Indian Orchard, Massachusetts 01151), an organization that has done more than any other to consolidate historical material on the disaster and to keep the memory of the R.M.S. *Titanic* alive. Through the courtesy of the THS, I was able to obtain prints, photographs, and information otherwise unavailable. And since the THS maintains the most up-to-date records of data on the disaster, the statistics on accommodations, survivors and deceased in this book supersede those of previously published books. I am particularly grateful to Mr. Edward S. Kamuda, secretary of the THS, who answered my many questions, who critically read portions of the manuscript, and whose interesting correspondence kept me stimulated throughout the course of this book's preparation.

I am also indebted to those survivors of the disaster who contributed general recollections and answered specific questions. For special thanks, I would like to single out the late Dickinson H. Bishop, Mr. Frank J.W.

Goldsmith, and especially Mrs. Ruth M. Blanchard (née Becker). I am also grateful to the descendants of August E. Wennerstrom, who gave me access to their father's private papers.

An equal debt is owed to the descendants of William Alden Smith, who illuminated my portrayal of the senator with numerous recollections and details. I would like to thank the late senator's daughter-in-law, Mrs. Marie McRae Temple; his granddaughter, Mrs. Marie Winner; and especially his warm and generous great-nephew, Mr. John Martin Huggett.

Several heads of manuscript repositories made my research particularly enjoyable and rewarding: Mr. Joseph Cherwinski, staff librarian of the Michigan Department of Education State Library; Ms. Mary Jo Pugh, reference archivist at the Alvin Bentley Historical Library; and especially Mr. F. J. Collins, reference librarian of the Michigan Room, Grand Rapids Public Library. I am also indebted to Mr. John C. Broderick, chief: Library of Congress, Manuscript Division; Mr. Gordon Olson, assistant director: Grand Rapids Public Museum; and Mr. George P. Perros, Legislative and Natural Resources Branch, General Services Administration: National Archives and Records Service (Washington, D.C.).

Other individuals supplied useful leads and supplementary information. Of these, I would like to thank Mr. LeRoy Barnett, reference archivist: Michigan Department of State, Michigan History Division (Lansing); Dr. Paul Bernstein, School of Social Sciences, University of California, Irvine; Mrs. Eslie E. Cann, Nevada Historical Society (Reno); Mr. Joseph Huebner, University of Notre Dame Library; Mr. Lee Montgomery Hutchins, Grand Rapids Historical Society; Mr. Ardie L. Kelly, The Mariners Museum (Newport News, Virginia); Mr. Bert Lindenfeld, managing editor of the *Her-*

ald-Palladium (St. Joseph, Michigan); Mr. Don Lynch, THS Advisory Board; Dr. William D. Rowley, Department of History, University of Nevada; Ms. Judith A. Schiff, chief research archivist: Yale University Library; Mr. Martin Schmitt, curator: Special Collections, University of Oregon Library; Mrs. James M. Sweedyk, THS member; and Mrs. Berenice E. Vanderburg of Dowagiac, Michigan.

I would like to acknowledge my indebtedness to the Alvin Bentley Historical Library, Grand Rapids Public Library, Grand Rapids Public Museum, and William Clements Library for allowing me to quote from material in their archives. Likewise I am grateful to the Yale University Library for permission to publish from the *Francis G. Newlands Collection;* and to Folkways Music Publishers, Inc., New York, New York, for permission to quote from Huddie Ledbetter's "De Titanic," collected and adapted by John A. Lomax and Alan Lomax, TRO © copyright 1936 and renewed 1964.

My deepest thanks to John Goodwin, Hal Landen, and Tony Lydgate who provided shelter, polemics, and regular periods of much-needed distraction. To my mother, who surrendered her dining room to boxes of research cards and typescript. And finally to Barbrie Ann, wife and wit, and to Derek Wyndel Wade, who loaned me his "President book."

Preface

Of all ships in history, the R.M.S. *Titanic* commands a mystique second only to Noah's Ark. In its day, the foundering of the *Titanic* was a twofold drama: One side of it was a shipwreck at sea; the other was society's response to it. The resulting composite of disaster at sea and upheaval ashore succeeded in generating a story of mythic proportions that has now survived seven decades.

In recent years, there has been an attempt to escape the *Titanic*'s mystique by focusing on the shipwreck and belittling the response ashore, which—so it has been argued—is full of pointless emotionalism and only obfuscates the "facts" of the wreck. The "facts" of the wreck are these: In 1912, 1,522 people drowned or froze to death after the palatial liner in which they were sailing was sufficiently mismanaged as to take a nose dive to the bottom of the North Atlantic. The disaster ashore was quite another matter. In the United States alone, it was a crisis of spiritual and political values sufficient to color indelibly the course of the twentieth century. I find it inseparable from the story of the shipwreck. And I do not believe that an appreciation of one precludes an understanding of the other. In this book, therefore, I have tried to give equal attention to the two special facets that make up this epic catastrophe.

A few words on method are in order. Part Two, the longest section of this book, recounts the United States Senate's formal inquiry into the disaster, in which the *Titanic*'s surviving owner, officers, seamen, and passengers gave sworn testimony, beginning just five days after the ship had foundered. For the most part, I have relied on the U.S. government's printed transcript of the testimony from these hearings. In 1912, however, there were no practical recording devices, and 80 percent of the testimony was taken down in shorthand by a single, harried but valiant young stenographer named William McKinstry. Consequently, various mistakes, typographical errors, and American misunderstandings of clipped British accents ("forty" for "fourteen") entered the record. I have corrected these on the basis of newspaper accounts of the investigation and also on the basis of information contained in the private papers of Senator William Alden Smith of Michigan, chairman of the Senate inquiry.

Throughout my recounting of the *Titanic* investigation, the reader will find italicized flashbacks describing the uncanny events that took place in the middle of the North Atlantic on the night of April 14, 1912. The content of these flashbacks is taken exclusively from survivors' accounts of the wreck; hence, a majority of it is in quotes. The process used to construct these flashbacks represents—like the *Titanic* herself—a wonder of twentieth-century technology; in this case, a computer.

Survivor data came from various sources. A sizable block represents testimony and affidavits given to the

U.S. Senate inquiry. The data also includes survivor accounts published soon after the disaster, carefully selected newspaper interviews, material from private archives, letters sent to the President, interview transcripts, and material supplied by survivors living today who were kind enough to share their recollections with me. For the flashbacks, all this data was programmed to be retrievable by such coded areas as time, place (deck), lifeboat number, etc. Naturally, the perceptions of nearly two hundred people entail inconsistencies, and while these are fewer near the onset of the disaster, they increase geometrically as the point of the *Titanic*'s foundering is approached. (At the end, one minute seemed to some survivors like one minute; to others, it seemed like a lifetime.) I was therefore obliged to make numerous decisions, and not everyone will agree with my conclusions. Occasionally, my decisions were made easier by the living survivors, who graciously answered some of the most absurd and trivial questions put to them in sixty-seven years. Nevertheless, the final decisions were mine and I take full responsibility for them.

This book focuses on the American inquiry held immediately after the shipwreck, an investigation as misunderstood as it has been misrepresented. Accordingly, I have not relied on the rehash of the accident conducted in London by the British Board of Trade—that is, with two exceptions. The British testimony was used for the flashback in Chapter 8 relating Officer Lightoller's conversation with the *Titanic*'s captain shortly before the collision; and also for the goings-on aboard the *Californian* in Chapter 16.

There are no reconstructed conversations in this book. Everything in quotations is taken from published, archival, or private sources. Also, the body language of testifying witnesses and other individuals is not my own fabrication but reflects instead the impressions of numerous news reporters. A complete list of newspapers used, as well as other sources, may be found in the Bibliography.

W.C.W.

Prologue

Pilots of the Purple Twilight

In the spring of 1851, the graceful expanse of London's Hyde Park was packed with a congregation awaiting the event of the century. People from all over the world had assembled to witness the most spectacular trade show ever conceived. Never before in its history had London been so crowded. In spite of the size of the assembly, a respectful order was maintained, for the event was in many respects a religious festival. The temple about to be opened was a shrine to technological progress; the exhibition itself, an unparalleled celebration of the Victorian spirit.

The International Exhibition of Industrial Arts, thereafter called the Great Exhibition, had been the dream of Britain's Prince Consort. The colossus that housed it, the Crystal Palace, was a monstrous greenhouse constructed by master engineers Messrs. Brunel and Russell from a prize-winning design sketched by a gardener on blotting paper. Beyond sheer size, part of its sensation lay in its paradoxical union of steel and glass—England's most durable and most transient products. Even the temple of the exhibition was a testament to the wily ingenuity of this new age of industrialism, an age of paradox materialized.

Inside the gaping, sunlit dome of the palace, spectators could thrill at exhibits of machinery, commerce, culture, and decoration from every civilized nation on earth. Special events took place on the hour. One could witness the operation of the world's largest steam engine, a frightening, hissing behemoth whose sole function was to entertain and awe, or listen to the heavenly thunder of simultaneous performances of the palace's four pipe organs. The Edinburgh *Review* quickly realized that the Great Exhibition was a monolithic symbol of the age that bore it, a "living scroll of human progress, inscribed with every successive conquest of man's intellect."

It was completely appropriate that England should have housed and hosted this spectacle. Great Britain's freedom from the fractious political revolutions of the previous century had permitted her to dole out moderate social reforms on a gradual basis, thus preserving her solidarity. This unity—combined with her islanders' ingenuity and abundance of coal—permitted her to win first place in harvesting the newly growing scientific wonders.

By 1840, the steam engine alone had transformed England's industries into sprawling, whirling beehives, and no part of her culture was free from the dizzying influence of a leaping technology. The telephone was invented; then came mechanical refrigeration. Faraday's electrical dynamo, then Edison's electric light permitted factories to stay open all night long, swelling production to a hitherto unimaginable degree. The turbine and internal combustion engines appeared. In time, the sorcery of Marconi's wireless telegraphy. As Winston

Churchill recalled, "Every morning when the world woke up, some new machinery had started running. Every night while the world had supper, it was running still."

As a result of new products and processes, the nation grew healthier and the population began to increase. From the time of the Great Exhibition until only twenty years later, the population of England rose by 5 million. The new technology continued to grow proportionally.

It was as exhilarating as only the experience of seemingly limitless growth can be. The feeling at a mass level spawned an optimism childlike in its innocence and adultlike in its determination. It was a consuming optimism, oblivious to the complications that would ensue once the natural limits of growth appeared. Furthermore, the breadth and immediate consequences of the growth were so unprecedented that people could no longer rely on past solutions for their problems. Instead, novel solutions had to be invented almost on a daily basis. In time, the need to keep eyes affixed on the future buoyed optimism even further, for the future had become tautly intertwined with the Victorian Dream.

Briefly stated, the Dream held that God's laws had been more precisely defined by the new sciences—those of social Darwinism as well as physical technology. Then came a teleological step: Man's condition had been improved by the new technology *so that* he could better meet the more perfectly manifested laws of God. Man's purpose, therefore, was to dedicate himself to applied technology and increased materialism; then, in time, the Kingdom of Heaven would be realized on earth. It was an admirably parsimonious formula for making Heaven and nature sing. Alfred Lord Tennyson's personal vision of the Victorian Dream accurately vented the aspirations of an entire age:

For I dipped into the future, far as human eye could see,
Saw the Vision of the world, and all the wonders that would be;
Saw the heavens fill with commerce, argosies of magic sails,
Pilots of the purple twilight, dropping down with costly bales; . . .

Not in vain the distance beacons. Forward, forward let us range;
Let the peoples spin forever down the ringing grooves of change.

When Prince Albert announced his plans for a Great Exhibition, the didactic function of the event had been very dear to his Prussian heart. The mammoth trade show would offer, he said, "A living picture of the . . . development at which mankind has arrived and a new starting point from which all nations will be able to direct their future exertions." In other words, the exhibition would be the first organized step toward the realization of the Dream. The British public could familiarize itself with the new technology, and nations of the world could share their respective achievements. Two weeks before the opening of the Crystal Palace, the Prince Consort's growing enthusiasm was more than he could contain. "We are living," he said, "at a period of most wonderful transition which tends rapidly to accomplish that great end to which indeed all history points—the realization of the unity of mankind."

Indeed the opening of the Crystal Palace, on the morning of May 1, 1851, was a nineteenth-century glimpse of Eden. As the London *Times* observed, it was "the first morning since the creation of the world that all people from all parts of the world" had assembled "and done a common act." The climax of the morning was the pageantry of the opening ceremony, at which Queen Victoria officiated. For his adoring wife, the Prince Consort had achieved, even if only momentarily, the role of the greatest queen bee in Christendom. The *Times* continued:

> In a building that could easily have accommodated twice as many, twenty-five thousand persons, so it is computed, were arranged in order round the throne of our SOVEREIGN. Around them, amidst them, and over their heads was displayed all that is useful or beautiful in nature or in art. Above them rose a glittering arch far more lofty and spacious than the vaults of even our noblest cathedrals. . . . Some were most reminded of that day when all ages and climes shall be gathered round the throne of their MAKER.

It was as if Dante's passionate vision of the heavenly throng in the form of a rose had been materialized before thousands who had never even heard of Dante. No matter that the materialized version was crassly vulgar. No matter that the combined choirs had sung out of tune and the four palace organs had been poorly synchronized. What a splendid noise it all had made! The Golden Age of Victorianism had arrived, and the palace and its exhibition constituted an event speculators would itch to duplicate down through and beyond the course of the nineteenth century.

Twenty years later saw the beginning of an era that lasted until 1912. The Second Industrial Revolution was born, and English-speaking nations achieved intellectual and social domination of the world. Progress in all its myriad forms continued, the Dream remained intact, but something was amiss. Advances in science had trammeled former religious beliefs, substituting a new credo in which people actually grew skeptical of anything that could not be proved in a laboratory. More and more, the real became equated with the material. The Dream slowly crystallized into a goal of mere acquisition.

There were sounds of warning, but these were voices crying in the wilderness. Thomas Carlyle reviled the "Gospel of Mammon," in which Hell—once a terror of the Infinite—had been reduced to simply "not making enough money." Matthew Arnold attempted in earnest to clarify the Dream. "It is in making endless additions to itself," he wrote, "in the endless expansion of its powers, in endless growth in wisdom and beauty, that the spirit of the human race finds its ideal." But expansion, he warned, had to be inward as well as outward. Trust in external expansion and "faith in machinery" were, to Arnold, "the most besetting danger to the Age."

The mood and momentum of the late Victorian era could not be tempered. By the end of the century, the Golden Age had become, in Mark Twain's famous epithet, the Gilded Age, a period of pronounced money-grubbing and ludicrous ostentation, when "excess" and "success" became interchangeable. Whereas England had reigned supreme over the Golden Age of Victorianism, she had to share the honor of ruling over the Gilded Age with a former colony.

In 1851, the contribution of the United States to the Great Exhibition had been embarrassingly deficient. *Punch* had noticed that the entire east end of the Crystal Palace had been set aside for the Americans, "but what was our astonishment, on arriving there, to find that their contribution to the world's industry consists as yet of a few wine-glasses, a square or two of soap, and a pair of salt cellars!" Even when a few more items were added, without a doubt the most interesting and influential "product" of the United States proved to be its minstrel show, which, like the palace's giant steam engine, went into gyrations on the hour.

After the Civil War, things were different. The United States' natural resources were swollen tenfold in the course of westward expansion and from the annexation of such territories as Hawaii, the Philippines, and Puerto Rico. Consequently, industrialization could proceed at a "glorious" rate. Railways stretched across the country, steel companies rose, and diverse, giant factories mushroomed overnight in the urban centers. As in England, the merchandising capitals of the United States began drawing in the rural population, and immigrants started flocking to her shores in hordes. In 1850, the population of New York City had been less than 700,000. By 1900, that number had grown to over 3 million.

Postbellum legislation and the absence of income tax had made it possible for individuals to accumulate vast sums of capital. Business trusts were formed by so-called captains of industry that quickly grew into huge amalgamations with far-reaching power. In 1901, J.P. Morgan organized U.S. Steel, which owned as much land as the states of Massachusetts, Vermont, and Rhode Island combined. "The public has nothing to fear from the bigness of a great corporation," said George W. Perkins, one of Morgan's directors. "No true American is afraid of a thing because it is big." In spite of his rhetoric, rough-riding Teddy Roosevelt preferred speaking softly to the trusts rather than wielding the big stick. There had been only three millionaires in the United States in 1861. By the dawn of the new century, there were over 3,800 of them. These captains of industry easily overran their European rivals and quickly made up for lost time. One of their dearest ambitions was that of acquiring all the trappings that signified affluence in Europe. Accordingly, they began building multiple mansions for themselves and ransacking Europe for treasures with which to stock them.

The foibles of the nouveau riche were not exclusively characteristic of America's moneyed classes. Since it was theoretically possible for any self-made man of the United States to equal the achievements of millionaires, the aspirations of the Gilded Age permeated the poorest levels of American society and spread to the naïve immigrants who daily arrived at the docks as well. Eventually, everyone grew fond of appraising things in terms of size, number and expense, and the popular press began writing in unbridled superlatives. To Holbrook Jackson, it was the inevitable "outcome of a society which had absorbed a bigger idea of life than it knew how to put into practice."

By 1907, the time was finally right for the elite of the Gilded Age to duplicate the stunning achievement of the Crystal Palace and the Great Exhibition of 1851. The new project was an amicably concerted effort between rich American capitalists and British manager-industrialists. Marriages between wealthy Americans and aristocratic Britons had already been in vogue for some time, and this new venture—comprising a union between Yankee greenbacks and British traditions—seemed assured of success where previous attempts had failed. Like the Prince Consort's vision, the monstrous size of the new palace required an enormous investment of capital. Even with a huge foundation in American stocks and securities, $6 million worth of 4.5 debentures had to be marketed and, in fact, were sold with relative ease. Like the former palace, the new one promised to be a spectacle of the latest in scientific technology—a colossal showcase featuring "all that is useful or beautiful in nature or in art." Once again it would provide a splendid setting for the celebration of the spirit of its age—presided over by Anglo-Americans, of course.

A crucial difference figured between the new and the old projects, however. Whereas the former venture had united the civilized nations in resplendent triumph, the new one was to unite the world in an appalling tragedy. The Gilded Age had pushed the Victorian Dream well beyond anything imaginable in 1851. The new palace had been designed to float.

PART ONE

Midnight Crossing

There was peace, and the world had an even tenor to its ways. True enough, from time to time there were events—catastrophes—like the Johnstown Flood, the San Francisco Earthquake, or floods in China—which stirred the sleeping world, but not enough to keep it from resuming its slumber. It seems to me that the disaster about to occur was the event, which not only made the world rub its eyes and awake, but woke it with a start, keeping it moving at a rapidly accelerating pace ever since, with less and less peace, satisfaction and happiness. . . . To my mind the world of today awoke April 15, 1912.

—John B. Thayer, *Titanic* passenger

1

Monster Ship

The twentieth century had just begun. At the end of its first decade, the youngest of a spectacular pair of oceangoing twins stood towering on the ways in Slip Number 3 at the Belfast shipyards of Harland and Wolff, Ltd. An observer at the construction site recorded:

> For months and months in that monstrous iron enclosure there was nothing that had the faintest likeness to a ship; only something that might have been the iron scaffolding for the naves of half-a-dozen cathedrals laid end to end. . . . at last the skeleton within the scaffolding began to take shape, at the sight of which men held their breaths. It was the shape of a ship, a ship so monstrous and unthinkable that it towered there over the buildings and dwarfed the very mountains by the water. . . . A rudder as big as a giant elm tree, bosses and bearings of propellers the size of windmills—everything was on a nightmare scale; and underneath the iron foundations of the cathedral floor men were laying, on concrete

> beds, pavements of oak and great cradles of timber and iron and sliding ways of pitch pine to support the bulk of the monster when she was moved, every square inch of the pavement surface bearing a weight of more than two tons. Twenty tons of tallow were spread upon the ways, and hydraulic rams and triggers built and fixed against the bulk of the ship so that, when the moment came, the waters she was to conquer should thrust her finally from the earth.

In front of the immense steel scaffolding, a small black sign with simple white lettering announced:

WHITE STAR
ROYAL MAIL STEAMER
"TITANIC"

Without question, she was the apogee of the steamship, the apotheosis of the ocean liner. Coincidentally, her sea birth would formally launch the epoch of the twentieth century.

The North Atlantic Ferry was already big business. Many years had passed since Dr. Johnson had compared crossing the Atlantic Ocean with "going to prison with the chance of being drowned." The new technology, which had entered shipbuilding as a direct consequence of the Great Exhibition, had changed all that. A dynamic transformation had been wrought in the form of ships. Light wooden hulls had given way to ponderous steel; graceful sails had been usurped by belching smokestacks. By 1900, the form of ships was still in transition, intensified now by the changing demands and the spirited competition of travel merchants who scrambled for the expanded and highly lucrative markets of exportation and emigrant traffic. As emigrants literally eddied in steady streams toward various, distant Lands of Golden Opportunity, steamship companies became corporations, and the big ships grew even bigger.

Eventually, for commercial magnates and the nomad rich, North Atlantic crossings became necessities. To all appearances, the most formidable ocean on the globe had been reduced to a common highway, traversable almost as swiftly, safely, and surely more agreeably than the continent.

For many years, a prosperous and friendly business relationship existed between shipbuilders Harland and Wolff of Belfast and the Ismay and Imrie Company (White Star Line) of Liverpool. Under White Star contracts, Harland and Wolff worked on a "cost plus" basis. The firm was free to build a ship along its own specifications, barring no expense; then a fixed percentage was added to the total expenditure which constituted its fee. It was agreed that Harland and Wolff would never build a ship for White Star's competitors, nor would White Star contract with rival shipbuilders.

Some of the most striking innovations in the North Atlantic liner had resulted from the collaboration of Thomas Henry Ismay, stolid Victorian businessman and cofounder of White Star, and Sir Edward Harland, Yorkshireman and marine-engineering prodigy. Their first triumph—the *Oceanic,* completed in 1871—was perhaps their greatest. This beautiful ship served as a paragon for subsequent White Star liners and influenced the course of rival shipbuilding as well. Ismay, always mindful of his customers' comfort, had realized that the more people felt at home, the less they experienced a terror of the sea and all of its nauseating consequences. On the *Oceanic,* therefore, he had moved all first-class accommodations, as well as the popular grand saloon, from the traditional stern to amidships, where vibration from the engines was minimal. He also had the roofs of the deck houses built out, the resulting space serving as lanes for passenger exercise—promenades, they were called. Additional innovations on subsequent White Star liners included running water in cabins, electric bells to signal stewards, and other minute but welcome conveniences.

Harland and Wolff were considered the highest-priced and most painstaking shipbuilders in Europe. The laborers were paid on a high scale, and a long waiting list was maintained for craftsmen who hoped to join the firm. Called "builders in the most complete sense of the word," Harland and Wolff were equipped and skilled in all facets of shipbuilding and few components were subcontracted. Consequently, a wonderful integrity permeated the whole of their creations. Moreover, beginning with the *Oceanic*, Sir Edward Harland had managed to streamline the hull of the passenger steamship, substituting for its tubby profile the long, sleek lines of a racing yacht—remarkable, considering the scale of the vessels.

Thomas Ismay died in 1899, Sir Edward Harland in 1895. White Star was taken over by Ismay's thirty-eight-year-old son, Bruce, who had always been employed in the family firm. Lord W. J. Pirrie, who had worked his way from boilermaker to baronet, succeeded to the chairmanship of Harland and Wolff.

By 1901, virtually all the major ocean lines were in serious trouble. Competition from new steamship companies, notably from Germany, and a slackening of emigrant traffic were followed by a ruinous rate war. If that were not enough, passenger lists were more and more taken up by nouveau riche tourists—mostly Americans—who demanded increased luxury as well as speed. Both demands required a staggering increase in the outlay of capital for building new ships.

At this point, American financier J. Pierpont Morgan

took a giant's step into the picture. Many Americans had been sizing up the financial prospects of overseas markets. Morgan, having bought up American railroads, coal, and steel, had now set his sights on something bigger—the Atlantic Ocean. Shortly after the U.S. Steel merger, a shipping magnate had asked him if it were possible to bring the various North Atlantic steamships under one ownership. "It ought to be," was Morgan's laconic reply. Now, at the height of the rate war, Morgan proposed an immense international trust, predominantly American-owned, which would essentially control all major European shiplines. Morgan's plan was to end the rate war simply by crushing competition and then fix prices at a comfortable profit.

British citizens were immediately unnerved by the clout inherent in Morgan's proposal. In the midst of this fear and outrage, the leaders of the Cunard Line succeeded in getting a loan of more than £2 million from the British government. The result was Cunard's *Lusitania* and *Mauretania*—the largest steamships the world had ever seen and which, by virtue of the latest design in marine turbine engines and hulls shaped by the Royal Navy, quickly captured the Blue Riband for speed across the North Atlantic. After this dazzling achievement by its archrival; White Star's viability as a competitor with Cunard depended on its submission to the Morgan scheme.

Bruce Ismay was understandably in a quandary over whether or not to part with his father's business. With the exception of augmenting the passenger over the freight service, Bruce's conduct as the new manager of White Star indicated that he intended to pursue Thomas Ismay's original plans and principles. Lord Pirrie of Harland and Wolff, however, was highly enthusiastic and argued convincingly for the Morgan plan. For Pirrie, it meant quite simply that Harland and Wolff would be able to expand its production by supplying ships to the entire International Mercantile Marine, the proposed moniker of the new monster trust.

Eventually, Morgan made an offer that the White Star shareholders couldn't refuse; he offered to buy them out at ten times the value of the line's earnings for the year 1900, which, owing to the traffic of the Boer War, had seen an exceedingly handsome profit. Assuaging the deepest British fears, Morgan further assured that ships of the White Star Line, though principally American-owned, would remain reserves of the British navy and could be completely taken over by it in the event of war.

The deal between International Mercantile Marine (IMM) and the White Star Line was finalized in December 1902. It was agreed that Bruce Ismay would remain the White Star's managing director and chairman.

Shortly afterward, the IMM nearly collapsed. A "rich man's panic" had led to a wave of selling rather than buying stocks. Morgan had oversubscribed the trust to the tune of $150 million; this, the panic, and the haste with which IMM had been formed put the trust in a perilous position. It was like an acute case of financial indigestion, and Andrew Carnegie howled with delight that Morgan had finally found something too big to swallow. Morgan beseeched Bruce Ismay to become president of IMM, an offer which, in spite of its enticing salary, Ismay did not want. For one thing, it would mean spending a lot of time in New York, and Ismay—a dedicated introvert—disliked being away from home. In the interest of his father's line, however, he acceded and became president of the giant trust. With Ismay's meticulous organization, plus the appointment of an energetic and resourceful American, P.A.S. Franklin, as vice-president, the International Mercantile Marine lumbered to its feet in four years.

One evening in 1907, the chauffeured limousine of Mr. and Mrs. J. Bruce Ismay arrived at the elegant Belgravia residence of Lord and Lady Pirrie for dinner. Both Ismay and Pirrie had been standing by patiently for the past several years while opulent German liners and the speedy Cunard sisters had steadily eaten away at their profits. With the solidarity of the new trust, the relationship with Franklin in the New York IMM office, and the immense capital standing behind them, the two men were finally in a position to parry their competitors right off the lanes. After dinner, over their cigars and port, Ismay and Pirrie began computing figures and sketching designs—doodles that would culminate in the *Titanic.*

Manager and builder were equally agreed that it would be foolish to attempt to compete with the speed of the new Cunard liners. Much more promising would be a gigantic pair of twin ships, later followed by a third, which could guarantee a week's crossing on a regular schedule without fail and under spectacular conditions. The new ships would not only exceed the Cunard sisters half again in gross tonnage, able to accommodate much more freight and passengers, but they would exemplify safety and economy of operation as well. Always in the end, though, these ships would be the last word in comfort and elegance. Incorporating the devices and decorations of a dozen different past and present civilizations, they would have something for everyone. They would be stunningly complete, seagoing exhibitions. More space would be devoted to the accommodation of deluxe travel than had ever before been possible—a promise that could not fail to seduce the wealthiest of North Atlantic passengers.

IMM had never floated very successfully, and its securities hadn't enjoyed much favor. The huge ships were exactly the kind of attraction the giant trust needed, and J.P. Morgan, who loved big things anyway, enthusiastically endorsed the proposal as soon as he heard it. Major alterations of the Belfast shipyards ensued.

The two vessels were going to be built side by side in twin slips. This necessitated clearing out space that had formerly served for the construction of three ocean liners. The flooring of the two new slips was piled throughout, reinforced with steel, and then covered with concrete four feet six inches thick in some places. Harland and Wolff expanded the size of its steel plating shop and constructed new joiner and boiler shops. When it came time for the ships to be "fitted out" (the postlaunch process of completing superstructures and interiors), the firm would be ready with a 200-ton floating crane, specially purchased for the occasion.

Most commercial interests regarded the new venture with admiration. The staid British journal *The Shipbuilder* saw the project as rightful heir to the Victorian Dream, noting that "the design and construction of these two magnificent ships would have been beyond the range of possibility but for the cumulative experience available from earlier efforts during the past half-century." Technological journals devoted to modern applications of electricity, engineering, radio, refrigeration, and the like were in accord in praising how all the latest technological advances were being ingeniously consolidated in the realization of such mammoth and splendid vessels.

There were a few detractors. The editors of the *Economist* growled at shipbuilders attempting to "lick creation." Their objections were entirely pragmatic: These "monster ships" would "involve too great a concentration of life and wealth in a single bottom"; moreover, the size of the ships surpassed existing underwriters' ability to insure them. Seaman and novelist

Joseph Conrad would become the most eloquent opponent of the "big-ship movement." Increase in the size of ships, said Conrad, was not progress: "If it were, elephantiasis, which causes a man's legs to become as large as tree-trunks, would be a sort of progress, whereas it is nothing but a disease, and a very ugly disease at that."

Complaints arose on the other side of the Atlantic as well. There wasn't a single dock on the American continent large enough to berth the twin giants. P.A.S. Franklin, with Morgan and the IMM behind him, prevailed upon the New York Harbor Board to permit two of the Chelsea piers to be extended 100 feet into the North (Hudson) River. The American journal *Engineering News* raised two questions about the request: Whether it would be safe for navigation in the North River, given its decreased width from pier extensions; and whether New York taxpayers could equitably be asked to shoulder the cost. The *News* continued:

> If these latest marine monsters represented a real advance in economic transportation—if their construction meant cheaper transatlantic freight transportation—it would probably be easy to answer both of these questions in the affirmative. We know of no reason, however, to suppose that these huge vessels really represent any such advance. They are built primarily to furnish the acme of luxury in passenger travel. Instead of representing an advance in economic transportation, they probably represent an actual increase in cost. . . . The curious thing is that [the IMM and White Star] should undertake to build these huge vessels without knowing beforehand where they could dock them at this end of their voyage. As the companies have put themselves into a dilemma, it would seem to be a good plan to let them find their own way out.

In the end, they did find their own way out. The power wielded by the House of Morgan was sufficient to convince New York authorities to extend the docks at city expense.

The first of the twin "marine monsters," the *Olympic*, sailed on her maiden voyage to New York on May 31, 1911. On the very same day, the R.M.S. *Titanic* was launched from Slip Number 3. White Star had chartered a Lancashire-and-Yorkshire turbine steamer to speed its guests across the Irish Channel to witness the launching at Belfast. Thirteen minutes after noon, "in the presence of an enormous company," the *Titanic* was launched, taking only sixty-two seconds from the time the hydraulic triggers were released to the time she smacked the Irish Sea. J.P. Morgan, who had traveled from London specially for the event, inspected the deck area of the *Titanic* where his own private suite would be constructed.

Leaving aboard the *Olympic* was J. Bruce Ismay, making the maiden voyage for the express purpose of determining any shortcomings in her appointments or general functions. Overall, Ismay thought the *Olympic* "a marvel," but several things couldn't pass his impeccable standards. The deck space on the *Olympic*, for example, Ismay thought excessive; it would be more feasible (as well as lucrative) to transform a good deal of the *Titanic*'s deck space into additional passenger accommodations. Furthermore, the reception room adjacent to the first-class dining saloon proved to be more popular than anticipated; it was considerably crowded after lunch, tea, and dinner. On the *Titanic*, the size of the reception room—as well as the number of seatings in the dining saloon—could stand expansion. The forward end of the vast promenade on A Deck, which adjoined a number of choice staterooms, wasn't sufficiently protected from the elements to suit first-class sensitivities. On the *Titanic,* this area should be completely enclosed with clever sliding windows. Other necessities were even more trivial; mattresses should be firmer, cigar holders were needed in the first-class bathrooms, and an electric potato peeler was required to keep up the pace of the crew's galley.

All of these observations introduced alterations in the blueprints of the *Titanic*—changes directed by experience and that seemed insignificant at first. The cumulative effort of the alterations would be such that the sister ships could no longer be regarded as *true* twins.

Following enactment of Ismay's recommendations, further "improvements" were made on the *Titanic.* Groupings of wicker furniture were replaced with handsome hardwood. Luxurious carpeting was fitted throughout the grand saloon. Since the saloon's reception room had proved so popular, another one was specially created to adjoin the first-class à la carte restaurant, where wealthy passengers could hold their own private dinner parties. Two extraordinary first-class suites were constructed on B Deck, one of them earmarked for J.P. Morgan. In addition to sumptuous stateroom accommodations, these suites featured a spacious parlor and a private promenade deck with half-timbered walls of the Elizabethan period; at the height of the season, the suites went for $4,350 one way. On the same deck, a Parisian boulevard was added to the restaurant, giving the satisfying illusion of a French sidewalk café. Space was found to accommodate 163 more passengers than on the *Olympic,* the majority of them in first class.

Ultimately, the *Titanic* became the *Olympic* perfected. Outweighing her sister by over a thousand tons, the *Titanic* became the largest and most luxurious vessel afloat. In newspapers on both sides of the Atlantic, she was soon being called "the Wonder Ship," "the Last

Word in Luxury," "the Unsinkable Ship," "the Biggest Ship in the World." On Wall Street, she was nicknamed "the Millionaires' Special."

In March, a great deal of overtime was worked by Harland and Wolff in order to have the *Titanic* ready for April. Following her sea trials, the *Titanic* loomed into Southampton Harbor on April 3, 1912. Her maiden voyage had been set for a week later. Docked at her special berth, she rose out of the water, according to one spectator, "like the side of a cliff." Her breathtaking enormity dominated all first impressions. She was nearly 900 feet long. The American journal *Power* advised its readers to run one-sixth of a mile "to appreciate in a small way the vastness" of the ship. From top to bottom, her nine steel decks made her equivalent in height to an eleven-story building. Atop her spangling superstructure, four gigantic funnels—22 feet in diameter—rose 62 feet above the casings; twin locomotives could drive through one of these funnels with plenty of room to spare. Fifty feet above the funnels, the aerials of her wireless swung suspended between two tall, exquisitely streamlined masts. A total of 3 million rivets (1,200 tons of them) had gone into her gleaming hull. Her three huge anchors represented a combined weight of 31 tons. Her 101-ton rudder, which had to be cast in six separate pieces by the Darlington Forge Company, was the height of a large house.

But statistics were overshadowed by the sheer aesthetic satisfaction in a ship of such incredible scale. Even considering her eventual fate, officials today at Harland and Wolff believe the *Titanic* to have been, without a doubt, the firm's finest achievement. "She was my last baby," said Alexander Carlisle, the chief designer of the ship, who by that time had been promoted to the position of master builder of the King's Royal

Navy. The hull of the *Titanic*, encircled by the bright golden band that had always identified steamships of the Ismay Line, still conveyed the gracefulness of Sir Edward Harland's original racing lines: sharpness of stem, slenderness, a high cutaway counter, and extraordinary length. "So perfect are her proportions," wrote *The Shipbuilder*, "that it is well-nigh impossible for the inexperienced to grasp her magnitude except when seen alongside another vessel." Her external form embraced the best of nineteenth-century traditions, while internally and on every account, she was a genuinc palace—a wedding of technology and convenience unique to the new century. The *Titanic* was a perfect realization of the juncture between two eras.

In the bowels of the ship was an awesome power plant, capable of moving the 46,000-ton vessel through the water with a combined strength of over 50,000 horses and a speed well over twenty-three knots. It could also supply power for evaporation and refrigeration plants; four passenger elevators; a fifty-phone switchboard; a five-kilowatt Marconi station; several hundred individual heating units; a gymnasium complete with all the latest electrical exercise devices from Wiesbaden; eight electric cargo cranes of a combined lifting weight of eighteen tons; numerous pumps, motors, and winches; and several ultramodern kitchens equipped with mechanical slicing, peeling, mincing, whisking, warming, and freezing machines. The latest model in water-tube ovens turned out the "very highest class of Vienna table bread."

The power plant was sectioned into a thoughtful arrangement of sixteen watertight compartments, divided by fifteen transverse steel bulkheads. Advertisements assured that "any two main compartments may be flooded without in any way involving the safety of the ship." In the unlikely event of an emergency, watertight doors would clutch down like sluggish guillotine blades, sealing the portals of every compartment. These doors could be operated all at once, electrically, from the bridge, or individually either by the action of a crewman or by the presence of water on the floor of a compartment, which would lift a float connected to the mechanical action. The watertight bulkheads extended from the cellular double bottom of the ship to five decks above, forward and aft; amidships, the bulkheads extended to the fourth deck above. In both cases, the extensions rose well above the waterline. On the passenger decks, the doors of the bulkheads required closing by stewards equipped with special keys. So ingenious was the entire system that *The Shipbuilder* pronounced the vessel "practically unsinkable," a phrase which, in less than two weeks, would become a haunting epitaph.

Full advantage of the gigantic proportions of the ship had been taken to provide passenger accommodations of unprecedented spaciousness and luxury. Amidships, the topmost five decks were allocated to a potential 735 first-class passengers. Amidships forward, the middle three decks could accommodate an additional 674 individuals traveling second class. These passengers could avail themselves of elegant dining saloons, lounges, smoking rooms, and libraries of various period designs.

The commodious grand saloon had concealed lighting behind its windows of cathedral-gray glass, giving the pleasant illusion of perpetual sunlight; as one admirer observed, "the effect is naturalness itself." The revamped reception room adjoining this palatial dining hall was simply splendid. The siren song of its advertising had been specially voiced to entice the American ear:

> . . . Upon a dark richly carpeted cloth which will further emphasize the delicacy and refinement of the paneling and act as a foil to the light dresses of the ladies, this company will assemble, the apotheosis, surely, of oceangoing luxury and comfort. What more appropriate setting than this dignified Jacobean room, redolent of the time when the Pilgrim Fathers set forth from Plymouth on their rude bark to brave the perils of the deep!

First-class passengers could also enjoy the gymnasium, the first swimming pool ever put on a ship, a regulation squash racket court, and ethereal palm verandas. A Turkish bath, complete with gilded cooling rooms and a masseuse, had been installed to meet the latest whim of plutocrats who had recently discovered the Middle East. According to *Engineering*, all of these pleasantries would "introduce acceptable varieties to life on board ship, which in the past has proved so monotonous to many passengers." The *Titanic*'s elite passengers would certainly not find the voyage monotonous.

The ship boasted other novel features. A special crane and compartment could load and store motorcars. (The self-starter had just been invented, and Henry Ford was turning out a new automobile every ninety-three minutes of the working day.) On the *Titanic*, the traditional "sick bay" had been transformed into a radiant hospital, completely equipped with a modern operating room. Space was found in the ship's vast refrigerated holds for mineral water and fresh-cut flowers. Barber shops with automated shampoo and drying appliances were available for all classes. A well-equipped darkroom permitted amateur photographers to develop their own pictures.

Third-class passengers were located aft on the middle three decks and forward and aft on the lowest passenger deck. The *Titanic* carried accommodations for a potential 1,024 third-class passengers, the vast majority of whom would be emigrants. Depending on the booking, portions of third-class quarters could be converted to freight and baggage compartments—a tradition lingering from the days when "steerage" had meant exactly that. In the 1860s, for example, it had been legal to transport human beings to one shore and then carry cattle in the same quarters on the trip back. One shipboard notice of that era adjured first- and second-class passengers "not to throw money or eatables to the steerage passengers, thereby creating disturbance and annoyance." Things had now changed considerably. American immigration laws still made it mandatory to keep gates securely locked between third-class and other passengers; the policy was intended to limit the spread of infectious diseases. But the same laws also demanded that British vessels provide 20 percent more third-class space per capita than what their own Board of Trade required. (Differences between American law and the Board of Trade would eventually become a scorching issue.)

Passengers traveling steerage aboard the *Titanic* would find very little to complain about. In fact, many steerage passengers would find accommodations more comfortable and food more plentiful than what they had known in their workaday lives.

2

Bon Voyage

The departure from Southampton of a new passenger liner was always a special event, and on the morning of April 10, the hotels were packed with prospective voyagers. Spectators and well-wishers queued along the docks and watched the extended preparations for the *Titanic*'s maiden voyage. Already the ship had experienced her share of problems.

The famous 1912 coal strike was on (memorialized in D.H. Lawrence's *The Daughter-in-Law*), and a number of North Atlantic vessels were short of fuel. The *Titanic* needed 650 tons of coal per day to feed her 159 hungry furnaces. Consequently, the White Star Line canceled the trips of its *Oceanic* and *Adriatic*, likewise scheduled for New York, and transferred the passengers as well as coal to the *Titanic*. White Star also bought coal from the holds of other ships—the small liner *New York*, for one. Other vessels, such as the *Philadelphia*, canceled scheduled departures, transferring many of their passengers also to the *Titanic*. While some of these transferred passengers thrilled at the prospects of sailing on the new leviathan, others had mixed emotions. For one thing, a booking in second class on the *Titanic* was more expensive than what they had paid for first-class accommodations aboard the canceled liners. Others felt strong foreboding at sailing on the maiden voyage of such an unusual and gargantuan ship. These were told by the purser, with documented consistency, that there was "nothing to worry about, since the *Titanic*'s watertight compartments would keep the ship afloat indefinitely."

Problems also rose among the *Titanic*'s crew. The *Olympic* had been laid up for repairs following a minor collision in the channel with a cruiser, the H.M.S. *Hawke.* The subsequent inquiry held the White Star Line responsible, concluding that the considerable wake of the *Olympic* had sucked the helpless little cruiser right off her course and into the hull of the giant liner. In any event, the chief officer of the *Olympic*, H.T. Wilde, was transferred to the *Titanic*, causing a reshuffle in the hierarchy of the other officers as well as in their respective duties. Crewmen had also come from the *Olympic*, as well as from the canceled *Oceanic*, a vessel considerably smaller than the new White Star giants. The *Oceanic*'s crew couldn't get over the vastness of the *Titanic.* For Second Officer Lightoller, an expert seaman of considerable experience, it took two weeks before he could confidently find his way from one part of the ship to another by the shortest route. More men came from the canceled *New York*—even smaller than the *Oceanic*—whose coal was now in the *Titanic*'s stokeholds. Many of the *New York* crewmen had joined the *Titanic* as late as the morning of sailing day, and although their impressions are unrecorded, they must have been befuddled.

In short, the men were a diverse group—what one dissatisfied passenger would later call "a scratch crew"—unfamiliar with the ship, their duties, and with each other. By Wednesday morning, a full complement of crewmen had been secured: 397 officers, engineers, seamen, firemen, trimmers, and greasers. There were an additional 518 employees aboard solely to run the ship's hotel: stewards and stewardesses, cooks, butchers and bakers, musicians, medical personnel, waiters, porters, cashiers, bellboys, scullions, and janitors. In all, a total of 915 people were employed for the *Titanic*'s maiden voyage—enough to fill to capacity many of the other liners offering passenger service to New York in 1912.

The *Titanic*'s passengers were well in excess of this number. In spite of the problems, the White Star Line had managed to achieve a very respectable booking. For one thing, the *Olympic* had provided wonderful advertising, and Manager Ismay had let it be known that the *Titanic* promised so much more than her sister ship. Earlier in the year, Ismay had been in New York City. Leaving there on the *Olympic* on January 24 in order to make the *Titanic*'s maiden voyage, Ismay had told the press that the *Titanic* was even more splendid, possessing in fact "one hundred more first-class cabins than the *Olympic*."

Everything had worked out well. The titled and the moneyed aristocracy had flocked to the *Titanic* as though it were a Gilded Age "happening." According to one passenger, there was "the artist of renown and the great writer, the man of theatrical success, the giant in the world of trade, the aide of a nation's president, the prettiest woman, the woman who represented social prominence, the indispensable American girl, presidents of railways, aristocrats of Europe—all these to add to the glory of the first sea-crossing of the biggest ship." To *The New York Times*, the first-class passenger list resembled the audience at a gala theater premiere. One important passenger was missing; although he had planned on making the maiden voyage, J.P. Morgan was prevented from doing so because of illness.

First-class accommodations had been filled to 46 percent of capacity, a total of 337 passengers. The majority of these were captains of industry, a mere dozen of them collectively worth $191 million. All of the first-class passengers were estimated to represent well over $500 million. Among them were Mr. and Mrs. Dickinson H. Bishop of southwestern Michigan. Dick Bishop was heir to the Round Oak Stove Company and his wife, Helen, was a belle of Sturgis society. The handsome couple had been married just the previous November and were honeymooning all over southern Europe, awaiting completion of their $200,000 home. After an extended tour of Egypt and Algiers, the Bishops had concluded their honeymoon in Cherbourg. They could have departed for the States on an earlier vessel, but they waited specifically "to come across on this monster new passenger boat."

Second cabin numbered 271 passengers or 40 percent of capacity. A number of them had been first-class passengers transferred from ships that had been canceled. Among them were Mrs. Allen O. Becker and her three children. Mrs. Becker was the wife of an American minister, then serving as a missionary in charge of an orphanage in Gunter, India. The Beckers' youngest child, two-year-old Richard, had come down with a serious illness, and they had been advised that the only hope for him lay in hospital facilities in the United States. On her own, Mrs. Becker had gamely made the journey from India to England with Richard and his two sisters—Ruth, age twelve, and Marion, age four. After dutifully trooping the three children through Westminster Abbey and Madame Tussaud's ("since they might never get another chance to see these places"), Mrs. Becker booked second-class passage on the *Titanic.* She was looking forward to the voyage, a respite from her exertions across the continent and through the hallmarks of London.

Steerage was booked to 70 percent of capacity—712 passengers in all. They were nearly all emigrants: English, Irish, French, Polish, Scandinavian, Italian, and a surprising number of people from the Middle and Far East. Steerage, in fact, was a microcosm of the globe. Among the third-class passengers were Mr. and Mrs. Frank Goldsmith and their nine-year-old son, Franky. Mr. Goldsmith, age thirty-three, was a machinist and had lived with his wife and son in Strood, County Kent, England. His wife's parents, Mr. and Mrs. Henry Brown, had already immigrated to Detroit and had consistently requested the Goldsmiths to come and join them. Mr. Goldsmith had been reluctant, however; he had heard stories of the insufferable conditions of steerage passengers and was not about to put his family through such an ordeal. But the *Titanic* had changed his mind. Inspecting the enormous White Star liner, Mr. Goldsmith had been delighted to discover that steerage accommodations were as fine as first class had been twenty years earlier. With a little help from his in-laws, he had been able to book passage and was looking forward to the voyage.

Traveling with the Goldsmiths was a mature and adventurous fifteen-year-old, Alfred Rush. His was a common situation for America-bound emigrants. Rush's brother, Charles, lived next door to the Goldsmiths' relations in Detroit. Hearing that the Goldsmiths were coming over on the *Titanic,* Charles immediately sent Alfred's fare and arranged for him to accompany them. Young Alfred, who had been living alone with his mother in London, was ecstatic about the prospects of seeking his fortune in the New World.

The *Titanic* was scheduled to leave at noon. Shortly before departure, her second and third class were on official display. A reporter from the London *Standard* was on board and was surprised at the complete absence of crowding anywhere in the ship. Fully an hour before she sailed, the gymnasium—managed by a professional gymnast—was in action. On one side, a lady was having a mechanical camel ride and recalling the delights of the pyramids. In another corner, two young men were racing on German bicycle machines that registered speed and distance. In the squash racket court, two Americans were "fighting the battle of their lives."

Passengers and visitors were exploring every nook and cranny. People were aimlessly and enthusiastically riding the elevators. They called at the post office, where the postmaster spoke on the responsibilities of delivering mail to the other side of the ocean. The kitchens were an extremely popular attraction, and the tasks their electrical appliances accomplished were simply amazing. Everyone touched the woodwork, the draperies, and the five grand pianos.

On the bridge, the spirited musicians of the ship's string band had switched from American ragtime to a medley from Oskar Straus's *The Chocolate Soldier*. Their executions of ragtime and operetta were equally delightful. Within hearing distance, serious-minded folk were examining the bindings of the books in the second-class library or learning wonderful things about the electrical buttons which controlled the 46,378-ton vessel, commanded its three steam engines, and marshaled its impressive array of services.

In steerage, the luncheon dining service and cutlery were being displayed. From the gleaming glasses to the textured linen, it was a sight fit for a king.

Shortly before noon, bells rang out, and the *Titanic*'s triple-throated voice ("the largest whistles ever made") boomed across the bay, thrilling inhabitants for miles around. The little tugs gave a snort, and the giant liner began gliding into the bay. Ashore, crowds were cheering from the midst of a forest of waving handkerchiefs; then, sudden silence. The *Titanic*'s triple-expansion steam engines had been set into motion.

The crowds had almost resumed cheering when, with "a series of reports like those of a revolver," the steel hawsers mooring the nearby steamer *New York* snapped in two and went coiling into the air. Spectators shrieked and scurried out of their path. The *New York* had been pulled by the tremendous force of the *Titanic*'s suction and was drifting right into the course of the giant liner. For a moment a collision seemed likely, a repeat of the *Olympic*'s accident with the *Hawke*. Captain E.J. Smith, commodore of the White Star Line and commander of the *Titanic*'s maiden voyage, immediately ordered a touch ahead on the port engine; the wash from this quick motion gently pushed the *New York* back. The monster ship was a whale rebuffing a dolphin with the flip of a fluke. Two tugs immediately drew aside and dragged the hapless *New York* back to her berth. Another example of the force of the *Titanic*'s suction would be revealed later when Southampton authorities discovered that a sunken barge had been dragged in the *Titanic*'s wake 800 yards across the harbor bottom.

Passengers had crowded along the ship's rail and watched the incident enthralled. It had, first of all, assured complete confidence in the *Titanic*'s able commander, "E.J." as he was called. But it had also emphatically demonstrated the power of this leviathan of progress on which they now held special places of honor. After leaving Southampton, the *Titanic* made two more passenger and mail stops—one at Cherbourg, France, and the other at Queenstown, Ireland. At one of these stops, Ship's Steward Seaton Blake dashed off a waggish postcard and mailed it to Mayor Gaynor of New York City. On one side of the card was a lithograph of the *Titanic*, steaming triumphantly through the waves. On the other side was:

> Guess you had better chain up the Statue of Liberty to a skyscraper in Fifth Avenue or to the ramparts of Fort Pitt, as I "reckon and calculate" that the foundations are liable to be swallowed up by the wash of this "octopus" from the other side, which sucked up from its moorings like a barnacle the Yankee Doodle liner *New York* yesterday in Southampton docks. Better instruct the United States fleet to tow her in, or I guess New York will be wiped off the map.

In all, the *Titanic* carried 1,320 passengers, which, with the crew and victual department, made a total of 2,235 people aboard. She also carried 3,435 bags of mail, 6,000 tons of coal, enough provisions to feed a town for several weeks, and 900 tons of baggage and "first-class package freight." For the most part, the freight was consigned to New York dealers for their spring display of European fashions and contained everything from diamonds and fine Calais lace to cases of live orchids and continental wines. In maritime history, the *Titanic*'s sumptuous accommodations and wealth, her beauty and bounty, had never before been seen. All this, plus her human cargo representing a panorama of civilization in its social extremes, would never be equaled. The image of this superb gigantic vessel racing over the North Atlantic to her chilling rendezvous at midnight would create the first enduring archetype wrought by the twentieth century.

The weather was excellent, and following the incident with the *New York*, every sign looked auspicious.

In New York City, readers of the *Times* were told to prepare to view a ship four blocks long, considerably broader than the height of the Singer Building. In London, the *Standard* proclaimed, "To the battle of Transatlantic passenger service, the *Titanic* adds a new and important factor, of value to the aristocracy and the plutocracy attracted from East to West and West to East . . . in the fight during the coming season, there will be a scent of battle all the way from New York to the shores of this country—a contest of sea giants in which the *Titanic* will doubtless take high honours."

3

The Backwash Ashore

Monday: April 15, 1912

At the offices of *The New York Times,* wireless bulletins received on the eighteenth floor were dropped down a shaft in a wooden box attached to a rope. When special news came in, the signal from the dispatcher was a vigorous shaking of the rope against the metal walls of the shaft. At midnight, things were quiet. Teddy Roosevelt had already won the presidential primary over Taft in Pennsylvania, and the paper had just been put to bed. At 1:20 A.M., the wireless box crashed down, and the rope thrashed violently at the shaft. The copy boy leaped at the scrap of paper, read the message, and promptly rushed it to managing editor Carr Van Anda. Van Anda scowled at it. The bulletin—from Cape Race, Newfoundland—stated:

> Sunday night, April 14 (AP). At 10:25 o'clock tonight the White Star Line steamship *Titanic* called

> "CQD" to the Marconi station here, and reported having struck an iceberg. The steamer said that immediate assistance was required.

Van Anda made phone calls to the White Star office and to *Times* correspondents in Halifax and Montreal and found out more information. Apparently at 11:25 the previous evening, the Canadian Allen Line had received the same bulletin and forwarded it to their steamer the *Virginian*, in transit from Halifax to Liverpool. The *Virginian* had altered course and was racing to the scene of the accident—41°46′ North, 50°14′ West. The *Titanic*'s sister ship, the *Olympic*, as well as another White Star liner, the *Baltic*, had already received the distress calls and were also rushing to the position. The *Virginian* later wired back that she had picked up what might be the last SOS signal from the *Titanic*. This message, received at 12:27, had been blurred and "cut off with great suddenness." Shortly after sending this information, the *Virginian* passed out of range of shore stations.

There was barely enough time for the *Times* to change the morning-mail edition. The Taft-Roosevelt campaign was pushed to the side, and the new, three-column, front-page headlines fairly screamed:

NEW LINER TITANIC HITS AN ICEBERG;
SINKING BY THE BOW AT MIDNIGHT;
WOMEN PUT OFF IN LIFEBOATS;
LAST WIRELESS AT 12:27 A.M. BLURRED.

Van Anda included details from prior bulletins on the *Titanic*'s passenger list. The names—available for first class only—were indeed impressive: Major Archibald Butt, President Taft's friend and White House aide; Mr.

and Mrs. John Jacob Astor; Mr. and Mrs. Isidor Straus; Mr. Benjamin Guggenheim; F.D. Millet, the artist and president of the Consolidated Academy of Rome; Charles M. Hayes, president of the Grand Trunk Railway; and J. Bruce Ismay, president of IMM and chairman of the White Star Line. Extra editions with longer passenger lists would be ground out all morning, engrossing families gathered at the breakfast tables of the nation.

It had been an odd season for ice in the North Atlantic; the fact was well known. A relatively warm winter had caused a great number of bergs to break off from the Greenland coast. Drifting northward, these had eventually hit the Labrador current and shifted in a southerly direction. Eventually, they had littered the steamship lanes off the Grand Banks of Newfoundland. On Sunday the fourteenth, the Cunard liner *Carmania* had arrived in New York reporting that she had navigated through vast ice jams off the Grand Banks. The *Niagara*, also now docked in New York, had even collided with the ice. Two holes had been knocked in her bottom, but she had managed to limp safely into port.

In the past, other ships had experienced severe blows with icebergs and survived. The *Arizona*, a famous case in 1879, the Donaldson liner *Concordia* in 1899, the *Kron-Prinz Wilhelm* in 1907, and the *Columbia* just the past year had all rammed headlong into North Atlantic bergs. Their bows had all crumpled like tinfoil, but the forward bulkheads had held and they were relatively unharmed. Indeed, there was no case in current recollection of any sizable ship going down as a result of an iceberg. Of course there had been many ships "missing without trace" prior to Marconi's wonderful invention; a number of these were believed to have had a fatal meeting with an iceberg. The famous Collins liner *Pacific*, lost in 1856, was a case in point. The only clue in this instance had been a note in a bottle, washed ashore on the west coast of the Hebrides:

> On board the *Pacific* from Liverpool to N.Y.—Ship going down. Confusion on board—Icebergs around us on every side. I know I cannot escape. I write the cause of our loss that friends may not live in suspense. The finder will please get it published.
> WM. GRAHAM.

Several hours after the first edition of the *Times* went out, Van Anda sat chewing on his cigar and puzzling over the available wireless messages. Mindful of the usefulness of history in the art of prediction, he had asked the *Times*'s morgue searched for any statistics on the *Titanic* and for items on ships that had encountered icebergs in the recent past. Although seemingly incredible, the cold facts suggested to Van Anda that there could be only one reason why the *Titanic*'s wireless had ceased abruptly after a flurry of distress calls. Playing a considerable hunch, Van Anda sent the city edition to press; it reported that the great liner had sunk. Van Anda then went about methodically arranging how the *Times* would handle subsequent confirmations. He had given *The New York Times* an international lead in the twentieth century it would never have to forfeit.

By 10:30 A.M., P.A.S. Franklin, vice-president and general manager of IMM, was beleaguered with visitors and phone calls. Franklin was extremely optimistic. Hearsay that the *Titanic* had foundered was preposterous. The cessation of the ship's signals was only due to a malfunction in the wireless or "atmospheric interference." White Star and IMM were "perfectly satisfied" that there was no cause for alarm regarding the safety of the passengers. After all, the *Titanic* was "practically unsinkable."

Soon the air was charged with wireless signals. The Marconi apparatus had become the newest toy of Americans, and unlike the situation in England, there were no laws regulating its use. Around noon, a message came from Cape Race via Montreal; it was the message everyone was waiting for, particularly the IMM and White Star. "ALL TITANIC PASSENGERS SAFE," reported the bulletin, "THE VIRGINIAN TOWING THE LINER INTO HALIFAX." Vice-President Franklin leaped into action with the kind of service that White Star customers had come to expect. A fast train was chartered to Halifax so that the *Titanic*'s passengers could be conveyed back to New York. White Star also cabled the Canadian government's Department of Marine and chartered a ship to meet and aid the *Titanic* into port; the steamer *Lady Laurier* immediately began coaling up. The train set out to Halifax with a number of passengers' relatives aboard, including the daughter of Mr. and Mrs. Straus. About this same time, a number of people—including Congressman J.A. Hughes of West Virginia, whose daughter was aboard the ship—received telegrams from the White Star's New York office: "ALL TITANIC'S PASSENGERS SAFE," read the dispatch, "LINER BEING TOWED TO HALIFAX."

The conservative *New York Sun*'s banner line was most reassuring: "ALL SAVED FROM TITANIC AFTER COLLISION." (The *Sun* also included an item disparaging the *Times*'s irresponsible report of the ship's foundering.) The *Worcester Evening Gazette* and *Baltimore Sun* printed similar banner lines assuring the liner's safety. *The Wall Street Journal* editorialized on the lesson of the "near-disaster":

> The gravity of the damage to the *Titanic* is apparent, but the important point is that she did not sink. Her watertight bulkheads were really watertight. The

forward part of the ship must have been flooded, and it is not surprising to hear that she was down by the head. Nevertheless, she kept afloat after an experience which might well appall the stoutest heart. . . . Man is the weakest and most formidable creature on the earth. His physical means of protection and offence are trifling. But his brain has within it the spirit of the divine, and he overcomes natural obstacles by thought, which is incomparably the greatest force in the universe.

By 2:00 P.M. another message was "reported from mid-ocean." From the Cunard liner *Carpathia* came word that "all passengers of liner *Titanic* safely transferred to this ship and S.S. *Parisian.* Sea calm. *Titanic* being towed by Allen liner *Virginian* to port." Since the *Carpathia* and *Parisian* were apparently steaming to New York, the special train en route to Halifax was stopped and began heading back to the city. Passengers were unnerved, but were quickly put at ease. It was only a change of plans. The *Titanic*'s passengers were going to arrive in New York after all.

England and the Continent were dependent on dispatches via Atlantic cable from the United States. They had heard from the *Olympic* that she was rushing to the scene of the accident; shortly afterward, the *Titanic*'s sister ship had moved out of range. After an initial panic, England was now considerably calmer. In the morning, the reinsurance rate on the *Titanic*'s cargo had risen to 50 and then 60 percent. After reassuring news from the *Virginian* about the *Titanic* being towed to Halifax, the rates had dropped from 50, to 45, and then finally to 25 percent. In the United States, IMM stock followed a comparable pattern.

John Wanamaker, the department store tycoon, had succeeded in installing the most powerful commercial radio stations in each of his Philadelphia and New York stores. It was officially announced that the stations would simply facilitate communication between the two stores. Actually, it was an ingenious stroke of advertising. Wanamaker's presented their wireless operators most visibly to the public, replete in headphones and tapping away in rapt concentration. The novelty had drawn additional hundreds of curious customers into the stores. The New York station had just hired a bright and aspiring twenty-one-year-old lad for the post of operator; in time his name would become nearly synonymous with broadcasting. At 4:35 P.M. atop New York Wanamaker's, young David Sarnoff received the message he later said "brought radio to the front . . . and incidentally, me." Amid static and jamming by amateur operators, Sarnoff managed to detect the faint signals of the *Olympic*, 1,400 miles out at sea. The message was concise, authoritative, and meticulously telegraphed: The *Titanic* had foundered at 12:47 A.M., New York time, and her only known survivors, about 675 people, were aboard the *Carpathia* now bound for New York.

The news was appalling. The paragon of the world's technology, the floating palace, the "practically unsinkable" ship had indisputably sunk. Nearly two thousand of her passengers and crew had gone to an unspeakable death. It was the worst marine disaster in history. It was a wholesale slaughter of innocents too unthinkable for its age. In after years, nothing—no event in any of the wars of the twentieth century—would equal the *Titanic* disaster in the breadth of its shock or the depth of its pathos.

"I have often been asked what were my emotions at that moment," David Sarnoff later said. "I doubt if I felt at all during the seventy-two hours after the news came. I gave the information to the press associations and newspapers at once, and it was as if bedlam had been let loose. Telephones were whirring, extras were being cried, crowds were gathering around newspaper bulletin boards."

The IMM–White Star office was now besieged by phone calls from across the nation and by telegrams from all over the world. By nightfall, a steady stream of visitors began trooping to the office. P.A.S. Franklin, deliriously optimistic, would hold on to the end. The *Carpathia*, said Franklin, may have *some* of the *Titanic*'s passengers, but no word had yet been received from the *Parisian*, which might also have had time to rescue passengers. Reporters steadily badgered Franklin and finally got the admission that there had been "a terrible loss of life." As the hours wore on and Franklin wore out, he finally admitted: "We are hopeful that the rumors which have reached us by telegraph from Halifax that there are passengers aboard the *Virginian* and the *Parisian* will prove to be true, and that these vessels will turn up with some of the passengers. It is the loss of life that makes this thing so awful. We can replace the money loss but not the lives of those who went down."

By midnight, Franklin was weeping. "I thought her unsinkable," he sobbed, "and I based my opinion on the best expert advice. I do not understand it."

By 1:00 in the morning, a crowd that would eventually number 4,000 people gathered in Times Square around the newspaper's bulletin, handwritten in 1912 by an agile scribe. There were several other bulletins available, but the *Times* had proved itself the only news source worthy of popular trust. Soon, the first list of survivors began trickling in: Mrs. Rose Abbott, Mrs. Edward W. Appleton, Mrs. John Jacob Astor—mostly women. Could it be that all those captains of industry had gone down with the captain of the ship?

At this time, far out at sea, novelist Theodore Dreiser was aboard the *Kroonland*. He had planned on taking the *Titanic* back home but opted instead to wait for the less expensive Red Star liner. He and several other passengers had just learned about the loss of the *Titanic.* "With one accord," Dreiser wrote, "we went to the rail and looked out into the blackness ahead. The swish of the sea could be heard and the intermittent moo of the fog-horn. . . . I went to my berth thinking of the pain and terrors of those doomed two thousand, a great rage in my heart against the fortuity of life."

The crowds had grown considerably larger at the White Star office. People were openly weeping and policemen had been called out. The worried face of young Vincent Astor, the multimillionaire's son, suddenly appeared and disappeared into the office. He soon came out, his face burried in his hands and sobbing. A Mr. Hoyt, whose brother and sister-in-law were on the ill-fated liner, forced his way into the office and also came right back out. "My God," cried Hoyt to the crowd, "we are ruined. They are all lost!"

Tuesday: April 16

The size and starkness of the morning headlines left no room for doubt. Many people, particularly in Europe and the western states, had retired the previous evening and had slept through the extras that screamed the news of the tragedy. The world now awoke only to be stunned into mourning. Nearly every major city on the globe had lost citizens in the disaster. No event in history had ever caused such a worldwide exchange of condolences. It was particularly hard on Anglo-Americans, who bore the brunt of the disaster. The *Titanic* had taken more than human lives; in her plunge to the deepest abyss of the North Atlantic, she had also taken the self-confidence and complacency of the English-speaking world. As the day progressed, grief would turn into outrage over facile issues as the two nations that had created the ship sought to fix responsibility for her loss.

At 8:00 in the morning, the IMM–White Star office was packed. By 10:00, the crowds gathered outside became so huge and unruly that the policemen on duty requested reinforcements. Two mounted policemen and six armed regulars quickly arrived; more would be called out all day long. As soon as an official of the line would appear at the main door, voices welled up in bitter reproach. "You lied to us!" they shouted. "Why did you lie to us?" Inside a grim procession was in progress. Friends and relations of passengers stood in long lines, awaiting their turns at the clerks' windows. As an individual's turn came, he would ask about a particular passenger. There would then be either "a grief-stricken cry" or "a joyous expression of relief." The former outnumbered the latter, two to one.

Officials were still making half-hearted suggestions that the *Parisian* and *Virginian* may have managed to save a handful of people clinging to wreckage. The suggestion only made things worse. The degree to which minds had become unhinged was revealed when the idea that maybe some fortunates had managed to find refuge atop the icebergs was voiced and quickly gained the endorsement of everyone jammed in the office. To allay all concerns, White Star announced that it was chartering a cable steamship, the *Mackay-Bennett* lying at Halifax, to search the disaster area and stay hovering about for days, even weeks if necessary. When the steamer finally departed, the day after, she would be carrying aboard a chaplain, an embalmer, a cargo of pine caskets, and a hold full of crushed ice.

Things were nearly as hectic at the offices of Cunard Line, which owned the rescue ship *Carpathia*. Everyone was trying to learn if friends or relations were aboard.

Names of first- and second-class survivors were still in the process of being sent. Press releases of the names had been fragmentary, misspelled, and misleading. A recent report had changed the number of survivors from 675 to 855. Every error renewed individual hopes, and of the possibly 300 names still unaccounted for, claims had been staked by the loved ones of over a thousand passengers.

C.P. Sumner, general manager of the Cunard Line, was as frantic as the crowd crammed in his office. He had sent five wireless messages to Captain Rostron of the *Carpathia*—all of them unanswered. The problem was presumed to lie in the *Carpathia*'s wireless set, which had a range of only 200 miles. Names sent from that ship had been dispatched earlier via the powerful set aboard the *Olympic*, which had now turned back on her original course and was also out of range.

President William Howard Taft ordered two fast scout cruisers, the *Chester* and *Salem*, to set out from Virginia, search the entire disaster area, and then make radio contact with the *Carpathia* and obtain a complete list of survivors. The President's order was not motivated entirely by humanitarian considerations. Taft was enormously worried about the fate of Archie Butt—his friend, adviser, and White House aide.

Names of survivors continued to trickle in till evening. Speculation was rife, however, as to who had definitely been lost. The morning newspapers were willing to concede certainty to the death of only one individual—Captain E.J. Smith. The New York papers published an interview with the captain obtained in 1907, an occasion when he had been successful in bringing a White Star liner, the *Adriatic*, to New York on her maiden voyage. E.J.'s impressions of the five years past were now tragically ironic and alarmingly prophetic of details yet to be learned:

> When anyone asks how I can best describe my experience in nearly forty years at sea, I merely say, uneventful. Of course there have been winter gales, and storms and fog and the like, but in all my experience, I have never been in any accident of any sort worth speaking about. I have seen but one vessel in distress in all my years at sea—a brig, the crew of which was taken off in a small boat in charge of my third officer. I never saw a wreck and never have been wrecked, nor was I ever in any predicament that threatened to end in disaster of any sort. You see, I am not very good material for a story.

E.J. was now excellent material for a story. His photograph, in fact, made the front pages of newspapers across the nation.

Among other places of activity in New York City, the office of Lloyds Underwriters witnessed its share of "exciting scenes." The *Economist* had been right; there hadn't been enough capital in two continents to insure the *Titanic* anywhere near adequately. The loss had been enormous and was then being conservatively estimated at over $12 million. The diamonds alone had been insured for $5 million. One passenger had taken out a $600,000 policy on a string of pearls. Looking up Wall Street from Water Street, one's vision was so obscured by flags at half-mast that one could not see the lower portion of Trinity Church. One broker told a reporter, "I cannot discuss it. See all those flags at half-mast; action *must* be taken by the government!" After an initial shock, Wall Street was now in a slow process of recovery. After all, a dozen of the financial pillars of the nation had been felled in a single swoop. Fortunately, as facts revealed, John Jacob Astor's holdings had been predominantly in real estate and not in stock.

In England, following the false reassurance of the previous day, Britons looking at their morning papers were shocked senseless. J.P. Alexander of Manchester, a member of Parliament, read the headlines and dropped dead. Southampton, where a majority of the crew lived, was a scene of relentless despair. By afternoon, Britain's sorrow would be partially mollified by anger. The *Chronicle* asked that an inquiry be made into the source of the falsely optimistic news. "Never again," it exploded, "must there be such an orgy of falsehood as raged in America on this occasion." (Taft and his attorney general were already urging Congress to hasten work on legislation controlling the use of the wireless.) Another British editor asked, "Who uttered these false tidings, and with what motives? Were they the rapid, reckless concoctions of American reporters, each bent on piecing out of half-intelligible fragments and rumors a telling, sensational story? Or, still more sinister conjecture, were they the deliberate concoctions of astute businessmen concerned to influence rates of reinsurance?" However pronounced Britain's outrage, it would pall before the fury growing in the United States.

It began with the fact that so little information was available during the day. American newspapers were forced to feature interviews with naval experts and marine engineers. Their opinions, though poignant, were not calculated to ease public distress. Stanley Bowdle, marine engineer, characterized the loss of life on the *Titanic* as "a sacrifice to degenerate luxury." Floating palaces like the White Star liner, said Bowdle, were "degenerate in size, foolish in enjoyment, and criminal in speed." Admiral Dewey, the hero of Manila, was quoted in the *Washington Post.* "I think that every passenger who crosses the North Atlantic takes his life in his hands every time," said Dewey. "For myself, I would rather go around the world in a well-equipped man-of-war than make a trip across the North Atlantic in a transatlantic vessel. The greed for money-making is so great that it is with the sincerest regret that I observe that human lives are never taken into consideration."

Naval constructor Robert Stocker looked into the *Titanic*'s specifications, evaluated the time the ship had stayed afloat, and offered a disturbing conclusion. "The *Titanic*," said Stocker, "must have been making full speed ahead when she collided with the iceberg and evidently her compartments must have been sprung from bow to stern." Simultaneously, alarming news broke from the U.S. Hydrographic Office in Washington, D.C. The *Titanic* had actually been forewarned of the iceberg menace. On Sunday the fourteenth, the day of the collision, the *Titanic* had passed onto shore stations this wireless message from the *Amerika:*

> April 14. The German steamer *Amerika* reported by radio-telegraph passing two large icebergs in latitude 41 degrees 27 minutes; longitude, 50 degrees 8 minutes—*Titanic* (Br. S. S.).

The position was twelve and a half miles from where the *Titanic* had foundered. Later in the day, the French liner *La Touraine* told that she too had warned the *Titanic.* Her captain said that he had sent a wireless dispatch reporting the presence of the icebergs to E.J. Smith on April 12; Smith had wired back his thanks. Referring to the *Titanic*'s route, the Hydrographic Office determined that she had steamed well north of the southern boundary of the bergs reported to her. Unfortunately, this news would be misunderstood as meaning that the *Titanic* had been on the northern fast route instead of the southern safe route.

Admiral F.E. Chadwick sent a letter in time for the

late edition of the *New York Evening Post.* "The *Titanic,*" claimed Chadwick, "was lost by unwise navigation, by running at full speed, though so amply forewarned, into the dangerous situation, which might easily have been avoided. This is the fundamental sad, and one important fact. It accounts for everything." It was a terse summing up of the information known so far. Bad navigation accounted for the disaster—bad *British* navigation. Increasingly, the finger began pointing at Britain. The worst was yet to come.

As a result of Carr Van Anda's careful research, the morning edition of *The New York Times* revealed the reason why so few people aboard the *Titanic* had been rescued: The lifeboat accommodations on the ship were adequate for barely half the number aboard. This appalling fact was a consequence of antiquated statutes by the British Board of Trade, which had not kept up with the rapidly increasing size of ocean liners. Its rules stated that any vessel exceeding 15,000 tons should provide no less than sixteen boats. The *Titanic* had complied with this rule and even gone beyond it, providing four additional canvas-collapsible lifeboats; but the *Titanic* had also exceeded the specified tonnage three times over. Briefly, her boats could accommodate a maximum of 1,178 people—over a thousand short of the number aboard on the maiden voyage.

The shortage was hardly a secret. American naval authority E.K. Roden had written some time back in *The Navy* about the lack of lifeboats on the new White Star liners. "In order to insure the safety of passengers and crew in case a ship is afire or on the point of sinking," Roden had written, "common sense will tell us that boats enough are needed to accommodate every person on board." Alexander Carlisle, the chief designer of the *Titanic,* had originally proposed fifty lifeboats for the ship instead of the twenty she had carried, but the line had demurred. Carlisle, who never believed "there was such a thing as an unsinkable ship," now made a statement that achieved widespread quotation: "Until the Board of Trade and the governments of other countries require sufficient boats to be carried, shipowners cannot afford such extra top weight."

That even Captain Smith had been aware of the deficiency in lifeboats was asserted by a Glenn Marston of Chicago. Marston had recently returned from Europe with E.J. on the *Olympic.* Pointing out the small number of boats to the captain, Marston was purportedly told by Smith: "If this ship should strike a submerged derelict or iceberg that would cut through several of the watertight compartments we would not have enough boats or rafts aboard to take care of more than one-third of the passengers. The *Titanic,* too, is no better equipped."

The grim irony of the lifeboat issue was more than the United States could stand. The information had been read in a stunned state in the morning. By evening, it was grasped in a context of rage. "Old-fogyism!" was the clumsy epithet hurled at Britain's Board of Trade by the *San Francisco Examiner.* "What satire on modern civilization!" it exclaimed. "What a commentary on national progress!" Hugo P. Frear, naval contractor for the Union Iron Works, wrote a scathing attack in time for late editions. "If the *Titanic* had been under United States Government supervision," Frear maintained, "its owners would have been compelled to equip it with forty-two lifeboats at least. These forty-two lifeboats would have accommodated 2,367 persons. The trouble with the English regulations is that they are behind the times. They have not kept up with progress."

A number of newspaper editors, led by Morgan Gable

of the *Pittsburgh Gazette-Times,* demanded that the American Congress intervene in British practices. Admiral Dewey provided ample justification. "The most unfortunate part of the fatality," said Dewey, "is that most of the drowned are American, and we Americans surely have some rights in the matter. . . . I sincerely hope Congress will attend to the matter of caring for the lives of passengers aboard our transatlantic liners. Is there any need for a more striking example?"

Each of the two English-speaking nations had now placed blame of some kind on the other. The issue was "lawlessness," but the manner in which Britain and America took sides on the issue was significant. For the British, it was the lawlessness of America's "little people"—the amateur wireless operators and news reporters. For Americans, it was the lawlessness of Britain's "big people"—the shipping magnates and the Board of Trade. The comforts of causation had been discovered, and an intercontinental foofaraw permitted the two nations to avoid facing their fears temporarily. Soon, however, this issue would not so much demarcate the two countries as it would divide the countries within themselves. In the United States, the division would have significant political consequences.

The psychological turmoil in the United States may be seen in some of the more far-fetched attempts to grapple with the disaster. It was revealed that Mayn Clew Garnett, a fiction writer, had written a story remarkably foreshadowing the wreck of the *Titanic.* Garnett's story, "The White Ghost of Disaster," had been run off the presses at the time the *Titanic* was preparing for her maiden voyage and would eventually appear in the May issue of *Popular Magazine.* Garnett's tale concerned a giant 800-foot liner which struck an iceberg and foundered, losing half the people aboard because of an insufficient number of lifeboats. (Rumor intimated that the author had dreamed the story while returning home from Europe aboard the *Olympic*.) People then discovered another piece of fiction—an obscure one, but even more uncanny than Garnett's premonition. Morgan Robertson's 1898 novel, *Futility*, also featured an 800-foot liner named, of all things, the *Titan*. Robertson's plot was frighteningly similar to the *Titanic* disaster. Finally, Celia Thaxter's 1887 book of poetry was uncovered; her poem "A Tryst" told the same story.

It was almost as if the catastrophe was prophecy fulfilled—an inevitable toppling of Titans by an outraged Divine Power. As certainty and uncertainty alternated in the flux of public opinion, Britain and the United States continued their respective descents into a miasma of angry confusion. By late Tuesday evening, Henry B. Adams—the Washington historian for whom "chaos was the law of nature, order the dream of man"—wrote a letter to a friend. "The foundering of the *Titanic*," wrote Adams, "is serious, and strikes at confidence in our mechanical success. . . . By my blessed Virgin, it is awful! This *Titanic* blow shatters one's nerves. We can't grapple it."

In the midst of a national nervous breakdown, the "Problem Editor" of the *St. Louis Post-Dispatch* prescribed occupational therapy. He presented a large cartoon showing the sinking *Titanic*. A man, followed by a woman, was descending an improbable-looking staircase along the ship's side; at the foot of the stairs, in the water, another woman stood upright in a lifeboat and beckoned the man to take the last remaining seat beside her. The caption asked, "Should the bridegroom take the last seat with his bride, or surrender it to the unknown woman behind him, and make his bride a widow?" Readers were invited to submit their solutions "to this real-life problem" over the remainder of the week, which they did with avidity.

Wednesday: April 17

Morning news snuffed all hopes of any survivors beyond those already reported. The captain of the *Olympic* had sent the White Star Line a message via the *Cedric*. "Please allay rumors that the *Virginian* has any of the *Titanic*'s survivors," wired Captain Haddock. "I believe that the only survivors are on the *Carpathia*." Shortly thereafter, the *Virginian* came back into wireless range and confirmed; she had simply arrived too late to be of any help. The *Parisian* forwarded the same message and added a note of grisly finality. The weather had been quite cold, the captain of the *Parisian* reported: "Any persons who might have clung to wreckage undoubtedly would have died of exposure." Around noon, a predicted eclipse of the sun said all that anyone had to say.

One of the scout cruisers sent by President Taft had succeeded in making radio contact with the *Carpathia* and was now sending a list of surviving third-class passengers along with a complete list of those persons known dead. A bleary-eyed and exhausted David Sarnoff was still at his key, taking down names of the deceased. "This was worse than the other list had been," Sarnoff later reported, "heartbreaking in its finality—a death knell to hope." Revised rosters of survivors now appeared in the newspapers, followed by black-edged lists of those who had perished.

In the U.S. House of Representatives, Chaplain Reverend Henry Couden expressed the anguish of the nation and underscored "the widespread sympathy going out from thousands of hearts to those who are suffering the untold agony of suspense, hoping, it may be, against hope." Eight hastily written bills were introduced in the House on Wednesday—five of them devoted to legislation compelling ocean liners to carry enough lifeboats.

In the Senate, a more far-reaching movement was

under way. As soon as the session was called to order, Senator Smith of Michigan presented a tightly drafted resolution calling for a formal investigation of the causes leading to the wreck of the *Titanic*. The investigators would have the power to subpoena surviving officers and officials of the *Titanic*, as well as personnel from the White Star Line. The resolution was somewhat daring, as most of the people it intended to subpoena were citizens of a foreign power. It was no more than what the nation was demanding, however, and Secretary of Commerce and Labor Charles Nagel determined that, legally, those operating vessels using United States harbors were accountable for information bearing on the loss of American lives.

Other investigations were taking place. The Department of Justice announced that it had sent out detectives to "run down the men" who had sent the false news Monday regarding the *Titanic*'s alleged safety. Although wireless officials doubted it, the department believed that the outrage had been committed by people attempting to extend the time for reinsuring the ship's cargo. Marconi himself was in the United States (he had planned on taking the *Titanic* back to England), and he and his American station managers were conducting their own investigation.

Citizens were still bewildered over why an experienced seaman like Captain E.J. Smith had driven his ship at full speed into a danger of which he had been fully warned. Word from Canada suggested a sinister solution to the puzzle. The White Star office in Montreal let it slip that someone in the New York office had alerted them Monday afternoon to the fact that the *Titanic* had foundered. If this were so, why had the New York office held out hope for so many hours later? America suddenly smelled a rat. And the biggest rat was alive and well aboard the *Carpathia*. J. Bruce Ismay—

chairman of the White Star Line and president of Morgan's monstrous trust—had obviously used his position to secure his own survival when hundreds of brave American men had gone to their doom. Since the success of ocean liners depended highly on their ability to stick to schedules, Ismay had undoubtedly "pushed Captain Smith" to risk the lives of those aboard by plunging his ship full speed ahead into the icebergs. Ismay was also undoubtedly behind the false messages and false hopes that had continually issued from his offices until the bitter news of the morning had quashed them.

In short, Ismay was given all the sins of the "big people" and promptly became the Ahab of the captains of industry. The American public had found a highly appropriate scapegoat, and since it couldn't prove the wild charges it was leveling at Ismay, it contented itself by venting anger over the fact that he was still alive. *The New York Times* damned him with innuendo; its editorial staff was certain that at the forthcoming Senate investigation, Ismay "who is now approaching this port, one of the few men saved from the *Titanic,* will be a witness." Cub reporter Ben Hecht penned this jingle for the *Chicago Record-Herald:*

> To hold your place in the ghastly face
> Of death on the sea of night
> Is a seaman's job, but to flee with the mob
> Is an owner's noble right.

Even such a friend of the trusts as *The Wall Street Journal* was forced to ask, "Is there any passenger who should not have found place in the boats before the greatest or least official of the line?" By the eve of the Senate investigation, the United States would be close to a lynching mood.

In the early evening, the *Carpathia* passed within range of a number of New England shore stations. The frenzied attempts of amateur wireless operators, however, "formed a hissing mixture from which scarcely a complete sentence" was intelligible. The Hearst organization had already dispatched a large tug, the *Mary Scully,* from Newport to establish radio contact with the rescue ship. At the console of the *Scully*'s elaborate wireless was Jack Binns, the hero of the wreck of the *Republic* in 1900. Binns had been the man who, despite the danger, had "stuck to his post to the last," managing to secure aid in time for the rescue of everyone aboard. He had been fèted all over the nation and remained the sterling kind of selfless hero that America loved to adore. (He would be succeeded in American imagery only by Charles Lindbergh.) The Hearst organization shrewdly figured that Binns would be given information that other news-hungry operators had been denied. Also aboard the *Mary Scully* were a first-class semaphore signalman, reporters, photographers, and Dr. Herbert Jones, formerly of Bellevue Hospital. Dr. Jones would be offering his services to the survivors, many of whom were believed to have "been driven insane" by the disaster.

The mission of the *Scully* was eventually aborted because of serious fog. The scoop would come instead from a simpler scheme by the *Boston Globe.* The *Globe* had sent ace reporter Winfield Thomas aboard Cunard's *Franconia,* which eventually established contact with the *Carpathia.* Thomas then wired an immediate dispatch back to the *Globe.* There were exactly 713 survivors from the *Titanic.* They were all quite sane and would be arriving in New York Harbor late Thursday evening.

4

Homecoming

Thursday: April 18

Anticipation of the *Carpathia*'s arrival dominated the day's events. For those concerned about loved ones there would finally be an end to revised passenger lists and to the ordeal of despair held in check by hope. For others there would be answers to why the largest steamship in the world had been lost on her maiden voyage. Reporters dispatched from all major cities in the United States and Canada were now en route to New York City. The arrival of the *Titanic*'s survivors promised to be even a bigger story than Dewey's sinking the Spanish fleet in Manila Bay.

In the morning, the Brooklyn Navy Yard wireless operator passed an item along that tapped into the mood of the previous day. To the telegrapher aboard Taft's scout cruiser, *Salem*, the *Carpathia* had transmitted only the names of the surviving steerage passengers. The *Salem* operator had indicated that he had an official inquiry from the President of the United States regarding

Archibald Butt, but the *Carpathia* hadn't okayed its transmission. To the press, this could mean only one thing. "TAFT WIRE REFUSED BY RESCUING VESSEL," said the header in the *San Francisco Examiner.* Editors rhetorically asked if there was "censorship aboard the rescue ship." Obviously there was; and Ismay was behind all of it!

The national paranoia deepened as a result of revelations made in the afternoon. Navy operators had also intercepted messages sent by Ismay aboard the *Carpathia* to Franklin at the IMM office. Three of these had been caught—the first:

> Most desirable *Titanic* crew aboard *Carpathia* should be returned home earliest moment possible. Suggest you hold *Cedric,* sailing her daylight Friday unless you see any reason contrary. Propose returning in her myself. Please send outfit of clothes, including shoes, for me to *Cedric.* Have nothing of my own. Please reply.

Then:

> Very important you should hold *Cedric* daylight Friday for *Titanic* crew. Answer.

And finally:

> Think most unwise to keep *Titanic* crew until Saturday. Strongly urge detaining *Cedric,* sailing her midnight if desirable.

All three messages had been signed "YAMSI," Ismay's code for his private, personal messages. It looked as though Ismay, in order to avoid U.S. repercussions for his heinous ways, was planning to skip with the crew back to England as soon as possible. The messages were given to Senator Smith in Washington, and the investigative team promptly altered its plans and set out for New York.

Meanwhile, in New York City, elaborate preparations were under way. Mayor Gaynor and Police Commissioner Waldo had been in conference all morning long. The streets adjacent to the Cunard pier, where the *Carpathia* would be arriving, would be completely cordoned. Special fences were now being built alongside the area at the pier where the survivors would be disembarking. Commissioner Waldo was calling out virtually the entire New York police force—200 mounted and regular officers as well as scores more in plainclothes. Given the unprecedented number of requests for press passes, the mayor decided to reduce the amount allowable to each newspaper.

The heart of the city had gone out to the survivors. The Municipal Lodging House offered 700 beds to those who would need them. The Hebrew, German, Irish, Italian, and Swedish Immigration Societies offered their facilities, as did the YMCA. General Booth assured that the Salvation Army would do everything in its power to meet the needs of the survivors. (The general had just sent a telegram to the President in which he stated that the disaster "speaks to the multitudes of the reality and nearness of the world to come, and of the urgency and overwhelming necessity of preparing for it.") Gimbel's even offered its department store as temporary quarters for over 200 people. In all, over 5,000 accommodations were promised, only a fraction of which would be necessary.

Special problems were envisioned and precautions taken. Space was cleared in every hospital in the city; there would be plenty of beds and medical services. The Red Cross Emergency Relief Committee sent out members and supplies. The Sisters of Charity, representing the Association of Catholic Churches, would be at the docks with spiritual and medical comforts. Fortunately, the two coroners and undertaker the mayor would send would not be needed.

Charities had secured an impressive amount of money for steerage passengers, who undoubtedly had lost everything in their possession. Mrs. W.K. Vanderbilt had been instrumental in organizing this, and members of the New York Stock Exchange had come through very nicely. Vincent Astor had contributed $10,000; Andrew Carnegie, $5,000; and John D. Rockefeller, $2,500. George M. Cohan, Broadway's Yankee Doodle Dandy, had raised nearly $9,000 among theater people and was arranging a benefit vaudeville show for Saturday night. John T. Brush, president of the New York Giants, announced that the team would play an exhibition game on Sunday, the proceeds going to destitute survivors. The Pennsylvania Railroad gave notice that any survivor going to Philadelphia or points west could travel at company expense.

Nevertheless, preparations by the city were amateurish in comparison to the meticulously orchestrated efforts of *The New York Times*. The *Times* had broken this story to the world and had no intention of pulling second place in the forthcoming event. Carr Van Anda had been planning for the homecoming ever since his spectacular morning edition of Monday the fifteenth. By Tuesday he had managed to rent an entire floor at the Strand Hotel, just a block from the Cunard pier. Four telephones had been specially installed and connected with rewrite desks in the *Times*'s newsroom. Each of the four phones was to be used for a specific story—from the arrival of the *Carpathia*, to stories by the survivors and those of the crew. Reporters were told to conduct their interviews and then rush the stories through the appropriate phones at the Strand. A bulletin board of the names of survivors already interviewed would be posted to avoid duplications. If the four phones were busy, three more would be available farther away; chauffeured cars would be waiting to take reporters to them. The *Times*'s switchboard operators had been ordered to keep every phone but one opened to "*Titanic* copy only."

In the afternoon, *Times* day editor Arthur Greaves corralled his entire staff, seasoned reporters as well as cubs; a pudgy-faced, bespectacled youth named Alexander Woollcott was among the latter. Greaves's address to his staff—much like a locker-room pep talk before the big game—is quoted by Meyer Berger in *The Story of the New York Times:*

> The *Carpathia*, with *Titanic* survivors, is due tonight around 9 o'clock. She has not answered wireless requests for information. A.P. just sent us this note: "We have no assurance that we will get any wireless news from the *Carpathia* as this vessel studiously refuses to answer all queries . . ." I'm sending sixteen of you down to the pier, though we have only these four passes. Men without passes will have to try to get through—to survivors, crew, and passengers—on their police cards. . . . Get all you can. Get Captain Rostron of the *Carpathia*. Get Bruce Ismay of White Star. Get every possible member of the *Titanic*'s crew, especially the four officers who were saved. We must get the *Titanic* wireless man's story, if he's alive, and we want the *Carpathia*'s wireless man.

Although word had been received that Second Marconi Operator Harold Bride was alive, nothing was certain about the fate of Chief Operator Jack Phillips, who had sent out the ship's SOS. Wireless men's stories were particularly hot items, ever since the epic of Jack Binns, the hero of the *Republic*, who had "stuck to his post to the last." Greaves told reporters that stories on the fates of Captain Smith, Archie Butt, and John Jacob Astor were also important.

People began lining up at the Cunard pier around 6:00 P.M., not very many at first. At seven o'clock, there were 200. By eight o'clock, 600. Over the next hour, the numbers increased, the crowd mushroomed, and eventually 30,000 people flanked against the patrolled cordons. An additional 10,000 spectators crowded along the Battery.

City officials had roped off the pier into alphabetical sections where friends and relations nervously waited. A little florid-faced man was seen chewing his cigar with such vigor, it looked as if he would swallow it. "I have five on board," he explained to a reporter. "I don't know if they're all alive—I can't tell. They've taken their names off the lists and put them back on again!"

The New York newspapers had chartered about fifty tugboats, ferry boats, steam launches, and yachts; these were filled with reporters and photographers who intended to follow the *Carpathia* into her berth. The fleet was led by a large tug containing the mayor and the official welcoming party. The sea was rough and choppy. A strong east wind was blowing and there was a light fog. By 8:30, everyone aboard the mayor's tug was peering through the mist. Suddenly, a dark form emerged on the horizon—it looked like a steamer.

"Liner ahead," called the lookout on the tug. Surely it was the *Carpathia*.

The hulk on the horizon veered slightly and, in a second, revealed a single funnel.

"It's the *Carpathia!*" exclaimed the tug's captain. "I can tell by her stack!"

The mayor's tug let out a whistle blast, quickly followed by the toots, bells, and sirens of every other boat in the harbor. The sound cascaded across the bay and was met by a cry that rippled through the crowd gathered at the pier and along the Battery. At the pier, rich men, poor men stood shoulder to shoulder, all of them united in the hope of seeing the faces of those they loved—some certain, others merely hopeful. Along the Battery, spectators jostled to get a glimpse of the people who had survived an epic disaster; by exalting these survivors, the spectators would share in the miracle of their reprieve.

Aboard the *Carpathia*, Captain Arthur Rostron looked out from the bridge toward the entrance of the harbor. It was at this time, he later said, that

> we got some idea of the suspense and excitement in the world. . . .
>
> As we were going up Ambrose Channel, the weather changed completely, and a more dramatic ending to a tragic occurrence it would be hard to conceive.
>
> It began to blow hard, rain came down in torrents, and, to complete the finale, we had continuous vivid lightning and heavy rolling thunder. . . .
>
> What with the wind and rain, a pitchdark night, lightning and thunder, and the photographers taking flashlight pictures of the ship, and the explosion of the lights, it was a scene never to be effaced from one's memory.

People at the pier began weeping quietly. There was no hysteria; everyone remained in control. But the Cunard liner was approaching at an exasperatingly slow pace. Eventually, the *Carpathia* came to a complete stop to pick up her pilot. The newsboats quickly clustered about her stern, and five reporters managed to clamber aboard the pilot boat. The *Carpathia*'s third officer, Mr. Rees, was stationed at the accommodation ladder and stared dumbfounded at the photographers' magnesium flashes exploding above the clamor of questions shouted by reporters through their megaphones.

"Pilot only!" Rees warned.

The reporters were determined and attempted to push in front of the pilot as he stepped onto the ladder. At this point, Officer Rees lunged forward, yanked the pilot by his arm onto the platform, and finished off by giving one of the newsmen a well-placed sock on the jaw.

Seeing this, another reporter used a different strategy. He popped either soap or some comparable substance into his mouth and began foaming and frothing like a rabies victim. Rolling his eyes, he screamed, "Oh! My poor sister! My sister is on board! I *must* see her! Let me up, mister, and I'll give you a hundred bucks."

"No!" said Rees.

"Two hundred bucks!"

"No! Stand back. Captain's order. Pilot only!"

Eventually the pilot got on board. So did a reporter. Captain Rostron immediately sequestered the invader and informed him that under no conditions could he interview the survivors. The captain left the newsman on the bridge on his own honor. "I must say he was a gentleman," Rostron later remarked.

The pilot now rang "full ahead" and, once again, the *Carpathia* began churning through the bay toward the Cunard pier. The newsboats followed alongside. By this time, a number of the *Titanic*'s survivors had gathered along the ship's rail to discover the source of all the commotion. As soon as their faces appeared, the photographers shot off a volley of magnesium bombs. One reporter thought he made eye contact with a young woman.

"Are you one of the *Titanic*'s survivors?" he called to her through a megaphone.

"Yes," the voice replied hesitatingly.

"Do you need help?"

There was a long silence. "No."

"If there is anything you want done it will be attended to," the reporter shouted.

"Thank you," came the reply. "I have been informed that my relatives will meet me at the pier."

More passengers began coming onto the *Carpathia*'s decks. Suddenly, reporters saw what looked like a group of the *Titanic*'s crewmen. The newsmen fumbled a moment, and then began waving fifty-dollar bills at the men.

"Jump overboard," they cried to the *Titanic*'s surviving seamen. "We'll pick you up!" No one jumped from the rescue ship.

A second reporter spotted what looked like another survivor. The all-important question was called to her: "Is Mr. John Jacob Astor on board?"

"No."

"Did he remain on the *Titanic* after the collision?"

"I do not know."

Then, silence.

The *Carpathia* proceeded right on past the Cunard pier where people were waiting in desperation. Gasps of surprise followed the ship as she steamed on slowly toward the White Star pier. The ship stopped. Something was happening on board. It was dark in the river, but flashes of lightning revealed that lifeboats manned by crewmen were being dropped from the *Carpathia*'s davits. Another flash and a deep sigh arose. They were the *Titanic*'s lifeboats. All that remained of the greatest ocean liner in history was being dutifully returned to the White Star Line.

Turning around, ever so slowly, the *Carpathia* came abreast of the Cunard pier where heavy steel hawsers were made fast to her in quiet solemnity. At 9:35 P.M., the canopied gangplanks were affixed and a chorus broke forth from the waiting crowd.

"Here they come!"

Then, a sharp, disappointed cry broke from the crowd. As revealed by the finery and completeness of their clothing, the passengers now disembarking were the *Carpathia*'s regular passengers. Another delay, now, before the *Titanic*'s passengers got off.

One by one, the finely dressed passengers trailed down the gangplanks. Then, a young woman appeared; she was hatless, her light brown hair disheveled. She stepped onto the gangplank and hesitated, her eyes darting about at the enormous multitude staring transfixed at her. Her steps quickened and she walked the rest of the way down. As she passed the cordoned section, she was enveloped by a bevy of reporters.

"Survivor?" they asked in unison.

"Yes."

"Your name, please?"

The game was afoot.

As the other survivors came down the gangplanks and into the arms of loved ones, staccato shrieks filled the night—rare expressions of mingled anguish and gratitude. Others waiting at the docks had not been so fortunate. To them, the ship had brought only a grim certainty they had been skirting all week long. Soon, their pitiful wails began blending in eerie consonance with the other sounds at the pier. In the distance, the Salvation Army began to play.

Survivors had disembarked in order of class. Mr. and

Mrs. Dickinson Bishop of southwestern Michigan were among the earliest to appear. They were met by a privately ordered limousine and whisked to the Waldorf-Astoria. The newlyweds would stay there the next few days, using the time to purchase complete new wardrobes before returning home.

A while later, second class disembarked, including Mrs. Allen O. Becker and her three children. Mrs. Becker looked terribly overwrought and was holding her sick two-year-old tightly wrapped in her arms. The family appeared to be led by twelve-year-old Ruth, looking chipper and self-reliant. It had been arranged for them to stay overnight, gratis, in one of the hotels before traveling on to Ohio. Before they boarded the westbound train, Mrs. Becker leaned down toward Ruth.

"Don't you *dare* tell anyone we were on the *Titanic,*" she admonished.

Third class had been detained aboard the ship. Secretary Nagel had ordered New York immigration authorities, in this special instance, to forego the humiliating ritual at Ellis Island. Steerage passengers being met by friends could leave immediately. For the others, State Inspector Williams arranged for seven inspectors to board the ship and examine the immigrants in their quarters. Among these were Mrs. Frank Goldsmith and Franky. Mr. Goldsmith had been lost, as had been young Alfred Rush, who had so gamely set out on his own for the New World. Mrs. Goldsmith, now widowed and penniless, would eventually be taken under the wing of the Salvation Army.

A few minutes after the *Titanic*'s passengers had begun disembarking, a briskly stepping man, in a long gray flapping coat and a derby, pushed his way through the gates toward the *Carpathia;* he was followed by five other men. After a moment's resistance from policemen, papers were flourished and the group was permitted to board the ship. It was Senator Smith and the investigative committee, obviously bent on finding Ismay.

Another team had been permitted past the gates—Guglielmo Marconi, whose invention was responsible for the few lives that had been saved, and a friend who turned out to be Jim Speers of *The New York Times*. Asking questions of crewmen, they found their way to the wireless room. Harold Bride, the *Titanic*'s Second Marconi Operator, was still operating the *Carpathia*'s wireless; he didn't even notice the two men come in. Wraithlike, he sat motionless at the key, only the blue spark dancing under his fingers indicating that he was alive. The skin was drawn so tightly over his face that the bones of his skull protruded, his eyes blackened into hollows. Yet to reporter Speers, Bride's face looked "spiritual, one which might be expected in a painting." Bride's frostbitten feet, now swathed in enormous bandages, were propped up on a chair. Marconi listened to Bride's efforts a few moments before saying, "That's hardly worth sending now, boy."

Bride suddenly looked up. His eyes flared upon recognizing the famous inventor, who quickly grasped his hand and held it warmly.

"Mr. Marconi," Bride said, "Phillips is dead. He's gone."

Speers whipped out his notebook and pencil.

Friday: April 19

The morning papers were filled with tales that, in just twenty-four hours, grew into enduring legends. Extras had been distributed throughout the previous evening and people in cities across the United States had stayed up all night to read them. English citizens had done the same.

Harold Bride's dictation to Jim Speers filled five columns of the front page of the *Times* and was one of the most thrilling sea stories ever told. It documented Jack Phillips's first CQD following the collision and how, at Bride's suggestion, the distress call had been changed to SOS, the new international signal. It told how the *Titanic* had slowly sunk by the bow, the inadequate number of boats being filled with women and children to the tune of ragtime played by the ship's band. The Marconi operator revealed the painful awareness of those in command who knew that rescuing craft were too far away to be of assistance in time. In the end, the ship took a crucial lunge at the bow and a wave had swept Bride overboard:

> There were men all around me—hundreds of them. The sea was dotted with them, all depending on their life-belts. I felt I simply had to get away from the ship. She was a beautiful sight then.
>
> Smoke and sparks were rushing out of her funnel, and there must have been an explosion, but we had heard none. We only saw the big stream of sparks. . . . The band was still playing, and I guess they all went down.
>
> They were playing "Autumn" then. I swam with all my might. I suppose I was 150 feet away when the *Titanic* on her nose, with her after-quarter sticking straight up in the air, began to settle—slowly.
>
> When at last the waves washed over her rudder there wasn't the least bit of suction I could feel. She must have kept going just as slowly as she had been.

Bride's story, one of the few accurate accounts published on Friday, carried a copyright notice by the

Times, which had paid Bride $1,000 for it; no other paper could quote it.

Stories by other survivors were not so accurate. But they certainly weren't lacking in sensation—undoubtedly a consequence of imaginative rewriting by the editors who had taken them down over the phone from harried reporters.

Seaman Billy Jones told how, "at the time of the collision, falling ice" from the rammed berg had "killed several persons on deck." Another man told how everyone on board "could tell from the first that she was sinking. The whole front part of the steamer, it seemed, was torn away. We knew from the first there was no hope. We were doomed. We were confident of that." Robert W. Daniel revealed that "Five minutes after the crash everybody seemed to have gone insane. Men and women fought, bit, and scratched to be in line for the lifeboats." In spite of several stories of male heroism and self-sacrifice, Mrs. C.G. Stengel let out that "Chinamen and stokers hid in the bottoms of the lifeboats before they were launched and men jumped into boatloads of women injuring them."

Mrs. Corinne Andrews, from a lifeboat about a mile from the sinking ship, had heard "a great explosion. It appeared to me as if the boilers had blown up and the *Titanic* had been lifted up amidships and broken in half." Jack Thayer agreed with her. According to Thayer, "she broke in two just in front of the third funnel." With the help of a *Carpathia* passenger, Thayer had prepared sketches of this spectacle which were printed in the *New York Herald.*

Editors had requested special copy on the fates of the millionaires and weren't disappointed. In one of the most famous accounts, Benjamin Guggenheim—president of International Pump Company—was reported to have returned to his room while the lifeboats were leaving the ship. Dressing resplendently in his finest evening clothes, Guggenheim had then reappeared on deck, saying to a steward:

> I think there is grave doubt that the men will get off. I am willing to remain and play the man's game if there are not enough boats for more than the women and children. I won't die here like a beast.
>
> Tell my wife, Johnson, if it should happen that my secretary and I both go down and you are saved, tell her I played the game out straight and to the end. No woman shall be left aboard this ship because Ben Guggenheim was a coward.

"People are better than we think we are," Reverend Johnston Myers later observed. "The millionaires are not all bad men as it turns out."

Major Butt and Colonel Astor were attributed soldiers' deaths. H.H. Haven reported that Astor "stood on the deck and fought off man after man until his wife was in a lifeboat. Then he remained on deck to the last. Major Butt was on the deck with a crowd of men to the last and went down with the ship." Mrs. Dan Marvin embellished this with vivid detail. In her version, Major Butt had stood on the deck "with an iron bar in his hand beating back the frenzied crowd who were attempting to overcrowd the lifeboats"—a perfectly glorious end for this popular military man.

Captain Smith had at least five different deaths, from heroic to ignominious. Seaman G.A. Hogg said, "I saw Captain Smith in the water alongside a raft. 'There's the skipper,' I yelled, 'Give him a hand.' They did, but he shook himself free and shouted to us, 'Good-bye boys, I'm going to follow the ship.' That was the last we saw of our skipper." Others remembered E.J. swimming with a child in his arms whom he managed to deliver to a lifeboat before being swept away in a wave. Another claimed that Smith had shouted, "Be British, boys, be British!" before going under with the ship. G.A. Drayton claimed that E.J. had simply been swept off the bridge when it lunged forward: "I saw him swim back onto the sinking ship. He went down with it in my sight."

Dr. J.F. Kemp, a passenger on the *Carpathia*, raised an ominous possibility. Kemp had spoken with a boy who had been one of the last children to have left the *Titanic*. The boy had seen "Captain Smith put a pistol to his head and then fall down." Others reported having seen Captain Smith commit suicide; crewmen, however, vigorously denied the possibility. Part of the momentum for E.J.'s alleged suicide may have come from the fact that six years earlier a climacteric German captain had caused considerable scandal by killing himself after accidentally beaching and injuring his ship. The story may also have arisen from passengers' confusing Smith with the ship's first officer.

Stories of Officer Murdoch's suicide tended to be quite consistent. Thomas Whitely, a waiter, reported that Murdoch "shot one man—I did not see this, but three others did—and then shot himself." Mrs. George D. Widener claimed, "I went on deck and was put into a lifeboat. As the boat pulled away from the *Titanic* I saw one of the officers shoot himself in the head." Steerage passenger Carl Jansen told how he had "glanced toward the bridge and saw the chief officer place a revolver in his mouth and shoot himself. His body toppled overboard." (Many years later, a novel about the disaster made significant use of this fable.)

The most alarming stories pertained to the ship's command. Seaman Jones let slip the fact that the Number 1 lifeboat held only thirteen people, though its capacity was forty. Mrs. George N. Stone claimed that she had been told to go back to bed after the collision. "I was not quite convinced," Mrs. Stone related, "but I went back to bed. If I had gone to sleep I should not be here." Asked if she had been warned in any way, Mrs. Stone replied, "Not a single warning was given in the part of the ship in which I was. No one came to tell us, no bell was rung, no horn was sounded. We could have died like rats in a trap for all the warning we received."

Mrs. Cornelia T. Andrews revealed, "When we finally did get into a boat, we found that our miserable men companions," as she called the boat's crewmen, "could not row and had only said they could because they wanted to save themselves."

Abraham Hyman told of dreadful circumstances for steerage passengers:

> When [the people from steerage] got on deck, they found a rope drawn closer to their quarters than usual, and this made some of them think there was danger. One or two of the women began to cry, and a panic began to spread. An officer came forward, stood close to the rope, and waved the people back. . . . The officer who was standing at the rope had a pistol in his hand, and he ordered everybody to keep back. First, one woman screamed and then another, and then one man (I think he was an Italian) pushed toward the boat and the officer fired at him.

Julius Sop, a Belgian emigrant, said that he had twice been threatened with death by officers with revolvers. The first time was on the boat deck. Then, after he had dived into the water and swam out to a lifeboat, another officer threatened to shoot him if he tried to climb into the small craft. An American woman in the boat had intervened. Brushing the officer's gun aside, she had purportedly said, "I can't see the poor fellow die. We might as well all go together."

Reporters had pressed vigorously for stories about Bruce Ismay's abominable conduct. Although most of these were wildly incredible, the account of Mrs. J. Cardeza, who claimed to have been in the same lifeboat with Ismay, stood out. "Mr. Ismay was safely seated in the lifeboat before it was anything like filled," said Mrs. Cardeza. "I noticed that he selected the crew that should row this boat. My husband is an excellent oarsman, and Mr. Ismay beckoned to him to get into the boat." According to Mrs. Cardeza, everyone helped with the rowing *except* Ismay. "I don't think very highly of Mr. Ismay's courage," she concluded.

By far, the most damning indictment against the command and management of the *Titanic* came from Major Arthur Peuchen, a first-class passenger from Toronto. Peuchen, a yachtsman, had been ordered into one of the lifeboats by the ship's second officer. Fearing censure for surviving, Peuchen had the foresight to have the officer sign a statement to this effect. The only Canadian reporter in New York City managed to take down Peuchen's account, which filled the front page of the *Toronto Globe.*

Asked for his opinion on the cause of the tragedy, Peuchen replied: "I say it was carelessness, gross carelessness. Why, the captain knew we were going into an ice field, and why should he remain dining in the saloon when such danger was about?" Peuchen elaborated on this charge to another reporter:

> Mr. Ismay was dining with Captain Smith—both of them in evening clothes—in a lower saloon when the captain, at least, should have been at his post of duty on the bridge. . . . In my opinion, as a man used to

> discipline and responsibility, Captain Smith should have been on the bridge, knowing, as everyone aboard the *Titanic* knew, that there were icebergs en route. I suppose, however, that he was invited to this dinner by the general manager of the line and that he had to go.

Peuchen also claimed that Ismay had known about telegraphed ice warnings, and yet the ship's speed had not been reduced—if anything, she had gone even faster. Peuchen suggested that the officers had been incompetent in loading the lifeboats; none had been adequately filled. He flatly stated that E.J. had been too old to have been given the responsibility of such a modern liner. He raised another possibility. Although everyone had been equipped with a life preserver, "It is strange," Peuchen observed, "that the life preservers did not result in more people being saved, or even in the bodies remaining on the surface. When the *Carpathia* passed over the spot, I went into the bow and peered closely among the wreckage, but I failed to see a single body floating." Peuchen's intelligent criticism quickly commanded public concern, and he would eventually voluntarily submit to questioning by the Senate investigation committee.

The accounts, which grew into lasting legends, were very special. Even before they were related (and today as well) special niches for the stories existed in the hearts of their audiences. Mrs. Helen Churchill Candee, a gracefully attractive and intelligent American interior designer, told the story of Mr. and Mrs. Isidor Straus; the story is true. According to Mrs. Candee: "An officer of the *Titanic* ordered Mrs. Straus into a boat. 'I will not leave my husband,' she said. 'We have been together all these years and I'll not leave him now.' I saw Mrs.

Straus waving her handkerchief to us as our boat left from the ship." In an article later published in *Colliers,* Mrs. Candee described the happy Straus couple as they appeared to passengers:

> With no parleying you knew they were people who had gained and accepted the sweets of success without intoxication. Sobriety and modesty were theirs; strength and calm showed on their faces.

Other wives had elected to meet death with their husbands: Mrs. H.J. Allison in first class, Mrs. E.C. Carter and numerous others in second class, and many wives in steerage. But they had no one to tell their stories.

It must be added that part of Mrs. Straus's sway over the American imagination was due to the fact that she was Jewish. In an era of flagrant anti-Semitism, her self-sacrifice permitted an unashamed adoration, tantamount to a therapeutic catharsis. In a memorial service held at the Broadway Theater two days after the item appeared, William Jennings Bryan compared the self-sacrifice of Mrs. Straus with the Old Testament story of Ruth ("Entreat me not to leave thee"). Such examples of "womanliness," said Bryan, "are the heritage of our people. They make us proud of those whom we know who are a part of us." The following day, Charles Carlisle, president of the Studebaker Corporation, wrote to President Taft asking that a monument be erected in Washington, D.C., with the names of all the victims of the disaster engraved on it. "First above all," wrote Carlisle, "I would suggest the name of Mrs. Isidor Straus be engraved." Mrs. Straus would be better memorialized in countless volumes of disaster fiction, persisting even to the present day.

Mrs. A.A. Dick appears to have originated the most

lasting legend. Although the facts are against her account, it became deeply ingrained in Anglo-American consciousness. She told a reporter: "What we remember best was that as the ship sunk, we could hear the band playing 'Nearer, My God, to Thee.' We looked back and could see the men standing on deck, absolutely quiet and waiting for the end." She elaborated on this to another reporter: "The last I remember of the *Titanic* was hearing the strains of 'Nearer, My God, to Thee.' Then there was a great sound of rushing water and the vessel sank beneath the waves."

This poetic vision was the perfect balm with which to salve the newfound terror of infinite chaos that the disaster had provoked in the civilized world. The image of the men, "standing on deck, absolutely quiet" as the band played this elegiac hymn, brought tears to all who envisioned it. The *London Standard* commented:

> We are usually an undemonstrative people, but the incident of the string band of the *Titanic*, its members gathered together to play the hymn, "Nearer, My God, to Thee," as the great ship settled for her last plunge, left men speechless with pity. It is a great incident of history, worthy to rank with the last parade on the *Birkenhead*.

The British troopship *Birkenhead* had struck a ledge and foundered off South Africa in 1852. Aboard were the 78th Highlanders, their families, and the crew. The ship sank in twenty minutes after almost all the women and children were gotten off in the few lifeboats. The waters were infested with sharks. The Highlanders and the sailors lined up on deck in military formation; so standing, they sank with the ship and were lost to a man. Rudyard Kipling had immortalized the incident in a poem:

So they stood an' was still to the Birken'ead drill,
Soldier an' sailor too.

Soon Mrs. Dick's story would be inspiring every doggerel bard in two continents. An excerpt from the efforts of one of them:

Over the waiting, starlit sea,
    Trembled the song of devotion.
The song of the souls that all would be
    'Nearer, My God, My God, to Thee,'
There on the lonely ocean.

Joseph Conrad railed at such sentimentality—"music to get drowned by," he called it:

> . . . it would have been finer if the band of the *Titanic* had been quietly saved, instead of being drowned while playing—whatever tune they were playing, the poor devils. . . . There is nothing more heroic in being drowned very much against your will, off a holed, helpless, big tank in which you bought your passage, than in quietly dying of colic caused by the imperfect salmon in the tin you bought from your grocer.

But the legend would not die. As late as the 1950s, a cinematic version of the *Titanic* disaster showed, at the end, every man on board the ship lined against the rail and singing the hymn sublimely along with the band.

There is no doubt that the band played to the end, as documented by Harold Bride, who was in a position to know. But Bride said the band was playing "Autumn," an Episcopalian hymn which doesn't sound like either of the settings of "Nearer, My God, to Thee." (There are English and American settings of "Nearer, My God, to

Thee"; both have been reproduced in various texts as *the* hymn the band played when the *Titanic* sunk.) The difference between "Autumn" and each of the other settings is rather interesting. "Autumn" is a robust tune, which in melody, cadence, and text denies the fear and imminence of death. "Nearer, My God, to Thee," in each of its versions is a quiet submission to fate. The fact that earlier the band had been playing (in the words of John Maxtone-Graham) a "numbing charade" of ragtime makes "Autumn" the hymn more likely to have been chosen by the band when the end was close at hand. People safely away in the lifeboats, as well as those ashore, evidently needed to believe that those who had been so cruelly sacrificed to "degenerate luxury" had met their fates with peaceful acceptance.

It is possible that Mrs. A.A. Dick, a Canadian, may have remembered that the survivors of the steamship *Valencia,* which foundered off the coast of British Columbia in 1905, had been discovered singing, "Nearer, My God, to Thee" by a surfboat that came to their rescue. Still, the hymn had a special niche in the mythology of the Gilded Age. It had been the favorite hymn of King Edward of England, and its title had purportedly formed the very last words uttered by the martyred President McKinley. Whether or not it was played aboard the R.M.S. *Titanic,* it was the most appropriate swan song of the Victorian Dream.

5

Journey's End

Saturday and Sunday: April 20–21

The weekend was a time for closure. Memorial services were held, and experts from every calling would grapple with the calamity as a whole, seeking its keystone or otherwise divining its meaning. These piecemeal attempts would amount to little, and nothing seemed forthcoming that could unify them. Too much information was yet lacking. Everyone was still too overwhelmed by the magnitude of the disaster to escape into objectivity. Efforts at closure would consist of renewed, more focused attacks on individuals in command—the bad baronets of the melodrama. Some would find in the disaster divine retribution for specific sins—card playing in the ship's lounge on a Sunday, for one. Still others asked that the tragedy be forgotten, that hearts and minds be turned instead to the heroic example of the martyred men and God's mercy on the saved few. Satisfactory closure to the catastrophe would not come to the nation for another five weeks.

On Friday, the day when the published stories of survivors held the world enthralled, the U.S. Hydrographic Office had officially shifted the North Atlantic steamship lanes 180 miles to the south. In England, a national day of mourning had been called; at one memorial service, Alexander Carlisle, the chief designer of the *Titanic*, had fainted. About the same time, Lord Pirrie had finally been told about the loss of Harland Wolff's greatest achievement and its attendant loss of life. Pirrie had planned on making the maiden voyage with Bruce Ismay, but had been prevented by illness. He had therefore sent a number of experts from the company aboard the ship, including his nephew Thomas Andrews; all had been lost. Those close to Pirrie had withheld news of the disaster, fearing its effect on his health.

In New York, the *Titanic*'s crewmen had been invited to attend a meager, pathetic memorial service provided for them by the Institute of the American Seamen's Friend Society. In the depth of its concern for needy passengers, the nation had overlooked the needs of the crewmen, many of whom had risked life and limb for the survivors now safely ashore. One of the seamen asked a visiting reporter if any of the money raised by charity would be going to crewmen. It seemed that he had a wife and children back in Southampton, and his pay had stopped on the fifteenth at 2:20 A.M.—the moment when the ship had disappeared beneath the waves.

The Senate subcommittee had begun its investigation in New York's Waldorf-Astoria. After the weekend, the inquiry as well as its witnesses would be moved to Washington. Ismay, the surviving officers, Harold Bride, and a number of crewmen were being detained under subpoena.

In the U.S. Senate on Friday, the anger against Bruce

Ismay had reached a fever peak. Senator Rayner of Maryland launched a vitriolic attack against the chairman of the White Star Line. In his address, Rayner had quoted a statement attributed to the daughter of Congressman Hughes, a survivor and widow of the disaster; her statement suggested that Ismay had received special consideration while getting into a lifeboat, as well as aboard the rescue vessel. This was more than Rayner could stomach:

> Mr. President, this is where the trouble lies. We punish inferior officers and subordinate employees for neglect of duty, but the men at the head who give the orders and reap the profit we permit to escape. All the civilized nations of the world will applaud the criminal prosecution of the management of this line, and if they can be made to suffer, as they ought and should be, no sympathy will go out for them; and if it does it will be hushed and drowned and submerged in the overwhelming lamentation, that today reechoes throughout every quarter and section of the civilized world, for the victims of their culpable carelessness, a recklessness that sent hundreds of their fellow beings into eternity, desolating homes and firesides, and turned this land into a home of mourning.
>
> In this hour of our calamity we appeal to the God of the universe for strengthening faith and we appeal to the majesty of the law to deal out retributive justice to this guilty company to the last degree.

This was strong stuff for the U.S. Senate of 1912, but the times were changing. Rayner had long been an archfoe of the trusts and vested interests, and the *Titanic* disaster was now rallying public support for his arguments. "Trust *vs.* the Populace" had now, in fact, become the dominant issue of the ongoing Taft-Roosevelt battle. The Republican party might even be split over it.

In New York, White Star officials were busily extrapolating official lists of survivors and deceased. So far, the statistics did not reflect a particularly democratic picture:

	Women and children saved	*Men saved*	*Total saved*
First Cabin	94%	31%	60%
Second Cabin	81%	10%	44%
Steerage	47%	14%	25%
Crew	87%	22%	24%

Although there appeared to be a difference between the percentage of second-class and third-class men saved, this difference is not statistically significant; both, however, are significantly different from the percentage of first-class men saved. The proportion of crewmen saved is accounted for by the fact that each lifeboat required at least two crewmen—a necessity that would be bitterly commented on later. As the weeks rolled by, the survivor figures would be amended here and there. The percentages would stay the same, though. The unequivocal fact remained that over 1,500 people had been lost and only 713 (a third of those aboard) saved.

During the weekend, the ballad mongers began writing the songs that would hopefully knit the nation back together. One of them, "It Was Sad When the Great Ship Went Down," eventually entered the folk literature and is still a favorite at American summer camps for children. There were also Edith M. Lessing's ditty,

"Just as the Ship Went Down," and a cloying piece, "The Band Played 'Nearer, My God, to Thee,' as the Ship Went Down," by Mark Beam and Harold Jones. Winton Baltzell, editor of *The Musician* and former editor of *The Etude*, felt the occasion called for a meaningful, serious composition. Accordingly, he wrote "The Wreck of the *Titanic*." This "descriptive composition for piano solo," replete with thundering bass rolls and agonized glissandi, was calculated to stimulate tears and thrill the digestion in the parlor after dinner on a Sunday afternoon.

All across the nation, citizens were moved to express their feelings in poetry. Newspaper editors were inundated with submissions. Many people sent their poems to the White House. President Taft received everything from hand-scrawled couplets to a beautifully printed, six-page epic by an Oklahoma cowboy and a comparable effort by a Norwegian dwarf, whose portrait was lithographed on the first page.

By Saturday evening, the papers were filled with letters to the editor, each of them nominating a specific element of the disaster as a contributing cause. A surprising number of people indicted the *Titanic*'s name. Wasn't such arrogance meant to "tempt Providence"? Even the captain of the *Carpathia* bothered to research the name and learned that the mythical Titans had been a race of people vainly striving to overcome the forces of nature. "Could anything be more unfortunate or tragic in its significance?" asked Captain Rostron. "Wasn't this just asking for trouble?" queried others.

The White Star Line had always named its ships after tribes of people with the suffix *-ic*. But to choose mythical giants as namesakes for the monster ships was stepping a bit beyond tradition. In doing so, White Star helped revive a fear of bombastic names for ships, an

Elizabethan superstition long forgotten. In John Webster's 1623 play *The Devil's Law Case*, the following exchange had occurred:

> ARIO: Come, come, come; you gave those ships most strange, most dreadful, and unfortunate names, I never lookt they'd prosper.
> ROM: Is there any ill omen in giving names to ships?
> ARIO: Did you not call one, *The Stormes Defiance*, another *The Scourge of the Sea*, and the third, *The Great Leviathan?*
> ROM: Very right, sir.
> ARIO: Very devillish names all three of them! and surely I think, they were curst in their very cradles, I doe meane, when they were upon their stockes.

The managing editors of newspapers were also zealous in placing blame. Typical was the *New York Herald*'s opinion: "Had this latest expression of mercantile naval construction been supplied with fewer fol-de-rols, such as gymnasiums, swimming-tanks, and other non-essentials to safety at sea, more boats and life-rafts could have been carried—and every life have been saved under the conditions that prevailed when the *Titanic* received her death-blow."

The liberal papers—particularly those of the Hearst organization—had a field day. The *New York American* stated:

> The *Titanic* had made a "record." It is a record of manslaughter unparalleled in marine history. Her maiden trip will indeed be a memory, one that the White Star Line will never be able to forget, and J. Bruce Ismay survives to tell how 1,400 lives committed to the care of his line and on his ship perished

> while he escaped. . . . Is the mere greed for extravagant cabin fares or the vanity of speed records to be made the excuse of multitudinous homicide?

The *Philadelphia North American*'s item was called "Murder":

> Human rights came into conflict with vested property rights on the decks of the *Titanic* during those hours of darkness and final parting. And the price was paid that will ever be paid until the will of nations forbids special privilege from using the bodies of men and women as counters in its private profit game. For that and no other is the silent message that seems to us comes from those men and women who lie murdered in the ocean depths.

Conservative papers tried to make more rational sense of the disaster. The *Chicago Tribune* concluded that "perfect safety in ocean travel is a fiction." The *Baltimore Sun* was reminded that "in spite of all our progress, perils still exist, and that before the forces of untamed nature man is often as helpless as an infant."

On Sunday, the churches of the American nation were filled to capacity. No event in clergymen's recollections had ever inspired such mass church attendance—certainly no Christmas ever had. People had come looking for answers, and the answer they most sought was God's explanation for His latest intervention in human affairs. For the most part, churchgoers would be disappointed. They would receive comfort, support for their indignation, justification for their continued complacency—but no answers. The church itself had been caught up in the spirit of the age that had launched the *Titanic* and could not extricate itself in time to perceive, much less reveal, a spiritual interpretation of the disaster. What Henry F. May has called "the Social Gospel of 1912" was simply a religious interpretation of the Victorian Dream: Suffering and tribulations could be borne as long as it was believable that mankind was improving and the Kingdom of Heaven was being materialized on earth. The *Titanic* disaster had shaken this belief to its foundations, and organzed religion was shaken with it. Soon, Americans would be turning to the federal government and politicians for things they had once sought from the church and its clergy.

Most Protestant services, on Sunday the twenty-first, began with a hymn (its name scarcely needs mentioning). It was sung as introits, as choral anthems, by soloists, and by entire weeping congregations. In that musical moment, all attempted to partake of the glorious vision of peaceful acceptance by which the ghastly deaths of 1,500 innocents had been so sentimentally obfuscated. In many churches, particularly the Episcopalian, the flags of the United States and Great Britain were draped together in a mournful caress. Reverend R.J. Hutcheon of Toronto announced, "We are . . . taught anew the truth of the old saying that suffering makes the whole world akin, and Great Britain and America are nearer today because citizens of both countries are lying together in a common ocean grave." However true that may have been on Sunday, by Monday the two nations were back on the warpath of mutual repudiation.

Many churches exalted the *Titanic*'s "heroes." The sterling deaths of John Jacob Astor and Major Butt were widely cited as examples for all Christians. In synagogues, Mr. and Mrs. Straus were eulogized. As Rabbi Samuel Schulman of New York's Temple Beth-El put it, "Beloved and adored of each other in life, in death they were not separated." In San Francisco, F.W. Clampett praised Captain E.J. Smith. "The brave captain was a sailor true," Clampett intoned. "Cannot we picture that last moment so that the message will come home to us all? The last boat was launched, the last grand plunge had begun. The strains of 'Nearer, My God, to Thee' floated to the ears of those pulling away. And what was the cry? 'Be British, boys, be British!' "

Many ministers preached about the "fact" that in the *Titanic*'s last moments, social caste had disappeared and all stood on the decks as equals. For example, Reverend Professor Eakin remarked: "There was no distinction on the ground of wealth or any other of those barriers that we in our folly have raised so high. . . . The prospect of death levelled all distinction." The extent of Reverend Eakin's own "folly" would stand revealed when the statistics of the survivors were published. Eakin, incidentally, also disparaged the love of luxury, of which women were "the greatest sinners of all in this regard."

From every pulpit, the self-sacrifice of the men in deference to the women and children was extolled. Reverend Clampett observed that the rescue of the few would never have been possible "unless the spirit of 'women and children first' had been shown. This sight of strong men lifting helpless women and children into boats and saying good-bye to them forever and to life is one that will never be forgotten." In New York the same argument was taken to extremes and concluded with an outright attack on the women's rights movement. The Reverend Dr. Leighton Parks of St. Bartholomew's Church said:

> You and I will be better in life and in death because of [the men's] good example. The real message of this great and overwhelming affliction is that it is the latest revelation of the power of the cross. . . . The men who stood on that deck, in the presence of disaster,

> exhibited a power of self-restraint, exhibited it so quietly, too, that it can not be explained on any ground of mere evolution. . . . But the Son of Man came into a world that was lost. And so the men on the *Titanic* sacrificed themselves for the women and children. The women did not ask for the sacrifice, but it was made. Those women who go about shrieking for their "rights" want something very different.

Indeed they did. In England, Mrs. Cecil Chapman stated that any suffragette would have preferred to meet her fate alongside her husband. "I would a thousand times rather go down with the ship under similar circumstances," she said. (*The New York Times* snarled at the "jangling note" Mrs. Chapman had added to the noble picture of male self-sacrifice.) Undoubtedly, Harriet Stanton Blatch, president of the American Political Woman's Union, had the best rejoinder. Ms. Blatch stated that since men had drafted the laws that governed the ship, they should have been the ones to go down with it. Asked what her position would be should women receive the vote, she replied, "Then we would have laws requiring plenty of lifeboats."

Only a handful of clergymen indicted the mentality of the Gilded Age. Reverend Dunbar H. Ogden of Atlanta stated, "It is easy to condemn when a great ship goes down, but is not our nation living, as the *Titanic* traveled that fateful night, in absolute disregard of human life?" By far the severest condemnation of contemporary civilization came from Dr. Charles H. Parkhurst of the Madison Square Presbyterian Church of New York:

> The picture which presents itself before my eyes is that of the glassy, glaring eyes of the victims, staring

> meaninglessly at the gilded furnishings of this sunken palace of the sea; dead helplessness wrapt in priceless luxury. . . . Everything for existence, nothing for life. Grand men, charming women, beautiful babies, all becoming horrible in the midst of the glittering splendor of a $10,000,000 casket! . . .
>
> The two sore spots which really run into one another and which constitute the disease that is gnawing into our civilization are love of money and passion for luxury. Those two combined are what sunk the *Titanic* and sent 1,500 souls prematurely to their final account.

Carlyle and Arnold couldn't have said it better.

Part of the significance of the many special memorial services and the phenomenal church turnout was the fact that no funerals had been possible. The bereaved as well as the general public had been denied one of the most basic rites of psychological closure following death. The Astors, the Guggenheims, and the Wideners apparently believed that even this limitation could be overcome with enough money. Collectively, the three families consulted the Merritt and Chapman Wrecking Company with a view toward raising the ship. It was undoubtedly the first in a long series of twentieth-century schemes to raise the *Titanic.* Merritt and Chapman knew the task was impossible; they did weigh, however, the possibility of dropping dynamite over the site with the chance of raising some of the bodies. The plan was abandoned on the basis of articles published by oceanographers. All marine experts agreed that, where the *Titanic* had gone down, a pressure of 6,000 pounds per square inch had already compressed the human bodies into the gelatinous murk that constitutes the ocean's bottom at such depths. Hopeful amateurs suggested that perhaps the *Titanic* had not sunk all the way to the bottom; the *Scientific American* presented theoretical evidence that it certainly had.

By Sunday afternoon, the cableship *MacKay-Bennett*, chartered by the White Star Line, had approached the *Titanic*'s grave. The sea temperature had plunged from fifty-seven to thirty-two degrees, and there were two icebergs and several overturned bergs ("growlers") about. The ocean was strewn with woodwork, cabin fittings, mahogany fronts of drawers, deck chairs, masses of loose cork, and bodies buoyed by life belts. All day long the crewmen worked at dragging the sodden, floating bodies onto the deck. It was agonizing work. The skulls and limbs of many of the victims had been crushed; some women had infants locked in their arms; faces were so bruised that they were almost beyond recognition. Eventually, Astor's body was found. All victims with identification were taken over by the embalmer, Mr. John R. Snow, who seemed to be enjoying his work. Those without identification were prepared for a proper burial at sea. By 8:00 P.M., Sunday the twenty-first (a week since the *Titanic* had entered this region), the first burials at sea commenced.

MacKay-Bennett engineer Frederick Hamilton kept a diary of the ship's mission, from which the following is quoted:

> The tolling of the bell summoned all hands to the forecastle where thirty bodies are to be committed to the deep, each carefully weighted and carefully sewed up in canvas. It is a weird scene, this gathering. The crescent moon is shedding a faint light on us, as the ship lays wallowing in the great rollers. The funeral service is conducted by the Reverend Canon Hind; for nearly an hour the words "For as much as it hath pleased . . . we therefore commit his

body to the deep" are repeated and at each interval comes, splash! as the weighted body plunges into the sea, there to sink to a depth of about two miles. Splash, splash, splash.

Early body counts wired from the *MacKay-Bennett* suggested that over a thousand "souls" had gone to the bottom with the ship. The observation Major Arthur Peuchen had made to the press Thursday night now came back ominously. "It is strange," Peuchen had said, "that the life preservers did not result in more people being saved, or even in the bodies remaining on the surface." Had there been a preserver shortage comparable to the boat shortage? "No," said the *Titanic*'s officers, who, with J. Bruce Ismay, were already en route to Washington, D.C., to continue testifying before the Senate committee. At the end, everyone had worn life belts.

Then where were the bodies? Harold Bride had remarked on the surprising lack of suction when the *Titanic* foundered. Had the preservers been defective? (Defective preservers had been one of the horrible legacies of the *General Slocum* disaster of 1904.) Worse yet, as Mrs. Stone had suggested, had stewards failed to alert in time the people on the lower decks who had "died like rats in a trap"? Questions like these were torturing the friends and relations of the "missing" passengers.

Other questions preoccupied the press. The *Washington Post* asked some good ones: Who was at fault "when it was common knowledge that the North Atlantic was a mass of floating ice"? Was the *Titanic*'s loss the result of "faulty construction"? Why, when the ship had stayed afloat for nearly three hours and lifeboats could have accommodated 1,178 people, had only 713 people been rescued? And why had 30 percent of those saved been members of the crew?

The questions were endless, and answers didn't seem forthcoming. Experts were in a hopeless muddle of conjecture. Authorities simply did not know. Reason and experience were equally impotent in the face of such an unprecedented calamity. Reason had pronounced the *Titanic* "practically unsinkable." Experience, with adequate prescience of the ice fields, had driven the ship at full speed headlong into them.

It would take a "born fool" to get answers to these questions.

PART TWO

The Investigation

Our course was simple and plain—to gather the facts relating to this disaster while they were still vivid realities. Questions of diverse citizenship gave way to the universal desire for the simple truth. It was of paramount importance that we should act quickly to avoid jurisdictional confusion and organized opposition at home or abroad. . . . Without any pretension to experience or special knowledge of nautical affairs, nevertheless I am of the opinion that very few important facts which were susceptible of being known escaped our scrutiny. Energy is often more desirable than learning. . . .

—WILLIAM ALDEN SMITH

6

A Bobbing Sort of a Cuss

The fairy tales of the Gilded Age were written by Horatio Alger. The exploits of "Jed the Poorhouse Boy," "Phil the Fiddler," "Mark the Matchboy," and other diamonds in the rough argued earnestly, if not convincingly, that hard work, enterprise, and grasped opportunities were sufficient to boost the lowest of American ragamuffins to the top of the social tree. The story of one of these street boys is not widely known. "Will the Popcorn Peddler" is a true story, and yet one so characteristic and improbable, it may as well have appeared in Alger's *Pluck and Luck* series.

Will's story began in the sleepy hamlet of Dowagiac, Michigan, one of the hundreds of nondescript, backwater villages that dotted the American Midwest in the late nineteenth century. Nestled unimposingly in the nation's heartland, Dowagiac, like many Michigan villages, was a haven for archaic Puritan culture and values, preserved almost intact from a mass migration of New Englanders to the state in the late eighteenth century. William Alden Smith was born in Dowagiac in

1859, the eldest son of George and Leah Smith—descendants of Revolutionary War general Israel Putnam and Henry Alden, the Virginian. Like every other Dowagiac youth, Will spent his schooldays studying the Bible and the McGuffey Reader and learning that the collapse of rural virtues had caused the fall of the Roman Empire. In his leisure time, he was off fishing in one of the small crystal-clear lakes that peppered the region or hailing the steam locomotives as they hissed and rumbled through the depot en route from Chicago to Detroit. Will would forever have a special attachment to the trains that had accelerated the tempo of American life and broken the monotony of even the smallest of American towns. Eventually he spent every spare moment at the Dowagiac depot, hawking newspapers to railway passengers and blacking the boots of weary Civil War soldiers, whose personal accounts of human sacrifice made the tears roll down his cheeks.

When Will was twelve years old, his family moved northward to the larger industrial city of Grand Rapids. Although it would not begin as he expected, the move would be the turning point of Will's life. Shortly after relocating in "Furniture City," his father became seriously ill with one of the lung diseases that plagued industrial laborers of the nineteenth century, and Will was obliged to drop out of school and seek menial work to sustain the family. He began selling the local newspaper. To this he added the evening duty of delivering telegrams for Western Union. But his dream was traveling as a newsboy-attaché on a train. A prominent citizen who much admired Will told him that if he applied to a friend of his, he was sure to secure such a position.

Will recalled: "I remember wearing for the first time a red rosette tie which my mother had made for this special occasion. I presented myself to the august personage. The railway official looked me over with evident satisfaction."

"So, sonny," he said, "you think you would like to be a railroad man, eh?"

Will nodded silently.

"Well, I guess you'll do," said the man. "Put up your deposit of ten dollars, and you can go to work on Monday."

"Ten dollars!" Will gasped. "I haven't got ten dollars!" He had not counted on the collateral that railroad newsboys were forced to put up, guaranteeing payment of their passage.

Will walked back home crestfallen, knowing fully in that moment "the wretchedness of poverty." Wishing to comfort him, his mother quietly slipped a quarter into his hand; it was a sizable sum, considering the era and the family circumstances. With the quarter in his pocket, Will paced the bricks of the Grand Rapids streets, weighing the possibilities as they raced through his head. As he watched the pushcart peddlers selling their wares to passersby, his face brightened with inspiration. He spent his entire quarter on unpopped popcorn and rushed home. By early evening, he was back on the street with little parcels of popcorn and took a place beside the other street vendors, who eyed him suspiciously. The old-timers didn't take kindly to gamins hustling their clientele, and Will's first few days were anything but auspicious.

The twelve-year-old was undaunted. A friend of Will's could play the banjo. Promising his buddy a share in the takings, Will took his place on the streets the next day, his musical companion at his side. He watched the passersby, carefully waiting for the streets to get maximally crowded.

"Now!" he shouted to his accompanist who responded with a strident jangle on the banjo. Will leaped into the center of the crowd, singing "Camptown Races" while simultaneously dancing a "breakdown" and waggling bags of his popcorn. (Many years later, friends of the U.S. senator from Michigan claimed that this experience had fomented Will's principal talent—his ability to seize Congress by carefully gauging the psychological moment, and hold it through sheer showmanship.)

The act was enormously effective. By the end of the day, Will had made $1.25. As he recalled, "It was capital I had not dreamed of, and with fifty cents I made another investment in corn. Out of this stock I realized three dollars." Business kept popping, and Will had to bring in his younger brother as a partner. Within a year, "Will's Popcorn" was reaping $75 a month—nearly double the average American income of the period—and providing the *sole* support of the Smith family.

Will soon became one of the most popular fixtures of the Grand Rapids streets, and his career began ascending like a rocket. When he was nineteen, sympathetic townspeople helped him win an appointment as pageboy in the Michigan legislature, where his keen senses and instincts quickly caught on to the tricks of oratory and a process that would always fascinate him—the politics of compromise. During this period, he also moonlighted as a correspondent for the *Chicago Times*, where he learned at an early age the relationship between politics and the media. At the age of twenty-one, he began studying law in the Grand Rapids offices of Burch and Montgomery, repaying his tutors with janitorial services.

In 1883, at the age of twenty-four, Will was admitted to the bar of Kent County and set up the offices of Smiley, Smith and Stevens. Almost immediately his firm became expert in the legal aspects of Will's oldest of affections—the railroad. He bought a railroad, financed another, and then sold both at a handsome profit which he put back into his law practice. Will won an unusually high percentage of his cases, and his reputation began spreading throughout the state. The Michigan Bar Association tried to assess the reasons for his phenomenal success:

> As a lawyer, Mr. Smith is diligent and indefatigable, and his loyalty to a client is unquestioned. He is shrewd to discover an advantage and quick to avail himself of it. . . . He enters upon a case thoroughly prepared. Not content with a general understanding of the controversy and its salient features, he seeks to familiarize himself with every interest and principle involved; to gain all possible knowledge of the points of his own case and that of his adversary.

What this assessment failed to grasp was the simple fact that Will often won his cases by wearing his adversaries out. He would patiently extract so much information from witnesses, they would either fag out or explode—in either case often furnishing vital information. Moreover, he was gifted with an almost photographic memory and could recall every detail of the testimony he had generated, whereas opposing counsel could not. His technique would eventually prove to be the most valuable and controversial aspect of the greatest case of his career.

Concurrently with his law practice, Will began launching his political career. In 1886 he became a member of the Michigan State Central Committee for the Republican party. The following year, Governor Cyrus Luce appointed him Michigan's first paid game warden. The post was a sinecure, as far as Will was concerned, and a mere stepping-stone toward his political aspirations. But he delighted in the portion of his duties that brought him into contact with the colorful people of the northern counties—like crusty Joe Bayliss, sheriff of the rough-and-tumble border town of Sault Ste. Marie, where the saloon doors still had signs posted saying, "Leave all firearms outside!" Michigan sportsmen were delighted with Will's appointment as game warden, confident that "City Boy Smith" wouldn't be able to "tell a ruffled grouse from a blue jay." They were unaware of the fact that Will was an astonishingly quick study. In the previous year there had been only 22 convictions. Under Warden Smith, the state secured 220.

Will remained a member of the Republican State Central Committee until 1892. By then, he was happily wedded to Nana Osterhout, the attractive, buxom, headstrong daughter of a Dutch lumberman. Two years later, at the age of thirty-four, he entered the race for congressman. His novel campaign in Michigan's fifth district was a "revelation" to his opponent. Instead of courting the influence of the most prominent citizens, which was customary in the days before electronic media, Will took his campaign directly to the people and energetically canvassed every single doorstep. Smith beat the incumbent, General L.G. Rutherford, by a plurality of 10,000 votes. With increasing majorities, he would be returned to Congress by his constituents, who idolized him; he eventually ran unopposed.

In 1895, Mr. Smith went to Washington, one of the youngest members of the House. Physically, William Alden—as everyone now called him—was an odd-looking statesman. An astute Washington correspondent noted that he had a peculiar face, easily malleable into the warmest affection and fiercest antagonism. His nose was broad. His close-set penetrating eyes flashed when he spoke. His full-lipped mouth held perhaps too many teeth, and his brushed-back mane of prematurely gray hair was forever falling in his eyes. His fast pace and lively movements suggested irrepressible energy. Although a small man, he bore himself with striking, often arrogant, self-confidence. As a correspondent for *The Nation* observed, his was more "the dignity of the prize bantam than of the eagle." In short, Congressman Smith looked pretty much what he was: a naïve but cocksure Midwestern rube.

Smith served his district with a fidelity and vigor matched only by his ambition. In his opinion, Grand Rapids, which dominated his district, was "politically speaking, a queer city. There is none other quite like it in this respect on the face of the earth." Consequently, there was no representative quite like Mr. Smith. He began his tenure unobtrusively enough, introducing a banal resolution making his idol Abe Lincoln's birthday a national holiday. (He eventually got it into law over the amused indifference of his colleagues.) In time, he hoisted his true colors.

House Republicans soon found him one of their most unpredictable members. On economic issues, such as the high protective tariff, he could be trusted to vote with the party. On other matters, particularly those affecting individual liberty and the rights of minorities, he could just as well be found leading the Democratic opposition. In one debate on the floor, House Democrats watched delightedly as the young Republican throttled his own party's bill for restricting immigration on the basis of a language test. In the fervent finale of his speech, William Alden exclaimed:

> I say that any attempt to impose an educational qualification upon citizenship is an abridgement of patriotism [applause] and an unfair discrimination against unfortunate people, whose hearts may be alive to every national responsibility.

Reflecting his state's interest in conservation, unusual for the day, he introduced legislation protecting national wildlife—"William Alden's tweetie-bird bill," his colleagues called it. He caused considerable amusement by proposing federal regulation over the nation's seemingly infinite supplies of timber and coal, arguing that America's natural resources would be "ruthlessly wasted and recklessly sacrificed until we are driven around the world seeking supplies for domestic purposes." *The Nation* noted of William Alden that "all that he has in the world, and all that he is, he owes to his faculty of being chipper in the teeth of every difficulty, and keeping everlastingly at it when he has made up his mind to accomplish something." These qualities would hold him in good stead when it came to the greatest challenge of his career.

He thrived on conflict and excitement. He was "plucky, genial, energetic," and a "regular hustler." While his colleagues contemplated weighty matters in a smoke-filled room, William Alden preferred thinking things through alone on horseback and would ride his thoroughbred Bobby Burns at a full gallop through Washington's Rock Creek Park. (He confessed distinct pleasure in having Bobby "kick up his heels at all the Washington aristocrats.") Proper Washington society began calling him "a born fool" and grew even more contemptuous when the epithet failed to faze him.

Fellow Republicans found him "a good lawyer, a rattling political worker, a charming companion socially, and yet so full of strict business methods" that he could often be overbearing. Although his political shrewdness was uncanny, there was no doubting the sterling quality of his integrity—his "aggressive honesty and devotion to principle," as one reporter called it. Those applying to him for political appointments were shocked to find they had to prove they were "endorsed by local sentiment." But integrity was not so much a moral issue with him as it was a practical one—it worked better than anything he knew, and he could wield it like a bludgeon. He was constantly offending fellow members of the Michigan delegation with his criticism of their political back-scratching. To an indignant Senator Russell Alger, Smith explained, "I have always been frank in my relations with my political friends. I will not allow any of them to make any mistakes through silence upon my part."

By the turn of the century, William Alden Smith had achieved the paradoxical distinction of being regarded as the most politically peculiar and yet "most representative Representative" in the House. He had also achieved quite a reputation as an orator. For a relatively small man, he had a remarkably powerful voice, coupled with a fine flow of words and an electric delivery. Democratic foe Champ Clark claimed that William Alden could "wring tears and force cheers from a grindstone." Although highly lauded, Smith's formal speeches followed the convention of alliterative hyperbole that, in the early years of the century, passed for eloquence. It was in his impromptu speeches—his "stampedes"—that Smith was at his best; these capitalized on his uncanny knack of sensing the mood around him and playing the psychological moment to the hilt.

In March 1904, President Roosevelt was about to be renominated for a second term. In order to silence a number of House members who were complaining too loudly about "executive usurpation" (Teddy hadn't asked Congress's permission to take the Panama Canal Zone), TR made public a report prepared by Assistant Postmaster Bristow. The Bristow report revealed that an appalling number of congressmen had overloaded the Post Office budget with political appointments for their friends.

The congressmen whose names were on the report were up for reelection themselves, and after several hours of gloom the House grew furious. The debate on the floor went on for days. Republicans demanded Bristow's immediate removal from office. Democrats branded him "an imbecile" and "an ass." William Alden sat back quietly amused, since his head wasn't on the block. (This was just the sort of thing he had been warning fellow members about for years.) But the opportunity was certainly ripe for something.

Upon being recognized, the congressman from Michigan began speaking with dramatic solemnity: "Mr. Speaker, I denounce this report that has been thrown voluntarily on the desks of Members as a gratuitous insult by a great Executive Department of this Government." The utterance brought a thunderclap of applause.

Spreading his lapels back with his thumbs and puffing out his chest to project his voice, Smith bellowed, "Whenever the people want a really popular candidate for President, they come to the House of Representatives to get him!" The cheers began.

Then, waving his fist, Smith roared, "And I hope the day is not far distant when the people will deservedly crown that great commoner, the Speaker of this House, with the Presidential office for which he is so admirably fitted!"

According to an eyewitness, the House, already worked to a high pitch of excitement, suddenly began "shrieking hysterically like a girls' seminary in a fire panic." Smith had all but nominated Speaker Joseph Cannon for the Presidency—"Uncle Joe," the "Iron Duke," the infamous boss who ruled the House like a martinet. The idea was absurd; Smith didn't even *like* Cannon.

Uncle Joe had been deep in conversation with one of

his lackeys and had not heard the cause of the commotion. Finally, a clerk came running up to him and gasped, "Mr. Speaker, you've been nominated for President, and they're cheering you!"

Dressed in one of the expensive suits specially tailored to make him look like a walking anachronism, Cannon leaped to his feet and spat in his cuspidor, teeth clenched and eyes blazing. He banged away at the gavel, but the tumult was far too great to be stopped so easily.

"Mr. Speaker, I ask unanimous consent that the gentleman from Michigan be allowed thirty minutes to conclude his remarks!" shouted Henry Clayton of Alabama.

"I ask unanimous consent that the debate be continued for three more days!" chimed Jesse Overstreet of Indiana.

But Mr. Smith would not be given back the floor—for several weeks, as a matter of fact. Smith's gambit had been carefully chosen to embarrass *both* Roosevelt and Cannon. It was embarrassing for Teddy, so close to his renomination, to have the House start a boom for the Speaker's candidacy. It was embarrassing for Cannon, who actually intended running for President in four years, to be set up against TR with whom he had been maintaining an uneasy truce and whose support he would eventually need in 1908. In one brief moment, William Alden Smith—the "born fool" from Michigan—had tripped up the two most powerful men in the capital.

The next morning, Congressman Smith was summoned to the White House. Reporters speculated that William Alden wouldn't fare too badly. After all, he had "as many teeth as the President" and could smile just as widely. Smith managed to convince Teddy that he had meant no harm with his little speech, and the President found himself accepting an offer from the Grand Rapids Furniture Association to fill the Red Room with its wares.

Leaving the White House, Smith was surrounded by reporters who wanted to know if he was going to follow his Cannon speech with another. "No," William Alden grinned sheepishly. "When you've made your bull's-eye, it won't do any good and may even damage your reputation as a marksman if you fire the other barrel."

By that time, Smith's marksmanship was already set on a seat in the U.S. Senate, but there were problems. At that time, senators were elected by the state legislatures, which in turn were controlled by the dominant corporate interests of the state. Consequently, there was a senator from steel, a senator from cotton, one from coal—nearly every one of them subsidized by a trust. Smith had tried for Michigan's U.S. Senate seat in 1903, but as a notorious independent, he had been defeated by the influence of a powerful corporate family, the McMillans of Detroit. Smith had railed against the "oligarchy of the Senate" and had condemned the "hidebound, unrelenting, uncompromising machine candidates" sponsored by the McMillans, but it would take more than tongue-lashings to dent the McMillan machine.

Early in 1906, as soon as the McMillans bought the powerful *Detroit Free Press,* Smith immediately responded by buying the tiny *Grand Rapids Herald,* whose editions he had once peddled on the streets. Walking through the pressroom of his new enterprise, Smith talked with all the newsboys and reporters, his attention riveting on a "tall, thin, tensely energetic" and bright young man called Van. Several days later, Smith asked Van into the front office. Carefully looking over the twenty-two-year-old in nerve-wracking silence, the congressman finally said, "Well, I'm going to make you managing editor of this paper and your salary will be twenty-five hundred dollars a year."

Van's jaw dropped; he was then making $832 a year. Van later recalled, "There was just no sense to it. It was one of the most amazing incidents. One of those fortuitous circumstances that change a whole life." The Alger scenario had been passed to another.

Feeling confident of his bid for the Senate if the people had a greater voice in the matter, Smith charged Van with launching a statewide campaign in the *Herald* for the direct election of senators and for a nominating primary. He also asked Van to organize a Michigan Republican Primary Defense League. Van's execution of his duties was masterly, and his editorials brilliant. (Many years later, Van—as Senator Arthur Vandenberg—would formulate a bipartisan model for foreign relations, sponsor the Marshall Plan, assist in drafting the charter of the United Nations, and in turn help launch the career of another Grand Rapids hopeful, Gerald R. Ford.)

Smith's campaign for the Senate, promising a transition of that body from "a closed, corporate board of control" to a "forum of the people," neatly coincided with sentiment already blowing in the wind. The Populist movement was fifteen years old, and what had once been considered radical was being called progressive in 1906. Periodicals were charging that the Senate had become a pawn of vested interests and special privilege. Increasingly, the cry was heard that the U.S. Senate was a marketplace for the millionaires and the trusts; and the cry came predominantly from the rural Midwest which, in all its naïve smugness, was convinced that its morality and methods could alone restore free government and private property.

In spite of its own inclinations, the Michigan legislature was forced by statewide sentiment to pass over two

McMillan candidates (both of them millionaires) and elect William Alden Smith to the U.S. Senate. He received the congratulations of every faction in the state—from typewritten letters on impressive business stationery to hand-scrawled blessings on scraps of paper. "Michigan is herself once more," wrote one. "Vox populi vox Dei!" "At last the people have a real 'live one' to represent them!" The newspapers trumpeted that "tremendous fortunes and old-line political machines are no longer necessary in the making of U.S. senators from Michigan."

The U.S. Senate was not among those rejoicing. William Alden's "stampedes" were well known on Capitol Hill, and the Senate was not amused. Smith simply did not fit in that sanctimonious body, and his friends in the House warned that the Senate bosses would make him "a pickle in the cold-storage reservoir." Smith, however, was undaunted. He began his tenure in the Senate as he had in the House—quietly and prudently. He secured an appointment on the powerful Committee on Foreign Relations, then on Commerce, and then on Territories, of which he became chairman. One year later, sensing he was on firm ground, he electrified the Senate by forcing from the Aldrich Emergency Currency Bill a railroad-bond feature tacked on by the J.P. Morgan interests. Smith was the first Republican who had ever challenged the undisputed sway of Nelson Aldrich, the czar of the Senate, and Aldrich capitulated to Smith's demand out of shock more than anything else. The incident was widely recounted, even in such apolitical weeklies as the *Saturday Evening Post.*

Other journals suddenly took an interest in this singular anomaly from Michigan. *Cosmopolitan,* which had just published a series of vignettes detailing the corruption of individual senators, wrote in praise of Smith:

"There is never any doubt as to where he stands on any public question. He is absolutely fearless in the statement of his convictions, and neither party caucuses, nor Senate traditions, nor autocratic chief executives embarrass or intimidate the expression of his honest views." These qualities, though not the sort to endear him to his senatorial colleagues, would sustain him over the course of the greatest ordeal of his career.

In early 1909, a New York power corporation had lobbied successfully for a treaty by which Canada would yield part of the Niagara for the company's use; in return, the United States would give Canada additional rights on the St. Mary's River in Sault Ste. Marie. The treaty had been drawn up by a Boston attorney and had the sponsorship of Henry Cabot Lodge, the formidable chairman of the Foreign Relations Committee. Smith denounced the treaty even though it had received President-elect Taft's support. The next day, William Alden was informed that his remarks in closed session had been given to a lobbyist for the treaty and that an argument based on his comments was ongoing in the Senate chamber. Furious at this violation of the rules for the sake of a trust, Smith rushed into the chamber, where he was immediately recognized.

"Mr. President," said Smith, "by what right are remarks of mine in executive session reported to a private individual outside this chamber?"

"To whom does the senator refer?" asked Cabot Lodge.

William Alden named the lobbyist.

"I deny that there is any truth in that assertion," Lodge replied.

"And I repeat it," said Smith.

"And I deny it," Lodge retorted. "It is not true!" Lodge, who held a Ph.D. in political science from Harvard, could barely conceal his contempt for this brash bumpkin "from the wilds of Michigan."

"And *again* I repeat it!" Smith snapped. "What is that lying upon the desk of the senator from Massachusetts?" A typewritten argument in favor of the treaty, written by the lobbyist named, lay on Lodge's desk. As Smith contended, it contained his remarks of the previous day. Lodge remained silent.

"Mr. President," Smith resumed, "if New York financial interests want to grab Canadian water power at Niagara and their friends in the Senate wish to help them do so, that is not my affair. But you *can't pay* for your *job* at Niagara by sacrificing the people of my state at St. Mary's!"

Amidst the nervous coughs reflecting the tension in the chamber, Lodge walked over to Smith's desk and quietly muttered, "We will ratify this treaty in spite of you."

Quite audibly, Smith retorted, "Senator, I don't like your irritating manners." Staring at Lodge a moment longer, Smith suddenly blared, "And furthermore, Senator, I don't like your looks!"

Lodge turned red, then white with rage. Democrats were "enjoying the debate hugely." Senator Tillman ("Pitchfork Ben") even hoped that "Michigan and Massachusetts would clinch." The evening papers capped the event with the headline: "SMITH TELLS LODGE HE DOESN'T LIKE HIS LOOKS." One correspondent, who thrilled at the vigor that had come into the moribund Senate, described the incident in verse:

> Oh, it does me good to hear it,
> And today I want to cheer it,
> It's the kind of reparteeing
> That we read about in books.

There was nothing harsh about it,
For he didn't even shout it;
William Alden simply told him
That he didn't like his looks.

Soon thereafter, Secretary of State Bacon notified President-elect Taft that if he wanted to save the treaty with Canada, he would have to "sit down hard on Smith." Taft's mentor, Theodore Roosevelt, was with Taft at the time and exploded, "By George, I would take the advice!"

"I *did* sit on him, I thought, this afternoon," Taft replied, "but William Alden is a bobbing sort of cuss and doesn't know when he is sat upon."

"Then I would get him by telephone and threaten him!" screeched the President.

Threats merely rolled off William Alden's back, but his ordeal was hardly over. Democrats didn't care to rally their strength to fight the GOP over the treaty, and every sympathetic Republican was too afraid of bucking the combination of TR, Taft, and Lodge. When the final day of debate on the treaty arrived, Smith was given the floor and promptly announced a one-man filibuster unless the treaty was amended. The Lodge forces quickly convened. Convinced that if anyone could pull off a solo filibuster Smith could, they gave in and William Alden added an amendment saving the St. Mary's for the people of the "Soo."

Liberal papers crowed with delight, acclaiming in paeans the man from Michigan

> who stood single-handed, alone with courage rare and fortitude unexampled, though his friends, his associates, two presidents, and their cabinets were all against him. When ages hence some poet sings the

> epic songs or writes the sagas of the American Senate he will find no brighter story than that of how William Alden Smith held the St. Mary's River, much as Horatius of old held Tiber's bridge. . . . the treaty now about to be consummated preserves water power rights of the American people—worth consideration in these days of battle for the conservation of American resources.

Later that same year, Smith became involved in a similar endeavor, but one that liberals were less willing to praise. It seemed that Jim Pelham, a black employee of the Census Bureau, had seen a black woman brutally clubbed by a policeman. While procuring the names of witnesses in order to make a protest, Pelham was himself placed under arrest. Though a nine-year resident of the capital, Pelham had originally come from Detroit, and when his friends found every route hopeless, they turned to Senator Smith. William Alden looked into the situation and said that, as a U.S. senator, he could do nothing. But, if Mr. Pelham desired, he would be willing to serve as his counsel, gratis. The offer was instantly accepted.

The case was heard in one of Washington's infamous lower courts, known as "nigger court." When Smith appeared for the defendant, Justice Kimball challenged the U.S. Senate's authority to intervene in the matter. Smith calmly explained that he was a member of the bar and admitted to Supreme Court practice, and was merely present as defendant's counsel. Kimball yielded, and Smith sat down, staring incredulously at the huge wire cage in which black witnesses were herded for trial. The senator grew incensed at the "rough-and-tumble way in which Negro prisoners are dealt with in Washington police court practices."

Smith made a motion for acquittal: "Tell me, had

Pelham been a white man would he have even been arrested?" The motion was deemed "irrelevant"; the case would be tried. Smith then devastated the three prosecution witnesses and called seven character witnesses for Pelham, who was acquitted.

When the news reached Capitol Hill, the incident was treated as a scandal. It was already clear that this "bumptuous nonentity" had utterly no respect for senatorial dignity, but this time he had gone too far. His dabbling in the Pelham case had besmirched the lofty traditions of the U.S. Senate. Other senators were merely amused and suggested that William Alden resign from the Senate and take up a full-time practice in "nigger court." The incident was not reported in the papers—there seemed something too shameful about it. Even most Michigan papers were reluctant to discuss it. Smith didn't mind, however; by now he was used to fighting lonely battles.

By 1910 a new wave began rolling over the Senate. Incoming Democrats and Progressive Republicans managed to form a viable progressive block, and the bosses found their authority challenged more consistently. Suddenly things grew ominous. Taft's proposal for a downward revision of the tariff exacerbated a growing schism in the once-invincible Republican party. Progressives were for a downward revision of the tariff, arguing that although the tariff may have once protected labor, it had not become the "mother of the trusts" and was causing inflation. The Old Guard members of the party, most of whom owed their seats to the trusts, were for "standing pat" on the tariff.

In its most obvious aspect, the rift between the Old Guard and the Progressive Republicans was a clash between centuries. The Old Guard clearly embraced nineteenth-century postbellum traditions of Anglo-Saxon privilege and constitutional conservatism. The Progressives expounded the necessity for broadly interpreting the constitution to meet the needs of a now greatly expanded and highly diversified populace. The philosophical basis of the division would sound the keynote of American politics for the twentieth century.

It was inevitable for William Alden Smith to find himself straddling both sides. In the first place, he was chronologically in between the two. He had entered the Senate at the nadir of the Old Guard and several years before enough "young Turks" had come in to forge a viable progressive faction. Secondly, everything about Smith's life, personality, and rise to power sprang from his inherent ability to see the strengths and weaknesses of each side of an issue; he was a genuine ambivert. Certainly he admired the Progressive Republicans, especially their values and zeal; but he didn't find them progressive in all the ways that were meaningful to him—they cared nothing about racial injustice, for example. (Only Smith and Old Guard Senator Foraker of Ohio stood firmly against Roosevelt's inequitable handling of the "Brownsville Affray.") Finally, and most importantly, Smith had come to value his political independence above everything else, and his independence rested squarely on his refusal to identify with any isolated clique—Progressives included.

Smith's best friends in the Senate, Dolliver of Iowa and Beveridge of Indiana, were both Progressives and continually invited him to attend their caucuses, but he refused. "I know of no faction of the party with which I am not on friendly terms," he said with obvious self-satisfaction. "I have no ambition to become a boss or to subdue one element in the party for the glory of another." In fact, Smith believed that *both* factions of Republicanism were essential to the party's vitality, and could not understand why the GOP couldn't be "broad enough and free enough to embrace Messrs. Cummings and LaFollette in its folds and in its leadership." As far as the tariff was concerned, he was content to let the two factions toss about "on the trough of the sea" while he busied himself with other matters.

From 1910 to 1912 he became deeply involved in his work as chairman of the Committee on Territories. According to Senator Shelby Cullom, Smith was an unusually "industrious and competent legislator," and for all his revels in the barnyard side of politics, he enjoyed legal draftsmanship. He was good at it and found the work relaxing. In 1911, he worked unceasingly to secure the statehoods of Arizona and New Mexico. In early 1912, he began spending long evenings on the codification and annotation of laws that would result in a huge printed volume and provide the first territorial government of Alaska.

On the evening of April 15, 1912, the senator was at work in his rooms on the fourth floor of the Senate Office Building, extremely engrossed in the problem of building railroads in Alaska. Suddenly, he heard a commotion outside in the corridors. The voices grew louder, and William Alden went out to investigate.

Word had just been received from New York that J.P. Morgan's latest venture, the enormous luxury liner R.M.S. *Titanic,* had foundered in the middle of the North Atlantic with a catastrophic loss of life. The greatest ordeal of William Alden Smith's career had arrived.

7

The *Congressional Limited*

On Tuesday morning, April 16, 1912, William Howard Taft sat glumly in the remodeled Oval Office. Reneging on his diet, the 320-pound President had just forsaken the salted almonds his wife, Nellie, had given him to subdue hunger pangs and had returned to his beloved bonbons. He was now in the final year of his term. Four years earlier a plurality of the nation had sung, "Get on the raft with Taft, boys, get in the winning boat." But the ship of state seemed to have sprung a leak. Taft's best endeavors had already been received by the American public as a series of disasters—and now this *Titanic* business! The anguish of the nation, however, was not the cause of the President's low spirits. In fact, public response to anything was rarely of interest to him. From federal judge, to governor of the Philippines, to Roosevelt's Secretary of War, Taft's public offices had consistently resulted from individual appointment. Consequently, he had never learned to woo, much less respect, popular sentiment—not even during his bid for the Presidency. Taft owed his presence in the White

House entirely to one man—his "friend, the Colonel," Theodore Roosevelt.

The Taft-Roosevelt relationship was one of those rare, quasi-mystical bonds between temperamentally opposite males in which a lack of commonality is manageable so long as the relationship realizes outside ambitions. Under President Roosevelt's leadership, Taft and TR had made a highly effective team. Where TR had been an energetic, content-oriented instigator, Taft had been a prudent, process-oriented administrator. After Teddy "took the Canal Zone," Taft had been dispatched to Panama to supervise the actual digging of the canal. When one of TR's unprecedented executive orders stirred up Washington, Taft kept things together by "sitting on the lid." The successful complementarity of their relationship, with its specious and heady aura of omnipotence, had been labeled "close friendship" by each of the men, even though it was nothing of the kind.

In 1907, TR had considered running for a third term, but for a number of reasons concluded that it was unfeasible. It was natural for him to appoint Taft his successor, and it had been a simple matter to foist his friend onto the GOP delegates at the convention and then personally oversee his successful campaign against William Jennings Bryan. With Taft in the White House, Teddy could relinquish the "bully pulpit," confident that his progressive policies would be perpetuated. It seemed the perfect solution to the politically unwise course of seeking a third term—or so Teddy thought, as he departed for an African safari amidst the cheers of his adoring countrymen.

As Chief Executive, Taft—with the benefit of neither Roosevelt's advice nor his manly support—had at first felt intimidated. Eventually, he had resolved to try things his own way. After all, he explained, "It's no use trying to be a Roosevelt with the ways of William

Howard Taft." Taft's "ways" were those of a literal constitutionalist, irrespective of the human frustration they incurred. He was earnestly dedicated to continued progressivism, but, in order to get his measures through Congress, he had allied himself with the Old Guard powers of Speaker Cannon, Representative Payne, and Senator Aldrich. TR had also cooperated with this conservative trio, but whereas Teddy had skillfully spun his public image above the "standpatters," Taft's methods seemed almost calculated to forge an indelible identification between himself and the reactionaries in the public mind.

This was ironic, since in many ways Taft's progressivism surpassed Roosevelt's. Whereas Teddy had hidden the fact that his 1904 campaign—studded with commonfolk rhetoric—had been financed by massive contributions from Wall Street, Taft pushed a bill through Congress requiring that campaign expenses in federal elections be made public. Disdaining TR's penchant for bypassing the merit system, Taft inaugurated a long-range plan whereby a huge number of federal offices would be placed under the civil service laws. Most important, in just four years Taft managed to prosecute nearly twice as many of the millionaires' trusts under the Sherman Act than TR had been willing to try in seven years.

Nevertheless Taft's achievements were obscured by his lackluster, uninspired public leadership. Teddy's charisma had cloaked the presidency in the garb of a Public Tribune. Taft cared little for images and stuck doggedly, almost mechanically, to realizing his campaign pledges, despite the way in which his methods grated on the populace. (Judge Taft could divine no reason for securing public endorsement of actions that were "basically right.") Teddy had been an adroit manipulator of people, but Taft's maneuvers constantly backfired. His legal mind was incapable of straddling fences, and virtually every attempt he made to bridge gaps in the party resulted only in widening them further. He despised the ceremonial side of the presidency. To friends who complained that he didn't keep himself in the headlines enough, Taft replied in his inimitable, convoluted fashion: "I couldn't if I would and I wouldn't if I could."

The situation grew critical in 1911 when Taft thrust Canadian reciprocity at Congress. In spite of its merits as modern foreign policy, the treaty's alleged harmfulness to farmers and lumbermen ignited the smouldering outrage of Progressive (mostly Western) Republicans. William Alden Smith, who helped lead the fight against reciprocity, had tried to warn Taft that if he pushed the bill Congress would "kill him with bird shot." (Smith told Archie Butt that the President would "be so full of little holes when they get through with him that his best friends won't recognize him.") Taft thought the treaty would only "break the Republican party for a while," but it did far worse. It split the party and the nation into east and west factions, with caluminous rantings unheard since the Civil War. Progressives finally concluded they could not endorse the President for another term.

For a while Progressive hopes rested on "Fighting Bob" LaFollette of Wisconsin. In February 1912, however, LaFollette—under the combined influence of ptomaine poisoning and a slug of whiskey to deaden the pain—delivered a reckless, slack-tongued speech before a group of journalists in which he damned the irresponsibility of the American press. Reviews of the incident were not the sort to sustain belief in the continued viability of LaFollette's candidacy.

Rumors of TR's coming back to the White House had captured the public imagination ever since the Colonel had returned from Africa with his big-game trophies. In time, his home in Oyster Bay became a mecca for distraught Progressives. Throughout 1911, Teddy refused entreaties that he run again in 1912. To his friend Henry Needham, TR said, "Now don't you get it into your head that there is a great tide in my favor. These things go up and go down."

Mostly they went up. Distorted accounts of Taft's desertion of progressive causes began agitating the Colonel. He started considering 1912 seriously when he was called on by financier George Perkins of the House of Morgan, who had been severely put upon by Taft's enthusiastic trust-busting—particularly the government's suit against U.S. Steel. After talking with Perkins, TR correctly reasoned that if Taft couldn't even carry standpat Wall Street, the Republican party was in genuine danger.

On February 21, 1912, TR made his celebrated announcement, "My hat is in the ring," and began preparing to challenge his old friend in the few state primaries in existence at the time. Roosevelt's immediate strategy suggested that his friendship with Taft had never existed, which in the final analysis was closest to the truth. In spite of an article he had published in *Outlook* praising the compromised Payne-Aldrich Tariff (Taft had signed it into law since "half a loaf is better than none"), Teddy now condemned it as an outrage to reform-minded folk. Earlier, TR had endorsed Canadian reciprocity; however, on April 8 in Mattoon, Illinois, he attacked it as a crime against the farmers. The ambivalence Roosevelt had always sensed beneath his fondness for Taft now began surfacing in the form of suspiciousness. In March, the Colonel was convinced that since Taft and his henchmen could not "murder the progressive movement, they wish to see the Republican party commit suicide." By April 16, he was telling a supporter, "I never have seen more infamous conduct than that of the Taft managers in this campaign and of course Taft is conniving at it and profiting by it."

This simply was not true. Taft, who unhappily chose to believe that the relationship with Teddy had been genuine friendship, was depressed by the whole sordid affair. In spite of entreaties from advisers, he refused to authorize political ploys against Roosevelt. Never an autonomous man, Taft began leaning on his aide and confidant Archie Butt in ways he had once leaned on the Colonel. "I don't understand Roosevelt," he told Archie. "I don't know what he is driving at except to make my way more difficult. I could not ask his advice on all questions. I could not subordinate my administration to him and retain my self-respect, but it is hard, very hard, Archie, to see a devoted friendship going to pieces like a rope of sand."

Major Archibald Butt was the proverbial man in the middle. The tall, distinguished-looking, softspoken Southerner had been TR's White House aide before serving Taft and had been privy to some of the duo's most intimate conversations. In spite of his affection for Roosevelt, he had been unswerving in his loyalty to the President and ingenious in placating Taft's endless self-doubts. At the White House New Year's reception of 1912, Archie had jacked up the Secret Service's guest-counting machines by a thousand, so that Taft would not have to be faced with such a stark statement of his abysmal unpopularity. He was nevertheless unable to forget his deep respect for the Colonel, nor could the Colonel forget him. Shortly after Taft had begun plaintively appealing to him for sympathy, Archie was confronted by indomitable Alice Roosevelt Longworth, who bore a personal message from her father: "Alice, when you get the opportunity, tell Archie from me to get out of his present job. And not to wait for the convention or election, but to do it soon."

Archie had then found himself in an onerous bind. He was one of the few who had irresolutely refused to take sides between the Colonel and the President. As a tangible link in their relationship, Archie found himself spiritually severed by their growing personal antagonism. Ultimately, he requested Taft's permission for a much-needed vacation in Europe, to which the President wholeheartedly agreed.

On April 14, TR trounced Taft in the Pennsylvania primary. Less than twenty-four hours later, homeward bound on the R.M.S. *Titanic*, Archie had gone to the bottom of the North Atlantic.

On Tuesday, April 16, the President was less concerned with his decimated political prospects than the undetermined fate of "our dear Archie." By midmorning, Taft was awaiting a reply from a telegram he had sent P.A.S. Franklin at the New York White Star office. It was pathetic in its plaintiveness:

> Have you any information concerning Major Butt? If you will communicate with me at once, would greatly appreciate.

Having received no reply in nearly two hours, Taft took what was for him prompt and decisive action. He dispatched the *Salem* and *Chester* to contact the *Carpathia* and inquire about his aide. Even so, his authority seemed flouted. Upon making radio contact with the rescue ship, Commander Chandler of the *Salem* wired the President that he could "get no information from *Carpathia* of any kind, although she is in easy radio communication." Occasionally the *Carpathia* would acknowledge calls, but would "not admit receipt of messages or make reply." Chandler could "not believe that she failed to understand the messages" he had sent her.

Naval officers said that the *Carpathia*'s refusal to answer an official inquiry from a president of the United States was "unprecedented." In back corridors of Washington, whispers intimated that if this sort of thing had happened to Teddy, he would have surrounded the little Cunarder with the Great White Fleet. President Taft merely moped. His reticence and inaccessibility seemed to grow in direct proportion to public concern over the shipwreck, and official Washington soon became irritated with him. As Henry Adams put it, "I do not know whether Taft or the *Titanic* is likely to be the furthest-reaching disaster."

It was inevitable for the *Titanic* to become a metaphor for the divergence between the Colonel and the President. This is borne out in letters bemoaning the disaster that were sent to the two men by awestruck citizens. Admirers of Teddy imagined that, had the Colonel been in charge of the *Titanic*, he would have been the dashing hero whose keen decisiveness would have somehow saved the ship in the nick of time—Taft would have sat back and watched her founder. Typical was a letter to TR saying, "since your hand has ceased to guide the helm that steers the good ship America, one disaster after another has overtaken her citizens."

Admirers of Taft, however, fancied that the President would have saved the ship with his prudence. As one friendly constituent expressed it: TR would have said, "Put on more steam, boys; we will knock hell of these icebergs—with the immediate result that all of the women and three thousand passengers would have gone with the ship instantly to the bottom." Captain Taft would have said, "Slow down, boys, and lay to until morning, when we move cautiously out of this dangerous sea."

In the face of what Taft himself called "the appalling character of this disaster," it was natural to worry whether or not the nation's skipper was securely at the helm. When telegrams, letters, poetry, questions, and advice began pouring into the White House, Taft's secretary, Charles Hilles, recognized the nation's plea for some form of reassurance from the Chief Executive and attempted to nudge the President toward a national proclamation. Taft's response was typical: Was there a precedent for it?

Straightaway, Hilles sent the State Department on a frenzied search for a precedent. Eventually Assistant Secretary of State Huntington Wilson, whose punctiliousness Taft despised ("I would like to sit on Wilson and mash him flat!"), located a precedent guaranteed to embarrass Taft. It has been established in 1906 by good old Teddy in response to the earthquake in Valparaiso, Chile.

Taft was thoroughly annoyed. If TR had issued such a proclamation, it couldn't hold as a precedent, since nearly everything Teddy had done was unconstitutional! By Thursday the eighteenth, Representative Bartholdt informed the White House that if the President wasn't at least going to lower the nation's flags, he would sponsor a resolution to that effect in the House. Although the President finally agreed to order flags at half-mast, he would issue no proclamation. Taft's obstinance on the matter was a political blunder, since in effect he tossed the ball right into Teddy's lap. TR, who was on the campaign trail out West—making the most politically of the raw nerves the disaster had exposed in the nation—soon dispatched a telegram to Mayor Gaynor of New York: "I wish I were present in New York to join with my fellow citizens in expressing our grief at the shocking catastrophe to the *Titanic,* and our deep sympathy with the kinsfolk of those who have perished."

William Taft simply wanted to be left alone to brood over Archie. On Wednesday, after learning the number lost and saved aboard the ship, the President gave up hope of Archie's rescue. "No other fate was possible with his soldierly spirit," he told the British ambassador. To a friend, Taft wrote, "Archie was the soul of honor. He was wholehearted and wholesome; courteous and courageous and a charming companion." At a memorial service for Archie, the President's profound grief bespoke not just the loss of his aide, but the loss of the relationship with Roosevelt which Archie had catalyzed and later symbolized. "I cannot turn around in my room," Taft said with tears in his eyes. "I can't go anywhere without expecting to see his smiling face or hear his cheerful voice in greeting."

While the President grieved and the Colonel ranted, the American nation grew more and more distraught.

Meanwhile in the Senate Office Building, Senator William Alden Smith of Michigan pored over the newspapers he had spread out on his desk. Struck by a curious coincidence, he extracted from his billfold a piece of yellowed newsprint he had clipped in 1902. It was a poem about a shipwreck:

> Then she, the stricken hull,
> The doomed, the beautiful,
> Proudly to fate abased
>   Her brow, Titanic.

He had been strangely moved by the poem ten years earlier and had all but forgotten that he still carried it around with him. *What did it all mean*?

The front pages of the papers featured prominent

portraits of a beaming, bewhiskered Captain E.J. Smith. Six years earlier, William Alden and his son had made a North Atlantic voyage aboard the *Baltic* under the command of E.J. As a U.S. congressman, Will had been invited to dine at the captain's table, where the conversation had turned from railway regulation to steamship safety. Subsequently, E.J. had invited him to the bridge, where he viewed the mechanism that activated the watertight doors. The captain had then conducted the congressman and his son on a tour through the ship, explaining everything in detail. William Alden had been duly impressed—as impressed as he was now dumbfounded. E.J. was no fool, nor was he "reckless," as some editors were then suggesting.

What had gone wrong? What about those ice warnings? Why had the world's largest, finest, and safest passenger ship foundered on her maiden voyage? Everyone was asking these questions, but the impetuous senator from Michigan was determined to have them answered.

He immediately phoned Charles Hilles at the White House to find out what the President was going to do; he was politely informed that the President would most likely do nothing. Smith then called the Michigan delegation to learn what was "brewing" in the House. There was talk of a number of bills to be presented for the future inclusion of sufficient lifeboats on steamships—mostly "panic legislation." Smith loathed panic legislation. Congress had been obsessed with it over the course of the Spanish-American War and for any temporary placation it achieved, it caused hundreds of knotty problems later. It appeared that if anything efficient were going to be done, it would have to be done by the Senate. And if anyone were going to jolt that sedate body into action, it would have to be Smith of Michigan.

The appropriate standing committee for dealing with

the *Titanic* matter was either Commerce or Foreign Relations. Which of the two didn't matter to Smith—he was a member of both. The Committee on Commerce was officially involved in waterway navigation and safety, though Smith's presence on it was due to his expertise on railroads. A good reason to focus on Commerce lay in its authority over the wireless; a bill for wireless regulation was already being batted about in the House, but standpatters were not particularly enthusiastic about seeing it through. After weighing the matter all Tuesday morning, Smith sat down at a typewriter and began banging out a draft.

On the morning of Wednesday, April 17, word had just been received that the only existing survivors of the wreck were those few already aboard the *Carpathia.* The size of the castrophe had now been grasped in Washington, and the dignified and decorous Senate was uncommonly agitated—a sight that privately pleased William Alden; it was about time it got upset over something of national importance. After Chaplain Ulysses Pierce droned a dolorous prayer, the secretary began reading the minutes, whereupon the reading was suspended and the floor given to Mr. Smith.

"Mr. President," said Smith, "I ask unanimous consent to introduce the resolution I send to the desk. I ask that it be read and referred to the Committee on Commerce."

The Smith Resolution directed that a subcommittee of Commerce be authorized to investigate the causes leading to the wreck of the *Titanic* "with its attendant loss of life, so shocking to the civilized world." Secondly, it empowered the subcommittee to summon witnesses, administer oaths, and serve subpoenas on all witnesses necessary for information. It delineated the specific areas of interest to the investigation, from lifeboats to prior safety inspection of the vessel. The resolution intended to forestall panic legislation by proposing new laws on the basis of facts uncovered. Finally, it recommended that the subcommittee's findings be used to draft "an international agreement to secure the protection of sea traffic."

There was only a glimmer of debate on the matter. Senator Martine of New Jersey had hastily put together a resolution for an international treaty, but was indifferent whether the Senate endorsed his or Smith's. As he put it, "Senators, let us act at once. True, we can not help the unfortunate souls who went to their watery graves; but lest another craft shall go to the bottom of the insatiable sea with her human cargo, I urge the passage of this resolution!"

The sole objection came from Senator Lodge of Massachusetts. From a legislatively correct position, Lodge coolly argued that while the bulk of the Smith Resolution was properly directed to Commerce, the component dealing with any prospective international treaty was clearly the prerogative of his own Committee on Foreign Relations.

"Mr. President," Smith explained, "my purpose in offering the resolution and its reference to the Committee on Commerce was prompted by the fact that the Committee on Commerce is now in session, and may take *immediate* jurisdiction of the resolution and make a prompt report thereon." Smith did not object to the treaty component going to Foreign Relations, but hinted that Lodge was nit-picking at an inappropriate time.

Possibly fearing the chance of another "clinch" between Massachusetts and Michigan, Senator Martine exclaimed, "I am perfectly indifferent to what committee it may be referred, so long as we can accomplish something. And in God's name let us do something!"

By unanimous consent, the part of Smith's resolution

ordering an investigation went to Commerce, and the treaty component went to Foreign Relations.

Afterward, Smith, met with Senator Knute Nelson, chairman of the Commerce Committee. Nelson instantly named Smith chairman of the investigative subcommittee and asked if he had any ideas as to the composition of the other members. Smith immediately replied in the affirmative. Above all else—nautical expertise included—the subcommittee must be perfectly balanced in political allegiances. It was already clear that the press intended on making the *Titanic* a political issue between the people *vs.* the trusts. If the members of the investigation became enmeshed in an inveigled political schism, it would rank as the second *Titanic* disaster. Smith and Nelson worked on the problem for the remainder of the day, eventually selecting a group entirely to Smith's satisfaction. There would be an equal number of Republicans and Democrats; and a liberal, moderate, and conservative representative of each party.

Liberal Republicans would be represented by "wild-eyed" Jonathan Bourne of Oregon, president of the Republican Progressive League; Bourne was still supporting LaFollette for President. Theodore Burton of Ohio, a Taft man and chairman of the National Waterways Commission, would represent the moderate core of the GOP; Burton had considerable experience in marine affairs. George C. Perkins of California, elderly chairman of the Naval Affairs Committee and himself an old sailor, would speak for the party's Old Guard.

Liberal Democrats would be represented by Francis G. Newlands of Nevada. Newlands had been a persistent champion of Bryan's campaign for free silver, and his soft-spoken honesty and persistence had earned him the respect of even the fiercest enemies of Bryan's cause; Newlands was now preoccupied with a plan to irrigate the nation's Western deserts. Moderate Democrat interests would be reflected by Florida's Duncan Fletcher, an astute attorney who had recently distinguished himself as a member of the investigative team that had exposed the shady campaign tactics of Senator Lorimer of Illinois. Finally, Furnifold Simmons of North Carolina would represent the conservative wing of the Democratic party.

The next day, Thursday, April 18, Smith was in his office dictating a letter to his friend, Governor Chase Osborn of Michigan. "I have something of very great importance that I want to say to you," he wrote the governor, "and I hope everything may remain in status quo until we have talked the matter over." Smith was up for renomination, but his own prospects in the forthcoming campaign were of little concern to him. By then Michigan had passed a statewide primary and Smith felt "no apprehensions whatever" over his renomination; it was now in the hands of the people. But Osborn was Michigan chairman for the committee to elect Theodore Roosevelt, and the Republican party in Michigan was a model of the nation in its bitter divisiveness. Smith was concerned over a possible outbreak of violence among prospective delegates to the national convention and was planning a trip back to his home state to discuss the matter with the governor.

No sooner had he completed his dictation than the Department of the Navy called Smith and informed him that they had intercepted several significant messages sent by J. Bruce Ismay aboard the *Carpathia.* These were the telegrams intimating that Ismay planned on skipping with the crew back to England without putting a foot on American soil. The senator thought the matter over no longer than a minute. If those responsible for the *Titanic* refused to come to Washington, then

Washington would go to them. He called the White House and arranged a noon meeting with the President.

In the Oval Office, Smith could see that Taft had been taking both the loss of Archie and his humiliating defeat by TR in the Pennsylvania primary quite hard. The President looked haggard; his flesh was waxen and—*mirabile dictu*—he had gained even more weight than the last time Smith had seen him. The senator liked Taft personally. He respected his Yale Law School education and resonated with his principles and sincerity. But the fact remained (as Smith had told his friend Al Beveridge) that Taft had "no political sagacity at all."

William Alden hoped Taft could appreciate the national importance of the forthcoming investigation and was pleasantly surprised when the President expressed his "hearty sympathy" with the resolution and his willingness "to do everything" in his "power to further the investigation."

Smith asked about the legality of placing British citizens under subpoena. Taft was confident that so long as they were in United States territory there could be no question about it; however, he conferred briefly with Attorney General Wickersham, who quickly confirmed its legitimacy. Furthermore, added the President, under the circumstances "it would be highly unlikely" for the British authorities to raise objections. (Taft was beginning to smart from the *Carpathia*'s refusal to answer his questions about Archie.)

Smith had three personal requests. He wanted Secretary of Commerce and Labor Charles Nagel, who was in charge of immigration, to accompany him to New York and expedite the handling of steerage passengers; Taft consented. Secondly, he also wanted U.S. Steamship Inspector General George Uhler, an acknowledged maritime authority, to join the senatorial party and provide nautical expertise to the course of the interrogation; again Taft agreed. Finally, Smith asked for the use of a U.S. Treasury revenue cutter to intercept the *Carpathia* before she docked; that way there could be no chance of Ismay's escaping. Again, Taft consented and said he would have Secretary of the Treasury Franklin MacVeagh arrange it that afternoon.

Leaving the White House, the senator gave waiting reporters only the barest details before arriving at the Senate Office Building, where he called the first meeting of the investigative subcommittee. After explaining about the Ismay marconigrams, Smith asked who wanted to come with him to New York to subpoena and interrogate the witnesses. Liberal Democrat Francis Newlands immediately agreed. Progressive Republican Jonathan Bourne was also interested, but his renomination in Oregon was coming up that weekend, and he wondered if he could join the group after resolving some unfinished business in the capital. Smith said that would be perfectly acceptable.

Moderate Republican Ted Burton explained that, although he would like to go, as chairman of the National Waterways Commission he would have to remain in the capital to evaluate a recent proposal for a ship channel from Chicago to the Mississippi River. Moderate Democrat Duncan Fletcher, an important member of Burton's commission, also begged off. Conservative Republican George Perkins was seventy-three years old and not in the best of health; he didn't feel like going.

Conservative Democrat Furnifold Simmons, however, objected to the entire idea. Senators "gallivanting across the country to subpoena foreigners," said Simmons, wasn't in keeping with "senatorial dignity."

"My God!" exploded William Alden. "If this isn't a time to let senatorial dignity go hang, I don't know what is!"

Simmons did not agree. The real issue at hand was the fact that Smith and Simmons were bitter political enemies. A vigorous anti-populist, Simmons had headed a movement in his home state of North Carolina that led to a constitutional amendment effectively depriving most Negroes of the right to vote—an achievement unlikely to endear him to the Michigan abolitionist. Eventually, the conservative Democrat would ask to be dropped from the investigation altogether, a request its chairman would steadfastly refuse.

Smith next called up the sergeant-at-arms of the Senate, Colonel Daniel Ransdell. How did Dan feel, Smith asked, about subpoenaing British citizens to come testify in Washington? Dan squirmed at the question, but agreed that if he had to, he'd do it. Although Ransdell was the only one legally empowered to serve subpoenas for the Senate, he had never been compelled to exercise that authority—much less "on foreigners."

William Alden sat fretting in his office; would Ransdell's nerve fail him at a critical moment? As if to guarantee the success of Smith's scheme, Joe Bayliss, sheriff of Chippewa County, Michigan, and Smith's old game warden crony from Sault Ste. Marie, unexpectedly dropped in. Called by his town "the greatest little sheriff in Michigan," Bayliss was on business in the capital, but couldn't leave for home without stopping by to pay William Alden a call. The senator asked the sheriff where he planned to go next.

"Back to the Soo," Joe replied.

"Oh, no you're not," retorted Smith, his eyes glinting. "You're going to New York with me!" By then, only an hour and a half remained before the *Congressional Limited* was due to leave Washington for New York.

"But I cannot!" Bayliss protested.

"Ask no questions," William Alden replied, "but be at the railroad station by three thirty."

Bayliss argued that he didn't have transportation to the station. The senator said he would send his private car for him. While Dan Ransdell might be squeamish about serving subpoenas, Smith reasoned that crusty Joe, in his battered boots and slouch hat, wouldn't have the slightest compunction about serving foreigners or anybody else for that matter. While Smith called up Dan to arrange Joe's deputization as an assistant sergeant-at-arms of the U.S. Senate, the sheriff dispatched a hasty telegram to his people at the Soo, explaining that he had been "kidnapped for a few days by William Alden."

Smith had attempted to keep the Senate's mission to New York quiet. But at 3:30, as he, Newlands, Bayliss, and Inspector General Uhler arrived at Union Station, the depot was ringed with reporters eager for the story. Amidst a volley of overlapping, unintelligible questions, Smith began recounting his conversation with the President while the party inched its way to the train.

"The officers of the White Star Line," Smith explained, "should respond to congressional action frankly and honestly if they are to enjoy the privileges of American ports and retain the confidence of the American people."

"Are ya going to arrest Bruce Ismay, Senator?"

Smith winced. "We are not going into this matter with a club," he replied. "We will proceed cautiously and conservatively."

"Senator, how can Congress have any jurisdiction over the British?"

"We may not have jurisdiction over the individual," Smith explained, "but the American Congress is not without jurisdiction over the harbors of the United States. It is for these men who make use of the harbors to meet the public demand for information in regard to the disaster. Good day, boys."

Aboard the *Congressional Limited,* Smith located Secretary Nagel in an adjoining car. Nagel had accompanied another Washington party comprised of Mrs. Champ Clark and her daughter (Champ was running for the Democratic nomination for President); Congressman J.A. Hughes of West Virginia, whose daughter was aboard the *Carpathia* and who had received a telegram on the fifteenth advising him of the *Titanic*'s complete safety; Congressmen Levy and Goldfogle of New York; and Mr. W.B. Hibbs, a friend of Archie Butt's whom the President had designated his personal representative. While Nagel remained with this group, Smith and Newlands conferred with Inspector General Uhler about lines of inquiry to be used in the investigation: precautions that ships take in the vicinity of ice, essentials of proper ship inspection, and other details.

During the stop in Wilmington, Delaware, Western Union delivered a telegram to Smith from Franklin MacVeagh of the Treasury Departmment. Taft had kept his word about arranging the use of a revenue cutter. In New York the senatorial party would be met by revenue and customs officers at the Thirty-fourth Street station, who would then escort them to the U.S.S. *Manhattan.* So far, everything was running like clockwork.

The *Congressional Limited* rumbled into Penn Station at 9:07 P.M., and the party was met by Messrs. Loeb and Henry, collector and surveyor of the Port of New York. Loeb and Henry, who were actually jumping up and down with excitement, breathlessly explained that the *Carpathia* was already in sight and was close to docking. Three cabs were standing by. The committee members took two of them, while the ladies took the third to the Waldorf-Astoria, where reservations had been made for everyone. Almost immediately, the party ran into the first of what would be a common twentieth-century phenomenon: a traffic jam. Cars had converged from every part of the nation, and it was 9:32 by the time the cab cut through traffic and arrived at Pier 54 at West Fourteenth Street and North River.

It was a pitch-black drizzling night, but the *Carpathia*'s single funnel could be seen rising above the other side of the brilliantly lit Cunard Pier. Ropes dotted with green lanterns stretched for seventy-five yards in front of the pier to help keep back the masses. Thousands and thousands of people were being shoved back by policemen standing five feet apart; in spite of their drawn nightsticks, "New York's finest" looked absolutely terrified. The entire North River was an Acheron of human moans punctuated by thunder and the flash explosions of cameras. At the check gate, Smith identified himself and was informed that the *Titanic*'s survivors had just begun disembarking. Pulling his bowler tight over his head, Smith dashed up the gangplank with Newlands, Uhler, Ransdell, Bayliss, and Bill McKinstry (Smith's private secretary) trailing close behind. Aboard the *Carpathia*, Smith asked two officers the location of Mr. Ismay and was promptly escorted to the surgeon's quarters. On the door of the indicated cabin, Smith read a hand-lettered sign: PLEASE DO NOT KNOCK.

The senator knocked.

A tall, stocky, pudgy-faced gentleman appeared and identified himself as Phillip Franklin, vice-president of IMM. Smith asked to see Ismay, but Franklin replied that Mr. Ismay was "far too ill" to be interviewed.

"I'm sorry," said William Alden, pushing the door aside with his umbrella, "but I will have to see that for myself." Leaving the sergeants-at-arms and McKinstry outside, Smith, Newlands, and Uhler entered the cabin.

A half hour later, on the lower decks of the *Carpathia*, Secretary Charles Nagel was standing by as customs inspectors examined the *Titanic*'s steerage survivors in their cramped quarters. Nagel suddenly noticed Senator

Smith watching silently at his side. The steerage people were a pitiful sight. Dressed piecemeal in borrowed articles of clothing, they were displaced, destitute, and frightened. One inspector was routinely asking a young colleen if she had an immigration card.

"Divil a bit of a card have I," she said, wide-eyed. "I'm lucky to have me own life."

Smith walked over to Bill Williams, New York's immigration commissioner and asked rather peevishly, "Can't you speed this up?" The commissioner went and spoke to the individual inspectors.

Smith then joined Francis Newlands on the *Carpathia*'s boat deck, where the awestruck Nevada statesman was surveying the waiting thousands' gradual descent into hysterical paroxysms. The laughter mingling with the shrieks sent chills up William Alden's spine. He watched a man jumping and twirling in strange pirouettes until, when accosted by a policeman, he collapsed on his knees in shrill wails of grief. William Alden later recounted the spectacle at the pier as one of "joy and sorrow so intermingled that it was difficult to discern light from shadow."

Leaving the *Carpathia*, Smith was converged upon by a herd of reporters with press passes tucked in their hatbands. All of them wanted to know about Ismay.

"The interview with Mr. Ismay and Mr. Franklin has been very frank and courteous," said the senator. "Mr. Ismay is to appear before the subcommittee tomorrow morning at the Waldorf-Astoria with the four surviving officers of the *Titanic* for examination."

"What will happen then, Senator?"

"The course the committee decides to take after that will be determined by tomorrow's developments."

"Do you expect much of a fight over the investigation, Senator?"

"I find no disposition on the part of the officers of the

White Star Line to thwart our purpose," Smith replied, "but, on the contrary, a disposition to aid us."

As the reporters dispersed, eager to get at a group of survivors, William Alden was suddenly engulfed by another crowd. They were relatives of *Titanic* passengers who had not come home. As they began speaking all at once, emotion overtook reason. They began voicing anguished suggestions that their loved ones might still be floating about atop icebergs, on wreckage, or picked up by hostile foreign ships. Smith tried to explain that the scout cruisers the President had dispatched were still checking on those possibilities. The people refused to accept the worst. Finally, they raised the possibility that their folk were in the *Titanic*'s watertight compartments—alive and well, but trapped and slowly suffocating at the bottom of the sea! Two women fell to their knees and began wailing at the ghastly thought of it, and by this time, tears were also in the senator's eyes. He had neither the heart nor the know-how to tell them that their wild hopes exceeded the bounds of possibility.

"I'll do what I can, I'll do *whatever* I can," Smith murmured over and over to them until Francis Newlands tapped him on the shoulder, and they left to catch their cab for the Waldorf.

Inside the taxi, Smith tried to grapple with the nightmare he had just entered. His premonitions of his mission had not come anywhere near close to gauging the unparalleled breadth of this tragedy. Shaken to his depths, Smith sat without speaking a word. Slowly a resolve began growing in him—a resolve that eventually would not only help ruin his party and rupture the relations between the United States and Britain, but one that would jeopardize his reputation to posterity as well.

8

The New York Hearings (1)

The East Room of the Waldorf-Astoria was an elegant reception hall of floraled walls and brocade drapes, offset by gleaming white woodwork and crystal chandeliers. On Friday, April 19, most of its furniture was removed and a large conference table placed near the center of the room. Straightback chairs were lined up in rows along the walls. At 9:00 in the morning, the doors were opened, and in three minutes there was standing room only. A swarm of buzzing spectators overflowed into the corridors. For the most part, the crowd represented New York's curious upper classes, but a sprinkling of modestly attired people with worried faces suggested those with a personal investment in the inquiry.

Given the mood of the nation, Smith had decided that information obtained by the committee should be made public at once, and the conference table was encircled by newspaper reporters with long stenographic pads, standing shoulder to shoulder.

Already seated at the table was Mr. Joseph Bruce Ismay, president of IMM and manager of the White

Star Line. Ismay was scrupulously dressed in a dark-blue suit with a black scarf running through his high lay-down collar. Reporters perceived the tall dark man in ethnic stereotypes. One newsman found his curly hair and swarthy complexion "distinctly Oriental." Another thought his large handlebar mustache gave "a German cast to his face." Most agreed that his fine delicate features "were aristocratic," and his personal mannerisms those of a "cultivated Englishman"—a type regarded suspiciously by the average American at the turn of the century. Seated alongside Ismay were his plump American vice-president, P.A.S. Franklin; the *Titanic*'s second officer, Charles Lightoller; two of IMM's top corporate attorneys; and two bodyguards detailed to protect Ismay in view of nationwide threats.

At 10:00, Senators Smith and Newlands and Inspector General Uhler strode into the East Room and took their official places at the table. A moment later, Representative Hughes, Sergeant-at-Arms Ransdell, and H.B. Hibbs (Archie Butt's friend) were seated. Chairman Smith called the session to order in a loud, clear voice and briefly explained the purpose of the subcommittee.

A tremor of excitement rippled through the crowd as Mr. Ismay was called to give testimony. Nervously adjusting his cuffs, Ismay gave his age at nearly fifty and was proceeding to answer other preliminary questions when three camera flashes went off at once with a deafening explosion.

"Get those photographers out of here!" William Alden snapped at a quaking Dan Ransdell. The cameramen left willingly, since their mission had been accomplished. In the evening papers, Americans coast to coast would be treated to a portrait of Ismay on the grill, his dark eyes glistening with anxiety.

Smith asked Ismay to tell the circumstances of the

voyage, along with any other information that he thought would be helpful to the inquiry.

"In the first place," said Ismay, "I would like to express my sincere grief at this deplorable catastrophe." The White Star manager's face was wreathed with a twitching, ingratiating smile that made people doubt the sincerity of his grief. Nodding ebulliently at the members of the committee, Ismay continued. "I understand that you gentlemen have been appointed as a committee of the Senate to inquire into the circumstances. So far as we are concerned, we welcome it. We court the fullest inquiry. We have nothing to conceal—nothing to hide. The ship was built in Belfast. She was the latest thing in the art of shipbuilding. Absolutely no money was spared in her construction."

Ismay reviewed the passenger stops the *Titanic* had made and explained that the number of revolutions had increased from 70, to 72, and then to 75 as the ship warmed up to her maiden voyage. The full speed of the vessel was estimated at 78 to 80 revolutions, but to the best of Ismay's knowledge, she had never exceeded 75.

"The ship sank," said Ismay, "at two twenty. That, sir, I think is all I can tell you."

"Will you describe what you did after the impact or collision?" Smith asked.

"I presume the impact awakened me," Ismay recalled. "I lay in bed for a moment or two afterwards, not realizing, probably, what had happened. Eventually I got up and walked along the passageway . . ."

Clad only in pajamas, Ismay went out in the corridor on B Deck and found a steward. "What has happened?" he asked. "I don't know, sir," the steward replied. The manager went back into his room, put on his coat and slippers, and scurried up to the bridge. It was bitterly cold out and the air had a strange odor "as if it came from a clammy cave." Ismay found the captain, who explained, "We have struck ice." "Do you think the ship is seriously damaged?" Ismay asked. E.J. looked him squarely in the eye: "I am afraid she is."

Returning to B Deck, Ismay met Chief Engineer Bell on the way. Although Mr. Bell agreed that the ship was seriously injured, he was confident that the pumps—already in action—would keep her afloat. Ismay dressed and went back to the bridge where he found E.J. and Thomas Andrews, one of the builders from Harland and Wolff, in a somber tête-à-tête. After a few minutes, the captain ordered the lifeboats uncovered.

"I assisted as best I could," Ismay continued, "getting the boats out and putting the women and children into the boats. I stood upon that deck practically until I left the ship in the starboard collapsible boat, which is the last boat to leave the ship, so far as I know. More than that I do not know."

Throughout his testimony, the White Star manager had nervously smoothed his handsome mustache with his right hand. A diamond ring glittered on his little finger and caught the attention of the newsmen. One of them thought that Ismay's "makeup" suggested "a life of ease rather than one of strength, as if he were accustomed to having his own way because it is given him rather than because he wins it." No matter how well Ismay defended himself, Americans seemed determined to continue scapegoating him—they hadn't reveled in this much doggery at an Englishman since the days of George III.

"You say that the trip was a voluntary trip on your part?" Smith asked.

"Absolutely."

"For the purpose of viewing this ship in action, or did you have some business in New York?"

"I had no business to bring me to New York at all," Ismay asserted. "I simply came in the natural course of events—as one is apt to in the case of a new ship—to see how she works, and with the idea of seeing how we could improve on her for the next ship we are building."

The third of White Star's monster trio was already on the stocks back in Belfast. Work had ceased on her shortly after the *Titanic* foundered. Rumor had it that the new sister was going to be called the *Gigantic*, a name White Star would undoubtedly wish to reconsider.

"How many passengers were in the lifeboat in which you left the ship?" Smith asked.

"I should think about forty-five."

"Forty-five?" Smith repeated. The crowd had begun muttering quietly. This and the poor acoustics of the East Room made things hard to hear. McKinstry, serving as court stenographer, was continually asking for repeats.

"That is my recollection," said Ismay.

"Was that its full capacity?"

"Practically."

Later on in the questioning, Senator Newlands asked Ismay if he had selected the men who had gone with him in this boat. Newlands had obviously been reading Mrs. Cardeza's account in the morning papers.

"No, sir!" snapped Ismay, clearly offended by the question. (It was eventually determined that Mrs. Cardeza hadn't even been in Ismay's boat.)

"What were the circumstances of your departure from the ship?" asked Smith. "I ask merely that—"

"The boat was there," Ismay interrupted. "There was a certain number of men in the boat, and the officer called out asking if there were any more women, and there was no response, and there were no passengers left on the deck."

The last remark was baffling. How had it transpired that no more passengers were left on the boat deck when so many of them had perished? Where had they been? It was a mystery that would obsess William Alden throughout the inquiry.

"There were no passengers on the deck?"

"No, sir," replied Ismay, "and as the boat was in the act of being lowered away, I got into it."

"Mr. Ismay, what can you say about the sinking and disappearance of the ship? Can you describe the manner in which she went down?"

Ismay's reply was very faint. "I did not see her go down," he answered, shaking his head mournfully.

If the manager had in truth taken the last lifeboat, Smith wondered how he could have missed the event. "You did not see her go down?" he asked.

"No, sir."

"How far were you from the ship?"

"I do not know how far we were away. I was sitting with my back to the ship. I was rowing all the time I was in the boat. We were pulling away."

"You did not care to see her go down?"

"I am *glad* I did not!" The manager's response left no doubt as to his sincerity on that point.

The committee quizzed Ismay on the manning and the quality of the lifeboats, of which he claimed to have no knowledge. Ismay also denied interfering with the captain's command of the ship. Smith then asked the manager about the *Titanic*'s floating capacity as affected by damaged compartments.

"The ship was specially constructed so that she would float with any two compartments full of water," Ismay replied. "I think I am right in saying that there are very few ships—" The manager hesitated in midsentence; it was rather late to be quoting the puffed-up claims of the ship's advertisement, but he decided to say it anyway. "I believe there are very few ships today of which the same can be said. When we built the *Titanic* we had that especially in mind. If this ship had hit the iceberg stem on, in all human probability she would have been here today."

A murmur filled the room, and the information hit the streets in the form of "extras" almost immediately. Tongues quickly began wagging at the irony of it all. If only the ship had hit the berg head on! Joseph Conrad would groan as he imagined the seamanship of the twentieth century: "When in doubt try to ram fairly—whatever's before you."

Senator Newlands asked how exactly the ship did hit the berg.

"From information I have received," Ismay replied, "I think she struck the iceberg a glancing blow between the end of the forecastle and the captain's bridge, just aft of the foremast, sir."

While Ismay was answering Newlands, Smith read a note passed to him by Inspector General Uhler. Smith now addressed Ismay on the subject of the note: "I understand you to say a little while ago that you were rowing with your back to the ship. If you were rowing and going away from the ship, you would naturally be facing the ship, would you not?"

"No," Ismay flushed. "In these boats some row facing the bow of the boat and some facing the stern. I was seated with my back to the man who was steering, so that I was facing away from the ship."

Uhler's insinuation had irritated the manager. Following his testimony, Ismay told a reporter that the senators were going about their inquiry "in a manner that seems unjust," and that the injustice seemed "to lie heaviest upon" himself. As an example, he cited the question about the way he had rowed the boat. The interviewing reporter was delighted to note that Mr. Ismay seemed "not far away from a complete breakdown."

"Were all the women and children saved?" Smith asked. So far, White Star had posted no official statistics.

"I am afraid not, sir," Ismay replied.

"What proportion were saved?"

"I have no idea. I have not asked. Since the accident I have made very few inquiries of any sort."

Shortly thereafter Senator Newlands raised the issue at which America was still furious: "What was the full equipment of lifeboats for a ship of this size?"

"I could not tell you that, sir," Ismay replied instantaneously. "That is covered by the Board of Trade regulations. She may have exceeded the Board of Trade regulations, for all I know." Ismay knew very well that she did. "Anyhow," he continued, "she had sufficient boats to obtain her passenger certificate, and therefore she must have been fully boated, according to the requirements of the English Board of Trade, which I understand are accepted by this country. Is not that so, General?" This last question had been directed to George Uhler.

"Yes," Uhler admitted.

Smith raised the other burning issue: "Mr. Ismay, did you in any manner attempt to influence or interfere with the wireless communication between the *Carpathia* and other stations?"

"No, sir, I think the captain of the *Carpathia* is here, and he will probably tell you that I was never out of my room from the time I got on board the *Carpathia* until the ship docked here last night. I never moved out of the room."

Smith would not have to verify the matter with the captain, since he had already done so the previous evening. As the examination of Ismay concluded, Smith asked if he would be available to the committee for future questioning.

"At any time you wish, sir," Ismay replied.

"And I suppose that includes the surviving officers?"

"Certainly, sir. Anybody you wish is absolutely at your disposal."

"What are your immediate plans?" Smith asked.

"I understand that depends on you," said Ismay, trying not to look too hopeful.

Smith was noncommittal. "I thank you in behalf of my associates and myself for responding so readily this morning and for your statements; and I am going to ask you to hold yourself subject to our wishes during the balance of the day."

In less than a week, Smith and Ismay would be exchanging formalities of a far less cordial nature.

The committee's next witness was Arthur Henry Rostron, master of the *Carpathia*. Captain Rostron, tall, trim, and balding, appeared to be in his mid-forties; he had a wide mouth and a disciplined yet gentle bearing. Although he had twenty-seven years' experience at sea, Rostron had been captain of the *Carpathia* for only three months. (His rescue of the *Titanic*'s survivors would prove the turning point of his career.) Rostron explained that the *Carpathia* had been bound from New York to Gibraltar and had been at sea only three and a half days when, on Monday the fifteenth at 12:35 A.M., the *Titanic*'s distress call had been received. It was "providential" that the *Carpathia* had caught the CQD, since her operator had been ready to shut off for the night.

"Immediately on getting the message," Rostron related, "I gave the order to turn the ship around; and immediately I had given that order, I asked the operator if he was sure it was a distress signal from the *Titanic.* I asked him twice."

Assured that the impossible had befallen the unsinkable, Rostron had set a course for the *Titanic* some fifty-eight miles to the northwest of his own position. He had ordered his engineers to shut off all the hot water on the ship and turn every available ounce of heat into steam. He had then called out the heads of all the shipboard departments and issued further orders.

"I do not know whether you care to hear what my orders were exactly," Rostron said.

"Yes, sir," Smith nodded, "we would like to hear them."

The captain then drew out a typewritten list of nearly thirty different commands he had given that eventful morning. Owing to his instantaneous decisions and clear-headed efficiency, Rostron was known as "the Electric Spark" among Cunard seamen, and the orders he had issued left nothing to chance. He had specified where the survivors were to be bedded and who would minister to their every need. He had posted extra lookouts and ordered all sorts of emergency gear brought out on deck, including canvas ash bags for hoisting infants and children aboard. Later, for the sake of complete candor, Rostron privately told Smith that he had also ordered large, heavy chairs put on deck along with ropes with which to securely bind any survivors who had been driven mad. Smith found Rostron's orders a "marvel of systematic preparation and completeness."

At 4:10 A.M., having driven the *Carpathia* at full speed three and a half hours, threading her through dangerous bergs and pack ice, Rostron had finally reached the *Titanic*'s lifeboats.

"We picked up the first boat," Rostron related, "and the boat was in charge of an officer. I saw that he was not under full control of this boat, and the officer sung out to me that he only had one seaman in the boat, so I had to maneuver the ship to get as close to the boat as possible. . . . By the time we had the first boat's people, it was breaking day, and then I could see the remaining boats all around within an area of about four miles. I also saw icebergs all around me."

No survivor would ever be able to forget the apparition of the icebergs as they materialized in the rosy glow of the dawn that April morning. At first, only "sinister points" loomed dark against the burst of the sun over the horizon. But as the sun rose higher the peaks became "pearly pink ice mountains glorified into celestial beauty." One English lady thought they looked like "giant opals." A male survivor gazed at them with overwhelming ambivalence: "Terrible as was the disaster one of them had caused, there was an awful beauty about them which could not be overlooked." An American girl was awed by the dazzling, twenty-one-mile span of pack ice: "The floe glistened like a never-ending meadow covered with new fallen snow. Those same white mountains, marvellous in their purity, had made of the just ended night one of the blackest the sea has ever known."

"I maneuvered the ship," Rostron continued, "and we gradually got all the boats together. We got all the boats alongside and all the people up aboard by eight thirty. I was then very close to where the *Titanic* must have gone down, as there was a lot of, hardly wreckage, but small pieces of broken-up stuff—nothing in the way of anything large. At eight o'clock, the Leyland Line steamer *Californian* hove up, and we exchanged messages."

Rostron suddenly paused, his eyes seeming to fix on a distant scene.

"I want to go back again, a little bit," he said slowly. "At eight thirty all the people were on board. I asked for the purser, and told him that I wanted to hold a service—" Rostron's eyes filled with tears and his voice broke down with emotion. "A short prayer of thankfulness for those rescued," he sobbed, "and a short burial service for those who were lost."

The sight of this gallant man's tears humbled everyone in the East Room. Many began weeping, including Senator Smith, who leaned across the table closer to the captain.

"I then got an Episcopal clergyman," Rostron continued, "one of our passengers, and asked him if he would do this for me, which he did willingly. While they were holding the service, I was on the bridge, of course, and I maneuvered around the scene of the wreckage. We saw nothing except one body."

"Floating—" Smith began hoarsely.

"Floating."

"—with a life preserver on?"

"With a life preserver on," Rostron nodded. "That is the only body I saw. . . . We took three dead men from the boats, and they were brought on board. Another man was brought up—I think he was one of the crew—who died that morning about ten o'clock, I think. He, with the other three, were buried at four in the afternoon."

Ruth Becker, twelve years old at the time, still remembers this afternoon funeral service—particularly the panic that briefly engulfed the survivors when the *Carpathia* stopped for the burial at sea. Everyone thought that the *Carpathia,* too, had struck a berg, and that their nightmare was about to be repeated.

But Rostron had nothing but praise for the survivors. "I must say, from the very start, all these people behaved magnificently. As each boat came alongside, everyone was calm, and they kept perfectly still in their boats. They were quiet and orderly; and each person came up the ladder, or was pulled up in turn, as they were told off. There was no confusion whatever among the passengers. They behaved magnificently—every one of them."

> *The* Carpathia*'s regular passengers were stirred to their depths by the mien of the survivors as they walked onto the deck. To Stanton Coit, they seemed not so much stunned and crushed as they appeared "lifted into an atmosphere of vision where self-centered suffering merges into some mystic meaning. . . . My feeling is that in the midst of all this horror human nature never manifested itself as greater or tenderer. We were all one, not only with one another, but with the cosmic being that for the time had seemed so cruel."*

The captain's account of those rescued varied considerably from the visions of lunacy, suicide, and hysteria that the American press had conjured. And his testimony, thus far, had been a vastly different experience for the committee and spectators than had been Ismay's. Direct contrasts between the two men became acute when Rostron began talking about the lifeboats. The captain was asked to describe a collapsible boat—the kind in which Ismay had achieved his escape. According to Rostron, the boat was "hardly collapsible. It is a flat raft boat, with collapsible canvas sides, about two feet deep."

"To hold how many people?" Smith asked.

"One of those boats would hold sixty to seventy-five comfortably."

Ismay had said that forty-five people was "practically" the collapsible's full capacity. Eventually, Smith got around to other questions bearing on Ismay's credibility.

"Did you personally know the captain of the *Titanic?*" Smith asked.

"I knew him, yes," Rostron replied.

"How long had you known him?"

"I had met him fifteen years ago. I only met him about three times altogether."

"In your company, who is the master of a ship at sea?"

"The captain."

"In absolute control?"

"In absolute control," Rostron affirmed, "legal and otherwise. No one can interfere." Pressed further on this issue, Rostron qualified his remark. "By law, the captain of the vessel has absolute control, but suppose we get orders from the owners of the vessel to do a certain thing and we do not carry it out. The only thing is then that we are liable to dismissal."

On the *Congressional Limited,* Smith had learned from George Uhler about the so-called Irish promotion, in which a captain disobedient to his company first got a transfer to a slower ship, and then went all the way down the line until claimed by oblivion as a master of a freighter. Smith decided to ask his question more pointedly.

"Captain, is it customary to take orders from a director or a general officer of the company aboard?"

"No, sir."

"From whom do you take orders?"

"From no one."

"Aboard ship?"

"At sea, immediately I leave port until I arrive at port, the captain is in absolute control and takes orders from no one. I have never known it in our company or any other big company when a director or a managing owner would issue orders on the ship. It matters not who comes on board the ship, they are either passengers or crew. There is no official status and no authority whatever with them."

Off to the side of the room, J. Bruce Ismay sat with a smile on his face. Rostron had just refuted the charge of which Ismay had already been tried and convicted by the American press. William Alden seemed to be pondering the issue. Finally, he asked Rostron if the captain's absolute authority provided the legal basis for Rostron's decision to go so far off his course and cut full speed through ice to rescue the *Titanic*'s survivors.

Rostron nodded. "I can confess this much, that if I had known at the time there was so much ice about, I should not; but I was right in it then. I could see the ice. I knew I was perfectly clear. There is one other consideration. Although I was running a risk with my own ship and my passengers, I also had to consider what I was going for."

"To save the lives of others?" Smith suggested.

"Yes, I had to consider the lives of the others."

"You were prompted by your interest in humanity?"

"Absolutely."

"And you took the chance?"

"It was hardly a chance. Of course it was a chance, but at the same time I knew quite what I was doing. I considered that I was perfectly free, and that I was doing perfectly right in what I did."

"I suppose no criticism has been passed upon you for it," Smith said quietly.

"No."

"The senator paused; his lips parted, but nothing came out. Quite unexpectedly his eyes filled with tears which he mopped with a handkerchief. "In fact," Smith choked, "I think I may say for my associates that your conduct deserves the highest praise." (According to his own account of this moment, Smith "could hardly speak the words.")

Rostron's eyes were also bedewed. "I thank you, sir," the captain said softly.

"And we are very grateful to you, captain, for coming here."

The two men arose spontaneously to shake hands and there wasn't a dry eye in the room. A reporter from Washington was so moved, he could only describe the scene with a bit of Kipling verse:

For there is neither East nor West,
Border, nor breed, nor birth,
When two strong men stand face to face,
Though they come from the ends of the earth.

Before dismissing Rostron, Smith recalled an important matter needing clarification. The American people as well as William Howard Taft were still perturbed over what they believed a deliberate snub of the President by the *Carpathia*'s wireless. Ismay had already denied responsibility for it. In the morning papers, Guglielmo Marconi had suggested that any censorship would have come not from the wireless operators but the master of the vessel.

"Some complaint has been made because the message of the President of the United States which was sent the *Carpathia* was not answered. Do you know anything about that?" Smith asked.

"I heard last night," Rostron replied, "that there was a message about a Major Butt. I asked my purser this morning if he remembers any message coming about Major Butt, and he said, yes, the *Olympic* sent a message asking if Major Butt was on board, and it was answered, 'Not on board.' That is the only thing I know about that message of that name."

"Did you know, of your own knowledge, of the attempt of the President of the United States to communicate directly with your ship?"

"Absolutely not. Nothing whatever of that."

"I gather that there was no intention whatever of either ignoring his message—"

"My word," Rostron interrupted, "I hope not, sir."

"—or neglecting it?"

"Absolutely no intention of any such thing, sir. It never entered the minds of anyone."

"And no one attempted in any way to put a censorship over the wireless of your ship?"

"Absolutely no censorship whatever."

Smith would search elsewhere for the cause of the so-called censorship, but as far as he was concerned, Rostron had been officially cleared.

After the hearing, Rostron privately asked the senator about the nature of the latter questions. Smith explained that the President was still harboring some hurt feelings over being rebuffed by the *Carpathia*. In light of the testimony, however, there could be no chance of blaming Rostron for the incident. Rostron was nevertheless concerned that his ship had caused the President to worry, and Smith swiftly suggested that a personal letter from the captain would surely dispel the President's resentment.

Rostron's letter to Taft, sent directly afterwards, was a masterpiece of deference and tact. He offered his profound regret that the President "should have the slightest cause to imagine that any act of me—or those under my command—could possibly be construed to intentionally or otherwise ignore or disregard any message which Your Excellency might honour me." Several months later, Taft was only too happy to present Captain Rostron with the Congressional Medal of Honor, granted by the Senate. The award resulted from a resolution thrust at the senators in a highly emotional moment by William Alden Smith—his first legislative motion subsequent to completing the investigation. The *Titanic*'s survivors also presented Rostron with an award—a loving cup, purchased by a collection taken among themselves and handed to the broadly grinning captain by a beaming Mrs. J.J. ("Unsinkable Molly") Brown.

When Rostron returned to New York, having in the meantime completed the *Carpathia*'s originally scheduled voyage, he found waiting for him a dozen bags of mail containing thousands of letters from the American people. Most of them came from thankful survivors or their friends and relations, and from Americans who in 1912 did not yet have mâtinee idols to adore. Others came from sincere admirers, from autograph hunters, and from people down in their luck. Some contained proposals of marriage. In addition to the letters were parcels containing Bibles, jewelry, cigarette cases, pens, teapots, binoculars, and photographs. Rostron asked his officers to help him answer every letter and acknowledge each gift. Later the captain was feted all over the United States, praised in countless speeches, and presented with testimonials and checks. A plaque of his head was placed in New York's Hall of Fame—an honor never previously accorded an Englishman.

But the important thing was Rostron's effect on the investigative committee. In the words of the captain's own second officer, who was present at the hearing, Rostron's testimony had been "seamanlike and forthright." Summing up his own impressions to reporters, William Alden called Rostron "not only an efficient seaman, but one of nature's noblemen." Unfortunately for a number of future witnesses, Rostron's superb seamanship would provide the senator with a standard against which every interrogated mariner would be measured.

The main feature of the afternoon session was the testimony of Charles Herbert Lightoller, the *Titanic*'s second officer. Lightoller was of medium height and impressed all the reporters as "strong and powerfully built." When he removed his cap, his square-jawed face looked virile and sea-worn; a projecting tuft of hair stood upright on his forehead. He seemed perfectly at ease as he gave his age at thirty-eight and reviewed his thirteen years at sea.

Smith's first questions concerned the *Titanic*'s sea trials, during which Lightoller had been on duty. Lightoller's answers were as terse as possible, and a number of reporters felt he was definitely bent on protecting the interests of Ismay and the White Star Line. After all, as the highest-ranking officer to have survived the disaster, Lightoller's chances for promotion in the line had been substantially increased. Initially, Lightoller managed to get away with a number of evasions by his charming manner of speech. His voice was deep, resonant, beautifully modulated, and suggestive to American ears of a slight Scots accent. Both Lightoller's bearing and speech conveyed intelligence aligned with competence.

A devoted Christian Scientist, Lightoller was self-reliant in the extreme. He was also tricky. For a while, Lightoller's evasions were met "good naturedly" by Senator Smith, who would merely pause at them, smile enigmatically, and proceed with further questions.

Inquiring about the ship's safety equipment, Smith

was assured by the second officer that the *Titanic* had been "perfectly complete." She had carried enough life preservers for everyone aboard—including the steerage.

"Was a test of the lifeboats made before you sailed for Southampton?" Smith asked.

"All the gear was tested," replied Lightoller, whose evasions capitalized on William Alden's obvious lack of experience in marine matters.

"Were the lifeboats lowered?"

"Yes, sir."

"Under whose orders?"

"The officers'. Principally my orders."

"Did you see the work done?"

"I did."

"Tell just what was done."

"All the boats on the ship were swung out," Lightoller explained, "and those that I required were lowered down as far as I wanted them—some of them all the way down, and some dropped into the water."

"I wish you would give the proportion that went into the water," said Smith.

"About six."

"Six went into the water?"

"Yes."

"And the others lowered—"

"Part of the way," Lightoller interposed. "As far as I thought necessary."

"Of course," said Smith, "part of the way would not do anybody much good on a sinking ship. I assume you did that for the purpose of trying the gear, and not for the purpose of testing the security of the lifeboats."

"It is principally the gear we test," Lightoller nodded. "The lifeboats we know to be all right."

The lifeboats were known to be "all right," since they had been tested previously by Harland and Wolff. However, the exact nature and results of those tests were never fully explained to the men who had shipped on the *Titanic*—an oversight which indirectly contributed to the loss of over 400 additional lives.

The next phase of Smith's interrogation pertained to the collision, a time when Lightoller had been asleep in his quarters. The officer reported having been awakened by a "slight jar and a grinding noise."

"You knew you had struck something?" Smith asked.

"Yes, sir."

"What did you assume it to be?"

"Ice."

"Ice?"

"Yes, sir."

"Why?"

"That was the conclusion one naturally jumps to around the Banks there."

"Had you seen ice before?"

"No, sir."

"Had there been any tests taken of the temperature of the water?"

"A test is taken of the water every two hours from the time the ship leaves until she returns to port," Lightoller replied.

"Do you know whether these tests were made?" Smith asked.

"They were. . . ."

"How were these tests made?"

"By drawing water from over the side in a canvas bucket and placing a thermometer in it. . . ."

"Did you hear anything about the rope or chain or wire to which the test basins were attached not reaching the water at any time during those tests?"

"The bucket, you speak of?" Lightoller asked.

"Yes."

"No, sir."

"Would a complaint of that character come to you if it had been true?"

"Very quickly, I should think, sir."

Smith's odd question had been prompted by a brief interview he'd held with Mrs. Mahala Douglas in the corridors of the Waldorf-Astoria the previous evening. Mrs. Douglas, who had lost her husband in the disaster, was extremely distraught and had sought out the senator to tell him that she and her husband had observed a sailor making the water-temperature tests on the deck of the *Titanic.* The rope attached to the test bucket apparently had not been long enough; after several unsuccessful attempts to reach the sea, the sailor had simply filled the bucket with the ship's tap water and placed the thermometer in it.

The issue of the water-temperature tests had been given to Smith by George Uhler, who offered it as one of the means by which mariners determined their proximity to large ice floes. The test was not without problems. It yielded a great number of false positives; the temperature would drop significantly, even in the absence of ice. But prudent sailors—old salts, fishermen of the Grand Banks, and such Arctic explorers as Sir Ernest Shackleton and Admiral Peary—still used the test. In the famous ship the *Great Eastern,* a colossus of 1858 designed by Brunel and Russell of Crystal Palace fame, the original plans had called for a special thermometer on the bridge, over which sea water was continually pumped. The device had been specifically intended by Brunel to assist in determining the proximity of ice. Although it would eventually be testified that the temperature of the water had dropped drastically prior to the *Titanic*'s collision, Lightoller consistently denied the usefulness of the test.

"Is this test taken for the purpose of ascertaining the temperature of the water?" Smith asked.

"Yes, sir."

"Merely?"

"Merely."

"What does the temperature of the water indicate to you?"

"Nothing more than the temperature of the air, sir."

"Does it not indicate the proximity of a colder area or an unusual condition?"

"No, sir. It indicates cold water, sir, of course."

Lightoller explained that his watch (6:00 to 10:00 P.M.) had immediately preceded that in which the collision had occurred under First Officer Murdoch's command. Smith asked him what the temperature of the water had been during his watch, and the officer guessed that it probably wasn't much over freezing.

"What did the tests show?" Smith asked.

"I do not know, sir."

"You mean they did not report to you?"

"It is entered in a book, sir."

"And the fact is not communicated to you directly after each test?"

"Not unless I ask for it."

"And you did not think it necessary to ask for it that night?"

"No, sir."

"You knew you were in the vicinity of icebergs, did you not?"

"Water is absolutely no guide to icebergs, sir."

"I did not ask that," said William Alden matter-of-factly. "Did you know you were in the vicinity of icebergs?"

"No, sir," Lightoller lied.

The senator promptly drew out of a portfolio a copy

of the *Amerika*'s marconigram about the icebergs, which the *Titanic* had relayed to the U.S. Hydrographic Office. Lightoller glanced at it from the corner of his eye, but remained completely unruffled. Asked about the marconigram, Lightoller recalled that *some* message had been received about ice, but he couldn't say if it had been from the *Amerika* or not. On further examination, Lightoller admitted that he had spoken with the captain about ice warnings on the afternoon of the fourteenth; and then again during his watch, two and a half hours before the collision. William Alden was immediately interested in what had been exchanged during this latter conversation.

"We spoke about the weather," Lightoller replied, "the calmness of the sea; the clearness; about the time we should be getting up toward the vicinity of the ice and how we should recognize it if we should see it—freshening up our minds as to the indication that ice gives of its proximity. . . ."

The captain looked out at the sea. "There is not much wind," he observed. "No, sir," replied Lightoller, "it is a flat calm." "A flat calm," the captain duly repeated. With a flat calm, there would be no breakers to help illuminate the base of an iceberg. It was a risky situation. "In any case," Lightoller offered, "there will be a certain amount of reflected light from the bergs." "Oh, yes," the captain agreed, "there will be a certain amount of reflected light." The two men were certain that even if the dark-blue side of a recently split-off iceberg were in the path of the ship, its white outline would give sufficient warning.

"Was any reference made at that time to the wireless message from the *Amerika?*" the senator asked.

"Captain Smith made a remark that if it was in a

slight degree hazy there would be no doubt we should have to go very slowly."

"Did you slow up?"

"That I do not know, sir," replied Lightoller.

"You would have known if it had been done, would you not, during your watch?"

"Not necessarily so, sir."

"Who would give the command?"

"The commander would send orders down to the chief engineer to reduce her by so many revolutions."

To the best of Lightoller's knowledge, however, the speed had not been reduced. The crucial factor had been the visibility. Captain Smith had definitely planned to slow down if the weather became in the slightest degree hazy, and that had not transpired during Lightoller's watch.

"What was the weather that night?" asked the senator.

"Clear and calm."

"Were you at all apprehensive about your proximity to these icebergs?"

"No, sir."

"And for that reason you did not think it necessary to increase the official lookout?" This was a critical issue.

"No, sir."

"And that was not done?"

"No, sir."

The spectators murmured at the information. Tension was mounting in the East Room, and Ismay finally left the hearing. He spent the rest of the afternoon pacing up and down the hall outside, chain-smoking, and muttering comments to reporters he would eventually regret.

"Did you talk with Mr. Murdoch about the iceberg situation when you left thc watch?" Smith asked.

"No, sir." (Lightoller would eventually recant this

part of his testimony. The night order book had had a footnote about keeping a sharp lookout for ice; and when Lightoller handed over the watch to Murdoch at 10:00 P.M. he had told him, "We might be up around the ice any time now.")

"Did [Murdoch] ask you anything about it?" asked the senator.

"No, sir."

"What was said between you?"

"We remarked on the weather, about its being calm, clear. We remarked the distance we could see. We seemed to be able to see a long distance. Everything was very clear. We could see the stars setting down to the horizon."

Lightoller was obviously holding back, and it began trying Smith's patience.

"It was cold, was it not?" the senator interrupted.

"Yes, sir."

"Sharp?"

"Yes, sir."

"How cold was it?"

"Thirty-one, sir."

"Above zero?"

"Thirty-one degrees above zero, yes, sir."

"Is that unusually cold for that longitude?"

"No, sir."

"At that time of the year?"

"No, sir."

With Lightoller's refusal to reveal how well the *Titanic*'s officers knew of the proximity of ice, the increasing coldness was the only angle William Alden could play. Lightoller doggedly denied the reliability of this indication, however, and Smith gave it up. The senator would eventually confirm the prudence of using water-temperature indications of the proximity of large ice floes from two captains and a number of other expert witnesses. It was abundantly clear, however, that confirmation wouldn't come from the second officer. By this time, it was also apparent to William Alden that those in command of the *Titanic*, though not yet demonstrably negligent, had been extraordinarily cavalier in the face of a known danger.

9

The New York Hearings (2)

The most tedious yet revealing part of Lightoller's interrogation concerned the lowering of the passengers in the lifeboats. As soon as Smith learned that Lightoller had been in charge of the boats on the *Titanic*'s port side, he launched a grueling, three-and-a-half-hour examination. Using endless repetitions, digressions, and then more repetitions, Smith slowly eroded the defensive armor of Lightoller's nautical expertise (for which Lightoller never forgave him). Although William Alden's old "wear-'em-out" trick generated a number of important pieces of information, they were few and far between.

Lightoller told that he had only put twenty-five people in the first boat lowered, and Smith asked if the boat had ever returned to the ship to take on additional passengers.

"Not to my knowledge, sir," Lightoller replied.

"As a matter of fact it was not much more than half loaded, was it?" asked Smith.

"You mean its floating capacity?" The officer hoped

to make a distinction between floating and lowering capacity.

"Yes."

"Floating capacity, no."

Although the lifeboats had been certified by Harland and Wolff to hold sixty-five people each, the distance from the leviathan's top deck, where the boats were lowered, to the water was a breathtaking seventy feet. Lightoller had been uneasy about the strength of the tackle for this much of a drop and was equally concerned about the chance of the boats buckling in the middle with sixty-five people in them. Harland and Wolff had carried out tests specifically on these two possibilities and had found the operation safe on both accounts. Not only were these tests unknown to the officers, but the captain had failed to carry out a scheduled boat drill during the maiden voyage.

"In a great emergency like that, where there were limited facilities, could you not have afforded to try to put more people into that boat?"

"I did not know it was urgent then," Lightoller asserted. "I had no idea it was urgent."

"You did not know it was urgent?"

"Nothing like it!"

Lightoller was obviously speaking the truth. Ismay had testified that E.J. had been aware of the urgency within minutes of the collision. The fact that the captain had not given more specific orders to his officers under the circumstances suggested to the senator a serious breakdown in the *Titanic*'s chain of command—specifically, a paralysis at the top.

Smith inquired about the boats Lightoller loaded, once he had become aware of the ship's peril; the officer replied that he had then taken "more chances."

"Were the people ready to go?" Smith asked.

"Perfectly quiet and ready."

"Any jostling or pushing or crowding?"

"None whatever."

"The men all refrained from asserting their strength and crowding back the women and children?"

"They could not have stood quieter if they had been in church," Lightoller replied dryly.

"If you had filled that third boat full, how many people would you have had in it?"

"What do you mean by full?" Lightoller asked.

"To its full capacity," replied William Alden, who by now had refused to recognize Lightoller's distinction between loading and lowering capacities.

"Sixty-five, sir," Lightoller replied faintly.

"Beg pardon?"

"Sixty-five, sir."

"Do you think you had that many in it?"

"Certainly not, sir."

"How many did you have?"

"Thirty-five, I would say, sir."

For Lightoller, taking "more chances" meant loading the boats still some thirty passengers short of their capacity. The magnitude of his error in the direction of overcautiousness would not be fully manifested until the subcommittee took the testimony of the crewmen.

Lightoller confirmed Ismay's statement that, near the end, very few passengers could be found on deck.

"Had the passengers the right to go on that deck from below?" Smith asked.

"Every right," Lightoller replied.

"There was no restraint at the staircase?"

"None."

"Was that true as to the steerage?"

"The steerage have no right up there, sir."

"Did they on that occasion?"

"Oh, yes."

"There was no restraint?"

"Oh, absolutely none. . . ."

"From what you have said," Smith began, "you discriminated entirely in the interest of the passengers—first the women and children—in filling these lifeboats?"

"Yes, sir."

"Why did you do that? Because of the captain's orders or because of the rule of the sea?"

"The rule of human nature," Lightoller replied solemnly.

A murmur of approval filled the East Room.

"The rule of human nature," Smith nodded. "And there was no studied purpose, as far as you know, to save the crew?"

"Absolutely not," came the indignant reply.

Smith's offensive question was prompted by the fact that, although no statistics had been posted on who had been lost, 30 percent of those saved were crewmen. Lightoller had testified that he had put only 2 or 3 crewman in each boat, a practice which if consistently followed would have resulted in only 60 crewmen saved instead of the 216 who survived. Lightoller was quick to point out that he had been in charge of only one side of the ship and had no knowledge of what had transpired on the starboard side.

Smith asked about the quality of the life preservers and was assured that the preservers were in good condition.

"Have you ever been into the sea with one of them?" Smith asked.

"Yes, sir," Lightoller replied.

"Where?"

"From the *Titanic.*"

"In this recent collision?"

"Yes, sir."

"How long were you in the sea with a life belt on?"

"Between half an hour and an hour."

"What time did you leave the ship?"

"I didn't leave it," replied the second officer.

At once, every chair squeaked in the room as spectators inched closer to catch every word of what promised to be a thrilling story from the officer.

"Did the ship leave you?" Smith asked.

"Yes, sir."

The end was near. The ship took an abrupt lunge forward, and the sea rolled up over the bridge. Standing on the roof of the wheelhouse, Lightoller dove and swam toward the sinking foremast. In a moment of panic caused by the icy water, he was about to hang on to the crow's nest—now level with the sea—before he realized the danger of clutching anything connected to the doomed vessel. He collected his wits, saying to himself, "Now I'll see how much I have learned from Christian Science." He began swimming toward starboard when, suddenly, he was drawn by suction toward an airshaft on the roof of the officers' quarters—directly in front of the first funnel. The sea was pouring down the shaft, and Lightoller found himself riveted to its wire grating; should the grating give way, he knew he'd be swept down 100 feet into the flooding forward stokehold.

Glued to the foundering ship, he closed his eyes as his head went under water, recalling the words of the Ninety-first Psalm: "He shall give his angels charge over thee." At that moment, a volume of hot air belched up from the shaft (probably a boiler explosion) and set him free. He struggled to the surface only to be sucked under by another ventilator, and he could never recall how he got away from this one. When he surfaced the second time, an overturned collapsible lifeboat was miraculously floating alongside. He grabbed ahold of its rope.

Drifting with the collapsible, Lightoller watched as the Titanic*'s bow plunged deeper and her stern, some four blocks away, rose groaning into the air. By then, the base of the first funnel was under water, and the grating that supported it collapsed under the pressure. The enormous smokestack, with its scores of tons, toppled over with a crash and a spray of sparks onto the hundreds of horrified people bobbing and gasping in the water.*

"It fell on all the people there were alongside of the boat—if there were any there," Lightoller said. The officer hadn't told Smith about the people in the water.

"Injure any of them seriously?" Smith asked.

"I could not say, sir."

"Did it *kill* anybody?" Smith persisted.

"I could not say, sir."

Even though he did not answer these questions, Lightoller deeply resented Smith's asking them. In his autobiography, published twenty-three years later, the officer wrote: "Amongst the many historic, and, what in less tragic circumstances would have been humorous, questions asked by Senator Smith at the Washington Enquiry was 'Did it hurt anyone?' " The questions were ultimately answered when the *MacKay-Bennett* arrived home with her cargo of corpses. Among these were the body of John Jacob Astor, crushed to a pulp—the entire corpse begrimed with thick soot. He was principally identified by his large diamond ring, set in platinum, and the $4,000 in his pocket.

Lightoller's reluctance to relate fully the details of the collapsing funnel may have been due to his ambivalence over the incident. In spite of what the funnel may have done to others it had proved a godsend for him. Its crash into the sea had caused a wave, sweeping the collapsible lifeboat with Lightoller attached some thirty yards clear of the ship. Eventually Lightoller had managed to climb on top of the overturned lifeboat, where he stood along with a number of others until the *Carpathia*'s arrival in the morning. Smith asked how many had managed to get on top of it.

"I should roughly estimate about thirty," Lightoller said. "She was packed standing from stem to stern at daylight."

"Was there any effort made by others to board her?" Smith asked.

"We took all on board we could."

"I understand that," Smith said, "but I wanted to know whether there was any *effort* made by others to get aboard."

"Not that I saw."

"There must have been a great number of people in the water," Smith insisted. The previous evening the senator had been made keenly aware that the undetermined fate of 823 "missing" passengers was a matter of agonizing conjecture for their friends and relations.

"But not near us," Lightoller explained. "They were some distance away from us."

"How far?"

"It seemed about a half mile."

Floundering in the water all about the collapsible was a mass of people clinging to wreckage and crying for help. Fireman Harry Senior tried to climb aboard, but "some chap" hit him over the head with an oar. Another begged for a hand, but was told, "Hold on to what you have, old boy; one more of you aboard would sink us all." The man in the water feebly replied, "All right, boys, good-bye and God bless you."

> *The incident nearly traumatized passenger Archibald Gracie. Already standing on the boat, Gracie turned his head away from the sights in the water, lest he too be forced "to refuse the pleading cries of those who were struggling for their lives."*

"I ask you again," Smith said to Lightoller, "there *must* have been a great number of passengers and crew still on the boat, the part of the boat that was not submerged, probably on the high point, so far as possible. Were they huddled together?"

"I could not say, sir," Lightoller replied. The officer became uncomfortable for the first time; his face was perspiring noticeably. "They did not seem to be. I could not say, sir. I did not notice. There were a great many of them. There were a great many of them, I know, but as to what condition they were in, huddled or not, I do not know."

Twenty-three years later, Lightoller's memory was better. He had indeed seen the people struggling hysterically up toward the rising stern of the ship. He wrote that they had been washed back

> in a dreadful huddled mass. . . . I knew, only too well, the utter futility of following that driving instinct of self-preservation and struggling up towards the stern. It would only be postponing the plunge, and prolonging the agony—even lessening one's already slim chances, by becoming one of a crowd. It came home to me very clearly how fatal it would be to get amongst those hundreds and hundreds of people who would shortly be struggling for their lives in that deadly cold water.

"Did they make any demonstration?" Smith asked.

"None."

"Was there any lamentation?"

"No, sir. Not a sign of it."

Smith was growing irritated. "There must have been about two thousand people there on that part—the unsubmerged part of the boat!"

"All the engineers and other men and many of the firemen were down below and never came on deck at all," Lightoller quickly explained.

"They never came on deck?"

"No, sir. They were never seen. That would reduce it by a great number."

Not only would it *not* have reduced it "by a great number," but Lightoller later recalled seeing the engineers and firemen come on deck after all.

It was near the close of the day. Since he had been unable to extract from the second officer an account of how people had perished, the senator decided to put on record (and get into the newspapers) Lightoller's authoritative response to the posssibility that had been posed to Smith the previous evening.

"Were there any watertight compartments in that ship?" Smith asked.

"Yes, sir."

"How many?"

"I could not tell you offhand, sir. Fourteen or fifteen."

"Were those watertight compartments known to the passengers or crew?"

"They must have been."

"How would they know it?"

"By the plans distributed about the ship. . . ."

"Are you able to say whether any of the crew or passengers took to these upper watertight compartments as a final, last resort?"

Lightoller appeared dumbfounded by the question.

"I mean," Smith amended for Lightoller's sake, "as a place to die?"

"I am quite unable to say, sir."

"Is that at all likely?" Smith asked.

"No sir; very unlikely."

Late Friday evening, the members of the subcommittee and Representative Hughes met in Smith's hotel room to review the testimony taken thus far. The essential facts of the matter were far from clear. It was impossible to determine what Officer Lightoller was concealing, and the worst of the nation's fears were still imaginable. Everyone shared the observation that White Star was bent on giving only the most perfunctory evidence, hoping to mollify American outrage as quickly as possible, so that Ismay and the crewmen could return to England.

Immediately before the executive meeting, Ismay had privately begged Smith's permission to return with the crew on the *Lapland*, scheduled to leave the next morning. William Alden had politely refused, later remarking to the press that "Mr. Ismay acquiesced with good grace in my request." At this point in time, the senator believed Ismay innocent of the worst of American suspicions. Much of what the White Star manager had said to reporters in the corridor that afternoon was consistent with his testimony before the committeee:

> What do you think I am? Do you believe that I'm the sort that would have left that ship as long as there were any women and children aboard her? That's the thing that hurts, and it hurts all the more because it's so false and baseless. . . . I have searched my mind with deepest care. I have thought long over each single incident that I could recall of the wreck. I am

> sure that nothing wrong was done—that I did nothing that I should not have done. My conscience is clear, and I have not been a lenient judge of my own acts.

But Ismay wasn't home free, by any means. The evening papers carried an interview with *Titanic* fireman John Thompson. From Queenstown out, Thompson said, "all the firemen had been talking of the orders we had to fire her up as hard as we possibly could." Thompson insisted that the ship was running at full speed at the time of the collision: "From the time we left Queenstown until the moment of the shock we never ceased to make from seventy-four to seventy-seven revolutions. It never went below seventy-four and as during that whole Sunday we had been keeping up to seventy-seven, surely she must have been making that speed then."

Ismay had testified that the ship had never exceeded 75 revolutions, about 21.5 knots.

Whether responsible for it or not, if Ismay was concealing negligence aboard the *Titanic*, the IMM could be in serious trouble. The Harter Act, written by Chief Justice Edward White in response to the *Bourgogne* disaster, stated that if a company owning a steamship had privity of negligence aboard, then individual passengers or their surviving kin could sue the company for damages. Though the *Titanic* may have been a British ship, she had nevertheless been owned by an American trust indictable under the Harter laws. Congressman Hughes, who had lost his son-in-law in the disaster and who was extremely bitter toward White Star for sending him a telegram proclaiming the ship's safety, agreed with William Alden that Ismay himself had probably not *caused* any negligence. But, as Hughes pointed out, the critical question was: Had Ismay, as president of IMM, been *cognizant* of negligence? If the answer to that was yes, then hundreds of American citizens could sue Morgan's trust under the terms of the Harter Act.

The possibility of individual Americans suing the House of Morgan was one that Smith could not treat lightly. In fact, the idea appealed to him immensely. As a Midwesterner, Smith had favored small independent businesses over the East Coast monopolies and was a strong believer in the spirit of competition that the trusts had sought so hard to crush. In the past, Smith had spent many hours in Congress contending with Morgan's steel and railroad trusts. He had had nearly as much trouble with Morgan in the Foreign Relations Committee. Very shortly before the *Titanic* disaster, Smith had expressed outrage at the State Department's willingness to back Morgan's Honduras investment scheme, saying, "I do not want to believe the American government wishes to accept the responsibility of so grave an act as forcing Honduras to agree to so hateful a thing as this—to rob Honduras of her sovereignty!" Subsequently, William Alden had successfully blocked the scheme, for which he had received the personal thanks of Policarpo Banilla, former president of Honduras. But he was still fuming over Morgan's gall in the matter.

Chairman Smith made a momentous decision as far as the inquiry was concerned. He concluded that, under the circumstances, it would be unfair to those Americans with grounds for lawsuits to permit Ismay and any White Star employee who was witness to negligence aboard the *Titanic* to return to England, where American law could not possibly have the reach to force their recall to the States.

The decision entailed immediate problems. IMM's

attorneys had notified Smith that the company could not be made responsible for the bed and board of over 200 British citizens for an extended time. Smith explained that he had no intention of subpoenaing that many; he would probably keep Ismay, the four surviving officers, and perhaps a dozen crewmen. Smith deliberately kept the exact number vague, since it ultimately depended on the outcome of a secret mission he had given "the greatest little sheriff in Michigan."

Around midnight on Friday, Sheriff Joe Bayliss came to Smith's room. Joe had been assigned to spend the day eavesdropping on the crewmen, and his efforts had proved highly fruitful. The sheriff presented William Alden with a list of twenty-nine crewmen who had either been in charge of a lifeboat or who were freely telling "horror stories" about the ship's navigation and management. The number of men quite exceeded the estimate Smith had given to IMM's attorneys, but the senator wasn't concerned. He told Joe to subpoena every man on the list as early Saturday morning as possible. Bayliss left and immediately woke up Sergeant-at-Arms Ransdell, and the two of them began the necessary paperwork.

Saturday morning, April 20, the subpoenas were served (Joe claimed that it had taken some "fancy steppin' " to accomplish the job), and a flurry of rumors got back to the subcommittee. The British consul at New York was purportedly on the train to Washington to lodge a complaint with the British ambassador. The directors of IMM were calling up friendly members of Congress, demanding to know what right a federal committee had to subpoena foreigners as well as Americans within the sovereign state of New York. It looked like the fight was going to be states' rights *vs.* the federal government. Smith expected that some form of organized opposition would break out, but if this was the best IMM could do, it was pretty lame.

The Saturday hearings were scheduled to begin at 10:00, but the subcommittee was still in private session at that time. Francis Newlands had worked out the strategy: All haste should be made in terminating the hearings in New York and resuming them at once in the capital; there, the IMM would not have states' rights to cloak their objections, and the authority of the U.S. Congress could be called upon to deal with future blocking and recalcitrant witnesses. Smith agreed, but said that he had to interview Harold Bride, the *Titanic*'s only surviving wireless operator, who was still ill and wouldn't be able to be transported to Washington immediately. It was decided that Bride would be interviewed, and then an official announcement would be made. Smith figured that he would be able to draft the announcement during the luncheon break.

At 10:30, the committee dashed down to the Myrtle Room. The Waldorf-Astoria had transferred the hearings to this larger room in view of the problems of crowding and acoustics the East Room had posed. The Myrtle Room was enormously popular with New York plutocrats who had held many an evening party there. On one occasion, a host had filled it with live nightingales rented from a local zoo. This ballroom now seemed curiously appropriatc for the *Titanic* inquiry, which was becoming something of an autopsy on the Gilded Age.

J. Bruce Ismay, seated alongside Franklin and Lightoller, was reading the morning papers and "smiling sardonically" at the accounts of his heinous conduct and disagreeable personality. The crowd was now larger than ever and included several New York politicians, former Assistant Secretary of the Navy Truman Newberry, and Inez Milholland—reputedly the loveliest suffragette in the nation. Ms. Milholland was not present in an official capacity; she was attending with her onetime financé Guglielmo Marconi, who had a personal investment in the witnesses scheduled.

"Gentlemen," Chairman Smith announced upon his arrival, "I am sorry to have delayed beginning the hearing beyond the hour set this morning, but a conference between my colleagues and myself made it necessary."

Smith then called Harold T. Cottam to the stand. Cottam, the *Carpathia*'s wireless operator, struck reporters as little more than a boy; in fact he was just twenty-three years old. His testimony deeply impressed everyone with its account of long and unregulated hours, grave responsibilities, and pitiful wages of about $20 a month. Reporters felt that Smith was deliberately gathering evidence to impress upon Congress the need for hastening the wireless-regulation bill.

During Cottam's interrogation, the committee was joined by Senator James A. Reed, who had been stumping in the East on behalf of the presidential candidacy of fellow Missourian Champ Clark. Reed had been taking some potshots at Clark's opponent for the Democratic nomination, the asthenic Princeton professor Woodrow Wilson—a "political dilettante" in Reed's opinion.

Toward the end of Cottam's testimony, Smith read the telegram Representative Hughes had received from the White Star Line on the evening of the fifteenth:

> Titanic proceeding to Halifax. Passengers will probably land there Wednesday. All safe.

The spectators murmured at the information. Cottam denied having sent any such marconigram. P.A.S. Franklin was biting his fingernails, and Ismay's ordinarily dark complexion looked rather pale.

At this high point of tension, Smith called for Harold Bride to take the stand.

The entrance of the star witness, in the words of one reporter, "was like an illustration of a gruesome story." The noise from the crowded corridors flowed into the Myrtle Room as the double doors banged open, and Harold Bride entered in a wheelchair, his head sunk deep in a pillow, his mouth slack, and his left foot still swathed in a large white bandage. He appeared as wan and hollow-cheeked as he had when Marconi had met him aboard the *Carpathia*. The crowd in the Myrtle Room had now grown so thick that the wheelchair couldn't be maneuvered to the conference table. Bride had to be carried over to the senators and was gently placed in a large, overstuffed chair.

Bride gave his age as twenty-two. He had attended the British School of Telegraphy and had been employed in the field since July of the previous year. Questioned about the *Titanic*'s wireless, Bride said that the ship had the only set equipped with a disk discharger; consequently, hers had been the most powerful apparatus afloat—a fact that surprised no one. Bride explained that he and Phillips, the senior operator, had been largely occupied in the relay of commercial messages for passengers. These had included everything from stock-exchange quotations to telegram greetings to friends and relatives.

On the afternoon preceding the collision, the apparatus had broken down, but Phillips had managed to repair it. The delay, however, had set him back with commercial transmissions, and he had been frantically busy all evening. About five minutes before midnight, Bride had awakened to take over the shift, completely unaware that a collision had taken place.

"During that time," asked Smith, "did Mr. Phillips tell you that the boat had been injured?"

"He told me that he thought she had got damaged in some way and that he expected that we should have to go back to Harland and Wolff's," Bride replied.

"Those are the builders at Belfast?"

"Yes, sir."

"What did you do then?"

"I took over the watch from him. . . ."

"Where did he go?"

"He was going to retire, sir."

"Did he retire?"

"He got inside of the other room, when the captain came in. . . ."

"What did the captain say?"

"He told us that we had better get assistance."

"Can you tell us in his language?"

Bride paused momentarily to reflect. Smith observed that although the wireless boy was ill, he wasn't quite as incapacitated as his dramatic entrance had suggested. (Someone at the Marconi Company had quite a flair for showmanship.) Bride's mental agility was readily apparent to spectators. His long fingers locked and interlocked as he searched his memory.

"This is exactly what he said," Bride began. "He said, 'You had better get assistance.' When Mr. Phillips heard him he came out and asked if he wanted to use a distress call. He said, 'Yes—at once.' "

> *Thirty-five minutes after the collision, Phillips sent the* Titanic*'s first distress call out over the frigid Atlantic: —·—· ——·— —·· The captain came back to the cabin and asked what he was sending. "CQD," Phillips replied. Bride was suddenly struck by "the humor of the situation." "Send SOS," Bride said. "It's the new call, and it may be your last chance to send it." Phillips chuckled at the sally, and the two opera-*

tors continued saying "lots of funny things to each other" as Phillips changed the signal: · · · — — — · · · · · · — — — · · ·

William Alden turned to the important matter of the ice warnings that the ship had received before the collision, and a Canadian reporter noted that the senator's "shrewd questioning" at this point "held enthralled the committee and the audience."

"Were you on duty when the wireless message was received from the *Amerika* regarding the proximity of icebergs in that longitude?"

"I have no knowledge of a wireless message received from the *Amerika* regarding any iceberg," Bride replied. He paused to reflect. "There may have been—received by Mr. Phillips—but I did not see one myself."

"Have you heard that such a message was received?"

"No, sir."

"Did Mr. Phillips say that such a message had been received?"

"No, sir."

"Did you ever talk with the captain about such a message?"

"There was a message delivered to the captain in the afternoon, sir, late in the afternoon—"

"Of Sunday?" Smith interposed.

"Yes, sir, regarding the ice field."

"From whom?"

"From the *Californian*, sir," Bride replied.

The crowd gasped. This was at least the third ice warning known to have been sent to the *Titanic*. Over the next month, the subcommittee would collect more ice warnings that had been sent to the liner, and even then the list would be incomplete.

In the midst of this testimony, the doors to the Myrtle

Room blew open, and a woman judged near hysterics barged in, weeping and asking those nearest if they had any information about Officer Murdoch. Apparently no one had the nerve to tell her that the first officer had perished, and her insistence grew louder. Finally, Chairman Smith looked over at the huddled trio of Ismay, Franklin, and Lightoller.

"Mr. Lightoller," Smith said, "would you be good enough to tell this lady whatever she wishes to know."

Lightoller didn't appear to relish the assignment, but he took the young woman to the far side of the room. Shortly thereafter she left.

Returning to Harold Bride, Smith learned that the North German Lloyd liner *Frankfurt* had been the first ship to answer the *Titanic*'s distress call. After receiving the message, the *Frankfurt* operator had gone to consult his captain. In the meantime, the *Carpathia* had responded. While the *Carpathia* was taking the information from Phillips, the *Frankfurt* operator had come back on the wire with a question from his captain: "What is the matter?" According to Bride, Phillips had been so outraged by the question, he tapped back: "You fool. Stand by and keep out." This revelation was met with a murmur of disapproval from the spectators, and Smith bore down on it.

"In such an emergency," the senator said to Bride, "do you not think that a more detailed statement might have been sent? Take, for instance, the message from the *Titanic* to the *Carpathia* that the boiler rooms were filling with water and the ship sinking; that could have been sent with perfect propriety to a boat that was in proximity, could it not?"

"No, sir," replied Bride, "I do not think it could have been, under the circumstances."

"Do you mean to say that the regulations under which you operate are such that in a situation of this character you have such discretionary power that you may *dismiss* an inquiry of that character—"

"You use your common sense," Bride interruped, "and the man on the *Frankfurt* apparently was not using his at the time."

Under the circumstances, Phillips's epithet was understandable, but there was more to it than this. Marconi and Telefunken, his German competitor, had long been waging a commercial war that had been eagerly acted out by their young wireless operators. The subcommittee learned later that the *Olympic*, after receiving the SOS, had also responded with a "foolish" question: "Are you steering southerly to meet us?" Phillips had replied fully and politely to this question: "We are putting the passengers off in small boats." In other words, Phillips had been willing to extend to a British ship—and a White Star liner at that—a courtesy he was unwilling to give a German. Germany had been angered by the *Frankfurt-Titanic* exchange, and her countrymen were now arguing that the disaster was due to "British inefficiency at sea." If the ship had been manned by Germans, they said, "her passengers and crew would be alive and the vessel afloat today." It was all a foretaste of the animosity that would soon erupt in a world war.

Senator Reed, technically a spectator, nudged Smith and whispered, "Ask him [Bride] how much longer it would have taken to send 'We are sinking' instead of 'You fool,' et cetera." Smith didn't think the question necessary. His chief object was to reveal the inept standards under which Marconi Marine was operating. It wasn't necessary to belabor a boy for faults that—as Smith knew from his own Western Union experience—had filtered down from the top of the company. Smith had already been through all this with railroad telegraphy (he had advocated and seen passed a bill making it illegal to keep a railroad telegrapher on duty for more than eight hours at a stretch) and was convinced that transatlantic wireless was just as bad, if not worse. No, the senator would wait until he got Mr. Marconi on the stand.

By this time, Bride was visibly tired. His voice had become faint, and he was slouching even deeper in his armchair; but Smith wasn't quite finished. He knew that Bride had escaped on the overturned collapsible with Lightoller, and he wanted Bride's version of the incident.

Bride told that he had fallen overboard clinging to collapsible "B" and had been underneath it in an air pocket for what seemed "a lifetime."

"Who was on top of the boat when you got on?" Smith asked.

"There was a big crowd on top when I got on," Bride recalled. "I had to get away from under the bottom. . . . I was the last man they invited on board."

Invited on board? Lightoller had just testified that most of those in the water had been "some distance" from the collapsible.

"Were there others struggling to get on?"

"Yes, sir."

"How many?"

"Dozens," Bride quietly replied.

A gasp filled the Myrtle Room as nerves snapped. It was the first glimpse of the horror of the disaster that any witness had given. Tears suddenly came to Senator Smith's eyes, and several women in the room began holding their heads and moaning softly. Bride seemed stunned by the spectators' response, and Senators Newlands and Reed began fearing for his health. They certainly didn't look forward to the possibility of the young man's dropping dead before the entire gathering. Newlands on one side of Smith and Reed on the other began nudging the chairman to terminate the testimony.

Smith leaned toward Newlands and muttered, *"Please do not interrupt me at this point*—I realize his condition."

"Dozens," Smith repeated. "In the water?"

"Yes, sir."

Officer Lightoller stood corrected. Now, what about the second officer's indignation at the suggestion that there had been efforts to save the crew?

"Do you know," Smith asked Bride, "whether the other occupants of that boat were officers or seamen or stewards or employees?"

"I should judge they were all employees," Bride freely responded. "They were all part of the boat's crew." (The actual ratio was twenty-seven crewmen to three passengers.)

William Alden thanked Bride for the frankness of his testimony and announced a recess until 3:00 that afternoon.

During the luncheon break, Joe Bayliss was waiting for the senator and told him that everyone on the list had been subpoenaed, but that new information had just come to his attention. They should have subpoenaed five more men, but unfortunately the *Lapland* had already sailed.

Smith figured that the ship couldn't have got very far. He called the U.S. Navy base, had the *Lapland* stopped by wireless, and sent Joe out on a tug to intercept her and bring the additional witnesses in. The plan succeeded.

The afternoon session came as a surprise to everyone. There was no afternoon session. As soon as everyone reassembled, Smith simply read the statement he had written during the break. He gave the names of those who had been subpoenaed. P.A.S. Franklin had been served as well as Mr. Ismay, and both wireless operators

Bride and Cottam were included with the four surviving officers. Smith also read the names of the twenty-nine crewmen Joe Bayliss had already served, but didn't mention the fact that the sheriff was on his way to bring back even more.

The senator then reviewed the circumstances that had brought the committee to New York and the purpose of the hearings. He announced that many passengers of the ill-fated maiden voyage had also been subpoenaed, but that their testimony would be taken following that of the ship's crew. Finally, Smith thanked the press for "their marked consideration and courtesy in this most trying situation" and assured them that open hearings would be continued before the full subcommittee in Washington.

With that, the committee strode out of the Myrtle Room and went up to pack their things. Reporters flying after Smith got only a brief remark from the chairman.

"The surface has barely been scratched," he said. "The real investigation is yet to come."

10

Back in Washington

On Sunday, April 21, the morning papers included a brief account of the released members of the crew who had sailed on the *Lapland* the previous day. They had been treated rather shabbily by IMM, and Ralph White, A.B., voiced the complaints of his fellow shipmates before departing. "We asked for some advance money on the wages due us," White said, "and although we were all without a cent, we were told that we would receive no money on our wages until our return to England. We signed up for the entire voyage, but the White Star officials claim that our wages ceased when the *Titanic* went under." Other seamen told that IMM had refused to cable their relatives in England that they were safe, giving the excuse that it would be "too great an expense."

But the crew's unhappiness wasn't nearly as big news as the consternation of Ismay and the IMM. Saturday evening, Ismay had once again asked Senator Smith's permission to return to England, and once again was refused. Ismay was now livid and proclaimed that he had "the utmost respect for the Senate of the United States, but the inquiry as it is proceeding now may wreak great injustice rather than clear up points in question." When the committee arrived at Penn Station for the trip back to the capital, William Alden was mobbed by reporters who had just heard that Ismay had lodged a formal protest to James Bryce, the British ambassador.

"No one has protested very seriously," Smith assured them with a smile. Asked what the complaint would mean to the future of the inquiry, the senator casually explained, "We are just going ahead and doing what the Senate instructed us to do, regardless of all and any consequences." Raising his eyebrows slightly, he added, "As far as that goes, I fail to perceive where there could be room or grounds for any protest."

The journey back to Washington was unusually somber. Everyone was emotionally drained. Only Francis Newlands, the genial Nevada giant whose hair hung in ringlets across his forehead, seemed chipper. Newlands was devouring the national newspapers. Accounts of the *Titanic* investigation had swept the front pages, squeezing Teddy Roosevelt's primary victories over Taft in Nebraska and West Virginia to an indifferent side column. *The New York Times* caustically observed that only a disaster "greater than that which he plans to inflict upon the country" could have upstaged Teddy so.

William Alden was sitting across from Senator Newlands in the coach, deep in thought. Newlands finally interrupted him to show him an editorial in the *New York Herald:*

> Where are the folk who have been saying the U.S. Senate is slow? They are not heard in public places today. One man has chased them away. That man is William Alden Smith of Michigan.

Smith smiled at the item, but quickly drew back into his thoughts. As of Thursday evening last, he had decided to abstain from reading the newspapers until the investigation was over. The stories were tempting—very tempting—but they were also puffed-up and contradictory. No, it wouldn't do to have the inquiry directed by the press. He retraced the testimony taken so far and the business he would have to finish in Washington before Monday. Suddenly he jolted.

"Jonathan!" he exclaimed to Francis Newlands. "Whatever happened to Jonathan?" Smith had completely forgotten that Jonathan Bourne had promised to join the group in New York by way of a later train.

Newlands immediately flipped a few pages back in his newspaper and showed Smith another item. Bourne had been defeated in his bid for renomination in Oregon and by now had probably lost interest in a good number of things. Smith shook his head in disappointment. He had warned the Progressives that they were too sure of themselves. Overconfidence seemed to be the disease of the year.

In Washington, Smith walked from Union Station to his residence at 1100 Sixteenth Street, about six blocks from the White House. As soon as he walked through the front door, his wife, Nan, told him to answer an urgent call from Margaret Molloy, the senator's "typewriter." Margaret was at the office—on a Sunday, no less. Over the phone, Smith heard Maggie bawl that the letters and telegrams were growing so thick, she was ready to pitch the whole lot of them out of the window.

Smith dashed to his rooms at 411 Senate Office Building, where he was stunned by the volume of the mail. Efforts at stacking it had come to little, though Maggie was still putting up a valiant, if losing, effort. The letters were expressions of appreciation from the American people. They also contained anguished requests that the senator look into the chance of survivors still atop icebergs or locked in the sunken ship's watertight compartments. Letters from relatives of steerage passengers expressed concern over the possibilities that their loved ones had been shot, locked in their quarters, or otherwise treated despicably before they were drowned. Much of the mail contained theories and hypotheses about the wreck that the inquiry might pursue. Others offered useful as well as floridly psychotic suggestions on how ocean steamships might be improved in the future.

In short, the letters represented the national interest, sentiment, and anguish that President Taft had ignored. And, as far as Smith was concerned, they constituted a mandate for the investigation to be pursued until the last shred of evidence bearing on the disaster was uncovered. By allowing the specific content of these letters from the American people to influence the course of the inquiry, Smith would exacerbate the already growing Anglo-American crisis, augment the Taft-TR battle, and bring a barrage of criticism onto his own head. In so doing, Smith would also transform the investigation into not just the first public forum of the American populace in the twentieth century but the first occasion of all time when a public corporation would be held accountable for its actions through an inquest determined in part by its customers.

Smith started reading the letters at random. One writer suggested turning "the cabins into lifeboats" which would float off the ship. Another applied the same principle to the bunk mattresses; they could be made of inflatable rubber. A gentleman from the Rocky Mountains conceived an original plan for equipping all ships with "iceberg hooks so that, when a vessel hits an iceberg, these hooks will grip and hold tight to it," thus buoying the ship. Another man recommended that ships carry "a cannon on the bow" which could blow any iceberg "to bits before the ship gets near it."

Not all the suggestions were so farfetched. A man from California described an elaborate way to attach a cable connected to a buoyant drum to the roof of the ship's bridge; if the vessel foundered, the mechanism would release the drum which would then float up, indicating the exact position of the ship's grave. The Curtiss Aeroplane Company argued with lofty optimism that an aeroplane carried "knocked down" on deck of a passenger liner could be "put together in fifteen minutes." Once assembled, enough room on most liners could be found to serve as a runway, and the plane could search out the closest neighboring vessel and secure its aid. In essence, it was a primitive plan for an aircraft carrier, but by then Smith was unable to tell the reasonable ideas from the crazy ones.

The senator told Maggie to forward *all* letters containing nautical suggestions to the Department of the Navy. As for the remainder, he wanted them the exact same way that he liked the mail from his constituents sorted: They should be organized into stacks according to content—the rational letters on top and the irrational ones on the bottom. When Marrie began sputtering in protest, William Alden quickly assured her that he'd find additional personnel to help out.

This was easier said than done. Smith did not wish to increase substantially the cost of the inquiry. In the first place, he had a penchant for economy when it came to spending the government's money. Secondly, he didn't wish the expense of the investigation to become a point against which IMM or Morgan's senatorial allies might rally. He finally concluded that extra help would have to come from volunteers and directed that, henceforth, any constituent who dropped by the office should be invited to help sort the mail. Although most Michiganders were delighted to participate, a playful admonition soon began appearing in a number of Michigan newspapers. Visitors from the Wolverine State to the nation's capital were warned not to call on their senior senator unless they were fully prepared to go to work.

Smith was not entirely happy with his solution. The sorting still needed competent direction by someone whom Smith could implicitly trust. After reflection, Smith wired William Alden Jr., his only child, at the University of Michigan. If Billy was willing to take a short leave from school, the senator would personally request the permission of Harry Burns Hutchins, president of U. of M. Response from Ann Arbor came immediately. Will Jr. would be happy to come to Washington and help out his dad, but would arrange things with Dr. Hutchins himself.

By 6:00 in the evening, Smith could no longer put off the reporters, whom Maggie Molloy had been sending away with stern Irish invective. All of them wanted desperately to know if they were going to be admitted to the Monday hearing.

"We're not going to have any star-chamber proceedings," Smith assured them. "The country has a right to know the truth about this terrible disaster." This was indeed the whole point of keeping the hearings open.

The reporters then wanted to know if the *Titanic*'s crewmen, who had just arrived in Washington, were under surveillance.

"Well, the fact isn't being advertised," Smith said with a slight smile, "but the sergeant-at-arms has a man with them."

The "man" stationed with the *Titanic*'s crewmen was Bill McKinstry, Smith's secretary whom the senator had sent to Union Station to escort the crewmen safely to the Continental Hotel. At the first sight of the crewmen, some of whom wore jumpers with TITANIC across the front, the Washington newsmen had instantly caught the fever. No matter how hard they tried, however, the reporters couldn't get a thing out of the stoically silent sailors. At the Continental, the rudeness of the newsmen as they looked over the crewmen's shoulders as they signed the register finally became too much for the *Titanic*'s impetuous fifth officer. "In England," barked Officer Harold Lowe, "I say a man would get a punch in the nose if he attempted to look over the guestbook!"

Elsewhere in the hotel, Bill McKinstry was wrestling with another problem. Second Officer Charles Lightoller, the highest in command, insisted that he should not be quartered in the same hotel as the crew. In fact, said Lightoller, all four of the surviving officers deserved a separate hotel—such as the posh New Willard, where Messrs. Franklin and Ismay were staying. Checking with the manager of the Continental, McKinstry was told that the management refused "to quarter the crew in this first-class hotel unless the officers stay with them." (The Continental was genuinely concerned over the havoc some thirty unsupervised sailors could wreak in their dignified establishment.) McKinstry went back to Lightoller and relayed the manager's position, but Lightoller remained obdurate. "As an officer," he insisted, "I'm not going to be quartered with the crew." The *Titanic*'s caste system, it appeared, had come all the way ashore.

"My God!" cried Bill McKinstry in desperation, "your captain now sleeps quartered with the crew under the waves!"

Lightoller was inclined to think that was quite another matter, but offered a compromise. He would remain with the men in the Continental if he could have a room on a separate floor and be guaranteed separate dining arrangements. McKinstry agreed, and Lightoller signed the register.

Oddly enough, a day later the crew was transferred to less elegant accommodations at the Hotel National. The official explanation was that the crew had been doubled up at the Continental and "disliked sleeping twins." At the National they could be permitted individual rooms. In view of the way the crewmen were accustomed to bunking aboard ship, this explanation seems highly unlikely.

Meanwhile, at the Senate Office Building, William Alden had turned his attention to the needs of the Washington phase of the inquiry. His Senate resolution had called for testimony from surviving passengers as well as crewmen. Now that the survivors had scattered across the country, it would be necessary to locate them and take their testimony in the form of affidavits. It was a job that would have routinely fallen upon the sergeant-at-arms, but those close to the senator claimed he had little confidence in Dan Ransdell. Joe Bayliss would have been ideal for the job, but Smith had reluctantly let the sheriff return to the Soo. Pondering the matter, Smith eventually sent telegrams to two more friends—Albert Carroll, former sheriff of Kent County, Michigan, and Edward O'Donnell, deputy U.S. marshal at Grand Rapids. Carroll and O'Donnell (later nicknamed the "Michigan Minutemen") immediately set out for Washington. When they arrived, Smith briefed them on the various trips they would have to make. As long as they were in the capital, however, they might "nose around wherever there is *Titanic* news and convey the results" back to the chairman.

In the remaining hours of Sunday evening, Smith received official calls from visitors. French ambassador Jules Jusserand, whom Taft had called "the slyest little diplomat in Washington," came to express his "gratification at what had been accomplished by the investigation" and to assure Senator Smith that France wished to cooperate with the United States in "improving conditions at sea." Jusserand's visit caused considerable gossip in Washington. England had recently attempted to sign an exclusive treaty (the General Arbitration Treaty) with the United States, whereby issues "justiceable in their nature" would be arbitrated by the Permanent Court of Arbitration at the Hague. According to Taft, the British ambassador, James Bryce, "had hoped to signalize the superiority of the English-speaking people by blazing the way for the millennium through this treaty with us." As soon as France and Germany got wind of the treaty, they asked to be included. Bryce did not wish the two alien nations included; but under pressure from Jusserand, Taft felt obliged to include France. The President, however, did not feel the same compulsion to include "the Huns" and, accordingly, Germany was excluded from the treaty.

A month before the *Titanic* disaster, the Senate Foreign Relations Committee refused to ratify the treaty, and Smith of Michigan had been the principal force behind the opposition. The senator's position had been simple: If the treaty was truly for the purpose of peace, as was loudly being proclaimed, then it should be extended to *all* the major European powers, including Germany. (There were a number of arcane aspects of the treaty. Several weeks later, the Irish New York *Gaelic-American* offered its personal explanation for British criticism of Smith's handling of the *Titanic* inquiry. In going against the Arbitration Treaty, said the *Gaelic-American,* Smith had refused the promise of U.S. support to England in her eagerly anticipated and obviously forthcoming naval war with Germany.)

Ambassador Bryce had been severely vexed over Smith's influence in killing the treaty. The ambassador had been sent to the United States especially for Canadian reciprocity and the Arbitration Treaty, and the "fool" from Michigan had been largely responsible for the defeat of both measures—not to mention the Canadian Waterways fiasco. Bryce was a great one for traveling in the United States and had made—what seemed at the time—a routine visit to Michigan shortly after the defeat of reciprocity. Afterward Bryce had sent this thoughtful note to William Alden:

> It has been a disappointment that I could not come to Michigan previously and have been obliged to come at a time when you are detained by your public duties in Washington. But I must not omit to tell you how very kindly your fellow citizens and constituents in Michigan have received me. It has been a very agreeable visit to your great state.

Smith had thought nothing of Bryce's trip until, a few days later, it got back to him that, during the visit, the ambassador had checked out with a number of prominent politicians the chances of defeating William Alden in 1912. (If the senator could be dumped, reciprocity could be resubmitted.) Even though the ambassador had been told by everyone that Smith would surely be reelected, William Alden had been furious. This kind of politicking was entirely out of place for a foreign dignitary, and relations thereafter between Bryce and Smith were icy.

Now, here was Senator Smith at the head of an inquiry that could cause Great Britain enormous embarrassment.

While Jules Jusserand was skillfully reserving a place for France in the senator's plans for an international maritime treaty, Lord Bryce was weighing Bruce Ismay's protest. The Senate was well within its legal rights in detaining Ismay; and if Bryce complained, William Alden (who might still be smarting from the ambassador's Michigan trip) could easily make things more unpleasant than they already were. Bryce sent word to Britain's foreign secretary that England would simply have to suffer the American inquiry, adding that William Alden Smith was "one of the most unsuitable persons who could have been charged with an investigation of this nature."

After Jusserand left, Smith was called on by the Austro-Hungarian ambassador, Baron Hengelmuller, whose mission was comparable to that of the French minister. Ambassador Hengelmuller also had an extraordinary "lead" for the chairman. A Hungarian sailor, Louis Klein, had shipped aboard the *Titanic* and was now in Cleveland, where he had made the shocking disclosure that the *Titanic*'s lookout had been asleep in the crow's nest and the crewmen intoxicated; stewards had served even the men on the bridge champagne left over from one of the first cabin's parties. Smith thought the accusation highly improbable, if not ridiculous, but diplomatic tact necessitated his assuring the baron that he would look into it fully. Smith gave the assignment to his Michigan Minutemen, and Ed O'Donnell was sent packing to Cleveland. It would turn out that Louis Klein had never even been aboard the *Titanic*.

Smith's final visitor on Sunday was George von Lengerke Meyer, Secretary of the Navy, whose visit Smith himself had requested. Meyer was a TR appointee and, under Taft, had established four permanent bureaus pertaining to naval operations. Under his skillful direction, the U.S. Navy had become broader and a good deal more competent. Meyer had been badly shaken by the *Titanic* disaster and told Smith that the merchant marine should build ships more like naval vessels—they should have longitudinal bulkheads and carry searchlights.

Meyer was particularly incensed over the *Carpathia*'s

refusal to respond to the *Chester*'s and *Salem*'s official inquiries from the President. In *The New York Times,* Harold Bride had explained that he hadn't refused the information to the U.S. Navy operators. The problem, he said, lay in the fact that the navy's wireless men had been "wretched operators. They knew American Morse, but not Continental Morse sufficiently to be worthwhile." Meyer had checked out the allegation with Rear Admiral Hutch I. Cone, chief of the Bureau of Naval Engineering, who called Bride's accusation absurd. "Continenal code is the code used by all the wireless operators in the navy," said Cone, "and they are successfully working with it all the time." Cone felt that Bride's allegation reflected his "harrowing strain" at the time.

Meyer went on to say that Bride's excuse simply did not hold up under critical examination. There appeared to be no difficulty in exchanges between the *Chester* and *Carpathia* on other matters. James Gaffney, the *Chester*'s operator, had his own explanation as to why the *Carpathia* had refused to communicate. "We carry aboard the *Chester* the DeForest wireless as well as the U.S. Wireless Specialty outfits," Gaffney said. "Whenever possible, the Marconi operators show their displeasure at the operators who are using or are known to carry the equipment of other makes." Meyer complained that, somehow, the Marconi Company was at the bottom of this mess. In spite of the International Wireless Convention of 1908, the Marconi operators had continued to boycott messages—other than emergency calls—between their stations and those that did not use their apparatus. This was the most likely explanation for the *Carpathia*'s failure to respond to the U.S. scout cruisers.

William Alden assured the distraught secretary he would look into the matter fully.

In the balance of their meeting, Smith asked Meyer numerous questions about North Atlantic navigation and requested some reading to help him keep abreast of technical aspects of the testimony. Meyer made a phone call and had some books delivered to Smith's home. He also promised the chairman that George Uhler would continue to be available to the subcommittee and that he'd also have someone from the U.S. Hydrographic Office attend the hearings. The secretary had a request of his own: Would it be all right if his two daughters attended the inquiry?

William Alden said it would be fine.

Although Smith had hoped to rest before the hearings resumed, he found it impossible. Returning home, the senator stayed up till dawn reading two books that Meyer had sent over: *Knight's Modern Seamanship* and *Ocean Steamships.* In the latter work, Smith became absorbed in a chapter entitled "The Region of Ice."

On Monday morning, April 22, at 8:45 A.M., Smith called all six of the subcommittee members to a preliminary meeting at his home. He reviewed the gist of the testimony taken in New York, discussed the Harter Act, and explained that given (1) negligence aboard the *Titanic* and (2) Ismay's privity of it, Morgan's IMM could be sued by the American people. Furnifold Simmons apparently balked at the questionable use of a Senate inquiry to lay the groundwork for individual suits of a trust. After Monday, he refused to attend another hearing.

The other members called the chairman's attention to the fact that Ismay's privity of negligence had already been established in a sensational story that had appeared in the papers. Mrs. Arthur Ryerson of Philadelphia, a survivor, was reported to have said that on the day of the collision, Ismay had passed her on deck and showed her a marconigram warning of ice. When Mrs.

Ryerson had asked if the ship would be slowed down, Ismay had purportedly told her, "Oh, no, we will put on more boilers and get out of it." (Ismay had since denied the story.)

Smith merely smiled at the information. He had not been reading the papers, but the incident had been related to him in the Waldorf-Astoria by Mrs. Douglas—the lady who had told him that the water buckets hadn't reached the sea. Smith had already placed Mrs. Ryerson under subpoena, but she remained ill at New York's Hotel Belmont and wasn't yet able to testify.

In the concluding moments of the meeting, Smith learned that his and Senator Martine's resolution for an international maritime conference had been reported favorably by the Foreign Relations Committee and had been sent to the President. Smith also learned, much to his amusement, that some of the senators up for reelection were jealous of the enormous publicity William Alden had been receiving in the newspapers.

The Washington hearings had been assigned to the immense caucus room in the new wing of the Senate Office Building. This chamber had just been pronounced "the handsomest legislative hearing room in the world." Politicians had dubbed it "the throne room." It had never been used and would be formally christened by the *Titanic* inquiry. The new chamber was indeed impressive—great panels of white marble and four enormous crystal chandeliers. But true to Gilded Age splendor, its acoustics were atrocious.

At 10:00 in the morning, the portals of the throne room were opened, and an enormous, excited throng of Washington women—dressed to the hilt—stampeded into the chamber and overtook space allotted to official witnesses and the press. The plumes atop their elegant coiffures jousted as the ladies, seated closely together, bubbled and chatted. A number of them had brought sack lunches.

The subcommittee and its chairman arrived at 10:30 and were barely able to squeeze into the room. After quietly appreciating the looks of awe on the faces of those members who had not accompanied him to New York, William Alden said to the assembly, "For my associates and myself, I desire to make an announcement." The senator paused, looking around for the source of an annoying racket. It was merely the hundreds of reporters who had scribbled down the words he had just uttered. Their conjoint stenography, reverberating in the echoes of the marble caucus room, had sounded like a horde of locusts.

The explosions from the photographers' cameras added to the noise. Turning around, Smith saw to his horror that one of the photographers had begun cranking a cinematic camera. The senator pushed his way through the crowd, and scurried down the corridors looking for the sergeant-at-arms and his assistants. William Alden dragged them back and helped them eject the photographers, remove an excess of protesting ladies, push the remaining crowd back, and move the newsmen several yards away from the conference table. Finally, the official visitors—who hadn't even been able to get inside—were escorted in and seated. They included Representative Nicholas Longworth (Alice Roosevelt's husband), numerous foreign ambassadors, Captain C.F.G. Sowerby (naval attaché of the British embassy), Inspector General Uhler, and Captain John Knapp, whom Meyer had dispatched from the U.S. Hydrographic Office.

"I desire to make an announcement," Smith resumed. "We are not at all concerned about the convenience of visitors upon the hearing. We are concerned primarily in obtaining the truth, and I desire each person here to understand that they are here solely by the courtesy of the committee, that the inquiry is not for their entertainment, and that any expressions of any kind or character will not be permitted."

The Washington hearings had officially begun.

The star witness of the day was Joseph Groves Boxhall, the *Titanic*'s twenty-eight-year-old fourth officer. Boxhall was a clean-cut young man, "small, delicate-looking," with coal-black hair. He seemed exceptionally nervous. He kept his hands firmly clasped so they wouldn't tremble and spoke so softly that constant repeats and calls for "louder" were necessary. (The acoustics of the throne room didn't help matters any.) But Boxhall's answers were framed with beautiful precision, which Chairman Smith found very welcome. He was, from all accounts, an intelligent and impressive witness.

Boxhall recalled that only two lifeboats had been lowered during the *Titanic*'s sole lifeboat drill, conducted at Southampton. All the boats had been in excellent condition and equipped with the necessary provisions; he had checked this himself. Boxhall's principal role aboard the *Titanic* had been that of navigator. He had spent a year in a special school studying navigation and nautical astronomy, and it was he who had plotted the positions of icebergs wirelessed from other ships, which Captain Smith had given him. William Alden wanted to know when the captain had given them to him.

"I do not know whether it was the day before or two days before [the collision]. He gave me some positions of icebergs, which I put on the chart. . . ."

"Did you know whether a wireless had been received from the *Amerika* that the *Titanic* was in the vicinity of icebergs?"

"No," replied Boxhall, "I could not say."

It is quite unlikely that Boxhall had ever seen the

Amerika's marconigram—or *any* of the critical warnings the *Titanic* had received on the afternoon preceding the collision. First of all, Boxhall was certain that no warning had been delivered to him Sunday the fourteenth. Secondly, all the positions he had plotted showed the reported ice to be well north of the *Titanic*'s track. If he had noticed any plottings near the track or south of the track, he explained, he would "have made a special note to the captain about them. If I had seen any bergs on the track or to the southward of the track I should have done that." (The *Amerika*'s warning specified ice south of the track.) Boxhall was confident that no such warning had come to the captain's atttention, otherwise, as he explained, "the word would have been passed around right away—everybody would have known it."

At noon on Sunday, April 14, E.J. handed Ismay a marconigram just received from the Baltic: *"Have had moderate variable winds and clear fine weather since leaving. Greek steamer* Athinai *reports passing icebergs and large quantity of field ice today in latitude 41:51 North, longitude 49:52 West." The reported ice was virtually on the* Titanic*'s track. Ismay glanced at the marconigram and casually slipped it into his pocket. At 7:10 P.M., the captain located Ismay in the smoking room and asked, "By the way, sir, have you got that telegram which I gave you this afternoon?" Ismay reached into his pocket. "Yes," he replied, "here it is." The captain took the scrap of paper, explaining, "I want it to put up in the officers' chart room."*

"Can you tell what the theory of the navigator is as to where the icebergs and growlers and field ice come from?" Smith asked. This portion of the senator's interrogation reflected the homework he had done the previous evening.

"As far as I understand," Boxhall replied, "they come from the Arctic region."

"What are they composed of, if you know?"

"Some people who have been very close to them tell me that they have seen sand and gravel and rocks and things of that kind in them."

"Rocks and other substances?"

"And earth," said Boxhall. "I have never been close enough to see that. . . ."

"Is it understood by mariners and navigators that they are more frequent in the latitude of the Grand Banks?" Smith asked.

"Around fifty West; forty-seven to fifty West, I think, as near as I can remember."

"From forty-seven West they are known to exist?"

"Yes."

"And it is customary to be particularly careful in that vicinity?" asked the senator.

"Oh, yes, sir."

"Well," said Smith, "how did it happen that in that identical vicinity it was not thought necessary to increase the lookout?"

"I do not know," Boxhall replied. "The lookout may have been increased; I cannot say."

Lightoller, however, had sworn that no additional lookouts had been posted and the only person who could adequately answer this question had gone down with his ship.

Senator Newlands asked the fourth officer why, given the reported clearness of the night, the fatal iceberg hadn't been seen in time.

"On such a night as that," Boxhall explained, "even if there is no moon, you can very, very often see an iceberg by the [breakers] on the sides of it; that is, if there is a little breeze. . . . I think if there had been a little ripple on the water we should have stood a very good chance of seeing the iceberg in time to miss it—in time to clear it."

Although the committee didn't realize it at the time, the most significant portion of Boxhall's testimony concerned a "mystery ship," which had been seen from the decks of the *Titanic* during the lowering of the lifeboats. From the time shortly after the collision until he left in lifeboat Number 2, Boxhall had been occupied in sending up distress rockets to catch the attention of the unidentified vessel. His testimony on the incident was so unexpected and so extraordinary, the committee at first had trouble comprehending it and, afterward, gave little credence to it.

"You say you fired these rockets and otherwise attempted to signal her?" Smith asked.

"Yes, sir," said Boxhall. "She got close enough, as I thought, to read our electric Morse signal, and I signaled to her. I told her to 'Come at once, we are sinking.' The captain was standing . . . with me most of the time when we were signaling."

"Did he also see it?" Smith assumed the captain would not have been prone to hallucinations.

"Yes, sir," Boxhall replied.

> *Boxhall had first spotted her "two masthead lights"—there was no doubt she was a steamer. The masthead lights were "pretty close together," indicating a four- or three-masted ship. He went over to the detonator and fired off some rockets. He then examined the mysterious vessel through the glasses. She was showing her green starboard light, as if she had come closer. More rockets were sent up. Boxhall could now see her red port light—even with his naked eye. It looked like the ship was turning around. He sig-*

naled her with the Morse lamp. No response. He then had a quartermaster send up the rockets while he worked the lamp and checked her through the glasses. Although some of the stewards on deck thought they saw her flicker back a message, Boxhall could see no response at all.

"From what you saw of that vessel," Smith asked, "how far would you think she was from the *Titanic?*"

"I should say approximately the ship would be about five miles," the fourth officer replied.

After the hearing, the committee reviewed Boxhall's testimony, and Inspector General Uhler was asked his opinion of the "mystery ship." "It is a strange story," Uhler replied. "But it is inconceivable that any vessel that could be seen from the *Titanic* should not have seen the rockets or the Morse signals from the *Titanic*. The rockets can be seen from ten to fifteen miles, and that was—from every account—a calm, clear night."

Smith was inclined to agree. It was unlikely that what Boxhall had seen was a ship. If it was a ship, she would have certainly seen the rockets and come to the *Titanic*'s rescue.

The reporters, who had been interested in the testimony, asked Chairman Smith if maybe it was the *Carpathia* Boxhall had seen. This was out of the question. The *Carpathia* was too far away at the time—she hadn't been seen until hours after the *Titanic* foundered. "No," William Alden told them, "the light—if there *was* a light—was not the *Carpathia.*"

It was, as General Uhler said, "a strange story."

The *Titanic* launched. Check lines grow taut as tugs begin towing her to the fitting-out basin. (*Titanic Historical Society, Inc., Indian Orchard, Massachusetts*)

The *Titanic* in Southampton Harbor. (*Titanic Historical Society, Inc., Indian Orchard, Massachusetts*)

The grand staircase of oak and wrought iron, sixty feet high and sixteen feet wide. The clock in the center is flanked by two carved figures, signifying "Honour and Glory crowning Time." (*Titanic Historical Society, Inc., Indian Orchard, Massachusetts*)

First-class cabin B-59. (*Titanic Historical Society, Inc., Indian Orchard, Massachusetts*)

Second-class passengers stroll on their allotted space on the boat deck. (*Titanic Historical Society, Inc., Indian Orchard, Massachusetts*)

Purser McElroy and E. J. photographed during the stop at Queenstown. (*Titanic Historical Society, Inc., Indian Orchard, Massachusetts*)

The men of the R.M.S. *Titanic:* (top left) First Officer William M. Murdoch, (top center) Captain E. J. Smith and friend, (top right) Chief Purser H. W. McElroy, (middle right) Chief Officer H. F. Wilde, and (bottom row, left to right) Ship's Surgeon Dr. J. E. Simpson, Fifth Officer Harold G. Lowe, Lookout F. Evans, Third Officer Herbert J. Pitman. (*Titanic Historical Society, Inc., Indian Orchard, Massachusetts*)

Storming the Broadway offices of the White Star Line on Tuesday morning, April 16. (*Wide World Photos*)

Franklin, Attorney Burlingham, and Ismay arrive in Washington, D.C. (*Historical Pictures Service, Inc., Chicago*)

11

Collision

Tuesday morning, April 23, the subcommittee agreed that in spite of the glamour of the throne room, its wretched acoustics made it necessary to hold the inquiry elsewhere. Smith offered his own Committee on Territories Conference Room, and his colleagues immediately accepted. This fifty-by-twenty-six attractive chamber of Vermont marble, colonial lamps, and mahogany furniture was less garish than the caucus room, and its acoustics far better. It was on the smallish side, with far less room for spectators; but that was just fine with Chairman Smith after the spectacle of the previous day.

When the Washington women, who had thrilled at Monday's hearing, found on Tuesday morning that they would not be admitted, they raised an unearthly fracas. At 10:30 A.M., those who hadn't been early enough to gain seats beat on the doors until the sergeant-at-arms opened them. At once, the forward phalanx of nearly 500 women who had filled the corridors and stairwells plowed into the room, knocking reporters onto the floor, physically moving the conference table, and fairly terrifying the committee members.

Smith politely asked them to leave. They would not budge—and there weren't enough sergeants-at-arms in the building to move them. Smith was forced to call out the capital police who eventually removed them, two at a time. A rather corpulent lady, elegantly attired and wearing an enormous chapeau decked with artificial flowers, was carried out screaming. "I'm the wife of a congressman, I'm the wife of a congressman!" she bellowed in protest.

William Alden leaned over and whispered to Senator Newlands, "My God, what are American women coming to?"

The hearings were delayed an hour as the women were escorted from the room. In the meantime, unbeknownst to the committee, reporters had smuggled in cameras piecemeal, using the spare time to assemble them on tripods. The committee had just relaxed and called its first witness when an explosion of flashes rocked the room. Smith leaped to his feet, his face flushed and nostrils flaring.

"This inquiry is official and solemn and there will be no hippodroming or commercializing of it!" Pummeling the conference table with his fist, he roared, "I *will not permit* it!"

The hearings had now begun to focus on junior officers and quartermasters, who offered information much more freely than had previous witnesses. Frederick Fleet, a short twenty-five-year-old Southampton man, had been stationed in the crow's nest at the time. Fleet now appeared before the committee, nervous and pitifully attired. His broken-down shoes were obviously a bequest from the American Seamen's Friend Society of New York. He clutched a worn-out cap in his hands which he periodically twisted during his testimony.

Speaking in a thick cockney accent, Fleet was often difficult to understand and appeared to have just as much trouble comprehending the senators' questions. One reporter couldn't decide whether the lookout man was "sleepy or stupid." Chances were he was nothing more than frightfully anxious, which he concealed the only way he knew how.

Fleet recalled how the night of Sunday, April 14, had appeared to the "eyes" of the ship.

> *From noon to nighttime, the temperature had dropped from fifty to thirty-two degrees. No one had ever seen the North Atlantic so calm—the imaginations of survivors would be taxed for the proper simile. The sea was "like polished glass," "like a millpond," "like a lake of oil," and "as calm and as full of reflected stars as the pool in a Moorish garden." Although there was no moon, the stars had never seemed to shine more brightly. They almost stood "right out of the sky, sparkling like cut diamonds."*
>
> *The men in the crow's nest had been warned to "keep a sharp lookout for small ice" and growlers. At approximately 11:39 P.M. (10:06 in New York) only twenty minutes remained of Frederick Fleet's watch. Peering out into the flat, twinkling calm, Fleet suddenly saw a faint, dark shadow. Focusing on it intently, he watched it emerge as "a small black mass" dead in the* Titanic's *track.*

"How far away was this 'black mass' when you first saw it?" asked Senator Smith.

"I have no idea, sir," Fleet replied.

The lookout began twisting his hat, silent and remote. Smith felt a definite compassion for this uneducated man.

"Did it impress you as serious?" the senator tried.

"I reported it a' soon as ever I seen it!" Fleet retorted with unexpected rancor.

It was difficult to tell what was gnawing at Mr. Fleet. He was obviously intimidated by the proceedings, but Smith watched him continually looking off to the side at Lightoller and Ismay. Was he hiding something out of fear of reprisal from his employers? Smith tried repeatedly to get Fleet to estimate the distance of the iceberg when he had first sighted it, but Fleet balked, telling the committee: "I am not a good judge of distance." Later in his testimony, Fleet mentioned that the lifeboat in which he had escaped had been approximately a mile away from the *Titanic* when she had foundered. Hearing this facile estimation of distance, Smith moved in on what sounded like a slip.

"How are you able to fix that in your mind—that you were a mile from the *Titanic* in this small boat?" Smith asked.

"I heard people talk about it?"

"Was that your own judgment, too?"

"I ain't got no judgment," the lookout replied.

The largely female audience tittered at Fleet's earnest self-observation and the chairman, whirling around at them, admonished that one more like that, and *all* spectators would be expelled from the chamber. Glaring at them a few seconds longer, Smith returned to his witness.

"I understand you to say you have no judgment of distance at all." The senator was no seaman, but he thought it a peculiar qualification for a ship's lookout.

"No more I haven't," Fleet asserted.

"So you based your conclusion that you were a mile away upon what others told you?"

"That's all."

"Could you tell how many ship's lengths you were away—*Titanic* ship's lengths?"

"No, I couldn't."

Mr. Fleet seemed hopelessly inaccessible. He was unable to guess how many minutes had passed before he reported the berg and the time the ship struck. He was unable to estimate how large the berg had appeared when he first spotted it. Smith finally managed to get Fleet to express the size by posing some choices.

"Was it the size of an ordinary house? Was it as large as this room appears to be?"

"No, no. It didn't appear very large at all."

"Was it as large as the table at which I am sitting?"

"It'd be as large as those two tables put together when I saw it first," Fleet volunteered. Here was the key. Fleet needed concrete alternatives to frame his answers.

"How large did it get to be, finally, when it struck the ship?"

"When we were alongside," Fleet answered, "it was a little bit higher than the forecastle head. . . . Fifty feet I should say."

Given the two estimates and the ship's speed at approximately 21.5 knots, the committee later calculated the berg at roughly less than a mile away when Fleet had spotted it. There were at least two reasons why Fleet had been unable to see it sooner. First of all was Joseph Boxhall's explanation that there had been no breakers to illuminate the base of the berg. But perhaps the more interesting actor contributing to the delayed sighting was the fact that *no binoculars had been issued to the crow's nest.* The lookouts had been given glasses on the trip from Belfast to Southampton, but at the latter port, these had been taken over by the bridge. It had irritated all six of the men specially assigned to lookout duty. One of them eventually told the committee that it was "always customary" on the White Star liners to have glasses in the crow's nest; he had no idea why the policy should have been changed for the maiden voyage of the *Titanic.* Another said that he had asked for glasses "several times," but was refused.

"Did you make any request for glasses on the *Titanic?*" Smith asked.

"We asked for them in Southampton," Fleet replied, "and they said there was none for us."

"Whom did you ask?"

"They said there was none intended for us."

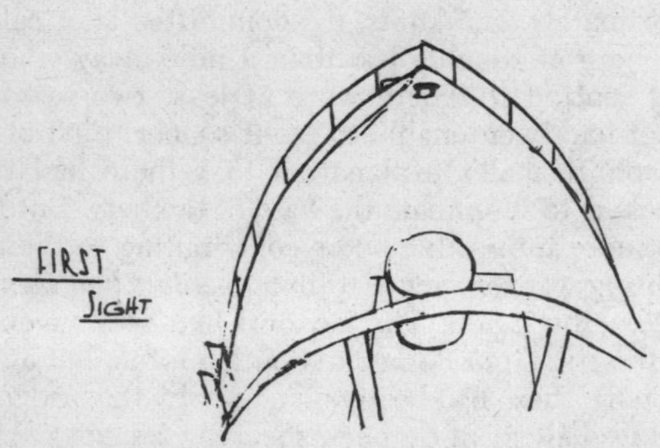

A drawing by Frederick Fleet, showing how the iceberg first appeared to the men in the crow's nest. (Credit: *Titanic Historical Society, Inc., Indian Orchard, Mass.*)

"*Whom* did you ask?"

"We asked Mr. Lightoller, the second officer," Fleet replied softly. Although somewhat relieved that his secret was out, Fleet glanced over nervously at the second officer and Mr. Ismay. Lightoller remained attentive and unruffled as usual. Ismay was busily preoccupied. He had borrowed paper from the reporters and was obsessed with sketching, over and over, a five-pointed star on a burgee—the pennant of his father's line.

"Suppose you had had glasses such as you had on the *Oceanic* or such as you had between Belfast and Southampton," the senator posed. "Could you have seen this black object a greater distance?"

"We could have seen it a bit sooner."

Drawing by Frederick Fleet, showing the nature of the collision. (Credit: *Titanic Historical Society, Inc., Indian Orchard, Mass.*)

"How much sooner?"

"Well," Fleet reflected, "enough to get out of the way." In this, the lookouts of the other watch would concur.

"Did you and your mates discuss with one another the fact that you had no glasses?"

"We discussed it all together between us," Fleet replied.

"Did you express surprise or regret that you had none?"

"I don't know what you mean."

Smith thought over the rephrasing of his question patiently. "Were you disappointed that you had no glasses?" he finally asked.

"Yes, sir," Fleet nodded.

White Star would minimize the importance of Fleet's testimony, the duty falling upon Second Officer Lightoller. "I never rely on *any* lookout," Lightoller later argued before the committee. "I keep a lookout myself, and so does every other officer." The second officer said that the usefulness of glasses in the crow's nest was a matter of opinion. "Different men have different ideas of the glasses, and of using them," he said. "Some keep them glued to their eyes altogether. I consider that very detrimental."

Fleet's assertion, however, would be supported by Admiral Robert Edwin Peary, Arctic explorer and discoverer of the North Pole. In an interview in the *New York World* just after Fleet's testimony, Peary claimed that the usefulness of glasses in sighting icebergs depended entirely on the visibility. "With a good clear night," such as had transpired April 14, "one could have seen farther, much farther with a binocular," Peary said. Asked how the finest ship in the world could have possibly failed to supply glasses to her lookouts, Peary merely chuckled. "Oh," he replied, "many things are forgotten during a ship's rush to its maiden voyage. Some common items because of their very commonness are overlooked."

Returning to Mr. Fleet, the committee learned that as soon as he had seen the "black mass" silhouetted against the stars, he had remarked to his mate, Reginald Lee, "There is ice ahead." Fleet had then yanked the bellpull three times, indicating an object dead ahead. Grabbing the phone in the crow's nest, Fleet had rung up the bridge and was answered at once by the sixth officer.

"He just asked me what did I see," Fleet recounted. "I told him an iceberg right ahead."

"What did he say then?" asked the senator.

"He said 'Thank you,' " Fleet replied.

The moan from the spectators packed in the room expressed their awe at the detachment that had prevailed at such a catastrophic moment in time. Some of the evening papers used "Thank You" as the header for Fleet's story.

On the bridge, Quartermaster Robert Hichens had been at the wheel. (Hichens was one of the key witnesses Joe Bayliss had brought back by tugboat from the *Lapland.*) The thirty-year-old seaman from Penzance spoke in a colorful Cornish accent and testified in a straightforward, effortless fashion. Few questions had to be asked of him, since he rambled so freely. With considerable detail, the quartermaster reconstructed the moment Fleet had rung up the bridge. It had been twenty minutes to midnight. First Officer Murdoch had been on the starboard wing. Sixth Officer Moody had picked up the phone and instantly relayed Fleet's warning to the officer of the watch: "Iceberg right ahead, sir."

Hichens recalled: "The chief officer rushed from the

wing to the bridge, or I imagine so, sir. Certainly I am enclosed in the wheelhouse, and I can't see—only my compass. He rushed to the engines. I heard the telegraph bell ring; he also give the order 'Hard astarboard!' "

In 1912, "hard astarboard" meant turning the stern of the ship to starboard and the bow to port. While Murdoch telegraphed the engine room "full astern," Hichens had obeyed the spoken order and threw his full weight to the wheel, spinning it counterclockwise. Sixth Officer Moody, standing by Hichens's left side, had affirmed the action: "Hard astarboard! The helm is hard over, sir."

In the crow's nest Frederick Fleet stood motionless, the phone still in his hand and his eyes bulging at the silhouette as it loomed larger and larger. The Titanic *kept moving dead ahead. After what seemed an eternity, her bows finally swung two points (twenty-two degrees) to port and were just beginning to clear the iceberg.*

Standby quartermaster Alfred Olliver, who had been checking the lights in the standard compass when he heard Fleet's three bells, was now walking toward the bridge. He entered the wheelhouse in time to hear Murdoch order the helm reversed: "Hard aport!"

Olliver was closely questioned on the reversal of the helm by Senator Burton.

"I heard 'hard aport,' " Olliver related, "and there was the man at the wheel and the officer. The officer was seeing it was carried out right. . . ."

"You do not know whether the helm was put hard astarboard first or not?" Burton asked.

"No, sir, I do not know that."

"But you know it was put hard aport after you got there?"

"After I got there. Yes, sir."

Fleet braced himself as the forecastle brushed against the berg, toppling nearly a ton of ice onto the forewell deck. Olliver dashed out of the wheelhouse in time to see the seventy-foot dark-blue pinnacle towering alongside. It glistened, wet and slick, and was pointed at the top. In the crow's nest, Fleet spun around and watched as the berg scraped along starboard and disappeared astern. It was all over in ten seconds.

"When she struck this obstacle, or this 'black mass,'" Smith asked Lookout Fleet, "was there much of a jar to the ship?"

"No, sir," Fleet replied.

"Was there *any?*"

"Just a slight grinding noise."

"Not sufficient to disturb you in your position in the crow's nest?"

"No, sir."

"Did it alarm you seriously when it struck?"

"No, sir," Fleet replied. "I thought it was a narrow shave."

Every passenger and crewman who appeared before the Senate committee would testify to the same effect. The collision had seemed no more than a close shave.

In the first-class smoking lounge on the deck beneath the bridge (A Deck), the aroma had become pleasingly masculine: tobacco smoke, whiskey, leather, and salt air. The gentlemen were still in their evening clothes—Archie Butt, Clarence Moore, Hugh

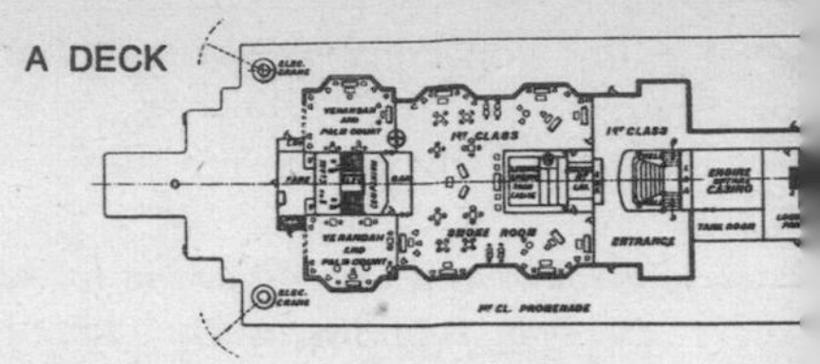

Woolner, and others absorbed in cocktails and card games. Woolner suddenly felt "a sort of stopping, a sort of—not exactly shock, but a sort of slowing down. And then we sort of felt a rip that gave a sort of slight twist to the whole room. Everybody, so far as I could see, stood up and a number of men walked out rapidly through the swinging doors on the port side, and ran along to the rail that was behind the mast. . . . I stood hearing what the conjectures were. People were guessing what it might be, and one man called out, 'An iceberg has passed astern,' but who it was I do not know. I never have seen the man since."

One deck lower, Steward Alfred Crawford was on duty in the forward part of B Deck. Hearing a slight "crunch" along starboard, Crawford scurried to the rail in time to see "a large black object" whisk alongside. He went back in "and there were a lot of passengers coming out." Among these were Dickinson Bishop of southwestern Michigan. While his bride, Helen, lay asleep in B-47, Bishop abandoned the

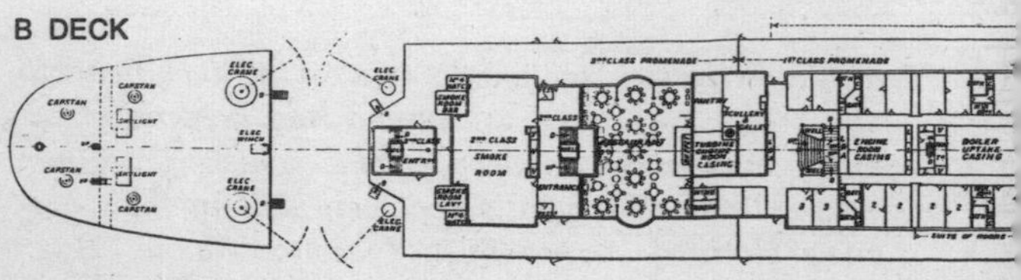

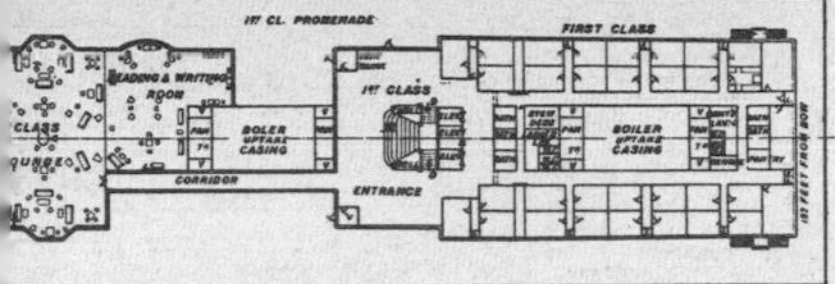

book he'd been reading and went out on deck, but "couldn't see a thing." He woke up his wife and the newlyweds cautiously ventured out together, remarking on "the intense cold." They looked "all over the deck" and walked up and down a couple of times before bumping into Steward Crawford, who chuckled at their obvious apprehension. "You go back downstairs," Crawford told them. "There is nothing to be afraid of. We have only struck a little piece of ice and passed it."

Farther aft, the men relaxing in the second-class smoke room began debating how large the berg had been. "Well," said a motor engineer, "I am accustomed to estimating distances and I put it at between eighty and ninety feet." The mood suddenly became jovial. Holding up his whiskey glass, one man said to his companion, "Just run along the deck and see if any ice has come aboard. I would like some for this."

Far aft on the poop, Quartermaster George Rowe was on duty on the afterbridge: "I felt a slight jar and I looked at my watch. It was a fine night, and it was then twenty minutes to twelve. I looked toward the

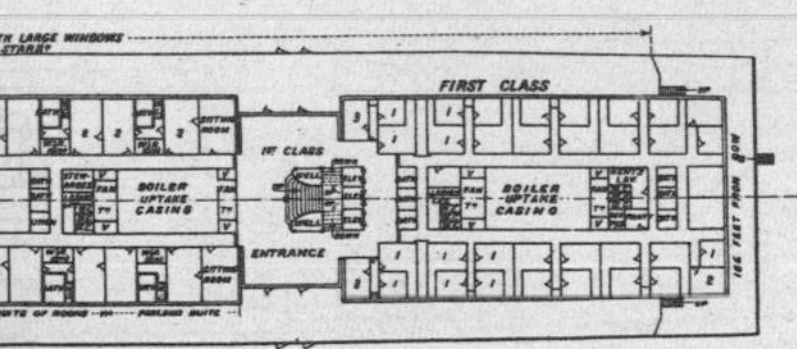

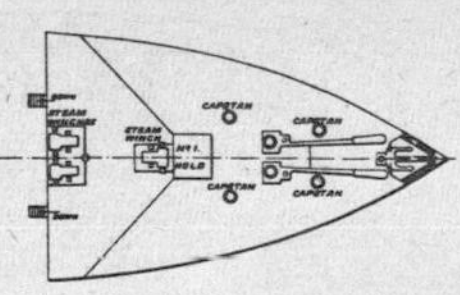

C DECK

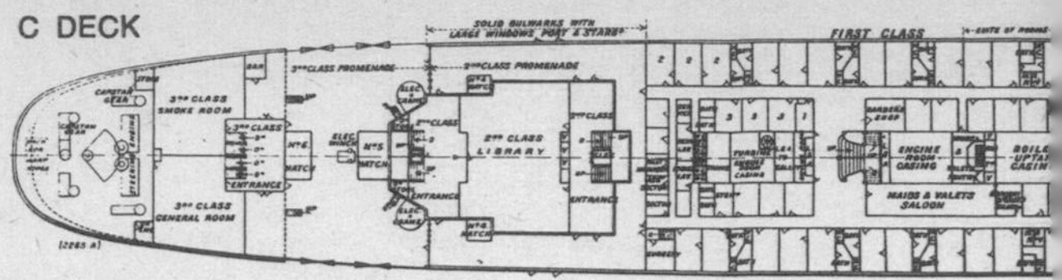

starboard side of the ship and saw a mass of ice. . . . It was very close to the ship, almost touching it."

Another level lower (C Deck), Seamen Osman, Buley, Brice, and Evans were in the forward mess hall on the port side. Sunday evening, there being nothing much to do, the men had been "smokin' and yarnin'." Some were quietly reading. Suddenly, they heard Fleet's three bells in the crow's nest directly above. In the next moment, Edward Buley felt "a slight jar. It seemed as though something was rubbing alongside of her at the time." Brice thought it "was like a heavy vibration." Frank Osman immediately went out into "the forewell deck, just against the seamen's mess room. Looking in the forewell square, I saw ice was there."

A few moments earlier, first-class passengers Mr. and Mrs. Walter Douglas had been strolling past the grand staircase, remarking to each other "that the boat was going faster than she ever had. The vibration as one passed the stairway in the center was very noticeable." Once in their stateroom, C-86, "the

D DECK

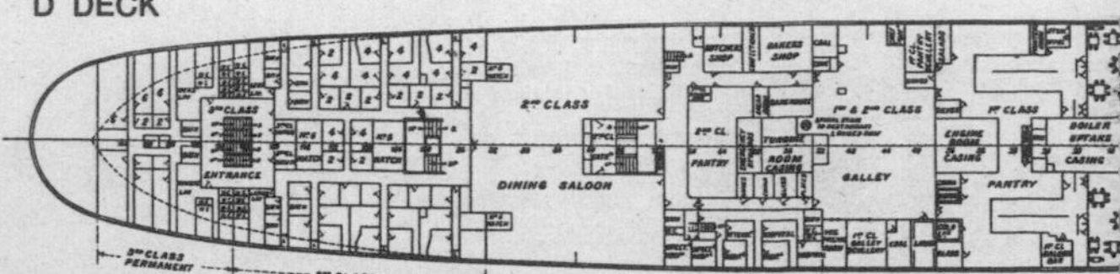

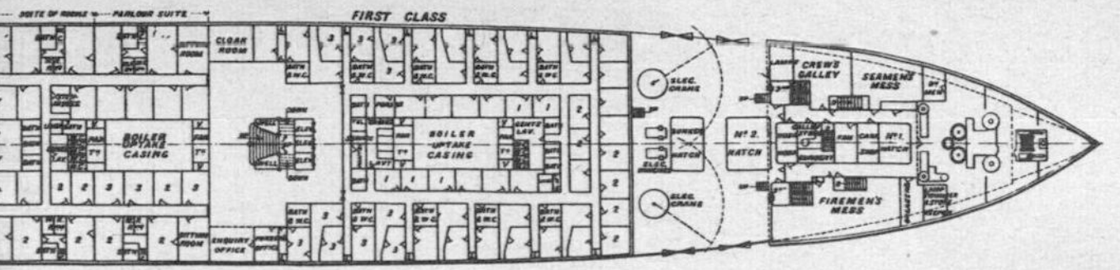

shock of the collision was not great" to them. Nor was it of much importance to Mrs. J. Stuart White: "It was just as though we went over about a thousand marbles. There was nothing terrifying about it at all."

Further aft, in C-116, C. E. Stengel was moaning in his sleep: "My wife called me and says, 'Wake up, you're dreaming,' and I was dreaming, and as I woke up I heard a slight crash. I paid no attention to it until I heard the engines stop. When the engines stopped I said, 'There is something serious; there is something wrong. We had better go up on deck.'"

The sailors who had accompanied Frank Osman out on the forewell square soon returned to the seamen's mess. One of them came back with a large chunk of ice in his hands and exclaimed to Frank Evans, "'Look what I found on the forewell deck!' and he chucked it down on the deck."

Another level down, D Deck was largely deserted. Near the forepeak, the firemen had awakened just minutes earlier to go on their watch at midnight. Fireman John Thompson "felt the crash with all its

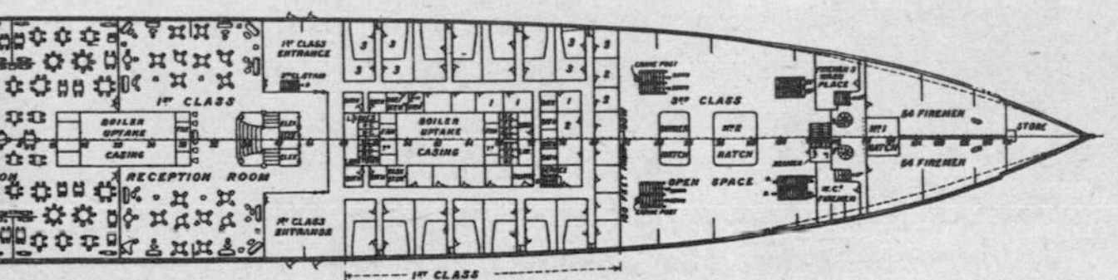

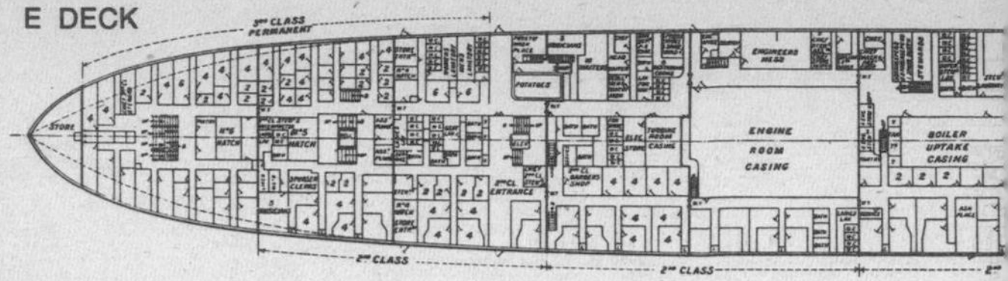

force up there in the eyes of the ship, and my mates and I were all thrown sprawling from our bunks. It was a harsh, grinding sound. . . . I ran on the deck and found the forward well deck covered with masses of ice torn from the berg. We went below to grab some clothes. Our leading fireman, William Small, rushed in and shouts, 'All hands below!' But we had no chance to go down the tunnels to the fireroom, for the water was rising and plainly to be seen. So we had to go up on the main deck. Next, the leading fireman rushed up there and orders us back to get life belts and go on the boat deck. We put out again for the forecastle, got our life belts on, and then up to the boat deck. The chief officer wanted to know 'what in the hell' we were doing up there and sent us down."

Another level down, E Deck began bustling with activity. Near the forepeak, Lamp Trimmer Samuel S. Hemming "went out and put my head through the porthole to see what we hit. I made the remark to the storekeeper, 'It must have been ice. . . .' I went up under the forecastle head to see where the hissing noise came from. . . . I opened the forepeak storeroom. Me and the storekeeper went down as far as the top of the tank and found everything dry. I came up to ascertain where the hissing noise was still coming from. I found it was the air escaping out of the exhaust of the tank. At that time, the chief officer, Mr. Wilde, puts his head around the hawse pipe and says,

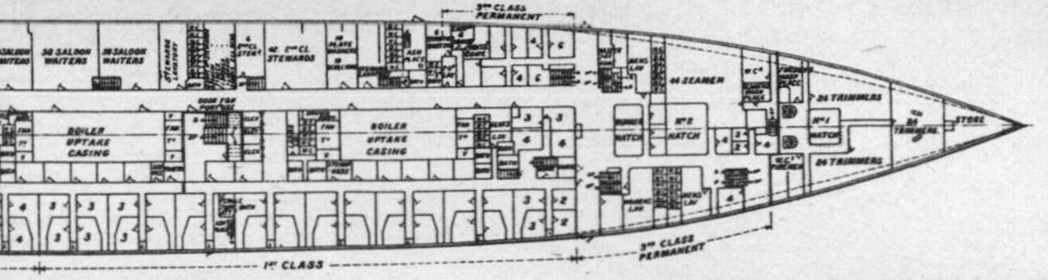

'What is that, Hemming?' I said, 'The air is escaping from the forepeak tank, but the storeroom is quite dry. . . .' We went back in our bunks a few minutes. Then the joiner came in and he said, 'If I were you, I would turn out, you fellows. She is making water one-two-three, and the racket court is getting filled up.' Just as he went, the boatswain came, and he says, 'Turn out, you fellows . . . you haven't half an hour to live. That is from Mr. Andrews. Keep it to yourselves, and let no one know.' "

Aft of the trimmers, Seaman Frederick Clench had been aroused "by the crunching and jarring, as if it was hitting up against something. . . . Of course I put on my trousers and I went on deck on the starboard side of the well deck and I saw a lot of ice" on "the well deck. . . . With that, I went in the alleyway again under the forecastle head to come down and put on my shoes. Someone said to me, 'Did you hear the rush of water?' I said, 'No.' They said, 'Look down under the [number 1] hatchway.' I looked down under the hatchway, and I saw the tarpaulin belly out as if there was a lot of wind under it, and I heard the rush of water coming through."

In the stewards' quarters amidships, Frederick D. Ray awoke to "a kind of movement that went backward and forward—I thought something had gone wrong in the engine room." Another steward, William Ward, got out of bed and "went to the port and opened it. It was very bitterly cold. I looked out and

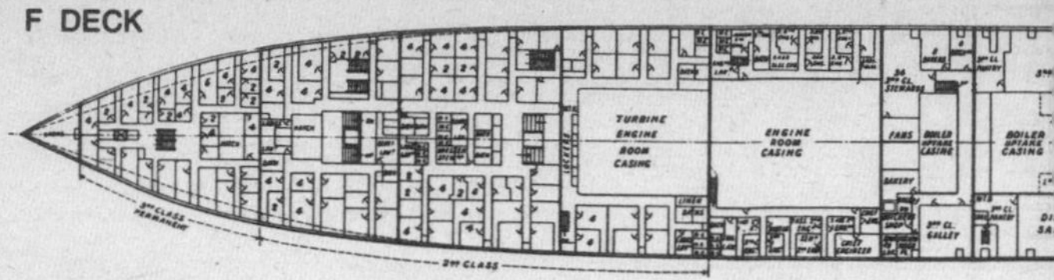

saw nothing. It was very dark. I got back into my bunk again. Presently two or three people came along there where we were all situated and said she had struck an iceberg, and some of them went and brought pieces of ice along in their hands. I thought at first it was the propeller gone, the way she went. I lay there for about twenty minutes, and in the meantime, the steerage passengers were coming from forward aft, carrying life belts with them. Some of them got their grips and packages and had them with them, and some were wet. Still I did not think it was anything serious."

In first-class stateroom E-8, Mr. Norman C. Chambers thought he'd heard "jangling chains whipping along the sides of the ship. This passed so quickly that I assumed something had gone wrong with the engines on the starboard side. . . . At the request of my wife I prepared to investigate what had happened. . . . I looked at the starboard end of our passageway, where there was the companionway leading to the quarters of the mail clerks and farther on to the mail room and, I believe, the mail-sorting room. And at the top of these stairs I found a couple of mail clerks, wet to their knees, who had just come up from below, bringing their registered mailbags. As the door in the bulkhead in the next deck was open, I was able to look directly into the trunk room, which was then filled with water, and within eighteen inches or two feet of the deck above. We were standing there joking

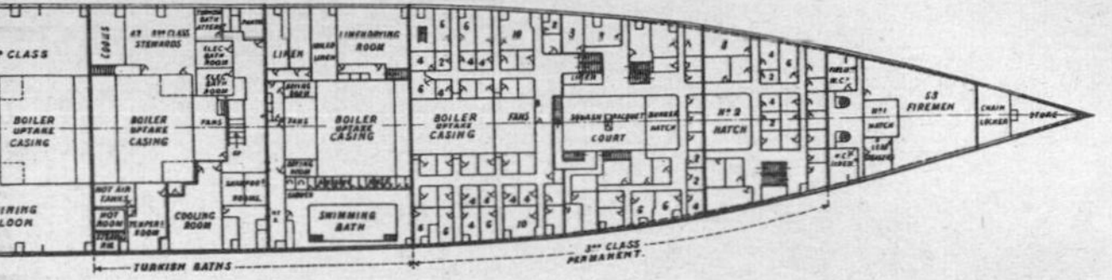

about our baggage being completely soaked and about the correspondence which was seen floating about on top of the water."

Another level down, far aft on F Deck, Mrs. Allen O. Becker and her three children had been awakened "by a dead silence. The engines had stopped. We heard people running through the halls and pounding above our cabin." Mrs. Becker became alarmed so she got out of bed to inquire of a steward the reason for stopping. "Nothing is the matter," he told her, "we will be going on in a few minutes." Mrs. Becker went "back to bed, but the longer she lay there the more alarmed she became. She decided to get up and inquire again." In the corridor she met the cabin steward and asked him what the trouble was. "Put your life belts on immediately and go up to the boat deck," he told her. "Do we have time to dress?" she asked. "No, madam," he replied, "you have time for nothing."

Shortly thereafter, Steward John Hardy came down onto F with twelve other men: "I went among the people and told those people to go on deck with their life belts on, and we assisted the ladies with the belts—those that hadn't their husbands with them—and we assisted in getting the children out of bed. I also aroused the stewardesses to assist them." When they finished with that task, Hardy and the others "commenced to close the watertight doors on F Deck."

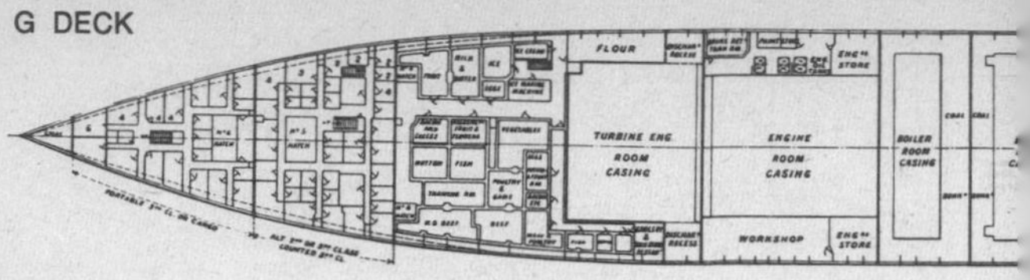

On G Deck, the lowest passenger deck, single male steerage passengers were accommodated forward, the women aft. Immediately upon impact in the forepart of the ship, steerage passenger Olaus Abelseth awoke startled. "What is that?" his roommate asked. "I don't know," Abelseth replied, "but we had better get up."

Close by, emigrant Daniel Buckley had slept a few minutes longer. When he finally awoke he "jumped out on the floor, and the first thing I knew my feet were getting wet. The water was just coming in slightly. I told the other fellows to get up, that there was something wrong and that the water was coming in. They only laughed at me. One of them says, 'Get back into bed. You're not in Ireland now.' I got on my clothes as quick as I could, and the three other fellows got out. The room was very small, so I got out to give them room to dress themselves. Two sailors came along and they were shouting, 'All up on deck, unless you want to get drowned!' "

August Wennerstrom and his companions from Sweden got up and went straight to the third-class

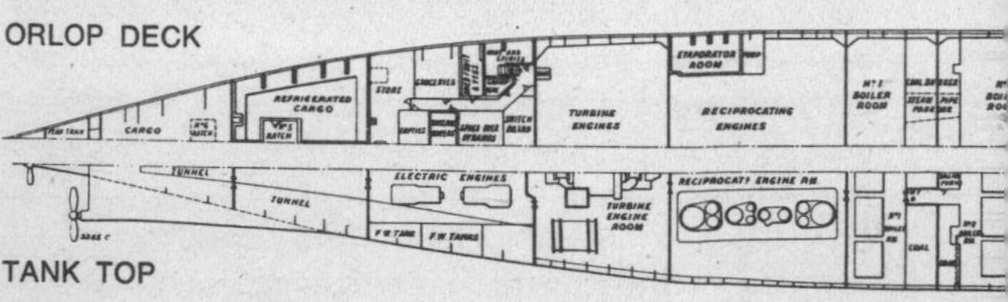

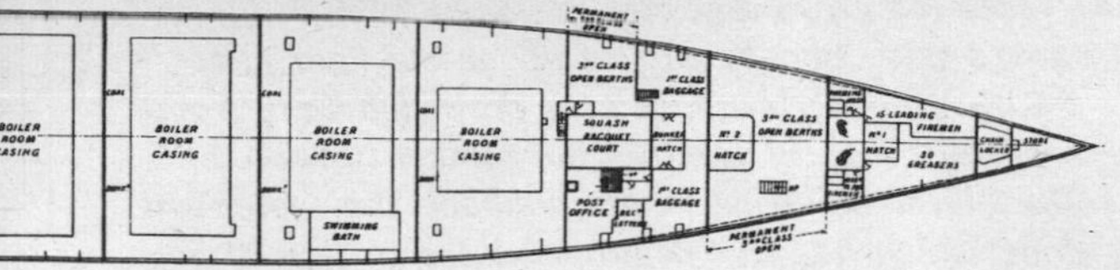

smoking room under the poop: "We tried to get something to drink, but the bar was closed. Nothing else to do, we got someone to play the piano and started to dance. During this, about fifty Italian emigrants came in, dressed in life preservers and carrying their baggage in bundles on their backs. They acted like they were crazy—jumping and calling on their 'Madonna.' We made a circle about them and started a ring dance all around them."

Two levels lower, through the predominantly open Orlop Deck—which surrounded the colossal reciprocating engines—and down to the tank top at the very bottom of the ship, Fireman Frederick Barrett had been hard at work stoking the furnaces in Number 6 boiler room, the fourth compartment abaft the forepeak. He had just paused to talk to the second engineer when Murdoch pulled the telegraph signal to the engine room. At once "the bell rang. The red light showed. We sang out, 'Shut the doors!' [meaning the ash doors to the furnaces] and there was a crash just as we sung out."

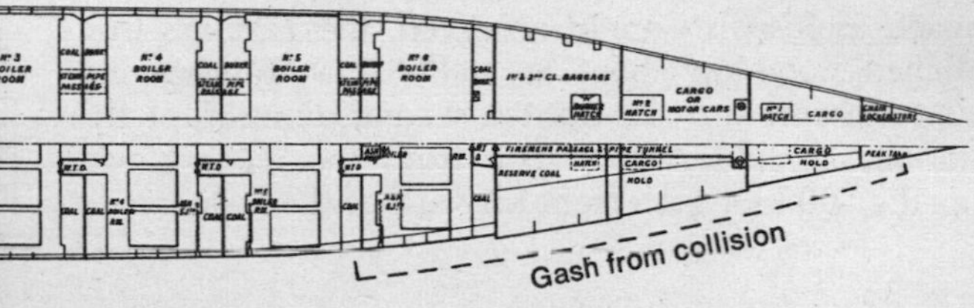

Foaming green seawater exploded through the Titanic*'s side "about two feet above the floor plates," shearing the starboard wall the entire length of Number 6 and slightly into the coal bunker in Number 5. The alarm bell was jangling above the watertight door, which had just begun to descend. Barrett and the engineer managed to leap through the doorway and into Number 5 boiler room as the door clanked shut.*

A few minutes later, Barrett climbed the escape ladder and looked down into Number 6 "and there was eight feet of water in there. I went to Number 5 fireroom when the lights went out. I was sent to find lamps, as the lights were out, and when we got the lamps we looked at the boilers and there was no water in them. I ran to the engineer, and he told me to get some firemen down to draw the fires. I got fifteen men down below."

Although the coal bunker kept the water from entering Number 5 for a while, the pressure ultimately proved too great. All at once Barrett "saw a wave of green foam come tearing through the boilers" in Number 5 and he "jumped for the escape ladder."

For the subcommittee's benefit, the U.S. Hydrographic Office later determined the blow with which the huge liner had struck the relatively small iceberg at approximately 1,173,200 foot tons, "or energy enough to lift fourteen monuments the size of the Washington Monument in one second of time." Under this kind of impact, as Joseph Conrad observed, the *Titanic*'s iron hull had stood up about as well "as a Huntley and Palmer biscuit tin." In the ten-second duration of the collision, an underwater spar from the iceberg had ripped a 300-foot gash from forward of the foremast to the Number 5 boiler room. Nothing could have saved her.

The committee was interested in what had happened on the bridge immediately after the collision, and those moments were recalled by Quartermasters Hichens and Olliver.

Hichens told how the captain had come rushing out of his room, asking: " 'What is that?' Mr. Murdoch said, 'An iceberg.' Captain Smith [then said] to Mr. Murdoch, 'Close the emergency doors.' Mr. Murdoch replied, 'The doors are already closed.' The captain sent then for the carpenter to sound the ship. He also came back to the wheelhouse and looked at the commutator in front of the compass, which is a little instrument like a clock to tell you how the ship is listing. The ship had a list of five degrees to the starboard."

According to Alfred Olliver, the *Titanic* had been ordered half speed ahead.

"Who gave that order?" asked Senator Burton.

"The captain telegraphed half speed ahead," Olliver replied.

"Did she have much way on?"

"When?"

"When he put the engines half speed ahead."

"No, sir," replied Olliver, "I reckon the ship was almost stopped."

"How long did he go ahead half speed?"

"Not very long, sir," Olliver replied. "I could not say the number of minutes, because I had messages in the meantime."

Burton could not understand why the captain had run his mortally injured ship half speed ahead for a few minutes following the collision, and the reason was never satisfactorily explained. Nor are there incontrovertible theories for the captain's order at the present time.

Having sat for two grueling days, the subcommittee met again Tuesday night for a private executive session. There were a number of issues for discussion. Senators Burton and Perkins, the most nautically informed members of the committee, thought the actions of First Officer Murdoch highly reprehensible. For example, why had Murdoch ordered the rudder "hard astarboard" and then—according to Alfred Olliver—changed it to "hard aport"? The question was eventually put to Joseph Boxhall, who said that Murdoch had intended "to port around" the iceberg. Asked to explain this more fully, Boxhall answered by way of a demonstration that couldn't easily be entered in the record. Years later, however, Charles Lightoller explained the maneuver in a BBC broadcast:

> Murdoch evidently saw the mass of ice practically at the same time as the lookout men [this is highly debatable] and shouted, "Hard astarboard, full speed astern!" His idea was to swing her bow clear and then put the helm hard over the other way and so swing her stern clear.

Even so, as long as Murdoch was trying to veer out of the iceberg's way, why had he "jammed on the brakes," so to speak, by throwing the engines full speed astern? The 1910 edition of *Knight's Modern Seamanship* clearly contraindicates such action:

> The first impulse of many officers in such a situation is to turn away from the danger, and at the same time to reverse the engines with full power. This course is much more likely to cause collisions than to prevent them. It may be right for [the ship] to turn away, if the emercency is such as to call for any actions on her part; but if she does this, so far from re-

> versing the engines, she sould, if possible, increase her speed as her whole effort must be directed to getting [out of the way of the obstacle] as quickly as possible. . . . *To turn away and slow is the surest possible way of bringing about collision.* [Italics in original.]

It should be added that the structural features of the *Titanic* compounded the effect of Murdoch's mistake. The *Titanic* had two four-cylinder reciprocating engines that ran the two wing propellers. Two cylinders from each of these exhausted into a low-pressure turbine engine that ran the center propeller, positioned directly in front of the rudder. The turbine engine was not reversible. When Murdoch had thrown the engines full speed astern, therefore, the center propeller had shut off, depriving the rudder of the slipstream from this propeller and seriously reducing its effectiveness. Hence, the *Titanic*'s deadly slow swing to port after the order "hard astarboard."

So long as Murdoch wished to veer out of the iceberg's way—certainly a natural desire—his best course of action would have been to reverse the port screw full astern, keep the starboard screw full ahead, and put the helm hard astarboard. (In the subsequent British inquiry, Harland and Wolff's chief engineer showed the court "turning curves" of the *Titanic,* including the case with one engine full ahead, the other reversed, and the rudder hard over. The "curves" were not published in the transcript of the British hearings.) Instead, Murdoch had maneuvered, according to *Knight's,* in a manner "more likely to cause collisions than to prevent them."

Senator Smith couldn't forget Ismay's New York testimony that had the ship rammed the berg head on, it would not have foundered; and this contention was subsequently verified by marine engineers. Although Joseph Conrad would vigorously deprecate such a proposed course of action, there is evidence that—in the *Titanic*'s case—this course would have been not only justifiable but obligatory. Lookout Frederick Fleet had testified to the effect that the iceberg had been seen very late. The lookouts had been given no binoculars. Also, the lack of definition between horizon and sky and the absence of a swell prevented the iceberg from being seen until it was very close at hand. Most authorities agreed that the ship was practically upon the berg when Murdoch took evasive action; *for such dire situations,* the recommendations of *Knight's Modern Seamanship* (1910) are again explicit:

> . . . so far as other considerations of law and seamanship permit, any vessel in danger of collision . . . should present her stem to the danger rather than her broadside.

Why did Murdoch, an otherwise comptent officer, choose the worst course possible for the *Titanic* under the circumstances? The evidence suggests that at the height of the emergency he went "against the book" and acted on instinct—his "first impulse," as *Knight's* calls it. It should be added in Murdoch's defense that the sea trials for *Olympic* and *Titanic* were decidedly deficient. These two ships represented significant increases in tonnage, and far more time ought to have been taken during their sea trials to test out their maneuverability than what, in fact, was spent. The testimony taken thus far on the *Titanic*'s sea trials suggested she had been whizzed through them. The fifth officer would eventually testify that the *Titanic*'s trial maneuvers had consisted of little more than a half hour of "twists and turns." Senator Smith would ask if any of these maneuvers had been conducted at full speed, such as the *Titanic* had nearly reached at the time of her fatal collision.

"No," replied the fifth officer, "she wasn't really put to it. She hasn't been put to it yet."

"And never will be," William Alden observed dryly.

There were other matters for the committee's consideration Tuesday night. The previous evening, Ismay had renewed his request to be released so that he could return to England. Ismay had promised to send hordes of experts over from Britain—marine architects, business personnel from White Star, engineers from Harland and Wolff—all of whom would be much more useful witnesses than himself. Generous as it was, Ismay's offer had been refused. Part Two of the Harter Act necessitated Ismay's availability after *all* evidence on negligence had been obtained, and Smith had denied permission for the third time. Now Ismay was making a more innocuous request; he wished merely to go back to New York for a few days, remaining, of course, at the committee's beck and call. Smith could not risk Ismay's skipping out from New York, and permission was denied.

The next order of business came from Knute Nelson, chairman of the Committee on Commerce. Nelson informed the members of the inquiry that the long-awaited, monumental bill on rivers and harbors had been sent over from the House and required the Commerce Committee's full and urgent attention. Could the *Titanic* investigation be postponed for the sake of this important bill? The subcommittee decided that it could not. The members, however, arranged a schedule whereby they would sit in shifts, alternating between the inquiry and the rivers and harbors sessions. William

Alden decided to stay with the inquiry exclusively, explaining to reporters, "We are being sought by Chairman Nelson of the Commerce Committee to suspend the investigation for a portion of tomorrow in order to meet with that committee to consider important portions of the rivers and harbors measure. We have decided not to interrupt these sessions for that or any other purpose."

In the White House lights were burning late. The President was in conference with his campaign managers, discussing the Colonel. Undaunted by the way in which the *Titanic* inquiry had upstaged him, Theodore Roosevelt had instead capitalized on the public outcry against corporate atrocities which the disaster had brought to the fore. With his customary sagacity, TR informed the people that Taft was behind everything: He was a "tool of the corporations" and in full sympathy with the precious whim of plutocrats. "I believe," said TR, "he has yielded to the bosses and to the great privileged interests."

For nearly a week the President's friends and advisers had begged him to fight back. Roosevelt's opportunism in the face of this appalling catastrophe and his ridiculous charges should be soundly trounced. But the President was still brooding. He had just received a heartbreaking letter from Mrs. John Thayer, a survivor of the disaster, who told about Archie's last days aboard the *Titanic*. "I was going to teach him a method of control of the nerves through which I had just been with a noted Swiss doctor," wrote Mrs. Thayer, "knowing it would be a very wonderful thing for him if he could get hold of it, for he was very nervous and did not know how he was going to stand the rushing life he was returning to."

With Archie's loss, a direct confrontation with TR

could not be mitigated, and the President gave in to his advisers. To a friend, Taft wrote Tuesday night: "I agree with you that the time has come when it is necessary for me to speak out in my own defense. I shall do so sorrowfully. I dislike to speak with directness about Theodore Roosevelt, but I can no longer refrain from refuting his false accusations." Newspaper editors working on the morning edition speculated that during the forthcoming primary battle in Massachusetts, the President would very likely "give the hat in the ring a swift kick."

12

Calumny

Leaving the Senate Office Building late Tuesday evening, Senator Smith was corralled by reporters who wanted his reactions to a number of developments in England. First of all, the Senate's *Titanic* inquiry had prompted a forthcoming British investigation. The decision for an independent British investigation had come about largely as a result of arguments advanced in the House of Commons by Will Crooks, a labor leader. Speaking of the Senate subcommittee, Crooks had said: "They did not wait to find out whether the law gave them power to subpoena and question people who could throw light on the matter. They at once sent a commission out to intercept even the owners of the vessel, together with any others wanted as witnesses. We have heard that they had no authority under the law to do so, but they did it, and England has applauded them for doing it."

But there seemed to be some question as to how much England was applauding. The reporters surrounding the senator also informed him that Britain's morning newspapers had been full of editorials condemning the American inquiry. The *London Daily Express* had called it "a parody of a judicial inquiry." The *London Daily News* had written, "We have no intention of prejudging the case or imitating the hasty, and often savage, verdicts pronounced in the United States." The *London Times* had remained sober but observed with some concern that Smith was conducting as much a preliminary hearing for "criminal prosecution" as he was an investigation. Unfortunately (though naturally enough) the *Times* had assumed that Britain—not the New Jersey-based IMM—was the defendant. The *New York World* would try to clarify the matter: "It is a Morgan, not a British shipping company, that is under investigation, and the relation of J. Bruce Ismay and other British subjects to the inquiry is only incidental." The explanation, however, would have little effect in abating Britain's mounting indignation.

Undoubtedly the most interesting theme in the British outcries was the personal condemnation of William Alden Smith. As America had latched onto Ismay as a scapegoat, Britain had now begun to reciprocate by attacking the senator from Michigan. The *Daily Express* expressed it coyly: "There is no need to suppose because Senator Smith is an asinine American that the inquiry is purposeless." The *London Standard* observed that "the Michigan senator is less qualified as an investigator than the average individual to be picked up in the average American streetcar." Whereas Ismay had been cast as the villain of the piece, Smith had now become the comic relief.

In the American newspapers of Tuesday evening, a few editors had thought it necessary to defend the senator. *The New York Times* claimed that the subcommittee was "digging into the work with the greatest care." The *Chicago Record-Herald* noted: "The American investigation was ordered in response to a natural public demand; it is doing good." Responding directly to the *London Daily News*, the *Chicago Evening Post* agreed that "America may make . . . 'hasty and often cruel verdicts,' but in the *Titanic* case, America is becoming more glad that the investigating committee of U.S. senators had the energy and vision to board the *Carpathia* before she docked. Else who knows how little of the truth about the wreck we would ever have known?"

Although William Alden assured the reporters that the British editorials "don't worry me at all," there would be a notable exception. Given the cost of sending information by Atlantic cable at ten cents per word, British news correspondents had wired the American testimony over in an abbreviated, rephrased, and often inaccurate form. Usually the interrogator was not identified, although it was consistently assumed by Britons to be Senator Smith. Moreover, lacking essential background information, British readers had found a number of the senator's questions peculiar. The *Daily Mail*, after examining one question in particular, had concluded that Smith must be an imbecile. It had editorialized that, in the forthcoming British investigation, "we shall not have a member of the court talking about watertight compartments as if they were bankers' safes, in which people could lock themselves to keep the water from their feet while they suffocate, as has been done by the most bitter and persistent of Mr. Ismay's assailants."

The quip had been prompted by the question Smith had put to Lightoller in New York, specifically to end the hysterical optimism of the friends and relations of "missing" passengers. That this same delusion was nationwide was confirmed by Smith when he examined his mail upon returning to Washington. Eventually, the "watertight-compartment gaffe" would become the most popular harangue of Smith's British critics. Smith himself would make light of the issue, even managing a jab back at England's editors:

> Of course, I have known for many years that a watertight compartment is not intended as an asylum for passengers, because this same captain, who went down with the *Titanic*, showed me over his ship on one of my voyages and I am quite familiar with the uses of the watertight compartment. But that these sorrowing people might receive some official reply as to whether that would be possible or not, I took chances of arousing the humor of a people—not generally accustomed to much humor—by asking that question. I assume all responsibility for it.

But he would neither forgive nor forget it. Those who were close to the senator say he remained bitter about it the rest of his life. It wasn't that Smith minded being made out a dolt. What hurt him was that he had been made a dolt for motives that were entirely humanitarian. The British press wounded Smith in the Achilles' heel of many Midwesterners—their altruism.

The morning of Wednesday, April 24, was full of surprises. Taft had just made public correspondence that showed that in 1907 Roosevelt had quietly suppressed a planned "busting" of International Harvester under the Sherman Act. Among the documents Taft permitted his campaign manager to give the press was a communiqué from Herbert Knox Smith, TR's commissioner of corporations. Knox Smith had advised Teddy against suing International Harvester, since it didn't behoove him "to throw away now the great influence of the so-called Morgan interests, which up to this time have supported the advanced policy of the administration." George W. Perkins, director of Harvester, was on the board of directors of IMM as well. He was also financing Teddy's present campaign. Soon the fur would fly.

In Southampton, the *Olympic* was in dock for sailing day, and her crew was causing worldwide interest by refusing to ship out until enough lifeboats were provided to serve everyone aboard. Bruce Ismay had already directed the IMM to do so, but on such short notice the company had been able to secure only forty collapsible boats, which the *Olympic*'s crewmen promptly dubbed "rotten and unseaworthy." In the afternoon, the entire staff of firemen, greasers, and trimmers shouldered their kits and walked back to town singing, "We're All Going the Same Way Home." Britain was in a quandary over how to handle this modern-day mutiny.

In spite of the British editorials of the previous morning, some of Britain's seafaring lower classes were expressing approval of the American inquiry. The representative of the National Sailors' and Firemen's Union said that in America "the truth is being brought out in a way that would be impossible in a court of inquiry" in England, which would be conducted "with such formality and be so dominated by lawyers that essential evidence would be obstructed at every turn." George Barnes, MP and former secretary of the Amalgamated Society of Engineers, remarked, "It may be humiliating to some to have an [American] inquiry into the loss of a British ship, but the general feeling, I think, is satisfaction. The average person realizes that Americans get to work very quickly, and the average person, I think, is rather glad it is so."

But apparently "the average person" wasn't writing the editorials in Great Britain. Wednesday's morning editions contained a renewed onslaught against Senator Smith. The *London Globe* called him "a gentleman from the wilds of Michigan, who possibly is compelled by the exigencies of electioneering to be as insolent as possible to Englishmen." The *Daily Express* dubbed the senator "a backwoodsman from Michigan" who was obviously enjoying "the limelight." (Michiganders were more amused than annoyed at British misconceptions of their state as "an unknown land populated by kangaroos and by cowboys with an intimate acquaintance of prairie schooners as the only kind of boat.")

A bitter personal attack on Smith by the *London Daily Mail* was particularly damaging, since it assumed the guise of an objective biographical sketch. The *Mail* contended that Smith "has been humorously caricatured as the wildest gesticulator in Congress. No matter what the subject under debate, whether he knows anything or not, Senator Smith is sure to be found on the list of speakers." The *Mail*'s Washington correspondent seemed keenly aware of Smith's role in thwarting Great Britain's past treaties and recalled "an occasion when Senator Smith, three years ago, intervened in a debate on American and Canadian waterways and called down upon himself the stinging rebuke from Senator Lodge that he knew nothing about the subject under discussion." Not only was this a garbled version of the event, but the article neglected to mention Smith's celebrated rejoinder to Lodge's "stinging rebuke." (When this article was brought to Smith's attention, he was convinced that the *Mail*'s correspondent had been talking to the senator from Massachusetts.)

The House of Commons was now beginning to react with the ire of the British press. Captain Waring, MP, asked the secretary of state for foreign affairs whether he was aware that, at the U.S. inquiry, a senator had asked a witness "if watertight compartments were intended for the reception of passengers in a time of danger, and that witnesses had been brought before the inquiry in a poor condition of health" (presumably a reference to Harold Bride). The foreign secretary replied that it was "undesirable by questions and answers in this House" to make reference to the American inquiry "on the basis of imperfect and possibly inaccurate reports."

Undoubtedly the most devastating criticism of Smith came in the form of burlesque. Sensing the tide of the moment, a London music hall got together an act featuring a low comedian, purportedly made up as the senator complete with umbrella, who went on stage and sang the following to the tune of "Lalago Potts":

> I'm Senator Smith of the U.S.A.,
> Senator Smith, that's me!
> A big bug in the enquiry way,
> Senator Smith, that's me!
> You're fixed right up if you infer
> I'm a cuss of a cast-iron character.
> When I says that a thing has got ter be,
> That thing's as good as done, d'yer see?
> I'm going to ask questions and find out some
> If I sit right here till kingdom come—
> That's me!
> Senator Smith of the U.S.A.

Wednesday editions in the United States quickly rallied to the senator's defense. The *Philadelphia Press* stated that "Senator Smith's inquiries have brought out and placed on permanent record the circumstances and conditions under which the great catastrophe took place. . . . If incidentally the examination disclosed that the chairman of the committee is not an expert in nautical matters and asked some questions that caused the seamen to smile, what does it matter? The value of this investigation is not in the questions, but in the answers."

The *New York Evening Mail* informed "the mariners of England" that "this is a landlubbers' inquiry and *ought* to be. The great public on shore asks the masters of the sea this question: 'How do you skippers and seamen manage to *do* this sort of thing?' It is the shore that wants to know; it is the sea that must answer. . . . Up to this point, Senator Smith has proved a very good interrogator, John Bull and all his sea dogs to the contrary notwithstanding."

The *New York Irish World and American Industrial Liberator* was particularly rankled: "If it had been an American ship that went down with a shipload of British subjects, because of such a desperate series of blunders, what an outcry would have been heard!" The *New York Herald* began lamblike and ended roaring: "Nothing has been more sympathetic, more gentle in its highest sense than the conduct of the inquiry by the Senate committee, and yet self-complacent moguls in England call this impertinent. . . . This country intends to find out why so many American lives were wasted by the incompetency of British seamen, and why women and children were sent to their deaths while so many in a British crew have been saved."

But the best defense of Smith came from an Englishman. Alfred Stead had recently succeeded to the editorship of the English *Review of Reviews* upon the death of his father, the illustrious William Stead, who had gone down on the *Titanic*. The son of the celebrated journalist was distressed over the criticism voiced in his country. To a friend at the *Chicago Daily News*, Stead Jr. wrote: "The growling of Parliament and the irascible comments of the newspapers relative to the Washington inquiry into the loss of the *Titanic* do not reflect the sentiment of the British public. . . . The newspapers tell us that Senator Smith, chairman of the Senate committee, is a 'backwoodsman,' ignorant of all nautical affairs. I do not care if he is a red Indian. His ignorance, if it exists, is excusable ignorance, whereas the ignorance of officers and seamen of their duties is criminal negligence."

In Washington, D.C., William Alden was unworried by the ongoing snit in England. He *was* concerned, however, with any reaction it might touch off on Capitol Hill. Fortunately, the Michigan Minutemen were on the prowl and gave the chairman a thorough report. Captain Sowerby, the naval attaché of the British embassy, was apparently complaining to everyone that "more naval experts" were needed on the committee. Senator McCumber of North Dakota was calling for "fair play for Ismay," hoping that the inquiry would somehow exonerate the man whom the United States had treated so unfairly. Senator Works of California hoped that the inquiry would finish with the crewmen as quickly as possible. (Smith had every intention of doing this.) Finally, it was heard that Senator Lodge of Massachusetts doubted whether the inquiry should be continued since, in view of the recent British reaction, it may be doing more harm than good. But whatever Lodge believed didn't matter—at least to William Alden it didn't. On the whole, Smith concluded that the minor irritation on Capitol Hill posed no threat at all to the future of the inquiry.

At 10:00 A.M. on Wednesday, J. Bruce Ismay, having been refused permission the previous evening to visit New York, called again on Senator Smith in his office. This time he had his attorney, Charles C. Burlingham, with him. Ismay beseeched the senator to *please* put him on the stand at once so he could conclude his testimony and return to England. Burlingham reiterated Ismay's prior promise to send over every kind of expert from Britain—all of them useless, as far as the Harter Act was concerned. After all, argued the attorney, the committee had been asking the *Titanic*'s crewmen questions that could be so much better answered by marine architects.

Smith was busy with his papers at the time and listened to the entreaties without responding. When the committee assembled in 414 Senate Office Building for the day's hearing, reporters at once noticed that "the air was surcharged with trouble." After a perfunctory recall of Frederick Fleet, Smith rose, saying, "I desire to make an announcement." The senator looked pointedly at the newspaper reporters, who quickly grasped that the announcement was intended for the American public.

"It is, of course," Smith began, "very apparent that the surviving officers of the *Titanic* are not shipbuilders having had to do with the construction of that vessel, and the committee have assumed that if these witnesses should tell what they themselves know of the circumstances surrounding the ship up to the time of the collision, and what transpired thereafter, this information would be about all that we could obtain from these witnesses.

"One word as to the plan: It has been our plan from the beginning to first obtain the testimony of citizens or subjects of Great Britain who are temporarily in this country, and this course will be pursued until the committee conclude that they have obtained all information accessible and useful to a proper understanding of this disaster.

"Now, one word about the difficulties: To the credit of most of the officers and crew, we have experienced no very troublesome difficulties in securing such witnesses as we felt were necessary. But from the beginning until now there has been a voluntary, gratuitous, meddlesome attempt upon the part of certain persons to influence the course of the committee and to shape its procedures."

Smith carefully avoided looking directly at Ismay, but out of the corner of his eye he could see that the president of IMM was ashen with tension.

Striking the desk with his fist, Smith blared, "The committee *will not tolerate* any further attempt on the part of anyone to shape its course. We shall proceed *in our own way,* completing the official record. And the judgment of our efforts may very appropriately be withheld until those who are disposed to question its wisdom have the actual official reports!"

The reporters were electrified as they took all this down. After the hearing they badgered the senator to know *who* was causing the trouble, but Smith remained resolutely silent. Everyone began speculating—particularly the British correspondents. The *London Times*'s man thought the announcement was a response to Parliament. The *Daily Mail* reporter figured the speech was against Smith's fellow committee members who were probably disgusted with their chairman. Other British papers opined that the American people themselves had caused the trouble, since Smith was embarrassing the American nation with his harebrained inquiry.

Nothing was further from the truth. The American people were solidly behind the inquiry and the man who had brought it into being. Typical was the *Chicago Evening Post*'s response: "Senator Smith will be but fulfilling the fair demand of his countrymen at large if he sweeps away the obstacles of which he speaks and sees to it that his committee gets the last possible particle of fact about the greatest of all sea tragedies."

Although Smith managed to keep the reason for his outburst out of the national papers, it was impossible for him to shun the entreaties of his old friend J. Wells Harvey, Washington correspondent of the *Grand Rapids Evening Press.* (The Michigan Minutemen were working out of Harvey's office.) In the *Press* on Wednesday evening, Harvey discreetly summarized what Smith told him in utmost confidence; and from it can be deduced Smith's interpretation of Ismay and his counsel's motives:

> The Senator's viewpoint is that the White Star Line has much at stake in this Inquiry and that its influence is being felt in every possible way. The question is not one of responsibility merely, but of liability for damages in civil suits. Should it be developed that reasonable diligence was not exercised in sailing the *Titanic,* the families of survivors have a good chance to collect damages.

Ismay had shuddered throughout the senator's impromptu speech. The White Star manager fancied that a mere mention of his name in the course of Smith's announcement would be sufficient to move someone to string up Ismay from a tree in some unspeakable backwater American town. The very next day, Ismay sat down in the Willard Hotel and composed an apologetic letter to the senator. He emphasized his "mental and physical strain as a result of the disaster" and his consistent "willingness to give . . . all information in my possession to the best of my ability." He also confessed that he was very concerned about the forthcoming British investigation, and was eager to get back to his family as well. "In view of my experience at the time of the disaster and subsequently," Ismay wrote, "I hope that the committee will feel" that the requests to return to England were "not unreasonable."

William Alden, too, was aware of the possible consequences that could result from identifying Ismay as the culprit (precisely why he had kept it a secret). But in view of the other pressures that Smith was steadily encountering, Ismay's demands had become annoying. Smith simply wanted Ismay to know that he had been pushed to his limits—a message Ismay grasped in no uncertain terms. In response to Ismay's letter, Smith wrote to him:

> Sir: Replying to your letter of this date, just received, permit me to say that I am not unmindful of the fact that you are being detained in this country against your will, and, probably, at no little inconvenience to yourself and family. I can readily see that your absence from England, at a time so momentous in the affairs of your company, would be most embarrassing, but the horror of the *Titanic* catastrophe and its importance to the people of the world call for scrupulous investigation into the causes leading up to the disaster, that future losses of similar character may, if possible, be avoided. . . . As I said to you in New York on Friday evening last, when you asked to be permitted to return home, and again on Saturday night, when you made the same request, I shall not consent to your leaving this country until the fullest inquiry has been made into the circumstances surrounding the accident. . . . I am working night and day to achieve this result, and you should continue to help me instead of annoying me and delaying my work by your personal importunities.
>
> Trusting you will receive this letter in the spirit in which it is written, I am, Very respectfully . . .

Throughout his career, nothing hardened William Alden's resolve like opposition. Adversity seemed only to energize him further. The British criticism and all its ramifications would merely intensify the investigation, prolonging it until every last scrap of evidence had been obtained. Like the *Titanic* that fateful April evening, the Smith committee would—in spite of warnings—continue plunging full speed ahead.

13

Twenty Boats and a Quiet Sea

The star witness of Wednesday's hearing was Harold Godfrey Lowe, the *Titanic*'s fifth officer. Even as a child, Harold Lowe had been a natural sailor. At the age of twelve, when his father's punt had capsized, the boy had swum a half mile to shore in his clothes and boots. When Lowe was fourteen, his father dragged him all over Liverpool, trying to apprentice him to a shipping firm; but Lowe had hated the idea. "I was not going to work for anybody for nothing," he said. "I wanted to be paid for my labor." Lowe's father had been adamant about an apprenticeship and Harold equally obdurate. "I am not going to be apprenticed," he told his father, "and that settles it!"

Consequently, Lowe ran away from home and followed the sea ever after. He spent seven years on schooners, switching to square-rigged sailing ships and finally to steamers when he earned all his certificates. He served five years in the West African Coast service. Once, on a trip homeward from Japan, a terrific gale arose. The captain asked for someone to undertake the dangerous task of mounting the rigging in the eye of the storm. Lowe immediately volunteered, saying, "I may as well die from the yard as from the deck." Following his West African service, Lowe joined the White Star Line.

Lacking formal education, this "boyish-looking" young man was an enthusiastic seaman and a plainspoken individualist. And the evidence argues that, given the *Titanic*'s particular set of circumstances on the evening of April 14, Harold Godfrey Lowe had been the most conscientious officer and the best all-around sailor aboard.

Now at the age of twenty-nine, Lowe sat in the witness chair—slim, dark, and rather good-looking, with dark eyebrows seeming to extend in an unbroken line across the base of his high forehead. His combed-back hair was inclined to curl. His projecting cheekbones and upturned nose gave his face a cocky appearance. His salty language, good looks, and virile mannerisms immediately endeared him to a group of students from a lady's seminary among Wednesday's spectators, and Lowe was not unmindful of their attention. To this cho-

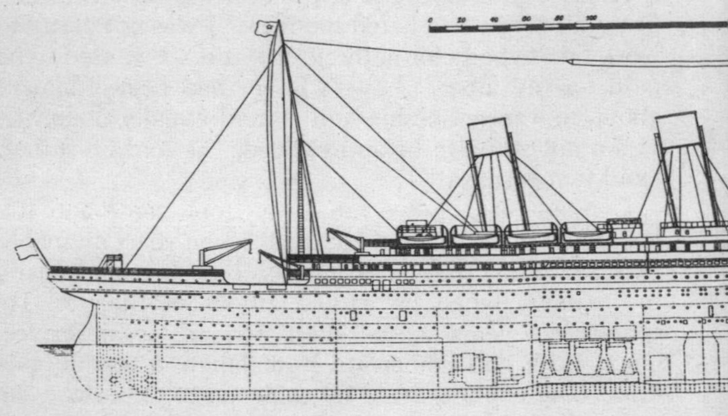

rus of rapturous maidens, it was as if Lowe had hornpiped right off the deck of the H.M.S. *Pinafore.*

Consistently enough, the exchanges between Chairman Smith and Officer Lowe often resembled the dialogue of a comic opera. The senator and the sailor were strangely akin. Their childhoods had encompassed an equal amount of premature autonomy, and both were matched in candor and impetuousness. But one was of the land and the other the sea, and when the two weren't entirely incomprehensible to each other, they were sailing by each other on opposite though parallel courses.

When Smith asked what part Lowe had taken during the *Titanic*'s sea trials, the officer answered in all sincerity, "I could no more tell you now than fly."

Smith had found the question he had put first to Boxhall (about an iceberg's composition) a good screening question for quickly checking the officers' familiarity with the North Atlantic. But when Smith asked Lowe what an iceberg was composed of, the officer replied, "Ice, I suppose, sir." The answer convulsed the crowd.

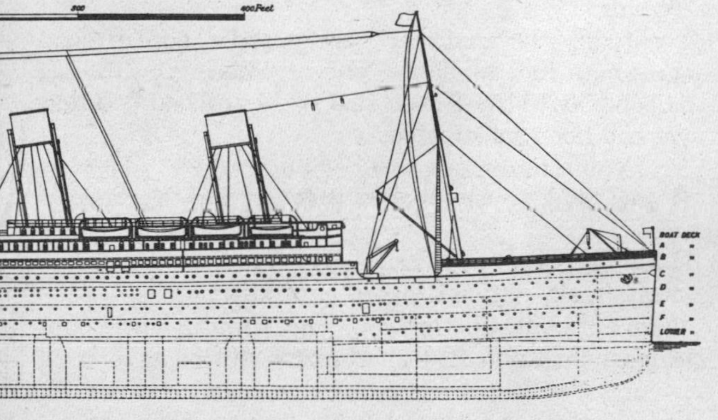

"Did you hear the testimony of your fellow officer Boxhall?" Smith asked.

"No, sir," replied Lowe.

"But you labor under the impression that they are composed entirely of ice?"

"*Absolutely*, sir."

Lowe mentioned that he had preserved the names and "lots of addresses" of the fifty passengers rescued with him in lifeboat Number 14, and Smith asked him to enumerate them. Pulling out a memoranda book, Lowe read three names.

"Go ahead a little faster, if you can," Smith directed.

"That's all," replied the fifth officer.

"Those are the only names you took down?"

"Out of my own particular boat," said Lowe.

"I thought you had a card there that they had signed with their autographs."

"Who?"

"These passengers who were in your own boat, Number Fourteen."

"No, sir," said Lowe, "I am no autograph hunter."

"I understand," said Smith, "but I thought you told me you had a card of that kind."

"No, sir."

Eventually the chairman was passed a note from a congressman in attendance, one of whose constituents had been aboard the *Titanic* that night and claimed that Lowe had been intoxicated.

"Are you a temperate man?" Smith asked.

"I am, sir, I never touched it in my life. I'm an abstainer."

"I am very glad to have you say that."

"I say it, sir, without fear of contradiction."

"I am not contradicting you," said Smith, "and I congratulate you upon it; but so many stories have been circulated. One has just been passed up to me now, from a reputable man, who says it was reported that you were drinking that night."

"*Me*, sir? No, sir! *This*," said Lowe hoisting a glass of water, "is the strongest drink I ever take."

The room tittered with laughter.

One would think the humor arising from the exchanges between the senator and Mr. Lowe incongruous, since the thrust of his testimony concerned the most deadly serious issue of the inquiry—the loading and lowering of the *Titanic*'s lifeboats.

"What time were you awakened?" Smith asked.

"I don't know," Lowe replied. "I was awakened by hearing voices, and I thought it was very strange, and somehow they woke me up and I realized there must be something the matter. So I looked out and I saw a lot of people around, and I jumped up and got dressed and went on deck."

"What did you find when you got up there?"

"I found that all the passengers were wearing belts."

First-class passenger Helen Candee watched as up the regal staircase came "a solid procession of all the ship's passengers, wordless, orderly, quiet, and only the dress told of the tragedy. On every man and every woman's body was tied the sinister emblem of death at sea, and each one walked with his life-clutching pack to await the coming horrors. It was a fancy-dress ball in Dante's Hell."

"Life belts?" Smith asked.

"Yes, sir. I also found that they were busy getting the boats ready to go overboard."

In fact, one boat had already been loaded.

12:45 A.M. Boat #7: *In the nearby gymnasium on the boat deck, Instructor McCawley was helping first-class passengers work out on the exercise machines while they waited for the boats. Mrs. Lucien Smith noted: "There was no commotion, no panic, and no one seemed to be particularly frightened; in fact, most of the people seemed interested in the unusual occurrence, many having crossed fifty and sixty times."*

A cluster of elite passengers stood near Number 7 mumbling. Officer Murdoch lowered the boat to the rail while Ismay sang out, "Gentlemen, please stand back." The passengers looked at each other, "more stunned than anything else." Helen Bishop heard a voice: "Put in the brides and grooms first." The Bishops entered Number 7 along with two other pairs of newlyweds. First-class passenger J. R. McGough felt powerful hands catch him by the shoulders—"Here, you're a big fellow; get in that boat!" McGough and some other men got in.

While Seaman Hogg clambered about the bottom of Number 7 trying to put the plug in, Steward Etches worked frantically at the falls—they kept catching in the passengers' feet. Three crewmen and twenty-five passengers got in. Murdoch shouted, "Lower away!" and began manipulating the Welin-patent davit. Helen Bishop peered down at the water seventy feet below. It was "like glass," she observed. "There wasn't even the ripple usually found on a small lake."

"You were not aroused from your slumber by *anyone?*" Smith asked Lowe.

"No, sir," replied the fifth officer. "Mr. Boxhall, the fourth officer, told me that he told me that we had struck an iceberg, but I do not remember it. . . . It must have been while I was asleep. You must remember that we do not have any too much sleep, and therefore when we sleep we die."

Lowe loved explaining himself, and did so exceptionally well.

"Now," said Smith, "what did you do after you went out on the deck and ascertained the position of the ship in the water, and saw what had occurred?"

"I first of all went and got my revolver."

"What for?" asked the senator, rather surprised.

"Well, sir, you never know when you'll need it."

"All right. Go ahead."

"Then I went and helped everybody all around. Let's see," he pondered. "I crossed over to the starboard side. I lowered away. The first boat I helped to lower was Number Five starboard boat. . . ."

"Do you known any of the men who assisted you in lowering that lifeboat?"

"No, sir, I do not—by name. But there's a man here"—Lowe glanced briefly toward his left—"and had he not been here I should not have known that I had ordered Mr. Ismay away from the boat."

"Did you order Mr. Ismay away from the boat?" asked Smith, rather interested.

"I did, sir."

"What did you say to him?"

"This was on the starboard side. I don't know his name—but I know him by sight—he is a steward. He spoke to me on board the *Carpathia.* He asked me if I knew what I had said to Mr. Ismay. I said, 'I don't know Mr. Ismay.' 'Well,' he said, 'you used very, very strong language with him.' '*Did* I?' I said. 'I cannot help it if I did.' He said, 'Yes, you did,' and he repeated the words." Looking intently at Smith, Lowe added, "If you wish me to repeat them I'll do so; if you do not, I'll not."

Lowe sat at solemn attention, awaiting the verdict

whether or not his cursing would be allowed into the record.

"I will ask you this," said Smith. "What was the occasion for your using this harsh language to Mr. Ismay?"

"The occasion for using the language I did was because Mr. Ismay was overanxious, and he was getting a trifle excited." Spinning his right hand in the air, Lowe began squeaking an outrageous imitation of J. Bruce Ismay: "Lower away! Lower away! Lower away! Lower away!"

The mimicry was superb, and the lady seminarians were overcome with giggles.

The chairman turned on the spectators. "I want to say that if there is any confusion here or any interruption to these proceedings, the persons who have been enjoying the courtesy of the committee will be excluded!" Smith nodded at Lowe, indicating for him to continue.

"I said—" Lowe began, but he apparently had reached the unspeakable part of his story. He slowly folded his arms across his chest, cocked an eyebrow at the ladies, and said, "Well, let it be."

"Give us what you said," piped Ismay from the side of the room. The White Star manager was glowering at Lowe.

"The chairman is examining me!" Lowe retorted to Ismay. This officer clearly owed no allegiance to the White Star Line.

"Mr. Ismay," said Smith, "you asked the witness to give the language?"

"I have no objection to his giving it," Ismay replied. "It was not very parliamentary."

"If the language is inappropriate—" Smith began.

"There is only one word that might be so considered," Lowe interposed.

"May I suggest," said Ismay, "that it be put on a

piece of paper and given to you, Mr. Chairman, and you decide."

"All right," Smith agreed, "write it down."

Bill McKinstry pushed a pencil and pad over to Lowe, who scribbled rapidly and handed the pad gingerly to Smith.

The senator glanced coolly at the pad. "You may put that in the record," he said to Lowe. "You said you—"

"You wish me to repeat it, sir?" asked the fifth officer.

"Yes."

"I told him, 'If you will get the hell out of that, I shall be able to do something.' "

The spectators remained deathly silent, but their thrill was nevertheless visible to reporters.

"What reply did he make?" asked Smith.

"He didn't make any reply. I said, 'Do you want me to lower away quickly? You'll have me *drown* the whole lot of them!' I was on the floor myself lowering away."

"When this first lifeboat, Number Five, was lowered, the gear and everything worked all right, did it?"

"Everything went all right sir, and it couldn't have been worked better."

"And it was lowered with perfect safety?"

"With perfect safety."

12:55 A.M. Boat #5: *"Are there any more women before this boat goes?" Ismay called out. "I am only a stewardess," a lady replied. "Never mind," Ismay said, "you are a woman—take your place." A stout gentleman leaned over to kiss his wife good-bye. "I cannot leave you," he moaned and tumbled into the boat beside her. "Throw that man out of the boat!" Murdoch shouted. Instead, three more men jumped in, dislocating two ribs of a lady passenger.*

"You go in charge of this boat," Murdoch barked at Officer Pitman, "and hang around the after gangway.

Good-bye and good luck." Turning to Lowe, Murdoch ordered, "That is enough before lowering. We can get a lot more in after she's in the water." Quartermaster Olliver was crawling along the bottom of the boat between the passengers' ankles to get the plug in before the boat touched the sea. "Lower away!" Murdoch called.

The paint was fresh on the pulleys (they had never before been used) and the falls kept sticking. The boat went down jerkily—first the bow dropped, then the stern. Mrs. Warren, a passenger, thought for sure she was going to be dumped out. Dr. Washington Dodge watched from the rail as Number 5 jogged down to the sea containing his wife and son; he felt "overwhelmed with doubts" as to whether or not he was "exposing them to greater danger than if they had remained on board the ship."

Quartermaster Olliver still hadn't managed to get the plug in, so Pitman blew his whistle at the men above. The boat stopped descending. As the QM put the plug in, a voice from above (undoubtedly Lowe's) bellowed, "It's your own bloomin' business to see that the plug's in anyhow!" Unhitching the falls was an ordeal; no one seemed to know how to do it. Finally free, Pitman ordered Number 5 rowed away, forgetting Murdoch's order to hand around the gangway door.

"When the boats and the gear are new and have been properly tested and work as they should, how many persons will a lifeboat the size of Number Five hold safely on a clear night and with no sea?" Smith asked.

The senator was approaching what had just become the lastest focal point of American outrage and anguish—the fact that the *Titanic*'s boats had been only halfway filled. According to his son, Smith's mail was full of protest on the subject.

"Do you mean to ask what she would hold in the water or what she would hold lowering?" asked Lowe. It was the same distinction Lightoller had wished to make in New York.

Smith permitted the distinction. "I want you to tell me how many she will hold lowering."

"That depends upon the caliber of the man lowering her," said Lowe, offering this entirely new outlook on the issue.

"Does it not depend upon the gear?"

"It depends upon the gear also, sir," Lowe agreed. "You will say to yourself, 'I will take the chance with fifty people in this boat.' Another man may say, 'I am not going to run the risk of fifty; I will take twenty-five or thirty.' "

"All right," said Smith, slowly becoming irritated with the fifth officer's colorful but nonetheless time-consuming illustrations. "You were in this boat, and the question depended upon the caliber of yourself?"

"No, sir, not upon me."

"Upon whom—Mr. Murdoch?"

"Upon Mr. Murdoch," Lowe nodded.

"From what you saw, was that boat loaded carefully to its proper capacity that night?"

"The lowering of that boat was not up to me."

"I am not asking that," flared the senator. "I did not ask you that *at all!*" To Bill McKinstry, Smith said, "Read the question." Addressing Lowe, he added, "If you will answer my questions we will make much better progress."

"From what you saw," read McKinstry, "was that boat loaded carefully to its proper capacity that night?"

Lowe seemed confused and even hurt by Smith's ordering the reporter to repeat the question. "You pull me up about going around explaining matters to you," he protested, "so I don't see how I can very well get at it if you pull me up on it."

"I am *not* pulling you up," Smith said resolutely.

"I say it is a matter of opinion whether that boat was properly filled or not," said Lowe.

"And I *want* your opinion," said the senator.

"And that depends on the man in charge of the said boat."

"Let me say this to you, Mr. Lowe. Nobody is on trial here, and this is not a court. This is an inquiry. You stood there and helped load this boat, and the man who had charge of it did not survive. Now I ask you whether, in your judgment, Number Five lifeboat was properly loaded to its capacity for safety, considering the condition of the weather and the condition of the sea. You certainly can answer that."

"Yes, she was, as regards lowering."

"What is the capacity of a lifeboat like that under the British regulations?"

"Sixty-five point five," Lowe replied. The Board of Trade specified 10 cubic feet per passenger, and the *Titanic*'s boats had 655-cubic-foot capacity each.

"I want that understood," Smith said. "Do you wish the committee to understand that a lifeboat whose capacity is sixty-five under the British regulations could not be lowered with safety, with new tackle and equipment, containing more than fifty people?"

Lowe nodded. "The dangers are," he explained, "that if you overcrowd the boat the first thing that you'll have will be that the boat will buckle up like that at the two ends"—Lowe positioned his hands in the form of a V—"'because she's suspended from both ends and there's no support in the middle. . . ."

"Then fifty would be the lowering capacity, in your judgment?"

"Yes, I should not like to put more than fifty in. . . ."

"You considered fifty safe?"

"I'm different from another man. I may take on more risk, we will say, than you." Lowe paused a moment. "Or you may take on more risk than me," he added diplomatically.

"*I* will pursue my inquiry," said the senator, stone-faced. "Did you hear Mr. Pitman's testimony yesterday?" Pitman had testified that only thirty-five people had departed in Number 5—a far more accurate estimate than Lowe's. "If Mr. Pitman was in this Number Five boat," Smith continued, "he was mistaken as to the number of people in it?"

"Why do you say he should be mistaken?" asked Lowe, suddenly interested.

"Because he said he was in a boat with thirty-five people and you say that he might have been in Number Five with fifty people."

"If he was in Number Five," Lowe said nonchalantly, "and he says there were thirty-five, he had a far better chance of ascertaining than I had. His judgment goes."

"If he occupied lifeboat Number Five and says that it contained only thirty-five people, in your opinion it would have accommodated at least fifteen more in the lowering and at least thirty more, altogether, on the water?"

"No, sir," Lowe disagreed, "not thirty more. I never said thirty more."

"We will not have any misunderstanding at all!" said William Alden, raising his voice. "You say that the capacity of this lifeboat, Number Five, was sixty-five people plus in the water?"

"Yes, sixty-five."

"If he says he had thirty-five people on his boat, there would have been room for thirty more on his boat, would there not?"

"You first said thirty-five and then thirty," said Lowe, genuinely confused.

"That makes sixty-five!" the chairman snapped.

Lowe thought he could clarify everything if he were permitted to talk extemporaneously. Smith reluctantly agreed, so long as it was to the point and wouldn't take too long.

"I was listening to Major—I forget his name—yesterday afternoon, and heard him say that the sailors could not row and manage a boat."

Major Arthur Peuchen had made a brief appearance before the committee, and his indictment of the seamanship aboard the *Titanic* had caused nationwide interest.

"Heard who say?" Smith asked.

"The major," Lowe replied.

"Major Peuchen?"

"Yes, sir."

12:55 A.M. Boat #6: *Major Peuchen watched as Number 6 was loaded. "We must get these masts and sails out of the boat," someone said, "you might give us a hand." Peuchen jumped in, cut the lashings with a pocketknife, and stepped back onto deck, dragging the mast with him. Molly Brown watched with great interest as Number 6 was lowered; she was about to turn around and see what was happening on the other side when strong hands caught her shoulders from behind. "You are going, too," a voice said from the shadows, and the hefty Mrs. Brown was plopped four feet into the descending boat.*

"I can't manage this boat with only one seaman!" came a man's voice from disappearing Number 6.

"Can I be of any assistance? I am a yachtsman," Peuchen said to Captain E.J. Smith. E.J. told Peuchen to go down to A Deck, break one of those clever windows specially built for the Titanic, *and get into the boat through a broken pane. The captain was not quite himself; his idea was impratical, if not downright dangerous. Instead, Peuchen grabbed a loose rope from the davit and lowered himself, hand-over-hand, into the boat.*

"What do you want me to do?" he asked the quartermaster in charge. "Get down and put that plug in," came the reply. As Peuchen dove for the plug, the QM rasped, "Hurry up. This boat is going to founder!" Peuchen thought he was referring to the lifeboat, but he wasn't.

Lowe began his extemporaneous explanation. "A sailor is not necessarily a boatman. Neither is a boatman a sailor, because they are two very different callings. I might pride myself that I am both—a sailor and a boatman. A sailor may go to sea for quite a number of years and never go into a boat, never touch an oar, whereas you put a boatman in a ship and put him to do a job, and he's useless. He doesn't know anything about it. . . . That's the reason why many of the sailors could not row."

"Is that the reason why the boats were not loaded to their full capacity?" asked Smith, who still hadn't heard from Lowe what he was looking for.

"No," replied Lowe, "that's not the reason why the boats weren't loaded to their full capacity."

"What is the reason?"

"That is about all I have to say, sir, about the sailors not being boatmen."

"Can you give *any* reason why they were not loaded to their full capacity?" Smith asked. The fifth officer's digressions were not particularly defensive—it wasn't so much that he was trying to conceal things. They seemed prompted instead by Lowe's inabililty to appreciate Smith's purpose, so Smith laid his cards on the table. "I want to know from what you did," the senator began, "whether you believe that the reason why these boats were not loaded to their lowering capacity was because they did not have skillful men to operate them."

> 1:00 A.M. Boat #3: *The first-class passengers sauntered out from the saloon. The band had come onto the boat deck, playing ragtime. A number of people were chatting—no one seemed in a hurry. One passenger was relaying the news that an officer said the ship could not sink in less than eight or ten hours and that several steamers, already contacted by wireless, would arrive well before then. Four first-class men got into Number 3, bringing with them two valets and a dog. At the last moment, a number of firemen jumped in. Elizabeth Schutes sat in the boat, watching the "rough seamen" attempting to lower it amid "the greatest confusion." Finally, Number 3 began jerking down toward the water—Miss Schutes was afraid it would capsize in midair. The boat eventually reached the sea, but the two crewmen couldn't coordinate their oars. They also had to continually stop and beat their hands, which were freezing from the cold.*

"No," replied Lowe to Smith's question about the lack of skilled crewmen. The fifth officer reiterated the fact that Murdoch had selected the number of people for the boat, and Lowe had merely complied with orders.

"You do not find any fault with the *shape* of the boats, do you?" Smith asked sarcastically.

"No, sir, you couldn't have better boats."

"Then you must find fault with the men that managed them."

"I find fault with the men to that extent that I've already stated," said Lowe, "that they were not boatmen. . . . Neither are boatmen sailors."

"Why did you let them in the lifeboat then?"

1:10 A.M. Boat #8: *Mrs. J. Stuart White observed that the crewmen getting into the boat were permitted to do so "under the pretense of being oarsmen." Dr. Alice F. Leader noticed that none of the seamen "seemed to know their places." Twenty-four women were already in the boat. Mrs. Straus approached Number 8, but stepped back to her husband. "We have been living together for many years," she glowed, "and where you go I go."*

The captain "seemed to be in a hurry to have" the boat leave and asked Seaman Jones if the plug was in. It was. "Any more ladies?" E.J. bawled through a megaphone. Two stewards and a cook entered Number 8—a total of twenty-eight people. The boat was lowered satisfactorily, but the men had trouble rowing. One of the stewards was poking his oar about every which way. "Why don't you put the oar in the oarlock," Mrs. White finally said to him. "Do you put it in that hole?" he asked. "Certainly," she replied. "I never had an oar in my hand before," he explained to her sheepishly. The men began arguing over how to manage the boat. One of them snapped at another, "If you don't stop talkin' through that hole in yer face, there'll be one less in this boat!"

The senator turned to the subject of lifeboat drill. There had been just one drill, when the ship was docked in Southampton, and only two boats had been lowered.

There had been another drill scheduled on the very day of the collision, but it had never taken place. The boat-lists had been put up, but the drill was never called—no one knew why. A steward would testify that maybe it was due to the number of steerage passengers, "because if we would all go to drill, meals would not be ready for the passengers." Another steward thought that the drill may have been skipped because, scheduled Sunday at 11:30 A.M., it would have overlapped with the church service at which E.J. so much liked officiating.

"What was the drill for at Southampton?" asked the senator.

"The drill at Southampton—I suppose it was for the Board of Trade," was Lowe's literal answer.

"Each of these lifeboats was manned by eight men," Smith began, alluding to the drill. "Where were these men who had gone through the trial test at Southampton when the danger arose? Do not get away from what I want."

"No, sir."

"Just let us understand one another," Smith said gently. "Now. You said that each man had his station?"

"Yes."

"And that each was required to go through a drill?"

"Yes."

"That drill, of course, was for the purpose of familiarizing those people with their duties if any accident happened, was it not? Where were those men when you were loading the lifeboat at Number Five?"

"You must remember, sir," replied Lowe, about to take off again, "in the first place we had the full ship's crew on our hands then at Southampton, when we manned those two boats; and we had the choice of the men. And in the second place, when this accident took place, there was a crowd of men—which accounts for the shortness of sailors—a crowd of men who went down with the boatswain to clear away the gangway doors in the hope that we should be able to send people down there when we had lowered the boats down."

"That did not require much skill, to clear away the gangway doors," Smith responded. "Anybody could do that. . . . But it did require some skill to lower and to satisfactorily man the lifeboats. And yet you are leaving the impression upon the committee and upon this record that the men who were familiar with those lifeboats and who had gone through the drill at Southampton were not available when those boats were loaded and lowered. Is that the impression you desire to leave?"

"No, sir, it is not."

"I know there was confusion," said Smith, "I know there was a *great* emergency there. But I wonder whether the discipline was right."

> 1:12 A.M. Boat #1: *The first-class gentleman asked the officer if he could get into Number 1. "Sure, jump in," came the reply. The passenger jumped over the rail and rolled into the boat. "That is the funniest sight I've seen tonight," said the officer, laughing heartily. Seven crewmen, three first-class gentlemen, a first-class lady and her maid were lowered away in Number 1—a total of twelve people, the smallest number of any boat.*

"The discipline could not have been better," Lowe asserted. "And what I mean to say is that you must remember that we did not have one boat to lower away. . . . You want at least eight or between eight and ten men to get a lifeboat ready, and you must understand that we are not getting all the lifeboats ready at once, or getting as many ready as we possibly can."

What Lowe was revealing in a roundabout way was the fact that although all the crew had taken appointed places during the so-called lifeboat drill, there had been only enough skilled boatmen to lower two lifeboats—a fact Lightoller had successfully skirted in New York. (In his autobiography, Lightoller revealed that, in 1912, the practice of appointed places at lifeboat drill was actually "just so much theory, concocted ashore with a keen eye to dividends.") Furthermore, there had been proportionately few seamen among the *Titanic*'s enormous crew. It had been inconceivable that on the "practically unsinkable" ship the need would ever arise for evacuating all the passengers at sea.

"Those that we get ready," Lowe continued, "we are swinging out and filling with women and children. I do not really remember the number of sailors we had on board."

Senator Perkins had been examining some papers. "It is in the testimony that there were eighty-three sailors," he announced. (This, out of a staff of over 900 people!)

"I don't know," said Lowe. "We were *brand new* to the ship, just the same as everybody else."

Here was the crux of the problem. White Star had been in a hurry to get the *Titanic* into service. Given the crewmen's lack of familiarity with the ship and with each other, the boat drill scheduled for the fourteenth was all the more important. For whatever reason, it had been omitted.

"Are you ready to admit," said Smith, "that the men on that ship whose duty it was to report to their stations when the order was issued to clear away the lifeboats and lower them with women and children were not available?"

Lowe was glumly silent.

"You can answer that very easily," Smith coached, "and we will not argue about it another minute."

"Do you mean to ask, sir, if the men were at their boat-drill stations?" Lowe asked.

"Yes."

"No, they were not," Lowe admitted.

Satisfied, Smith turned to another topic. "Did anyone get into either of these lifeboats, three or five, and get out again?"

"I do not remember," said Lowe, reflecting. "I don't think so."

> 1:20 A.M. Boat #9: *The elderly lady stepped into the boat and stepped right back; returning to the companionway, she forced her way down into the ship. Husbands were having trouble getting their wives to leave them. "For God's sake, go!" shouted Mr. Futrelle as he shoved his wife toward Number 9. A fireman sauntered by, threw his kit in the lifeboat, got in, and announced that he had been sent by the captain to take charge. Seaman Haines threw him out. More women entered Number 9 and it was lowered. The crewmen suddenly discovered that the oars were still lashed together. Steward Widgery luckily found a pocketknife, cut loose the oars, and they rowed away.*

"Did anyone get into either of them who was put out by your order?" asked the senator.

"No."

"Or anybody within your hearing?"

"No."

"Did any woman attempt to get in either of these boats and not succeed in getting in?"

"No, sir."

1:21 A.M. Boat #10: *The* Titanic *was beginning to list, and there was a three-foot gap between the port boats and the rail. The French lady jumped across to Number 10 but missed. Her hands clutched at the gunnels of the lifeboat while her feet fortunately caught on the rail of the deck below, where she was pulled in. She returned to the boat deck and safely entered Number 10. Children were being "chucked in." Seaman Evans, standing in the boat, managed to catch a baby by its gown and swing it over, dangling, to a lady in the boat. As Number 10 descended, "a foreigner" jumped into it from A Deck; he looked like "a crazed Italian."*

"Was the conduct of the people when you were loading these boats excited or otherwise?" Smith asked.

"Everything was quiet and calm. The only thing—and of course you would expect that—was that the people were messing up the falls, getting foul of the falls, and I had to halloo a bit to get them off the falls. Everything else went nicely, very nicely. Quietly and orderly."

"Did you see families separated?"

"I did."

1:25 A.M. Boat #11: *The boat had been lowered to A Deck, where second- and third-class women were waiting in a large crowd. Mrs. Allen O. Becker had placed her two youngest children in the boat when Number 11, without warning, began to descend. "Oh, please let me go with my children!" she cried. She was picked up and dropped in, but Ruth—her eldest—was left on the deck. "Get into the next boat," Mrs. Becker called to Ruth as Number 11 dropped out of sight. "Is there a seaman in the boat?" someone called from the deck. No answer. Seaman Brice slithered down a fall and got into the boat. Number 11 contained over seventy people—the largest number of any boat. Simultaneously, Number 12 dropped down from the port side.*

"Do you know who they were?" Smith asked, referring to the families Lowe had seen separated.

"Yes."

"Was there anything special that occurred at such times?"

"No."

"Everything was quiet?"

"Everything was quiet and orderly."

"Was there any weeping or lamentation?"

"No," replied Lowe, "none that I heard."

1:27 A.M. Boat #13: *"Don't put me in the boat!" screamed the fat lady. "I don't want to go in the boat. I have never been in an open boat in my life!" Steward Ray said to her, "You have got to go and you may as well keep quiet." An infant wrapped in a blanket was thrown to Ray, which he luckily managed to catch. "Who'll take this babby?" he asked. The "babby" was tossed to a young lady seated in the boat. Ruth Becker went up to the officer and asked if she could get in. "Sure," he replied and chucked her into Number 13. When a last call for women went unanswered, several men tumbled into the boat, which began descending.*

A three-foot-diameter discharge of water (the condenser exhaust) was flowing out of the ship's side—directly in the path of Number 13's descent. It was obvious that any moment the boat would drop beneath the discharge, get swamped, and capsize. Using the oars, the men pushed Number 13 sufficiently clear of the pouring outlet. Once lowered, a call was made for a knife to cut the falls. Someone suddenly looked above; Number 13 had drifted aft in the wash of the condenser discharge and was now directly beneath another descending boat. "Stop lowering Number Fourteen!" everyone shouted. (It was actually Number 15.) The boat hovering above stopped. "One! Two!" said a fireman as he cut the falls, and Number 13 rowed out into the night.

"Where did you go next?" Smith asked the fifth officer.

Lowe explained that he had crossed over to the port side, taking charge of Number 14. He had put a large load—fifty-eight passengers—in this boat, and Smith wanted to know what proportion were women and children.

"They were all women and children," replied Lowe, "bar one passenger, who was an Italian, and he sneaked in, and he was dressed like a woman."

"Had women's clothes on?" The senator was shocked.

"He had a shawl over his head, and everything else, and I only found out at the last moment."

This particular incident from Lowe's testimony would in time become a legend. For the moment, Smith turned to an issue that had already reached mythic proportions. "Did you hear any pistol shots?" Smith asked.

"Yes."

"And by whom were they fired Sunday night?"

"I heard them and I fired them," Lowe replied.

1:30 A.M. Boat #14: *A young boy, "hardly more than a schoolboy," climbed over the rail and fell in among the women in Number 14 who covered him up with their skirts. Lowe dragged the stowaway to his feet and ordered him back onto the ship. The boy didn't want to go. Lowe thrust his revolver into his face, saying, "I give you just ten seconds to get back onto that ship before I blow your brains out!" The boy only begged harder, and Lowe changed his tone. "For God's sake, be a man," he admonished. "We've got women and children to save." A little girl in Number 14 tugged at the fifth officer's sleeve. "Oh, Mr. Man," she whimpered "please don't shoot the poor man." Lowe shook his head with a smile and somehow got the boy to get back on the* Titanic. *Almost immediately "an Italian" jumped into Number 14 whom Lowe forcibly ejected. This "coward" was last seen in the hands of a dozen men from second class, who were "driving their fists into his face, and he was bleeding from the nose and mouth." Number 14 began descending.*

Lowe explained how he was forced to use his pistol during Number 14's descent. "As I was going down the decks, I knew—or I expected every moment—that my boat would double up under my feet. I was quite scared of it, although of course it would not do for me to mention the fact to anybody else. I had overcrowded her, but I knew that I had to take a certain amount of risk. So I thought, 'Well, I shall have to see that nobody else gets into the boat or else it will be a case! . . .' I thought if one additional body was to fall into that boat, that slight jerk of the additional weight might part the hooks or carry away something, no one would know what. There were a hundred and one things to worry about. Then I thought, 'Well, I'll keep an eye open.' So, as we were coming down the decks, coming down past the open decks, I saw a lot of Italians all along the ship's rail—understand it was open—and they were all glaring more or less like wild beasts ready to spring. That's why I yelled, 'Look out!' and let go, bang! right across the ship's side. . . ."

"How far from the ship's side was the lifeboat you were in?" asked the senator.

"I really don't know," Lowe replied. "I should say—oh, three or four feet."

"It cleared each deck three to four feet? . . ."

"I'll withdraw four feet and say three feet," Lowe amended. "As I went down I fired these shots and without the intention of hurting anybody and also with the knowledge that I did not hurt anybody."

"You are positive of that?"

"I'm absolutely positive."

The issue of firearms was yet a subject of strong speculation and rumor in the nation. It, too, was a conspicuous subject in Smith's mail. William Alden questioned Lowe closely on how he could have avoided hitting anyone, when he had only a three-foot space in which to fire.

"I had more," Lowe replied. "I had the width of the boat. I was standing up in the after part of her. From the center line of the boat would give another two feet or so. That would be five feet."

"If you had fired downward toward the water," Smith considered, "you would have been limited to that space."

"Yes."

"If you fired upward you would fire along the ship's side."

"Well," replied Lowe, "I fired horizontally."

There was conflict on this point. The Michigan Minutemen had several seamen gabbing that Lowe had fired directly into the crowd. Future testimony would include statements that "he shot straight down in the water," as well as "he fired either downward or upward." Lowe was maintaining that he had direct horizontally along the side of the ship.

"Upward?" Smith gestured.

"Horizontally," Lowe repeated. The officer mimed the action, holding his arm out straight from the shoulder, closing his left eye, and sighting along his arm. The gesture drew a raptured chorus of "Oooh!" from the lady seminarians.

"You are positive you did not hit anybody?" Smith asked.

"I am absolutely *positive* I hit nobody," Lowe replied.

The senator was satisfied that, if anyone had been shot, it had not resulted from Lowe's actions. Only one person was dissatisfied with the fifth officer's account, and that was Signor Cusani, the Italian ambassador and an official visitor at the hearing. By this time it had become obvious to Cusani that whenever despicable conduct by a passenger was related, it was attributed to "an Italian." In his testimony, Lowe had them glaring "like wild beasts." Southern Europeans had only recently begun immigrating to the United States and were a source of widespread suspicion among Anglo-Americans.

Approached by the ambassador after his testimony, Lowe agreed to write an amendment for the record:

> I do hereby cancel the word "Italian" and substitute the words "immigrants belonging to Latin races." In fact, I did not mean to infer that they were especially Italians, because I could only judge from their general appearance and complexion, and therefore I only meant to imply that they were of the types of

the Latin races. In any case, I did not intend to cast any reflection on the Italian nation.

This is the real truth, and therefore I feel honored to give out the present statement.

H. G. Lowe

William Alden explored one further issue with the fifth officer: When so many people had perished, why could none of them be found on the boat deck near the end? Smith had the overriding feeling that class distinctions were involved.

"Now," said Smith, "as they came along, you would pass them, one at a time, into a lifeboat. What orders did you have—to pass women and children?"

"I simply shouted, 'Women and children first—men stand back!' "

"Do you know how many women there were on the boat?"

"I do not, sir."

"You put them aboard as they came along, the first being served first?"

"The first, first; second, second."

"Regardless of class, or nationality, or pedigree. . . . No distinction whatsoever."

1:35 A.M. Boats #15 and #16: *The two boats were located at the extreme stern of the boat deck, alongside the second-class companionways. The ship's watertight bulkheads, in addition to their safety function, served to separate passengers by class. Steerage passengers following their habitual routes upward found themselves stranded on either the forewell or afterwell. While some of these people waited there dazed, others went into the third-class smoking and general rooms, where they "were dancing, smoking, playing cards, and telling jokes." Still others climbed the vertical ladders and even the electric cranes up to the boat deck.*

The only direct route from steerage to the boats was aft through the second-class quarters at C Deck. Steward Hart found a flock of steerage passengers there and shepherded them up to Number 15. Both Numbers 15 and 16 were being loaded with mostly second- and third-class women and children. While August Wennerstrom had been content to stay in the smoking room, he escorted a couple of Swedish girls up to Number 15.

The boats were dropped to A Deck, where they were then filled to capacity. Containing about sixty people each, they were finally lowered the rest of the way down. Wennerstrom stood watching and smoking a cigar as the boats disappeared down the side: "We had our eyes wide open and noticed everything that was going on, but could not feel any sorrow—or even fear. It was more like we were part of an audience in a wonderful, dramatic play."

Senator Smith also wanted to know how long Mr. Ismay had helped in lowering the boats. "You found him there when you turned from Number Five to Number Three?"

"He was there," replied Lowe, "and I distinctly remember seeing him alongside of me—that is, by my side—when the first detonator went off. I will tell you how I happen to remember it so distinctly. It was because the flash of the detonator lit up the whole deck. I did not know who Mr. Ismay was them, but I learned afterwards who he was, and he was standing alongside of me."

1:40 A.M. Starboard Collapsible "C": *Ismay stood back as Murdoch fired his pistol in the air, shouting,*

"Get out of this! Clear out!" A group of "Italians and foreigners" had sneaked into collapsible "C." The gunfire drew a number of men over from the port side who pounced on the interlopers and pulled them out of the boats by their legs; they all scampered away toward the stern and disappeared. The women and children were then put in. They had to be lifted into the boat, since they were all "very limp. They had not much spring in them at all."

On A Deck, the lights were beginning to glow an ominous red. The starboard was now clear of boats, and no passengers were in sight. Ismay could feel the bow of the ship sinking palpably beneath his feet. "Any more women and children?" Collapsible "C" began to be lowered, and Ismay and a first-class gentleman jumped in. The Titanic's *list to port had grown worse, and "C" began catching onto the rivets of the hull. The passengers pushed against the side of the ship to free the boat, which quickly hit the water and was rowed away.*

Referring to Ismay again, Smith said, "You saw him in the flash—"

"Of the detonator," Lowe interposed.

"Did you hear what Mr. Boxhall said about firing these rockets?"

"No, sir."

"Did you hear any such thing?"

"Any what, sir?"

"Firing rockets."

"I am now speaking of it," Lowe said.

"I know you are," said the senator, "and that is the reason I am asking you about it."

"Yes," replied Lowe, "they were incessantly going off. They were nearly deafening me."

1:45 A.M. Boat #2: *Thus far, the rockets had sounded the dominant note of apprehension. Through the artillery of her distress signals, "the great ship seemed shrieking in despair." Fourth Officer Boxhall had fired off a total of eight rockets when the captain told him to take charge of Number 2. There was a minor skirmish when Lightoller discovered the boat was full of men. They looked like stokers to several passengers, but Lightoller was convinced they were all "Dagoes." "Get out, you damned cowards," Lightoller shouted, flourishing his revolver at them. "I'd like to see every one of you overboard!" A lady passenger watched as "a solid row of men, from bow to stern," crawled out from Number 2 onto the deck. The lady entered the boat, asking her husband to please come with her. "No," he told her, "I must be a gentleman." Boxhall and three crewmen, a steerage male, and twenty-five women—30 people in all—got in Number 2 and were lowered away.*

Smith tried a final time to discover why some 1,500 were absent from the boat deck.

"There didn't seem to be any people there," Lowe told him.

"You did not find *anyone* that wanted to go?" Smith asked.

"Those that were there didn't seem to want to go. I hollered out, 'Who's next for the boat?' and there was no response."

"Was the top deck crowded?"

"No," replied Lowe. "There was a little knot of people on the forepart of the gymnasium door."

1:55 A.M. Boat #4: *The passengers were confused as to which deck had been designated for assembly. A large group had been escorted to A Deck and later told to go up to the boat deck. When a steward then ordered them to return to A Deck, a first-class passenger complained, "You ordered us up here and now you are taking us back!" Number 4—the last wooden boat remaining on the ship—was hanging at A Deck, level with the special windows which the men had finally succeeded in opening. Steamer chairs were being used as stair steps up to the boat.*

Although the ship was tilting forward, everyone "seemed unconcerned." One lady expressed misgivings, but a gentleman reassured her, saying, "Don't you hear the band playing?" Many were discussing their belief that the Olympic *and* Baltic *would soon be there to rescue everyone. A husband casually handed his wife some money. "We may be separated," he told her, "and you might need this." John Jacob Astor asked if he could accompany his wife—she was pregnant. "No, sir," Lightoller replied, "no man is allowed on this boat or any of the boats until the ladies are off." (Astor asked the number of the boat so he could find his wife later.) To a lady with her arm around her son, Lightoller said, "That boy cannot go." The boy's father insisted, "Of course that boy goes with his mother—he is only thirteen!" They entered Number 4 while Lightoller muttered to the assisting crewmen, "No more boys."*

"How many women are there in the boat?" someone called from above. "Twenty-four," came the answer. "That's enough—lower away!" The boat quickly reached the water, and its occupants could see at once how seriously the ship was sinking. She was very much down by the head—the angle of inclination steadily increasing. One could actually watch the portholes disappearing; and from inside the ship came "a crashing noise resembling china breaking."

Number 4 was rowed toward the stern hatchway, but the gangway doors had never been opened. Lamp Trimmer Sam Hemming lowered himself down on a fall and swam to Number 4 where he was hauled in. Two others then swam to the boat, telling its occupants that the ship didn't have many more minutes left. From the boat deck, barrels, steamer chairs—anything that could serve for flotation—were being thrown overboard. Number 4 quickly rowed away.

"Do you know whether the staircase was guarded that led up to the top floor?" Smith asked.

"No."

"Were people permitted to roam as they desired over the ship?"

"Everybody was free to go where they wanted to," Lowe replied.

"No restraint?"

"No restraint."

14

Dies Irae

On Thursday, April 25, President Taft went to Massachusetts, preparing for battle with TR in the state's primary. In speeches scheduled from Springfield to Boston, the President was expected to refute the Colonel's charges and finally make some of his own. It would be the turning point of the campaign.

In England the weeklies had just begun hitting the newsstands. To the *London Outlook*, America's *Titanic* inquiry was "a burlesque" played out by "Senatorial busybodies." *The Spectator* pronounced the subcommittee "not worthy of the body from which it was drawn." The *London Saturday Review*—always critical of things American—had special words for William Alden Smith: "If this gentleman really represents the fine flower of American legislative wisdom, we cease to wonder that the Yankee eagle is doomed to flap its wings in a twilight of semi-civilization. Why should British subjects be detained against their will at Washington in order that a blustering ignoramus may tease them with questions about the difference between 'the bow' and 'the head' of a ship, the origin of icebergs, and the use of watertight compartments?"

Smith's music-hall imitators were now doing so well that the manager of London's Hippodrome thought he could corner the market by getting the real thing. Accordingly, he wrote to Smith, inviting him to lecture "on the question of navigation and the safety of liners at sea." Smith wired back a curt refusal: "It would be impossible and inconsistent with my position as a United States Senator to accept your invitation." The Hippodrome manager, convinced that a performance by William Alden would be immensely entertaining, very much regretted the senator's decision. "He could have named his own price," said the disappointed impresario.

In Parliament the debate was becoming more heated. A number of members had grown irate over the length of America's detention of British subjects. Alexander MacCullum Scott asked the foreign secretary, "Are you aware that those called before the Senate committee are not receiving fair and honorable treatment? Will you take steps to secure fair and honorable treatment for British subjects?" But Mr. Ackland asserted, "No such complaint has been received by us."

It may be recalled that, for a variety of reasons, Ambassador Bryce had decided not to voice Ismay's original complaint. The rumor to which Mr. Scott alluded arose from a publicized visit the *Titanic*'s crewmen had made to Ambassador Bryce Wednesday evening. Bryce was leaving for New Zealand Thursday morning, and, according to Officer Lightoller, the men had merely called on the ambassador prior to his departure simply as British subjects calling on the official representative of their country. Concerning the rumor of complaints, Lightoller said to the press, "I am sorry such a report has gone abroad."

In his autobiography, published twenty-three years later, however, Lightoller said that near the end, the crewmen "refused to have anything more to do with the enquiry" and it "was only with the greatest difficulty I was able to bring peace into the camp." Not so, said the Michigan Minutemen, whose duties included eavesdropping on the crewmen. O'Donnell and Carroll maintained that the officers were indeed expressing annoyance at being detained in Washington and at Smith's nautical ignorance—but the crewmen were posing no problems at all. They were now on a first-name basis with Senator Smith, who had managed to get Congress to raise their witness fees from three to four dollars per day. Wednesday evening they were followed all over the capital by a reporter from the *Milwaukee Journal* who said "they seemed to be enjoying the time of their lives."

There was no doubting, however, that the situation was becoming "sticky." A number of American newspapers were expressing uneasiness at the tenor of Britain's outrage. Senators Burton and Fletcher were becoming steadily pressured by their important roles in the debate over the rivers and harbors bill, now being considered by the full Committee on Commerce; they would soon have to drop out of the inquiry altogether. There were twenty-four crewmen yet to be interviewed, and, at William Alden's request, a number of passengers had now arrived in Washington ready to testify. How could everyone be interrogated without causing a delay that would further damage British-American relations? Smith had already proffered a solution, but it meant the committee members had to work overtime: If each senator took a sample of the crewmen and interviewed them privately, the depositions of all twenty-four men could be disposed of in a single evening. The senators who had balked on this plan earlier now acquiesced.

Burton and Perkins each took three men; Newlands, Fletcher, and Smith each took four; and Bourne—now a lame duck—took six. All twenty-four men were interviewed Thursday evening, shortly after the day's hearing before the full subcommittee.

One of the more striking facts that came out of the individual sessions was how little the sailors and stewards suspected the ship would sink. Many of those who left in the lifeboats thought they were leaving merely as a precaution and would row back to the ship in the morning. Steward John Hardy told Senator Fletcher about it.

"Of course," Hardy related, "I had great respect and great regard for Officer Murdoch, and I was walking along the deck forward with him, and he said, 'I believe she is gone, Hardy,' and that's the only time I thought she might sink—when he said that."

"How long was that before your boat was launched?" asked Fletcher.

"It was a good half hour, I should say, sir." Hardy told about portside collapsible "D." "We launched the boat parallel with the ship's side, and Mr. Lightoller and myself loaded the boat."

2:05 P.M. Port Collapsible "D": *The Goldsmith family, Alfred Rush, and a friend of Mr. Goldsmith's were making their way up from steerage when they were stopped at a gate through which only women and children could pass. Mr. Goldsmith embraced his wife and gave his son's shoulder a squeeze. "So long, Franky, I'll see you later," he said to the nine-year-old. Mr. Goldsmith's friend took off his wedding ring and handed it to Mrs. Goldsmith. "If I don't see you in New York," he told her, "see that my wife gets this." A steward pulled Mrs. Goldsmith and Franky through the gate and was about to do the same to*

Alfred Rush, but the lad, who had turned sixteen just a few days prior, jerked his arm from the steward's grasp. "No," he said, "I'm going to stay here with the men!"

The little group reached the boat deck and scurried forward along port to collapsible "D," now hitched to Number 2's davits. Lightoller had ordered the men to stand, arms locked together, in a semicircle around the collapsible, letting only women and children through. Mrs. Goldsmith and Franky got into the boat, followed by a group of chattering Assyrian women with babes in arms. A Frenchman passed his two little boys through, who were chucked into the boat.

Lightoller and Hardy were standing in "D," helping the ladies hurdle a high bulwark rail. One of the ladies was intimidated by it and walked away. Twenty-five passengers were in the boat when Chief Officer Wilde came over from starboard and said, "You go with her, Lightoller." Instead Lightoller jumped back on deck. "Not damn likely," he retorted and manned the davit.

Two gentlemen on A deck watched as the collapsible dropped alongside. "There's nobody in the bows," said the one to the other, "let's make a jump for it. You go first." They tumbled head over heels into "D." As it dropped past B Deck, Franky Goldsmith could see several teenaged ship employees sporting about—it looked like they were playing hide-and-seek.

The boat reached the water, now nearly level with C Deck in the foward part of the ship. A man whose wife was in "D" leaped from the boat deck and was pulled into the collapsible from the water. "D" was already pointing astern, and the quartermaster in charge ordered it rowed toward the end of the ship.

One hundred fifty yards farther off to starboard, the QM could see a little cluster of lifeboats together (Number 14, Lowe's boat, along with Numbers 10 and 12) and ordered "D" pulled over toward them.

"We got clear of the ship," Hardy continued, "and rowed out some distance . . . and I remember quite distinctly Officer Lowe telling us to tie up to each other, as we would be better seen and could keep better together."

"I want all these boats tied up by their painters, head and tail," Lowe barked, "so as to make a more conspicuous mark!" The fifth officer was directing the lashing of the boats in language "so blasphemous" that a number of ladies in the boats were convinced "he was under the influence of liquor." To their criticism, Lowe snapped, "I think the best thing for you women to do is to take a nap."

With "D" gone, only two collapsibles had remained on the ship. Both of them had been put aboard for the sake of exceeding the number of boats required by the Board of Trade. Mere accouterments in the *Titanic*'s exaggeration, they had been impractically stowed on the roof of the officers' quarters abreast of the first funnel. Harold Bride described how he got to the one on the port side: "Just at this moment, the captain came into the [Marconi] cabin and said, 'You can do nothing more; look out for yourselves. . . .' Leaving Mr. Phillips operating, I went to our sleeping cabin, and got all our money together, returning to find a fireman or coal trimmer gently relieving Mr. Phillips of his lifebelt. There immediately followed a general scrimmage with the three of us. I regret to say we left too hurriedly in the end to take the man in question with us, and without a doubt he sank with the ship in the Marconi cabin as we left him.

"I had up to this time kept the [wireless logbook] entered up, intending when we left the ship to tear out the lot and each to take a copy, but now we could hear the water washing over the boat deck and Mr. Phillips said, 'Come, let's clear out. . . .' Leaving the cabin, we climbed on top of the houses comprising the officers' quarters and our own, and here I saw the last of Mr. Phillips, for he disappeared walking aft.

"I now assisted in pushing off [collapsible "B"], which was on the port side of the forward funnel, onto the boat deck. Just as the boat fell I noticed Captain Smith dive from the bridge into the sea."

Meanwhile, on the starboard side of this same funnel, First Officer Murdoch, passenger Archibald Gracie, and a number of others had been wrestling with the other collapsible. Gracie—a friend and neighbor of William Alden's—quickly responded to the senator's request to testify before the full committee, and described the struggle with collapsible "A." Gracie had loaned the sailors his penknife to cut the ropes securing "A" and was annoyed at the "want of some tool for the purposes for which it was intended." The collapsible had been cut loose and slid down to the boat deck on ways of propped-up oars. "Finally," Gracie related, "this boat came down on the deck. I do not know whether it was injured or not by the fall, but we were afraid that it had been injured."

"How long after this did the boat go down?" Smith asked.

"Soon after that," replied Gracie, "the water came up on the boat deck. We saw it and heard it. I had not noticed in the meantime that we were gradually sinking. I was engaged all the time in working, as I say, at those davits, trying to work on the falls to let [collapsible "A"] down." He and a friend "could see then that there was no more chance for us there—that there were so many people at that particular point—so we decided to go toward the stern, still on the starboard side."

Gracie and his companion had walked astern, passing by Assistant Cook John Collins, running forward with a baby in his arms; the mother, another child, and a steward were pattering close behind.

"We saw the collapsible boat taken off of the saloon deck," Collins explained in his session with Senator Bourne, "and then the sailors and the firemen that were forward seen the ship's bow in the water, and seen that she was intending to sink her bow. And they shouted out for all they were worth [that] we were to go aft . . . and we were just turning around and making for the stern end when"

the Titanic *took a sudden plunge forward, and a couple of reports rang out over the sea "like a volley of musketry." An immense wave struck the bridge and splayed back over each side of the boat deck. Collins, the baby, and the others of the party were washed overboard; the assistant cook never saw any of them again. Officer Murdoch was also knocked overboard. Collapsible "B" overturned and was floating away with Harold Bride hanging underneath, Seaman Hagan clinging to the tail end of its keel, and others close behind. Collapsible "A" was also afloat, but still attached to the falls of Number 1's davits. On the roof of the officers' quarters, Charles Lightoller took a good look behind him, faced forward, and "took a header" toward the sinking foremast.*

The submerged forecastle was now beginning to

shudder, "shaking very much" as the sea poured into A and B Decks and flooded the first-class quarters, the lounges, and the saloons. The impending crisis jolted everyone still aboard the ship. Far astern, Father Thomas Byles and a German priest became the focal point of a frantic crowd of emigrants. "Prepare to meet God!" exclaimed Father Byles. While many fell to their knees and began chanting the rosary, others dashed to the companionways and ladders.

The gentlemen's lounge on A Deck continued to be a bastion of aplomb. Men in evening clothes were still playing cards on grotesquely slanting tables. Liquor was now "on the house" and available to all classes. Several minutes earlier, Firemen Paddy Dillon and Johnny Bannon from Belfast had "made for the whiskey and got our share." Paddy had already downed three slugs, when the ship lurched forward. Stuffing a bottle of brandy into his jacket, he careened out onto deck and fell overboard.

On the boat deck Archibald Gracie, traipsing astern, was suddenly horrified at the "mass of humanity" that surged up onto deck. (There were a good many women in the crowd, and Gracie had thought for sure that all the women had already departed in the boats.) Those in the distant lifeboats could easily see this "thick mass of people" as they swarmed over the upper deck. To Helen Bishop in Number 7 it was a "veritable wave of humanity." They "surged up out of the steerage and shut the lights from our view. We were too far away to see the passengers individually, but we could see the black mass of human forms. . . . One dining room steward who was in our boat was thoughtful enough to bring green lights—the kind you burn on the Fourth of July. They cast a ghastly light over our boat. Whenever we would light one of these diminutive torches we would hear cries from the people aboard—they thought it was help coming."

Those who had come up from the forward companionways now spun toward the stern, only to run into the iron fence and railing that separated first- from second-class deck space. Gracie and his friend saw that they could make no progress whatsoever abaft, while a glance toward the bow revealed a wall of water roaring up on them. They looked upward. A man's legs were dangling over the roof of the officers' quarters. Gracie and his friend jumped, but couldn't reach the roof. The wave was now almost upon them, and Gracie crouched down, preparing to leap with the roller as if he were body surfing. It worked. Billowing upward, Gracie grabbed ahold of the railing on the roof and clung to it while he thrashed about in what seemed like a whirlpool. He looked to the right and left, but could see no one. The wave that had rescued him had engulfed everyone forward—including his friend and even the man on the roof whose legs he had seen earlier.

Astern, everyone was huddled as far from the rail as possible, clambering abaft and trying to keep from sliding on the slanting deck, which was growing even steeper. Some clutched at the deck houses, while others lost their footing and slid into the icy water that was creeping up the boat deck. In this crowd were August Wennerstrom and his companions Mr. and Mrs. Edvard Lindell; also seventeen-year-old Jack Thayer and a friend. "We were a mass of hopeless, dazed humanity," Thayer recalled, "attempting, as the Almighty and Nature made us, to keep our final breath until the last possible moment."

The sea was climbing up more quickly now.

Thayer could feel the ship moving "forward and into the water at an angle of about fifteen degrees. This movement, with the water rushing up toward us, was accompanied by a rumbling roar, mixed with more muffled explosions. It was like standing under a steel railway bridge while an express train passes overhead, mingled with the noise of a pressed-steel factory and wholesale breakage of china."

Wennerstrom and the Lindells suddenly lost their footing and slid, holding hands, down the deck and into the water—and "as a wonder," right into collapsible "A." The three of them climbed into the boat, which was half full of water, and quickly untied the falls at each end. The collapsible was now bumping precariously against the sinking forward tunnel.

Jack Thayer and his companion straddled the starboard rail abreast of Number 2 funnel. Thayer's friend put both legs over and, facing the ship, clung to the rail by his hands. "You're coming, boy, aren't you?" he asked Jack. "Go ahead," Thayer replied, "I'll be with you in a minute." Jack's companion let go of the rail, slid down into the water, and was swallowed up in the pounding torrent that was pouring into A Deck. Ten seconds after his friend disappeared, Thayer sat on the rail; facing outward, he gave a powerful thrust with his arms and leaped out as far from the ship as possible.

The shock of the freezing water knocked Thayer's breath out of him. When he recovered, he began furiously swimming away, but rested some forty yards from the side of the ship. Buoyed by his life jacket, Thayer turned around and stared at the Titanic: *"The ship seemed to be surrounded with a glare, and stood out of the night as though she were on fire. I watched her. I don't know why I didn't keep swimming away. Fascinated, I seemed tied to the spot."*

Those safely away in the lifeboats were also staring transfixed at the liner—a behemoth now groaning in its death throes. Bow down, she was steadily tilting forward, her first funnel partly submerged. To Charlotte Collyer in Number 14 she looked "like an enormous glowworm, for she was alight from the rising water line, clear to her stern—electric lights blazing in every cabin, lights on all the decks, and lights on her mastheads." Even the lights in the submerged portion of the ship continued burning, suffusing the water around her with a murky, soft-green radiance.

Suddenly, no sound could be heard from the Titanic *by those in the boats except the music of the band, which wafted over the sea. Many became aware of the music for the first time. They were playing "Autumn":*

> *God of mercy and compassion,*
> *Look with pity on my pain;*
> *Hear a mournful, broken spirit*
> *Prostrate at Thy feet complain . . .*
> *Hold me up in mighty waters,*
> *Keep my eyes on things above—*
> *Righteousness, divine atonement,*
> *Peace and everlasting love.*

The Titanic *continued her slow, forward descent, and Jack Thayer—still forty yards away—could hear "distinct wrenchings and tearings of boilers and engines from their beds." At once, the structure supporting the first funnel collapsed. The mammoth smokestack seemed to lift off like a missile—its steel hawsers tearing the planking out of the decks—be-*

fore it toppled onto the people in the water. The occupants of collapsible "A" were so close to it they could only think the entire forepart of the ship had exploded. It seemed to "rip the bottom out of our boat and throw us clear around the Titanic *to the other side." To Mrs. Collyer in Number 14, it was as if "something in the very bowels of the* Titanic *exploded, and millions of sparks shot up to the sky, like rockets in a park on the night of a summer holiday. This red spurt was fan-shaped as it went up, but the sparks descended in every direction, in the shape of a fountain of fire. Two other explosions followed, dull and heavy, as if below the surface."*

Her bulkheads were now giving way. Crushed between the pressure of the sea and the gargantuan tonnage of the foundering liner, the celebrated watertight bulkheads crumpled with "big booms." The dense cork lining inside the bulkheads shot up in sprays and spread out over the surface of the sea. Sliding forward, the Titanic *now reached a point of equilibrium astern of midships. The second funnel was partly submerged. The forward motion of the ship ceased, and with a wrenching moan the stern began slowly rising into the air.*

Lifeboat Number 8 and several others were obeying E.J.'s last command and rowing toward the "mystery ship."

In Number 6, everyone heard "a rumbling sound . . . then a sort of an explosion, then another."

In Number 5, it sounded "like the reports of a big gun in the distance." The passengers suddenly became nervous. "Let's row out a little farther," they begged the officer, who complied with the request.

In Number 9, the bosun's mate ordered the boat pulled farther away from the ship "for the safety of the people in the boat."

In Number 4, which had already picked up three people in the water, someone cried, "Pull for your lives, or you'll be sucked under!" Everyone began rowing "like mad."

In Number 2, a seaman stared at the steam and thick black smoke—even what looked like lumps of coal—belching out of the Titanic*'s funnels.*

In collapsible "D," Mrs. Goldsmith grabbed Franky by the back of the neck and crushed him to her bosom so he couldn't witness his father's fate.

In Number 1, one of the first-class gentlemen turned his head away. "I cannot look any longer." The other exclaimed, "My God, she's going now!"

The Titanic*'s stern steadily lifted upward, the ship pivoting on a center of gravity, until suddenly her lights snapped off. They came on again with a searing flash and then went out forever. Steerage passenger Carl Jansen was still on board: "We were suddenly plunged into darkness, save for the cold, clear light of the heavens, for it was a starlit night. I could not accustom myself to the change for several minutes. I think I was in a sort of daze and have no clear recollection of what happened afterward or how long a time had elapsed. Suddenly I heard shrieks and cries amidships. . . . People began to run by me toward the stern of the ship, and as I started to run I realized that the boat was beginning to go down very rapidly . . . her nose was being buried. A wave struck me and I went overboard."*

Jack Thayer had now managed to climb onto the bottom of overturned collapsible "B" and watched as the Titanic *attained a vertical position: "Her deck was turned slightly toward us. We could see groups of the almost fifteen hundred people still aboard, clinging in clusters or bunches, like swarming bees;*

only to fall in masses, pairs, or singly as the great afterpart of the ship, two hundred fifty feet of it, rose into the sky."

She now stood perpendicular and motionless, "looking like a gigantic whale submerging itself, headfirst." Her immense hull, silhouetted against the stars, pointed "like an enormous black finger" toward the heavens. The spectacle of her three massive propellers towering in the sky wavered between awesome and obscene.

She hovered "in this amazing attitude" for what seemed like five minutes, while the engines, boilers, furniture, fittings, and everything else in the ship wrenched loose and fell toward the bow. As Lawrence Beesley in Number 13 recalled: "It was partly a roar, partly a groan, partly a rattle, and partly a smash, and it was not a sudden roar as an explosion would be; it went on successively for some seconds, possibly fifteen to twenty, as the heavy machinery dropped down to the bottom (now the bows) of the ship. . . . But it was a noise no one had heard before, and no one wishes to hear again: it was stupefying, stupendous, as it came to us along the water."

The cacophony eventually ceased. The Titanic *corkscrewed slightly to port, and with a groaning shudder her stern began settling back to an angle of about seventy degrees.*

There was considerable controversy over what had happened next. A number of witnesses (particularly those closest to the wreck) perceived the sudden silence along with the settling of the stern from ninety to seventy degrees as evidence that the *Titanic* had broken in half. Through a combination of dim illumination, oblique angles, and undoubtedly wishful thinking, many thought the broken afterpart was righting itself and would float. Frank Osman, AB, stated, "After she got to a certain angle she exploded, broke in halves, and it seemed to me as if all the engines and everything that was in the afterpart slid out into the forward part, and the afterpart came up right again."

"She almost stood up perpendicular," said Steward George Crowe to Senator Bourne, "and her lights went dim, and presently she broke clean in two, probably two-thirds of the length of the ship."

"That is, two-thirds out of the water or two-thirds in the water?" asked Bourne.

"Two-thirds in the water," Crowe replied, "one-third of the aft funnel sticking up."

"How long did that third stick up?"

"After she floated back again."

"She floated back?"

"She broke, and the afterpart floated back."

But the bulk of the evidence was against this hypothesis. Technical journals agreed with the committee's conclusion. The electric lights had remained on until the *Titanic* had upended, at which time the dynamos had torn loose and crashed to the bows. To the *Marine Review*, this showed "conclusively that the immense hull held together without shearing her riveted longitudinal connections," otherwise, the wires would have stretched and snapped and the lights gone out earlier. *International Marine Engineering* was also convinced that she had gone down intact: "Such an occurrence [breaking in half] has taken place on at least three steel ships which foundered, but in those cases the ratios of breadth and depth to length were abnormal. In modern ship design the maximum shearing and longitudinal stresses are proportioned for cases as extreme, if not more extreme, than that in which the *Titanic* was placed, although the *Titanic* was in about the worst condition as far as the stresses are concerned that a ship can be in."

2:20 A.M.: *As the great ship settled back, she also began slipping under. The water engulfing her gurgled, foamed, and caught the starlight—ringing her sinking hulk with a nether halo. Scarcely fifty feet away from her in collapsible "A," August Wennerstrom was so close he couldn't really grasp all that was happening: "It was horrible; but at the same time, in a way that I am unable to explain, wonderfully dramatic." Looking upward, Wennerstrom watched as a man lowered himself from the stern down the logline. He was actually descending alongside the one-hundred-ton rudder. The ship was sinking so slowly that even at such close proximity Wennerstrom felt not the slightest trace of suction.*

The Titanic *suddenly picked up momentum in her plunge, but then paused abruptly. "Oh," said someone in collapsible "D," "she's going to float!" Mrs. Goldsmith released Franky from her bosom, and the nine-year-old focused on what was left of the ship. Nearly one hundred feet of her stern again reared up vertically and pointed at the heavens. A "huge column of black smoke" rose upward from her, "flattening out at the top like a mushroom." Franky stared at the strange outline of her rudder, which remained motionless for twenty seconds.*

"At the last," said Helen Candee, "the end of the world. A smooth, slow chute." Muffled thunder sounded deep beneath the surface of the sea, and "she went down with an awful grating, like a small boat running off a shingley beach." As her flagstaff

disappeared, the slightest ripple cascaded outward, gently rocking the debris and carnage she had left behind.

"I was taken down with the ship," Archibald Gracie told the committee. "I was hanging on to that railing, but I soon let go. I felt myself whirled around, swam under water, fearful that the hot water that came up from the boilers might boil me up—the second officer told me that he had the same feeling. I swam, it seemed to me, with unusual strength, and succeeded finally in reaching the surface and in getting a good distance away from the ship."

"How far away?" Smith asked.

"I could not say," Gracie replied, "because I could not see the ship. When I came up to the surface there was no ship there. The ship would then have been behind me, but all around me was wreckage. I saw what seemed to be bodies all around. . . . There was a sort of gulp, as if something had occurred behind me, and I suppose that was where the water was closing up where the ship had gone down."

Late Thursday evening—near the time the senators were completing their individual sessions with the crewmen—the President sat in his private coach in Boston, waiting to return to Washington. It had been a long day. As his train had cut across Massachusetts, the President's attacks on TR had grown bolder at each whistle-stop. Finishing up in Boston's Arena, Taft had finally condemned the inconsistencies of Teddy's positions, pointed out the few number of trusts the Roosevelt administration had prosecuted in contrast to his own, and listed the names of individual bosses backing the Colonel. A reporter now found Taft slumped forward on a lounge in the coach of his private train. The President suddenly buried his face in his hands, sobbing, "Roosevelt was my closest friend." The Grand Old Party—monolithic since the Civil War, the Guiding Spirit of America's Gilded Age—had now been torn in two. It would never be the same again.

15

"Pull for the Shore, Sailor"

The grimmest legacy left by the *Titanic* lay in her half-filled lifeboats, whose occupants collectively refused to return to the mass of nearly one thousand people left freezing in the water after the ship sank. William Alden pursued the subject in relentless detail, a decision many (especially in Britain) thought in the poorest possible taste. London's *Morning Post* was particularly bitter that "a disaster in which there was at least a certain dignity, in which British and Americans showed themselves on the whole worthy of their common race," had now been stripped of chivalrous romance. Attacking Chairman Smith, at whose ignorance "a schoolboy would blush," the *Post* charged that "honest Americans will feel with shame that not merely the White Star Line, but American civilisation is on its trial, and the country is coming worse out of the ordeal than the company."

The propriety of Smith's resolve in disclosing the matter depends on whether one identifies with those who had been in the lifeboats or those left struggling for their lives in the icy water. Jack Thayer, who had been in the water, had no compunction about his feelings on the subject: "The partially filled lifeboats standing by, only a few hundred yards away, never came back. Why on earth they did not come back is a mystery. How could any human being fail to heed those cries?"

In one of his most controversial interviews, Senator Smith addressed this question to Third Officer Herbert J. Pitman.

"Did you hear any cries of distress?" Smith asked Pitman.

"Oh, yes," replied the thirty-four-year-old ruddy-cheeked officer with heavily oiled and "closely patted-down" hair.

"What were they—cries for help?"

"Crying, shouting, moaning," Pitman replied.

"From the ship or from the water?"

"From the water after the ship disappeared—no noises before. . . ."

"Did you attempt to get near them?" Smith asked.

"As soon as she disappeared," said Pitman, "I said, 'Now, men, we will pull toward the wreck.' Everyone in my boat said it was a mad idea, because we had far better save what few we had in my boat than go back to the scene of the wreck and be swamped by the crowds that were there."

Pitman had lashed Number 5, his boat, to Number 7. Between the two of them there had been room for sixty more passengers.

"Tell us about your fellow passengers on that lifeboat," Smith said. "You say they discouraged you from returning or going in the direction of these cries?"

"They did," Pitman replied. "I told my men to get their oars out and pull toward the wreck—the scene of the wreck. . . . I said, 'We may be able to pick up a few more.' "

"Who demurred to that?"

"The whole crowd in my boat. A great number of them did."

"Women?"

"I couldn't discriminate whether women or men. They said it was rather a mad idea."

"I'll ask you if any woman in your boat appealed to you to return to the direction from which the cries came," said Smith.

"No one."

"You say that no woman passenger in your boat urged you to return?"

Pitman was becoming tense, and Charles Burlingham, IMM's attorney, interrupted: "It would have capsized the boat, Senator!"

"Pardon me," said Smith coolly, "I am not drawing any unfair conclusion from this. One of the officers told us that a woman in his boat urged him to return to the side of the ship. I want to be *very* sure that this officer heard no woman asking the same thing." The senator again addressed the witness: "Who demurred, now that you can specifically recall?"

"I could not name anyone in particular," Pitman replied.

"The men with the oars?"

"No, they did not. No. They started to obey my orders."

"You were in command," Smith observed. "They ought to have obeyed your orders."

"So they did," said the third officer.

"They did not—if you told them to pull toward the ship."

"They commenced pulling toward the ship, and the

passengers in my boat said it was a mad idea on my part to pull back to the ship, because if I did, we should be swamped with the crowd that was in the water, and it would add another forty to the list of drowned. And I decided I wouldn't pull back. . . ."

"How many of these cries were there?" Smith asked. "Was it a chorus, or was it—"

"I'd rather you didn't speak about that," interrupted Pitman who was becoming visibly distressed.

"I would like to know how you were impressed by it," said the senator.

"Well, I can't very well describe it. I'd rather you not speak of it."

"I realize that it isn't a pleasant theme," Smith persisted, "and yet I would like to know whether these cries were general and in chorus or desultory and occasional."

At the moment the ship disappeared "an awful shriek" arose from the wreckage. To Helen Candee, who was almost one mile away in Number 8, there was neither "wail nor frantic shout. Instead, a heavy moan as of one being from whom final agony forces a single sound."

Franky Goldsmith, one hundred fifty yards away, would never be able to forget it; after reaching Detroit, he resided near Navin Field, and the first time the Tigers hit a home run, he was instantly transported back to the thousand cries that shattered the frigid silence.

To Jack Thayer, right on the periphery of the victims, atop collapsible "B," it sounded "like locusts on a midsummer night . . ."

In collapsible "A," August Wennerstrom was right in the thick of it: "Close around us in a two-hundred-

foot circle lay a thousand souls, crying, praying, yelling, and doing their best to save their own lives. . . . They swam to us, hanging all around our canvas boat, and we all turned over. For how long a time I was away from the boat, I don't know. When I recovered consciousness I was floating on top of three human lives interlocked together. . . . When I came back to our boat, it was filled with water and all that held us up was the cork railing around the boat."

Wennerstrom climbed back in the swamped collapsible. His friend Edvard Lindell had also got aboard, but Mrs. Lindell was missing. Looking around, Wennerstrom saw her in the water and clasped her by the hand; he didn't have the strength to pull her aboard. After a half hour, he lost his grip and saw her disappear beneath the sea. Helplessly, he turned toward Mr. Lindell and, at first glance, thought his friend had aged sixty years. "His face had sunk in, his hair and mustache were gray, his eyes had changed. . . . He just looked straight ahead, never made a move or said a word." Closer inspection revealed that Mr. Lindell had frozen to death.

The "long continuous wailing chant" persisted, greatly disturbing everyone in the lifeboats. A number of women, particularly emigrants, suddenly remembered those they had left on board and "sent screams for them ringing to the stars in a maniac babytalk" In Number 13, several people began rowing away and singing "to keep from thinking of them":

Pull for the shore, sailor, pull for the shore!
Heed not the rolling waves, but bend to the oar;
Safe in the lifeboat, sailor, cling to self no more!
Leave the poor old stranded wreck, and pull for
the shore.

Seaman Fred Clench in Number 12 we tried to console the ladies: "I told them it was men in the boats shouting out to the others to keep them from getting away from one another." In Number 11, someone led the passengers in a cheer, and everyone "cheered and cheered to drown the screams." In Number 14, Officer Lowe also suggested "a good song to sing":

Throw out the Life-Line! Throw out the Life-Line!
Someone is drifting away;
Throw out the Life-Line! Throw out the Life-Line!
Someone is sinking today.

"There was a continual moan for about an hour," Pitman said, his eyes tearing with the memory.

"And you lay in the vicinity of that scene for about an hour?"

Pitman's voice suddenly broke with emotion. "Oh, *please,* sir, don't! I cannot bear to recall it. I wish we might not discuss the scene!"

Smith tapped stenographer Bill McKinstry on the wrist, indicating that the third officer's breakdown was "off the record." To Pitman, Smith said very softly, "I have no desire to lacerate your feelings. But we must know whether you drifted in the vicinity of that scene for about an hour."

"Oh, yes," Pitman sobbed. "We were in the vicinity of the wreck the whole time. . . ."

"Did this anguish or these cries of distress die away?"

"Yes, they—they died away gradually."

"Did they continue during most of the hour?"

"Oh, yes—I think so. It may have been a shorter time—of course I didn't watch every *five* minutes!"

"I understand that," Smith said quietly, "and I am

not trying to ask about a question of five minutes. Is that all you care to say?"

Pitman wiped his eyes with a handkerchief. "I'd rather you'd have left that out altogether."

"I know you would," said the senator, "but I must know what efforts you made to save the lives of passengers and crew under your charge. If that is all the effort you made, say so and I will stop that branch of my examination."

"That is all, sir! That's all the effort I made."

In the senators' private interviews with the crewmen, the story was the same. Many, like Pitman, blamed the predominantly female passengers in the boats. Frank Osman in Number 2 explained, "The women were all nervous and we pulled as far as we could get from her, so that the women could not see, and it would not cause a panic." George Moore in Number 3 told Senator Newlands: "All the people in the boat wanted to get clear of the ship. They didn't want to go near her. They kept urging me to keep away—to pull away from her." Fireman W.H. Taylor in Number 1 claimed that "a majority" of the passengers (there were only five of them in his boat) said "pull on," because of the anticiapted suction, which never occurred.

Several passengers and one steward, however, blamed the crewmen in charge. Major Peuchen had been furious with Quartermaster Hichens in Number 6. When a number of ladies in the boat asked to row back, Hichens had said, "No, we are not going back to the boat. It is our lives now, not theirs." Peuchen related: "He said it was no use going back there; there was only a lot of 'stiffs' there, which as very unkind, and the women resented it very much. I do not think he was qualified to be a quartermaster."

Ernest Archer told about a lady who asked that Number 16 be taken "back and see if there was anyone in the water we could pick up," but Archer never heard any more about it after that. Fred Ray, a softspoken but doughty steward in Number 13, related: "I was not in charge of the boat—I was only pulling an oar. I objected to pulling away from the ship at all . . . but of course my voice wasn't much against the others. We had six oars in the boat, and several times I refused to row, but eventually gave in and pulled with the others."

In the midst of so many similar accounts, the behavior of three men—Lowe, Perkis, and McCarthy—offered a striking contrast. Quartermaster Walter Perkis and his mate W. McCarthy had been in charge of Number 4.

> *Number 4 had already picked up the three men who had let themselves into the water from loose ropes on the ship's davits. When the* Titanic *went down, their boat was about a ship's length away. Perkis and McCarthy conferred and began rowing toward the periphery of the mass in the water. Several women shrieked and protested, going so far as to throw themselves on the oars so the men couldn't row. "There was a great deal of commotion" at this point, and a few women—notably Mrs. Astor—were instrumental in calming the nervous ladies. As Number 4 approached the edge of the bobbing, moaning horde, a few in the water saw it and began swimming toward it. McCarthy and another oarsman pulled in five men, among them Paddy Dillon. Paddy's bottle of brandy was discovered and pitched overboard; the fireman himself was dumped in a heap in the bottom of the boat and a blanket thrown over him. Of the five men, two died before Number 4 reached the* Car-

pathia. *Perkis then saw Officer Lowe's boat, Number 14, along with numbers 10, 12, and "D," and rowed toward the little group.*

Officer Harold Lowe had already told the committee what he had done after the ship foundered, and his account was consistently borne out in testimony of the crewmen.

When Number 4 came alongside Number 14 with the eight soaking men they had pulled aboard, Lowe made up his mind. In a loud voice, the fifth officer announced to everyone that the lifeboats had been unsatisfactorily filled and that he was now going to distribute the fifty-eight occupants of Number 14 into the other four boats. There were a few protests, but Lowe began snappily executing the transfer. A lady from Wisconsin apparently hesitated too much to suit the fifth officer. "Jump, goddamn you, jump!" he blared at the woman, who was speechless with indignation. When Number 14 was empty, Lowe picked a crew of seamen from the other four boats; he also took a passenger who volunteered.

Lowe had already ordered the mast up in Number 14, but there wasn't yet enough wind to hoist the sail. For the next hour and a half he waited for "the yells and shrieks" to subside—"for the people to thin out." Lowe listened to the unholy sound with cold-blooded detachment. At a certain point he suddenly decided it was safe to take the boat into the mob. The officer failed to anticipate that those who had endured were sparsely scattered among the carnage. By the time he maneuvered Number 14 into the mass of floating bodies, it was barely possible to tell where and from whom the few faint cries were coming.

"Were there many dead?" Senator Fletcher asked Seaman Edward Buley, one of Number 14's oarsmen.

"Yes, sir," Buley replied, "there were a good few dead, sir. Of course, you couldn't discern them exactly on account of the wreckage, but we turned over several of them to see if they were alive. It looked as though none of them were drowned. They looked as though they were frozen. The life belts they had on were that much"—Buley pointed at the top of his chest—"out of the water, and their heads laid back with their faces on the water, several of them. Their hands were coming up like that." Buley wafted his arms up abreast of his head.

"They were head and shoulders out of the water?" Fletcher asked.

"Yes, sir. . . ."

"They were not apparently drowned?"

"It looked as though they were frozen altogether, sir."

Finally, a man was found alive. He was enormous and his clothes completely waterlogged—it took the boat's entire crew to haul him into Number 14. The survivor, who turned out to be a passenger from New York, was propped up in the stern of the boat. He was bleeding from the nose and mouth. A steward took his collar off and chafed his limbs, but the pressure at the depth he had gone down with the ship ultimately proved too much for him, and he died before Number 14 reached the Carpathia. *Another cry was heard soon thereafter, but in the half hour it took for the men to reach him, he too had perished.*

"Going farther into the wreckage," Steward Crowe related, "we came across a steward or one of the crew, and we got him into the boat, and he was very cold and his hands were kind of stiff, but we got him in and he recovered by the time we got back to the *Carpathia.*"

"Did he survive?" asked Senator Bourne.

"Yes, sir. Also a Japanese or Chinese young fellow that we picked up on top of some of the wreckage."

The Oriental had somehow managed to lash himself onto a door and was lying face down on it, perfectly still, the sea washing over him as the door bobbed on the water. "What's the use?" exclaimed Lowe. "He's dead, likely, and if he isn't there's others better worth saving than a Jap!" Lowe later changed his mind, and the Oriental was taken aboard. He recovered and babbled a few words into the uncomprehending faces he found staring at him. He then arose, stretched his arms over his head, and began stamping his feet. In five minutes he was at an oar, pulling for all he was worth. Lowe stared at him agape. "By Jove!" blurted the fifth officer, "I'm ashamed of what I said about the little blighter. I'd save the likes o' him six times over if I got the chance."

Altogether, Lowe and his men had been able to rescue only three people alive. In the meantime, Numbers 12, 10, 4, and collapsible "D" had been left drifting. Fred Clench had been left in charge of Number 12 and related: "While Mr. Lowe was gone, I heard shouts. Of course I looked around, and I saw a boat in the way that appeared to be like a funnel."

Terrified at the impossible specter of the lost *Titanic*'s funnel coming at them, the four boats had cut loose.

"We started to back away then," said Clench. "We thought it was the top of the funnel. I put my head over the gunwale, and looked along the water's edge and saw [instead] some men on a raft. Then I heard two whistles blown."

Overturned collapsible "B" had barely been able to stay afloat with all the men standing on its bottom. Two had already died and slipped over the side. Gracie, Thayer, Carl Jansen, Bride, and twenty-five others were still standing, with Officer Lightoller in charge. Gracie had been focusing on some distant lights which he was hoping was the rescuing steamer. "Finally," Gracie related, "dawn appeared and there on the port side of our upset boat where we had been looking with anxious eyes, glory be to God, we saw the steamer Carpathia *about four or five miles away, with other* Titanic *lifeboats rowing towards her."*

The wind came up and the sea suddenly turned choppy. Lightoller was barely able to keep the boat trim by having the men lean this way and that. Lightoller than thought he saw a lifeboat in the distance. Putting his officer's whistle to his cold lips, he blew two shrill blasts.

Seaman Clench continued: "I sang out, 'Aye, aye; I'm coming over,' and we pulled over and found it was a raft—not a raft exactly, but an overturned boat—and Mr. Lightoller was there on that boat, and I believe, I do not know whether I am right or not, but I think the wireless operator was on there too. We took them on board the boat and we shared the amount of the room that was there. . . ."

"Then what did you do?" Senator Bourne asked.

"Mr. Lightoller took charge of us," said Clench, "and sighted the *Carpathia*'s lights. Then we started heading for that."

In the meantime, collapsible "D," her seamen having been removed earlier by Lowe, had floated about aimlessly. By this time, Lowe had completed his search and, taking advantage of the breeze, hoisted the sail forward.

Under sail, number 14 was "bowling along very nicely" at about five knots when Lowe spotted "D." He sailed over to her, piping, "Are you a collapsible?" "Yes," came the answer. "How are you?" Lowe asked. "We have about all we want." (They were afraid the fifth officer was again going to dump passengers into their heavily laden boat.) "Would you like a tow?" Lowe asked. "Yes, we would!" A rope was tossed to the collapsible, and Lowe ("both a sailor and a boatman") pulled her toward the Carpathia.

Lowe had then discovered collapsible "A," in a "worse plight" than the one he was towing. He at first considered cutting loose of "D" for the sake of speed, but decided he could manage it in time. Seaman Evans, one of Number 14's crew, told Senator Smith that the fifth officer had fired four shots when he came up to "A." "She was half full of water," Evans recounted, "and they were up to their ankles in water. There was one collapsible boat that we had in tow, and we went over to this one that was swamped, sir. . . ."

"How far was this swamped collapsible lifeboat from lifeboat Number Fourteen when you started to it?" Smith asked.

"About a mile and a half, sir," Evans replied.

"How near were you to the swamped boat when Lowe fired those shots?"

"About a hundred and fifty yards, sir."

"Did he say anything at the time he did it?"

"No, sir, he just mentioned the fact that they must not rush the boat, as it was liable to capsize her."

The occupants of collapsible "A" didn't have the strength to "rush" Lowe's boat. August Wennerstrom noted, "All the feeling had left us. If we wanted to know if we still had legs (or any other part) left, we had to feel down in the water with our hand. . . . The only exercise we got was when someone gave up hope and died, whom we immediately threw overboard to give the live ones a little more space and at the same time lighten the weight of the boat."

There were twelve people still alive in "A," including one woman. When they perceived the miraculous spectacle of "a sailboat" coming up on them, they synchronized their shouts: "One-two-three, HELP!" Lowe sailed up to them and took off the twelve survivors. There were three bodies left in "A." "Are you sure they're dead?" Lowe asked. "Absolutely sure," someone replied; they had been dead for some time. Before the survivors of "A" were taken into Number 14, they draped life belts over the faces of the three corpses. Lowe was sure the swamped collapsible would capsize and sink in a matter of minutes.

On Wednesday, Senator Smith had asked Lowe, "After taking these passengers from that collapsible that was injured, you headed in the direction of the *Carpathia?*"

"Yes," said Lowe, "I left for the *Carpathia.*"

"Did you succeed in landing them?"

"I landed everybody."

"All of them?"

"And the corpse included."

"Including the corpse of the man that had died on your boat?" This was the corpulent gentleman, the first person taken from the water by Number 14.

"Yes," Lowe replied.

"What, if anything, did you do after that?"

"There was nothing to do, sir. What was there to do?"

"I did not say there was anything," said William Alden. "I simply asked what you did."

"Nothing, sir. There was nothing to do."

Chairman Smith had already obtained testimony on the *Carpathia*'s rescue from Captain Rostron in New York. At this point in the proceedings, the committee focused its attention on another ship that had been close by.

16

The *Californian* Incident

William Alden had not forgotten Fourth Officer Boxhall's testimony about the "mystery ship" that had purportedly failed to come to the *Titanic*'s rescue. Every witness interrogated after Boxhall had been asked about the strange lights in the distance. Smith had earmarked the issue for special probing by the senators during their private sessions with the *Titanic*'s crewmen, and by the end of the week a substantial amount of data had been collected on the mystery ship.

Joseph Boxhall had implicated a steamer in Monday's testimony, and his account now stood corroborated by an able seaman and a steward. Seaman Buley was emphatic. "You could see she was a steamer," he said. "She had her steamer lights burning." Buley believed that the unidentified vessel could not have helped but see the *Titanic*'s rockets. "She was close enough to see our lights and to see the ship itself and also the rockets. She was *bound* to see them." Buley also introduced the interesting fact that although the ship's failure to respond to the *Titanic*'s distress had proved fatal for 1,522 people, she nevertheless served the useful purpose of a focus for those who had been lucky enough to escape in a lifeboat. E.J. had ordered the lead boats to row toward the lights of the mystery ship, and other boats had followed. "That's what kept the boats together," Buley explained.

Steward Alfred Crawford was calmly certain that "Captain Smith could see the light quite plain, as he pointed in the direction that we were to make for." Crawford was convinced that the ship had been a steamer, since it had carried two lights. "They were stationary masthead lights, one on the fore and one on the main." Crawford had seen the steamer lying dead in the water "not further than ten miles away."

Other witnesses testified to seeing the strange vessel, but were far from certain she had been a steamer. Officer Pitman and Lookout Fleet had seen only one stationary light, which Fleet had taken to be "a fisher sail." Quartermaster Hichens thought she'd been "a codbanker." Quartermaster Rowe thought he had seen the stern light of "a sailing ship." Seamen Frank Osman and George Moore and Steward Henry Etches had seen only one light, which they believed was "a sailing vessel from the Banks." Charles Lightoller had also seen just one light, but hastened to add that this had been with the naked eye. (Only Captain Smith and Joseph Boxhall had viewed the ship through glasses.) Passengers yet to be interrogated would confirm the presence that night of a strange light in the distance, shining eerily as if projected through "a frosted windowpane." The passengers, however, couldn't tell if it had been a steamer, a sailing ship, or a star's reflection off an iceberg.

In logically analyzing the inconsistent accounts of the mystery ship, the first obstacle is that of determining the compass point at which she had appeared. Lightoller was specifically asked the compass bearing of the light, but had no idea. The *Titanic* had been heading west-southwest at the time of the collision, but no one could say in which direction she had foundered. Accounts were consistent, however, that the mystery ship had been seen off the *Titanic*'s bows shortly after the collision. Some believed she had been directly off the bows. Boxhall thought she'd been a half point off the port bow, Lightoller two points off the port bow. But in what direction had the *Titanic*'s bows been pointing?

That question can be answered only circumstantially. It may be recalled that at the time of the collision, when the ship was heading westerly, Murdoch had ordered "hard astarboard" and then "hard aport" in his unsuccessful attempt to dodge the iceberg. In addition to the 3,000 feet the *Titanic* would have traveled before stopping, the captain had subsequently ordered his ship half speed ahead a few minutes—the rudder remaining throughout in the hard-aport position. This would have brought the *Titanic*'s bows in a northerly direction, for which there is supportive evidence. Passenger Lawrence Beesley—an acute observer by any standard—recorded:

> We rowed forward in the direction the *Titanic*'s bows were pointing before she sank. I see now that we must have been pointing northwest, for we presently saw the Northern Lights on the starboard, and again when the *Carpathia* came up from the south, we saw her from behind us on the southeast and turned our boats around to get to her.

Other passengers who had pulled away from the *Titanic*'s sinking bow talked about rowing directly toward the Northern Lights or following the North Star. Also, Seaman George Moore remembered than the lifeboats had been heading into the wind, which had come up from the north.

Following Boxhall's introduction of the mystery ship on Monday, a rash of rumors came to William Alden's attention. The Canadian liner *Mount Temple* had attempted coming to the *Titanic*'s rescue, but had been stopped by an immense ice barrier some eighteen miles southwest of the *Titanic*'s radioed position. After speculation mounted in the newspapers, a Toronto physician who had been a passenger on the *Mount Temple* that night told the press that he had seen the lights of the *Titanic* in the early hours of April 15, but that the *Mount Temple* had stopped her engines and done nothing. Smith instantly dispatched one of the Michigan Minutemen to Toronto. After interviewing Dr. Quitzrau, however, "Ab" Carroll decided his trip had not been worthwhile. Dr. Quitzrau's evidence was hearsay—he had seen no lights himself. Secondly, the *Titanic* was supposedly seen from the *Mount Temple* hours after she had foundered. (Dr. Quitzrau apparently was quite upset that he hadn't been taken to Washington and complained to the vice-consul at Toronto, who appealed to Smith, who invited the doctor's useless affidavit as a matter of diplomatic tact.)

Then, on Tuesday, news came from Boston that eventually broke the case wide open. The Leyland liner *Californian,* also owned by IMM, had docked in Boston on Friday the nineteenth (the day the New York hearings began). On the morning of April 15 she had been in the North Atlantic, stopped by pack ice somewhere *north* of the *Titanic*'s position. After she came into port, rumors spread ashore that the *Californian*'s crew had seen the *Titanic*'s distress rockets. Stanley Lord, master of the *Californian,* told the Associated Press:

> About 10:30 that Sunday night we steamed into an immense ice field and immediately, as a matter of safety, our engines were shut down to wait for day-

> light. With the engines stopped, the wireless [operator] was, of course, not working, so we heard nothing of the *Titanic*'s plight until the next morning.

To the *New York World*'s correspondent, Captain Lord added:

> Up to the moment of shutting down, no message of distress or any signal was received or sighted. The first thing the *Californian* operator got was a confused message from the *Frankfurt*, from which he finally made out that the *Titanic* was in distress.

Lord claimed that the *Californian* had been "from seventeen to nineteen miles distant from the *Titanic* that night," quite outside normal visual range. The captain gently smiled at the reporters' questions about the scuttlebutt attributed to his crew. "Sailors will tell anything when they are ashore," he explained.

One sailor would not be put off so easily. After reading what his captain had given the press Tuesday, Ernest Gill, an assistant engineer aboard the *Californian*, became indignant. On Wednesday, Gill went with a reporter and four fellow engineers and swore out an affidavit that was printed the next day in the *Boston American:*

> On the night of April 14 I was on duty from 8:00 P.M. until 12:00 in the engine room. At 11:56 I came on deck. The stars were shining brightly. It was very clear and I could see for a long distance. The ship's engines had been stopped since 10:30, and she was drifting amid floe ice. I looked over the rail on the starboard side and saw the lights of a very large steamer about ten miles away. I could see her broadside lights. I watched her for fully a minute. They

could not have helped but see her from the bridge and lookout.

It was now 12:00 and I went to my cabin. I woke my mate, William Thomas. He heard the ice crunching alongside the ship and asked, "Are we in the ice?" I replied, "Yes, but it must be clear off to the starboard, for I saw a big vessel going along full speed. She looked as if she might be a big German."

I turned in, but could not sleep. In half an hour I turned out, thinking to smoke a cigarette. Because of the cargo I could not smoke 'tween decks, so I went on deck again.

I had been on deck about ten minutes when I saw a white rocket about ten miles away on the starboard side. I thought it must be a shooting star. In seven or eight minutes I saw distinctly a second rocket in the same place, and I said to myself, "That must be a vessel in distress."

It was not my business to notify the bridge or the lookouts; but they could not have helped but see them.

I knew no more until I was awakened at 6:40 by the chief engineer, who said, "Turn out to render assistance. The *Titanic* has gone down."

I exclaimed and leaped from my bunk. I went on deck and found the vessel under way and proceeding full speed. She was clear of the field ice, but there were plenty of bergs about.

I went down on watch and heard the second and fourth engineers in conversation. Mr. J.C. Evans is the second and Mr. Wooten is the fourth. The second was telling the fourth that the third officer had reported rockets had gone up in his watch. I knew then that it must have been the *Titanic* he'd seen.

The second engineer added that the captain had been notified by the apprentice officer, whose name,

I think, is Gibson, of the rockets. The skipper had told him to Morse to the vessel in distress. Mr. Stone, the second navigating officer, was on the bridge at that time, said Mr. Evans.

I overheard Mr. Evans say that more lights had been shown and more rockets went up. Then, according to Mr. Evans, Mr. Gibson went to the captain again and reported more rockets. The skipper told him to continue to Morse until he got a reply. No reply was received.

The next remark I heard the second pass was, "Why in the devil they didn't wake the wireless man up?" The entire crew of the steamer have been talking among themselves about the disregard of the rockets. I personally urged several to join me in protesting the conduct of the captain, but they refused, because they feared to lose their jobs.

A day or two before the ship reached port the skipper called the quartermaster, who was on duty at the time the rockets were discharged, into his cabin. They were in conversation about three-quarters of an hour. The quartermster declared that he did not see the rockets.

I am quite sure that the *Californian* was less than twenty miles from the *Titanic*, which the officers report to have been our position. I could not have seen her if she had been more than 10 miles distant, and I saw her very plainly.

I have no ill will toward the captain or any other officer of the ship, and I am losing a profitable berth by making this statement. I am actuated by the desire that no captain who refuses or neglects to give aid to a vessel in distress should be able to hush up the men.

ERNEST GILL

The *Boston American* wired Gill's complete affidavit to Senator Smith the same night it was taken. By sheer coincidence, Smith had already planned to subpoena Captain Lord and his wireless operator for their evidence on the ice warning they had sent the *Titanic* and which Harold Bride had been rather vague about in New York. Smith quickly added Ernest Gill's name to the list of those he wanted subpoenaed and wired the list to the U.S. marshal in Boston.

The men from the *Californian* arrived in Washington Friday, April 26, at 1:00 P.M. P.A.S. Franklin was on the stand at the time; turning the questioning over to Senator Fletcher, Smith slipped out of the room. Introducing himself to Ernest Gill, Smith directed the twenty-eight-year-old sailor to his private office. At this point in time, the senator was unconvinced that Gill's fabulous story was anything more than another canard. In view of the fact that the subcommittee members were now rotating in shifts between the *Titanic* inquiry and the full Committee on Commerce, their time had grown precious. If Smith could quickly discredit the assistant engineer's story, the committee could be spared the waste of pursuing a red herring.

Inside his office, Smith showed Gill a copy of the affidavit and asked if it were true. The "rather wild-looking young man" with strawberry-blond hair and a shaggy mustache was skittish and fidgety, but stuck doggedly to the essentials of his affidavit. Smith then asked outright how much the *Boston American* had paid him for the story. Five hundred dollars, came the snappy reply. But the story was true, Gill insisted. He couldn't have given out the story unless he'd been paid for it; he fully expected to "get the sack" as soon as the captain got wind of it, and he'd need the money between his present job and the next. Smith asked if he'd been dismissed. Not yet, Gill responded. The senator suddenly found Gill's unsophisticated candor appealing. After only fifteen minutes, William Alden terminated the private interview and whisked Gill to the hearing room.

Smith read the affidavit to the committee, who listened incredulously. They had been given no warning of this development—Smith had not bothered to mention it until he had checked out Gill's credibility. Gill was led through the details of his statement. He had seen two rockets to the south that night, either "pale blue or white" in color. There was no mistaking they'd been distress rockets; they had exploded in the air, and "the stars spangled out" from them. Gill claimed to have first seen a large liner. About thirty-five minutes later (12:42 *Titanic* time), he had seen the two rockets. There had been no sign of the ship then—the rockets had come up over the horizon. "I am of the general opinion that the crew is," Gill concluded, "that she was the *Titanic.*"

The committee broke for lunch. While Senators Newland and Fletcher left the building muttering about Gill's testimony, William Alden slipped into the Committee of Commerce sessions and found Senators Bourne, Burton, and Perkins. He informed them what had just transpired and asked if they could break away a few minutes in the afternoon to hear the testimony of Captain Lord himself. They immediately agreed.

Captain Stanley Lord took the stand directly after the recess. Tall with a slight stoop, Lord was an extremely red-faced man with what was described as "an enormously high forehead and a lantern jaw." He sat in the chair clutching his logbook, which Smith had specifically requested that he bring. Lord spoke in a low monotone, and although somewhat stiff and formal, he gave his utmost cooperation to the committee. Before delving into what has since become known as "the *Californian* incident," Smith milked the captain for his expert opinion on a variety of issues already of concern to the committee.

Lord testified to the remarkable quantity of ice in the region—a rare phenomenon for that latitude. After he had received an ice warning from the *Coronian,* Lord himself had remained on the bridge for almost the entire day and had posted an extra lookout on the forecastle head; the situation, he thought, warranted the extra lookout. Although the captain disclaimed the need for binoculars in the crow's nest, he did confirm that the temperature of the water was a practical indicator of large bodies of ice. He mentioned that in fog, when he was "anywhere near the ice track," he always took the temperature of the water every five to ten minutes. When Lord had perceived the ice situation hazardous in the extreme, he closed his ship down for the night. There was no doubt in anyone's mind that Captain Lord was a most prudent master. The issue at hand was whether he was a conscientious one as well.

Although Lord read a number of passages from his logbook describing the events of the night, Smith heard no mention of rockets. (In fact, the sighting of rockets was to be found *nowhere* in the log.) Finally, Smith introduced the subject.

"I think you had better let me tell you that story," Lord offered.

"I wish you would," replied William Alden, settling back in his chair.

"When I came off the bridge at half past ten," Lord began, "I pointed out to the [third] officer that I thought I saw a light coming along. It was a most peculiar night; we had been making mistakes all along with the stars, thinking they were signals." The signals Lord was referring to at this point in his testimony were ship's steaming and masthead lights.

"We could not distinguish where the sky ended and where the water commenced," the captain continued. "You understand, it was a flat calm. [The officer] said he thought it was a star, and I did not say anything more. I went down below. I was talking with the engineer about keeping the steam ready, and we saw these signals coming along and I said, 'There is a steamer coming. Let's go to the wireless and see what the news is.' "

In the Marconi cabin Lord asked Operator Cyril Evans what ships he had. "Only the Titanic,*" Evans replied. Lord was sure the steamer he'd seen wasn't the* Titanic; *she was far too small. Perhaps this ship to the south didn't have wireless—that's why Evans hadn't heard anything from her. The captain told Evans to let the* Titanic *know that due to "the dangerous proximity of ice" the* Californian *had stopped for the night.*

Lord then returned to the bridge where he found his third officer scrutinizing the unidentified steamer to the south. Although the officer had at first mistaken the ship for a star, she had now come close enough for him to make her out as a passenger liner. At 11:50, the officer had watched her lights flash out—either they had been put out for the night or else the ship had turned sharply. She now seemed to be stopped, pointing north toward the Californian; *the officer could see her red port light.*

"Can you make anything out of her lights?" the captain asked. "She is evidently a passenger steamer coming up on us," the officer replied. "That does not look like a passenger ship," Lord said. "It is, sir," affirmed the officer.

The captain told him to call her up on the Morse lamp.

"We signaled her at half past eleven with the Morse lamp," Lord continued. "She did not take the slightest notice of it. . . . We signaled her again at ten minutes past twelve, half past twelve, a quarter to one, and one o'clock. We have a very powerful Morse lamp. I suppose you can see that about ten miles, and she was about four miles off, and she did not take the slightest notice of it. When the second officer came on the bridge, at twelve or twelve ten, I told him to watch that steamer, which was stopped, and I pointed out the ice to him. . . . At ten minutes to one, I whistled up the speaking tube and asked him if she was getting any nearer. He said, 'No, she is not taking any notice of us.' So I said, 'I will go and lie down a bit.' At a quarter past one, [the second officer] said, 'I think she has fired a rocket.' "

It had first appeared as "a white flash in the sky." With his glasses, the second officer saw four more of them—definitely white rockets—sent up at three- or four-minute intervals. They didn't seem to go up as high as distress rockets and he could not hear them exploding, but the officer called up the captain regardless. Lord wanted to know if they were "company signals"—colored flares used between ships for identification purposes. The officer replied that he didn't know, but that they were all white. Captain Lord told him to "go on Morseing."

"So," Captain Lord continued, "he put the whistle back and apparently he was calling. I could hear [the Morse lamp] ticking over my head. Then I went to sleep."

Lord had apparently reached the end of his story and paused, awaiting questions from the senators. According to reporters, he seemed oblivious to the intense state of arousal he had caused in the committee.

"You heard nothing more about it?" Smith asked hoarsely.

"Nothing more until about between [1:15] and half past four," Lord replied.

Five rockets had already been seen by the second officer. The apprentice took up the Morse lamp and resumed signaling. For a moment he thought he was getting a response from the ship to the south. He observed her through the glasses. No, he finally said to the officer, it was "just her mast light flickering." The glasses still to his eyes, the apprentice saw a sixth rocket: "a white flash on the deck followed by a faint streak towards the sky which then burst into white stars." Two more rockets followed. It was now 1:50 A.M.

"Look at her now," the officer said, pointing at the unidentified vessel. "She looks very queer out of the water—her lights look queer." It seemed as if the strange ship was listing. Then she began "disappearing in the southwest." By 2:15, they could no longer see her, so the officer sent the apprentice down to tell the captain.

The captain had been sleeping, but he sat up, eyes opened, when the apprentice entered his room. The apprentice told him that, altogether, the strange ship had fired eight rockets and "had gone out of sight to the southwest." "All right," said Lord, "are you sure there were no colors in them?" "No," the apprentice replied, "they were all white." The captain asked what time it was and then went back to sleep.

Lord continued his testimony. "I have a faint recollection of the apprentice opening my room door—opening it and shutting it. . . . I believe the boy came down to deliver me the message that this steamer had steamed away from us to the southwest, showing several of these flashes or white rockets."

The men on the bridge had never said that the strange ship had "steamed away." They said she had "disappeared" or "gone out of sight" to the southwest.

"Captain," said Smith, "these Morse signals are a sort of language or method by which ships speak to one another?"

"Yes, sir. At night."

"The rockets that are used are for the same purpose and are understood, are they not, among mariners?" Smith was building a case.

"As being distress rockets?" asked the captain.

"Yes."

"Oh, yes," Lord replied. "You *never* mistake a distress rocket."

"Suppose the Morse signals and the rockets were displayed and exploded on the *Titanic* continuously for a half to three-quarters of an hour after she struck ice. Would you, from the position of your ship *on a night like Sunday night,* have been able to see those signals?"

"From the position [the *Titanic*] was supposed to have been in?"

"Yes."

"We could not have seen her Morse code. That is an utter impossibility."

"Could you have seen her rockets?"

"I do not think so. Nineteen and a half miles is a long ways. It would have been way down on the horizon. [Gill's affidavit and the testimony the *Californian*'s officers eventually gave before the British inquiry were consistent with the rockets appearing 'way down on the horizon.'] It might have been mistaken for a shooting star," Lord continued, "or anything at all."

But no one aboard the *Californian* mentioned shooting stars. What had been seen were described as rockets—*eight* white rockets.

Captain Lord's interrogation had been remarkably brief. During the noon recess, the captain had mentioned to Smith that he hoped to catch the next train back to Boston so that he could keep his schedule and sail back to England the next morning. The committee therefore turned to the *Californian*'s wireless operator, twenty-year-old Cyril Evans.

Evans's presence had been originally requested so that the committee could learn more about the ice warning the *Californian* had sent to the *Titanic* Sunday afternoon. In light of Lord's testimony, however, the senators were more interested in what message Evans had sent by the captain's orders shortly after the *Californian* had spotted the strange vessel to the south. The exchange between the *Titanic* and the *Californian* that moment epitomized the two ships' bizarre inability to communicate, and the faces of the senators were chalk-white with tension as Evans related it.

"The captain told me he was going to stop because of the ice," Evans explained, "and the captain asked me if I had any boats, and I said, 'The *Titanic.*' He said, 'Better advise him we are surrounded by ice and stopped.' So I went to my cabin, and at five past nine New York time [less than an hour before the collision] I called him up. I said, 'Say, Old Man, we are stopped and surrounded by ice.' He turned around and said, 'Shut up, shut up, I am busy. I am working Cape Race and you are jamming me.' "

In New York Harold Bride had testified that Phillips had been working feverishly up to ten minutes before the collision, clearing the passengers' marconigrams through the relay station at Cape Race. Evans now explained to the committee that Phillips's rebuff wasn't all that rude or unusual. The *Titanic*'s signals had "come in with a bang," and Evans figured his own must have hit the *Titanic* the same way, thus jamming Phillips's reception of Cape Race. Of course, the idea of commercial traffic taking precedence over navigational warnings was appalling—at least it was to Chairman Smith—but there were no hard regulations governing the Marconi Marine on such matters. (William Alden would see that there *would be*, once a railroad man got through with marine legislation!)

Also relevant was the fact that Evans's message could very well have appeared to Phillips as operator-to-operator chitchat. Evans had given no indication that he was sending a warning from his captain. Although Captain Lord could have chosen to send a Master Service Message to the *Titanic*—which Phillips would have been obliged to receive, deliver to the bridge, and acknowledge—this had not been done.

Only minutes before the *Titanic*'s collision, Evans had heard Phillips still working Cape Race. Then he had hung up his headphones and turned in for the night.

"When were you awakened?" Smith asked.

"About three-thirty A.M., New York time," Evans replied.

"And who awakened you?"

"The chief officer. . . . He said, 'There is a ship that has been firing rockets in the night. Please see if there is anything the matter. . . .' "

"What did you do?"

"I jumped out of bed, slipped on a pair of trousers and a pair of slippers, and I went at once to my key and started my motor and gave CQ. About a second later I was answered by the *Frankfurt*. . . . He said, 'Do you know the *Titanic* has sunk during the night, collided with an iceberg?' "

The chief officer of the Californian *rushed the message from the wireless to the bridge. Lord was stunned by the news. "Go back again and find the position as quickly as possible," he said. The officer soon returned with the* Titanic*'s last radioed position. Lord looked at the slip of paper.*

"You must get me a better position," the captain finally said. "We do not want to go on a wild-goose chase."

Senator Fletcher began checking Ernest Gill's testimony against that of Operator Evans. "Do you know of the conversation or statement that was made to Gill about which he has testified here?" Fletcher asked.

"I do not know, sir," replied Evans. "Nearly everybody on the ship has talked amongst themselves and in front of other members of the crew about it. . . ."

"In a general way, what was the talk with reference to that you heard on the ship?"

"Well, I could not say. It was just simply the usual talk about the rockets." Evans clearly disliked the topic Fletcher had introduced.

"Were the rockets described?"

"Not to my knowledge, no, sir. I never heard them described."

Senator Burton intervened: "You say *everybody* was talking on board among themselves about these rockets?"

"Yes, sir."

"Do you mean by that that they were saying that they themselves had seen the rockets, or that there was merely talk about it on the ship?"

"There was talk about it," Evans replied, "and some

of them said they had seen it, and some said they had not."

Smith raised another issue. Recalling that the *Titanic*'s wireless had "come in with a bang" to the *Californian,* Smith asked if this in any way indicated proximity of the two ships. Evans said he didn't think so, but later, before the British inquiry, he would answer in the affirmative to the same question.

"Do you know why you were not called when the rockets were first seen?" Smith asked. This, indeed, remains the most baffling question that can be asked about the *Californian.*

"No, sir."

"What did the first mate or any other officer on the ship or member of the crew tell you about Captain Lord being notified *three times* that a vessel was sending up rockets?" Lord had admitted to hearing about the rockets only twice, the second time in a state of semiconsciousness. The "three times" had been related to Smith by Ernest Gill during his private interview.

Evans was visibly shaken by the question. "Well, we have talked among ourselves, but—"

"One minute," Smith interrupted. "I do not want any idle gossip. If you can recall anything that was said by an officer of your ship about the matter, I would like to have you state it; and if you can not, say so."

"I know that the mate did not say anything to me. No. . . ."

"Did any other officer of the *Californian* say anything to you about having notified the captain three times that a vessel was sending up rockets?"

"I think the apprentice did. . . . From people taking up the conversation I knew it was said that rockets had been seen—had been fired. They did not know what rockets they were. I know they said that rockets had been fired off, and the captain had been roused."

"How many times?"
"Three times, I think it was, sir."

From the testimony of the *Californian* witnesses—one of the shorter segments of testimony taken during the inquiry—the Smith committee would draw its furthest-reaching conclusion, one that has divided nautical experts in bitter controversy even to the present day. As far as Smith was concerned, he had heard everything he needed to hear. The *Californian*'s master had sworn to the fact of extremely hazardous conditions off the Grand Banks that night. He also admitted to extraordinarily deceptive visual conditions. Rockets had been seen from the bridge of the *Californian*—eight rockets, the same number Mr. Boxhall had fired—and had been reported to Captain Lord twice, possibly three times. But the master had remained sleeping in his chartroom, ordering his officer simply to "keep on Morseing." *He had never aroused the wireless operator.* And as far as William Alden was concerned, that was that.

There were at least two additional factors that made Captain Lord fare poorly in Smith's final evaluation. The first concerned the captain's misguided attempt to conceal the *Californian*'s sighting of rockets—no matter where they had come from. In Boston, Lord's reports to the press and others said nothing about rockets; he had even gone so far as to discredit his own crewmen, whose gossip about the rockets proved remarkable accurate. Without a doubt, the *Californian*'s logbook should have included at least some mention of the rockets—a subject conspicuous by its absence.

The second reason was even more subjective. Smith had already grown accustomed to his feelings of dismay whenever his seawise witnesses blithely testified to what seemed to him the most unregulated, unwary, and unwise practices. Compared to the railroads, Smith found the 1912 North Atlantic passenger service an almost laissez-faire operation. Without knowing more, Smith might have begrudgingly excused Lord's casual response to the rockets as on a par with his peers.

But then there was Captain Arthur W. Rostron.

The senator could not help but imagine what Rostron would have done had he been in Lord's place that night. Even today the staunchest defenders of Captain Lord shrink from speculating how Rostron would have reacted to a second officer's announcement that an unidentified vessel, near an extremely hazardous ice barrier, had sent up rockets. Rostron would have aroused the wireless operator.

Still, William Alden was no seaman, and he knew it. There were a great number of discrepancies in the testimony. The vessel Captain Lord had seen to the south was, he thought, only four miles away (Gill said ten). Most witnesses aboard the *Titanic* thought the mystery ship was no more than five miles away (Crawford said ten). But Lord claimed that the *Californian* had been at least nineteen miles away from the *Titanic*, well outside visual range of her sidelights.

Captain John Knapp of the Hydrographics Office dutifully attended every day of the Washington hearings, and Smith turned the problem over to him. Knapp spent three weeks working out detailed graphs of the reported ice near the *Titanic* when she foundered and the positions of the *Titanic* and *Californian.* With no more justification than a desire to reconcile conflicting elements in the testimony, Knapp concluded that the two ships *could* have been closer together than what Lord reported.

Smith asked Knapp if there was any evidence for a third steamer in between the two, but Knapp doubted it. "I am led to the conclusion," he said, "that if there was any vessel between the *Californian* and the *Titanic* at the time referred to she does not seem to have been seen by any of the ships near there on the following morning, nor have there been any reports submitted to the Hydrographic Office which would indicate that there was any such steamer in that locality."

In the end, Smith held Lord accountable for not attempting to come to the *Titanic*'s rescue, a conclusion later upheld by Lord Mersey's British inquiry, which was enlightened by the presence of a number of nautical experts.

The "*Californian* incident" has provoked more controversy and inspired more books and articles than any other single aspect of the *Titanic* disaster. Defenders of Captain Lord (sometimes called Lordites) believe their man was crucified unfairly because the two inquiries obviously wanted a scapegoat for the disaster. Their arguments make a good deal of sense.

Lordites are inclined toward a reductionistic examination of the evidence. Focusing predominantly on nonhuman issues, they emphasize the wide discrepancies and abundant inconsistencies in the testimony concerning positions, bearings, lights, colors, sounds, estimates of distance, and the like. They point out that the majority of the *Titanic*'s survivors thought the mystery ship had been a sailing vessel. In fact there may have been two or more sailing vessels. Mrs. Walter Clark, for example, claimed that she and the other occupants of boat Number 4 "saw three or four fishing smacks in the vicinity. We knew that they were not other lifeboats for the reason that lights could be seen high above, as if on masts." Lordites argue that such a sailing vessel, or vessels, or another steamer undoubtedly lay between the *Titanic* and the *Californian* and constituted the mystery ship(s) each had seen that night. Furthermore, the mystery ship seen by the *Titanic* had been moving toward the stricken liner, according to Boxhall, and therefore couldn't possibly be the *Californian,* which was stopped in the water, her bow slowly turning NE–SW with the drift all night long.

Lordites assume a rational basis underlying human behavior. They argue that E.J. had ordered at least two lifeboats to row some ten miles to the mystery ship, land the passengers, and then come back and take on more passengers. It was an inconceivable task. How could a man as experienced as E.J. have given such an irresponsible order—unless, as Boxhall suggested, the mystery ship was moving toward the *Titanic.* In which case: (1) E.J.'s order makes sense; and (2) the mystery ship was not the *Californian,* which was stationary all night.

Lordites take a conservative position on individual responsibility and accordingly find the maligned Captain Lord innocent of negligence.

On the other side, anti-Lordites sweep away the discrepancies and emphasize the irrationality of human behavior in a crisis and Captain Lord's duty under the circumstances. Rational sense does not have to be made of the inconsistencies in the testimony. It has been amply demonstrated that witnesses in a state of anxiety tend to perceive a singular phenomenon in vastly different ways. There may have been more than fifty different mystery ships sighted; there could well have been but one.

Boxhall's perception of movement in the mystery ship was a deduction, not an observation. He had first seen her masthead lights—and fired some rockets. He had seen her green starboard light—and fired some rockets. Finally, he was able to see her red port light. Given this sequence of perceptions plus an urgent hope (and ideal conditions for the photokinetic effect), Boxhall had concluded the ship was moving toward the *Titanic.* An alternative explanation for Boxhall's conclusion is that the mystery ship was pointing northeast and then turned to the southwest, exactly as the *Californian* had done that night.

Anti-Lordites agree that E.J.'s ordering at least two lifeboats toward the mystery ship does not make any sense. Nor do several other things that E.J. did in the course of the fatal voyage. What makes the least sense is the fact that the captain had driven his ship at nearly full speed, with no extra lookouts, directly into a hazard of which he had been amply forewarned. Without a doubt, the captain did a number of irresponsible things—his order to the lifeboats being just one of them. The senselessness of his actions cannot be discounted simply because they are senseless.

But the crucial issue for the anti-Lordites is the rockets. The *Titanic* sent up eight rockets; the *Californian* saw eight rockets. No other ship firing rockets has ever been uncovered. It matters not whether there was a sailing ship(s), a third steamer, or the entire Spanish Armada between the two vessels—rockets are rockets. Even if the rockets were those of a spectral third ship, Captain Lord was no less culpable. He knew very well the hazards of the vicinity and the significance of distress rockets at sea. He should have awakened the wireless operator.

Anti-Lordites broadly define individual responsibility and find Captain Lord guilty of negligence.

The two positions on "the *Californian* incident" represent a nearly perfect dualism. It is almost possible to study the two different sets of arguments objectively and conclude that in one context Lord's only mistake was being tragically too close to the greatest marine disaster of all time; in the second context, that he was deplorably negligent, and fortunate in having escaped prosecution. This is *almost* possible, for it must be said that the arguments of the Lordites suffer a consistent flaw. In spite of their predilection for rationalism, Lordites seem to revel in ad-hominem logical fallacies. They say, for example, the Captain Lord was condemned in Washington because Senator Smith was so stupid and that he was condemned in London because Lord Mersey and his panel of marine experts were so clever. If so, it may account for the entrenched popularity of the verdict against Captain Lord: It is a judgment on which fools *and* wise men agree, and penetrating it with rationality alone leads to the height of absurdity.

17

Corporate Culpability

Chairman Smith was beginning to show signs of strain. Throughout eight days of hearings he had averaged four hours of sleep a night, and his already small frame had shed twelve pounds. His usually infallible memory was beginning to get dates and times confused; other minor lapses were creeping into his interrogations. Michigan newsmen based in the capital discovered far more disturbing symptoms in their senior senator: William Alden was unaware where the Detroit Tigers were playing—even worse, he didn't know why Ty Cobb was batting. Smith was also growing disappointed. Although his inquiry had produced a remarkably accurate and complete portrait of the epic disaster, it had not succeeded in satisfying the basic provisions of the Harter Act. As far as the senator was concerned, he had failed in his most tangible goal. The House of Morgan could not be held responsible, and Americans suffering losses in the disaster would be unable to collect from International Mercantile Marine.

Smith had spent nights studying American merchant

marine laws, and there could be no doubt about it. Incredible as it seemed, what common sense judged as negligent navigation was blameless under existent American statutes. There were no hard rules governing the speed of passenger ships in ice zones. The only regulation of the Merchant Shipping Act on lifeboat drills directed that each drill had to be properly recorded in the ship's logbook. The absence of binoculars in the crow's nest, a dearth of seamen, inadequately trained boat crews, insufficient lifeboats—none of these constituted legal negligence in 1912. The only thing Smith could hope for was a hand in reshaping marine legislation.

Having finished with testimony on the disaster itself, Smith spent the final days of the inquiry focusing on issues that had inflamed the American public immediately following the disaster: the phony message that the *Titanic* was being towed to Halifax, the long delayed confirmation that the ship had been lost, the *Carpathia*'s radio silence en route with the survivors, and Ismay's alleged misconduct. The first issue—the bogus newsflash—had already been investigated and reported by the press. It seemed that a frenetic amateur wireless operator had picked up fragments of two unrelated marconigrams and combined them. "Is the *Titanic* safe?" and "*Asian* 300 miles west of *Titanic* and towing oil tanker to Halifax" thereby became: "*Titanic* safe—towing to Halifax." The amalgam had been endorsed and distributed by the Associated Press, since it was far more believable than the truth of the matter.

White Star's long delay in releasing the news of the *Titanic*'s loss remained a matter of public bitterness. P.A.S. Franklin had already sworn under oath that his first knowledge of the ship's foundering had come by way of the *Olympic* on Monday, April 15, at 6:16 P.M. A good deal of confusion remained about this point. According to testimony, as soon as Ismay had been taken aboard the rescue ship (about 8:15 A.M.), he had dispatched the following marconigram to his New York office:

> Deeply regret advise you *Titanic* sunk this morning, 15th, after collision with iceberg, resulting serious loss of life; further particulars later.

This message had not arrived in New York, however, until the following Wednesday—two full days later. Why had it taken so long? Mr. Marconi blamed Captain Rostron; and Senator Smith, who had the utmost faith in Rostron, wired the captain on the matter.

Rostron replied from Gibraltar:

> . . . purser asked my permission to send [Ismay's message], which I granted. As it was official message, Ismay mentally very ill at time, our purser asked him to add last three words; now find sent through Sable Island 17th April. Message given to purser afternoon of 15th; purser took message to Operator Cottam personally and gave my permission to send early as possible. I did not forbid relaying message to any ship. On contrary, I particularly mentioned doing all possible to get official messages, names of survivors, then survivors' messages away by most convenient means. By *Olympic* were sent messages signed by self to Cunard, Liverpool, and New York, White Star, and [Associated] Press messages, Ismay's almost identical with mine; worked *Olympic* as long as possible. Only messages I prevented sending were further press messages. I desire full investigation my actions.
>
> ROSTRON

Notwithstanding Rostron's orders to send the official word as early as possible and through other ships if necessary, Operator Cottam of the *Carpathia* had delayed it two days, eventually transmitting it through Sable Island. Grilled on this matter by Senator Smith, Cottam explained that it was "not customary to put official news through any other ship at all" except those of "the same line." This was not true—as the senator learned during a special interview he held with Gilbert Balfour, operator of the *Baltic* and official inspector for the Marconi Company. Balfour explained that he certainly would have transmitted such dire information through other ships in the vicinity. "Every Marconi station is supposed to assist in relaying the traffic of other ships," he explained. Asked why Cottam had handled the matter in the way he did, Balfour replied, "I could not account for it, unless perhaps he lost his head a bit."

But Cottam hadn't "lost his head." Something was going on. Smith had earlier shared with the *Washington Post* his consternation over the fact that the wireless operators "are under the control of *both* the captain of the ship and the wireless companies. It must be determined whether this divided authority is the best thing." Information eventually reached the senator suggesting that the "divided authority" issue was at least partially responsible for the problem.

On April 18, when the *Carpathia* had brought the *Titanic*'s survivors into port, the U.S. Navy had intercepted two messages sent by the Marconi Company to its two operators aboard the rescue ship. The first one:

> Say, old man, Marconi Company taking good care of you. Keep your mouth shut, and hold your story. It is fixed for you so you will get big money. Now please do your best to clear.

And the second:

> Arranged for your exclusive story for dollars in four figures, Mr. Marconi agreeing. Say nothing until you see me. Where are you now?

This was interesting. The Marconi Company had arranged for exclusive sale to *The New York Times* what its wireless operators had curiously been unable to transmit to the world. It was time to get Mr. Marconi on the stand.

After an initial period of financial hardship, the Marconi Company had slowly grown prosperous. Immediately after the *Titanic* disaster, Guglielmo Marconi had been pronounced a public savior, and stock in his corporation had risen from 55 to 225. Three days later, the company succeeded in swinging a merger with the Western Union Telegraph Company, giving it virtual control over the wireless business of the world. Long in favor of governmental regulation of the wireless, Marconi had now begun cautioning against "too much" federal interference. After all, he said, "we don't want the waves of the ether enveloped in red tape." In spite of the public accolades for the inventor, Senator Smith saw the Marconi Company as just another trust; and as such, it was fair game.

Guglielmo Marconi appeared before the committee, a slight man of average height. Although he remained an Italian citizen, his livelihood was in England (he had married the daughter of an Irish baron), and he spoke with only the slightest accent. Reporters found him "dapper, spry and smiling," and looking much younger than his thirty-seven years. Asked about the incriminating messages intercepted by the navy, Marconi explained his feeling that the two operators should be permitted to make "some small amount of money out of the information they had." It wasn't an established policy of the company to permit this, but the precedent had been set with Jack Binns, the hero of the wreck of the *Republic.* Marconi emphasized that the secrecy injunction had been transmitted just as the *Carpathia* was entering New York harbor. It therefore could not in any way have prompted the operators' silence en route.

Smith was unconvinced and came back with astonishing vehemence. "With the right to exact compensation for an exclusive story detailing the horrors of the greatest sea disaster that ever occurred in the history of the world, do you mean that an operator under your company's direction shall have the right to *prevent the public* from knowing of that calamity—"

"No!" Marconi interrupted, his face flushed.

"Hold on a moment!" Smith admonished. "From knowing of that calamity *except* through the *exclusive* appropriation of the facts by the operator who is cognizant of them?"

"I say not at all," Marconi replied. "I gave no instructions in regard to withholding any information, and I gave no advice or instructions in regard to any exclusive story to anybody. The only thing I did say or did authorize was that if he was offered payment for a story on the disaster, he was permitted, so far as the English company went, to take the money."

Marconi was skirting the truth, and William Alden knew it. The senator had already sent his nephew Martin C. Huggett and a Kalamazoo crony specially to New York to investigate the matter, and they had wired back a report. It seemed that the Marconi Company and *The New York Times* had a close relationship of long standing. The company had contracted with the *Times* for the first transatlantic wireless service, and this shared venture had proved advantageous and lucrative for both parties. Nearly six hours before the *Carpathia* docked, managing editor Carr Van Anda had persuaded Marconi to leave his supper early and go with *Times* reporter Jim Speers to the *Carpathia*. Marconi's chief engineer, at Marconi's instructions, had then sent off the two messages the navy intercepted. The *Carpathia* was off limits to all reporters, and the only way Jim Speers could have gotten aboard was on the coattails of the illustrious Italian inventor.

"Mr. Marconi," Smith asked, "did you expect the operator to syndicate this information, or to give it exclusively to one newspaper?"

"I did not expect him to give it exclusively."

"Did you expect him to put the story up to the highest bidder?"

"No, sir . . ."

"You expected that he would impart his information to *some* newspaper?"

"To *some* newspaper. I did not care which."

"Are you yourself 'interested' in any way in *The New York Times?*"

"No. . . ."

"Is any director of your company interested in *The New York Times?*"

"No!"

On it went, Marconi never admitting to any of the chairman's allegations. The other members of the investigative committee suddenly felt Smith was on dangerous ground. Marconi had been lionized by the nation, and here was William Alden treating him like any other entrepreneur of a dubious trust. Senator Newlands, whose devotion to the inquiry was second only to Smith's, became especially nervous. After the first bout, the other committee members warned Smith that it was political suicide to grill a man as popular as Marconi, but Smith didn't seem to care. As he later confided to friends, he could never resist swinging at "handmade halos."

Newlands emphasized Marconi's sworn testimony that the "secrecy injunction" had been sent just as the *Carpathia* had entered the harbor; and that the wireless boys had been given no prior motive for withholding information. But Smith reasoned that the boys would have had to be jackasses to forget the fame and fortune Jack Binns had garnered in nearly identical circumstances. Smith checked out this hypothesis with Melville Stone, general manager of the Associated Press. Stone was inclined to agree: "I think the opportunities to make money on their part would tend [toward news suppression], but I have no knowledge that anything of that kind was done. I do know this—that we were striving from Tuesday morning until Thursday night, when the *Carpathia* arrived, by every known means to get some word from the *Carpathia.*"

Smith was quick to point out that in no way did he hold the wireless boys or even the *Times* responsible for the affair. The Marconi Company alone was at fault. He agreed with Mr. Marconi that the wireless operators undoubtedly deserved monetary reward for their heroic service in the course of the disaster. But whereas Marconi had sought the solution in the exclusive sale of their information to a paper friendly to Marconi interests, Smith's solution was simpler: "Why not just pay the operators a decent wage?"

The senator, himself a newsman, was keenly aware of the potential of this newfangled gadget called radio. Speculation was already commonplace that it would surpass existent forms of mass communication, and, if so, it was imperative that the federal government intervene in the new media and regulate its practices before it grew any larger. The Marconi Company's deal with the *Times* was no more than a typical muscle flex of newly created monopolies. The disaster had demonstrated how deeply public interests could be affected by the wireless, and Smith was convinced that the goodwill of the company was insufficient to guarantee protection of those interests in the future.

Unable to get Marconi to reveal the entire story, Smith settled for the inventor's public renunciation of the policy of silencing operators for the exclusive sale of their information.

"I am entirely in favor of discouraging the practice," Marconi finally stated, "and I naturally give very great weight to any opinion expressed by the chairman of this committee."

The press went wild over the Marconi-*Times* collusion. Revealed directly before and after the *Californian* testimony, it easily overrode any interest that the mystery ship might have generated. The *Times* had been smugly congratulating itself for securing Harold Bride's copyrighted story, and now the other news services were only too happy to drag it through the muck. The Associated Press was straightforward: "TITANIC STORY IS HELD UP FOR CASH." The Pulitzers were poetic: "TRAGEDY COINED INTO DOLLARS." The Hearst organization was sensational: "NEW YORK PAPER KEPT WORLD IN AGONY WHILE DICKERING FOR WRECK NEWS."

Carr Van Anda tried to quench the accusations with cold logic: The "silence injunction" had been posed *after* the *Carpathia* had begun entering the harbor. But logic couldn't even dampen the ebullience of the other papers. Ultimately Van Anda made a major decision. The *Times* would publicly discredit the man who had revealed the information to the world.

The *Times*'s editorials immediately before and after the revelation of its collusion with Marconi make fascinating reading. Before, the *Times* had been one of Chairman Smith's staunchest defenders. It had admonished British critics not to be "too harsh" with Smith, even though he asked unseamanlike questions. After all, the senator responded to the nation's need "with laudable energy" and he "has brought out what we all wanted to know and had a right to know about the loss of the big ship—he has enabled us all to form a clear idea as to where the responsibility, direct and indirect, for that loss lies." Given a choice between eating its words and changing its tune, the *Times* changed its tune. In an editorial entitled "The Preposterous Smith," the *Times* suddenly asked, "Did the Michigan Legislature elect him as a joke?" It was melodramatically indignant that Smith "with his insulting questions and suspicions" had slurred the character of a public savior like Marconi. It opined that Smith "was put up to this wretched business by newspapers jealous of the *Times*."

Not content with this, Van Anda sent scouts on a mission to uncover what corporate payrolls the senator was on; the search was immensely disappointing. The *Times* therefore fired back with bird shot: The senator was a nautical nincompoop. He was known to walk ahead of ladies into public elevators. His *Titanic* inquiry had become an embarrassment to the nation. His fellow committee members were so "disgusted" with his stupidity, they had begun boycotting the hearings! (Actually, the senators were splitting their time between the investigation and the rivers and harbors bill.) Finally, the *Times* reprinted an outrageous cartoon of Smith which had recently appeared in the *London Graphic*.

The *Times*'s attempt to nationally discredit both Smith and his inquiry was an abysmal failure. Only a handful of conservative Republican papers jumped on its bandwagon, the bulk of these—like the *Springfield Republican* and *Boston Globe*—from Senator Lodge's home state and accustomed to criticizing Smith anyway. About this time, a surprising editorial—what one reviewer called "a sparkling article"—written by the illustrious G.K. Chesterton appeared in the *Illustrated London News:*

> I see all the English papers are sneering at Senator Smith for not knowing certain facts about shipping. Now, I can quite understand a contrary feeling in this affair. I can understand people thinking that it does not much matter whether Senator Smith knows the facts; what matters is whether he is really trying to find them out. It is not a complete answer to say that we could have appointed a president who knew much more about shipping. We might have appointed one in his place who knew far too much about shipping He might have known far too much to let any one tell the truth about it. The Americans affect me altogether as foreigners; but I know enough about foreigners to know that foreigners can correct and complete a nation.
>
> This American excitement is a thing that hardly exists in England at all. It is a thing called Public Opinion. It is impatient, inquisitive, often ferocious; but I assure you, it has its uses. Do not despise it.

A few days later, Hearst's *New York American* published an open letter. This editorial was widely reprinted and eventually read into the Congressional Record by a Democrat, Senator Davis:

> The work of the Senate committee was worthy of the best traditions of the Senate—the old-fashioned traditions, free from all empty formalism and the taint of favor and privilege.
>
> Senator Smith deserves the strongest commenda-

> tion. It was mainly due to his energetic initiative, to his searching, indefatigable patience and thoroughness, to his keen insight and strong common sense that the work was done and finished in a manner that leaves nothing to be desired.
>
> There were powerful financial interests opposed to this inquest, and there was a powerful inertia of senatorial habit that had to be overcome. But under the driving hand of the sturdy Senator from Michigan the committee took to its task without the loss of a day or an hour, and kept at it steadily . . . until the last scrap of material testimony had been wrung from the most unwilling witnesses.
>
> Americans are not greatly concerned with the criticisms that have passed upon this investigation by inspired organs of corporate influence and political red tape. . . .

With this, the *Times* shut up. It even managed adroitly to come back to the fold of Smith's admirers. "Whatever else may be said about Senator Smith," it editorialized, "he cannot be charged with trying to 'whitewash' anybody or to conceal any facts." The *Times* had learned this the hard way.

On April 29, the investigative subcommittee released the *Titanic*'s crewmen who returned to England, but J. Bruce Ismay was held an additional day. The White Star manager had already been cleared of the worst of American suspicions. He had emphatically denied that the *Titanic* had been out to set a speed record. It would, in fact, have been patently impossible. When the ship was being designed, her manager and builder had opted for luxury instead of speed; there was no way the *Titanic* could have wrested the Blue Riband away from the turbine-driven *Mauretania*. Ismay had further denied ordering the captain to a speed higher than what E.J. himself had chosen. Captain Rostron had backed Ismay up on this. So had Captain Inman Sealby, former commander of White Star's *Republic* and now a law student at the University of Michigan. Sealby had given an interview in Ann Arbor that had been forwarded to Michigan's senior senator. "It has always been my experience," said Sealby, "that owners of the White Star Line would absolutely refuse to offer any suggestion to the captain of the craft, so long as she was at sea. . . . I cannot believe [Ismay] would interfere with Captain Smith's command."

Another fact clearly brought out in the evidence was that Ismay had helped load the lifeboats and had tried to impress upon the officers the urgency of the situation—a duty E.J. had neglected. Ismay had departed not in the first lifeboat, but in one of the last; and he had jumped into it as it was being lowered. The same thing had been done by other first-class men, and Ismay emphasized that aboard the ship he had been little more than a first-class passenger. Although this is largely true, a first-class passenger automatically carried disproportionate weight aboard the *Titanic*. William E. Carter, the American who had jumped into collapsible "C" with Ismay, told the press: "One of the officers . . . declared that if [Ismay and I] wanted to, we could get into the boat if we took the place of seamen. He gave us this preference because we were among the first-class passengers." Although this account is undoubtedly false—Ismay refuted it in his evidence—it nevertheless gives a glimpse of the attitudes that prevailed among first-class passengers. But no one criticized the other fifty-three first-class men who had saved their own lives. Instead, Ismay was singled out and condemned for his lack of chivalry in refusing to go down with the ship. Eventually, the White Star manager would bear the shame for all surviving males.

Although the evidence brought out thus far in the inquiry had silenced the vocal outrage against Ismay, it had become clear to Smith that Americans had not changed their minds over the heinous crimes the White Star manager had supposedly committed. Senator Newlands had recently received a letter from Brooks Adams, the eminent Boston historian, who held Ismay responsible for the captain's negligence as well as for deficiencies of the British Board of Trade:

> [Ismay] is responsible for the lack of lifeboats, he is responsible for the captain who was so reckless, for the lack of discipline of the crew, and for the sailing directions given to the captain which probably caused his recklessness. In the face of all this he saves himself, leaving fifteen hundred men and women to perish. I know of nothing at once so cowardly and so brutal in recent history. The one thing he could have done was to prove his honesty and his sincerity by giving his life. I hope that you gentlemen will make it plain that such men cannot be kept in control of passenger ships if we can help it.

If this was the opinion of an objective historian, what must the average American be thinking? For the sake of America's peace of mind, Smith decided it was necessary for Ismay to spend another day denying all the rumors.

Following the confrontation with the senator the previous Wednesday, Ismay had become cooperative in the extreme. In contrast to his nervously guarded behavior in New York, he was now almost waxy in his compliance. He looked tired—as tired as Senator Smith.

Smith began by reviewing Ismay's intercepted marconigrams, which had implied his intent to skip back to England with the crew—the issue that had prompted William Alden's race to New York with the subpoenas. Although it was revealed that the idea of holding the *Cedric* for a speedy return to England had been Lightoller's, Ismay readily admitted that he had endorsed the plan and took full responsibility for it: "At that time, you understand, I had not the slightest idea there was going to be an investigation of this sort."

"When did you first learn of the investigation?" Smith asked.

"Five minutes before I saw you, sir."

"Who informed you?"

"Mr. Franklin. I think you came on board the ship with him, did you not, or about the same time?"

"I followed very shortly," Smith replied softly. It now seemed an eternity since the encounter which had taken place just twelve days prior.

Smith reviewed the issue of the ship's speed. "You were not looking for any greater speed, and were not crowding her for that purpose?"

"We did not expect the ship to make any better speed than the *Olympic*. No, sir."

"Did you have any talk with the captain with reference to the speed of the ship?"

"Never, sir."

By this time Smith had spoken to Mrs. Ryerson about her published interview in which she claimed that Ismay had said "we will put on more boilers" and go faster to "get out" of the ice fields. Mrs. Ryerson refused to swear to this "fact" in an affidavit. It had been "an exaggeration."

"Did you, at any time, urge [the captain] to greater speed?" Smith asked.

"No, sir."

"Do you know of *anyone* who urged him to greater speed than he was making when the ship was making seventy revolutions?"

Ismay gave a brief sigh. "It is really impossible to imagine such a thing on board ship," he said. . . .

"What can you say, Mr. Ismay, as to your treatment at the hands of the committee since you have been under our direction?" the senator asked.

"I have no fault to find," Ismay replied. "Naturally, I was disappointed in not being allowed to go home, but I feel quite satisifed you have some very good reason in your own mind for keeping me here."

There was a silence in the room—an unfathomable silence.

"You quite agree now that it was the wisest thing to do?" Smith asked.

"I think under the circumstances it was."

"And even in my refusal to permit you to go you saw no discourtesy?"

"Certainly not, sir."

On Tuesday, April 30, Ismay was released from American jurisdiction and immediately departed for England and the inquiry of his own countrymen. On the very same day, a grisly curtain call to the American investigation came by way of the funeral ship *MacKay-Bennett*'s arrival in Halifax. By this time a plausible solution to the mystery of the missing bodies had emerged. The buoyed bodies of the *Titanic*'s dead—perhaps a thousand of them—had apparently got caught up in the immense ice mass moving northeasterly in the Gulf Stream. The reason ships had failed earlier to discover the bodies was due to the fact that, in view of the disaster, they had cautiously not ventured too close to the ice. With the movement of the Gulf Stream and the breaking up of the ice, the bodies were dispersed, the numerous ships began depicting the North Atlantic as a floating graveyard. The steamer *Winifredian* saw a body twenty-five miles from where the *Titanic* had gone down. The *Minia* reported sighting seventeen corpses some forty-five miles east of the *Titanic*'s radioed position. The *Algerine*, a sealer, found more. The *Bremen* saw nearly a hundred and fifty bodies: a man in evening dress atop a door; several others on steamer chairs; two men locked arm and arm; and a woman floating with her nightgown billowing on the surface of the sea.

The *MacKay-Bennett* had found altogether 306 bodies; 116 of these were buried at sea, the rest brought in. Although it was given out that only bodies lacking identification or those in too deteriorated a condition were buried at sea, it was later revealed that the bodies of first-class passengers, no matter what their condition, were brought to the mainland. The bodies lay in a curling rink, and people from all over the United States were en route to Halifax to claim them. The President sent a member of the War Department to see if Archie Butt's body was there. It wasn't.

The *MacKay-Bennett* had of course been unable to scour the entire North Atlantic, and for weeks afterward ships continued to sight victims of the "practically unsinkable" ship. Some Scandinavian immigrants en route to Minnesota related an incident so heartbreaking and ghastly a transcription of it was sent to President Taft. "In several instances," the immigrants reported, "bodies were struck by our boat and knocked from the water several feet into the air."

The *Titanic* inquiry was now officially over. Smith spent the next day dutifully attending the Committee on

Commerce's sessions on the rivers and harbors bill, but his heart wasn't in it. His mind kept retracing themes in the testimony that disturbed him. The arcane practices of the Marconi Company demanded further exposure. Rumors were still afloat that the New York White Star office knew about the tragedy far earlier than it had admitted. And the steerage passengers. William Alden had accepted the accounts of Lightoller and the other officers that there had been no restraint of immigrants from the lifeboats. Then, near the end of the proceedings, Archibald Gracie had testified to the "mass of humanity" that poured up onto the boat deck after all the boats had gone.

Smith left the Commerce session early and went to his office where his son and secretary continued the herculean task of reading and categorizing his mail. "Go pack your things," he told them. "We're going to New York tomorrow morning."

The senator's surprise return to New York was welcomed by reporters. Asked the purpose of his visit, he explained that he was there "to take the testimony of several *Titanic* passengers and also to clean up some of the conflicting testimony on a few points." The *World* asked why he wanted to interview more passengers.

"The horrible impression remains on my mind," Smith replied, "that the people of the steerage did not get half a chance. Colonel Archibald Gracie, who was one of the last to leave the *Titanic* before she went down, testified to having seen in the last minutes a crowd of men and women from the steerage appear on the upper decks. Why hadn't those steerage people appeared on the deck before? Had they been restrained from doing so?"

A reporter from the *Times*, still attuned to Van Anda's desire to discredit the senator, asked him what he thought of the London Hippodrome's invitation to come over and perform. To the reporter's surprise, the question "seemed more to please" Smith "than annoy him."

"What did I *think* about it?" said William Alden, grinning broadly. "I thought I didn't care for it!"

Smith took up a room once again in the Waldorf-Astoria, where he and his son, Billy, arranged the interviewing of additional witnesses. Faithful Bill McKinstry was still serving as court reporter. The senator called up the Irish Immigration Society, the Hebrew Immigration Society, and the Salvation Army, asking if any steerage passengers who could speak English were still in town. Nearly all had departed for points west, but each agency managed to send over a survivor.

It came as quite a surprise to Smith that, although attempts to restrict steerage from the boats were implicit in at least two accounts, all three steerage witnesses minimized it. Irishman Daniel Buckley voiced the strongest complaint: "They tried to keep us down at first on our steerage deck. They did not want us to go up to the first-class place at all. . . . There was one steerage passenger there, and he was getting up the steps, and just as he was going in a little gate a [sailor] came along and chucked him down—threw him down into the steerage place. . . ."

"Was this gate locked?" Smith asked.

"It was not locked at the time we made the attempt to get up there," explained Buckley, "but the sailor, or whoever he was, locked it. So that this fellow that went up after him broke the lock on it, and he went after the fellow that threw him down. He said if he could get hold of him he would throw him in the ocean."

"Did these passengers in the steerage have any opportunity at all of getting out?"

"Yes, they had."

"What opportunity did they have?"

"I think they had as much chance as the first- and second-class passengers."

"After this gate was broken?"

"Yes."

Olaus Abelseth, a Norwegian immigrant and survivor of collapsible "A," recounted how a gate had been shut, but then opened for ladies to pass through. The gate was finally opened for the men.

"Do you think the passengers in the steerage and in the bow of the boat had an opportunity to get out and up on the decks, or were they held back?" asked the senator.

"Yes," replied Abelseth. "I think they had an opportunity to get up."

"There were no gates or doors locked, or anything that kept them down?"

"No, sir; not that I could see."

"You were not under restraint?" the senator persisted. "You were permitted to go aboard the boats the same as other passengers?"

"Yes, sir."

Since Smith was unable to get from the steerage witnesses any solid complaints about being barred from the boats, the issue did not figure in his final report. Certainly, the senator had expended considerable effort (particularly for 1912) toward discovering class discrimination in the *Titanic*'s lifesaving methods. But he had approached the issue from a legal standpoint and had sought the barriers in too concrete a form. Class restraints were clearly present aboard the *Titanic*—just as they were in society—but they were more subtle and far more pernicious than mere iron gates.

First of all, there was the ship's architecture. Steerage passengers were located on the lowest passenger decks, fore and aft; bulkheads separated them from midships, and they had no ready access from their own upper decks to the boat deck. As the boats were filled on a first-come-first-serve basis, it was inevitable for first-class passengers to fare some 35 percent better than steerage.

Secondly, compared with first or even second class, there were far fewer stewards to assist in organizing and directing the steerage passengers. The numerous language barriers only heightened the confusion. Berk Pickard, Smith's witness from the Hebrew Immigration Society, recounted this confusion: "There were no doors locked to prevent us from going back. I did not take much notice of it, and I went on deck. The other passengers started in arguing. One said that it was dangerous and the other said that it was not. One said white and the other said black. Instead of arguing with those people, I instantly went up to the highest spot."

Pickard had found the door between the second and third class unlocked; passing through, he had gone up to the boat deck. "The steerage passengers," he said, "so far as I could see, were not prevented from getting up to the upper decks by anybody, or by closed doors, or anything else."

Undoubtedly, the worst barriers were the ones within the steerage passengers themselves. Years of conditioning as third-class citizens led a great many of them to give up hope as soon as the crisis became evident. August Wennerstrom, who could not speak English at the time and wasn't called by Smith, later left a detailed account of the phenomenon. He had been astonished at how all the people gathered in the third-class lounges, one by one, surrendered to Fate:

> One of our friends, a man by the name of John Lundahl who had been home to the old country on a visit and was going back to the United States, said to us, "Good-bye, friends; I'm too old to fight the Atlan-

> tic." He went to the smoking room and there on a chair was awaiting his last call. So did an English lady. She sat down by the piano and, with her child on her knee, she played the piano until the Atlantic grave called them both.

Wennerstrom had been appalled at the number of people who cast their lot with God and Father Byles:

> Hundreds were in a circle with a preacher in the middle, praying, crying, asking God and Mary to help them. They lay there still crying till the water was over their heads. They just prayed and yelled, never lifting a hand to help themselves. They had lost their own will power and expected God to do all the work for them.

Barriers to steerage? Yes, but of a kind less indictable to the White Star Line than to the whole of civilization.

During his New York stay, Smith interviewed more passengers. He spoke with the manager of the Associated Press and the manager of the Dow-Jones ticker on which "news" of the *Titanic*'s tow to Halifax had first appeared. He also interviewed wireless experts—including Jack Binns—and tracked down the rumors that White Star had known earlier about the ship's foundering. He attended to a dozen other small details. The essence of it all was that there had been considerable confusion, but no subterfuge during the first week of the disaster. Franklin's claim that the New York White Star office had been unaware of the ship's true fate till late Monday was amply supported.

Smith returned to Washington and on May 10 began writing the formal report of the investigative subcommittee. The report was already slated for presentation to the full Senate in a little over two weeks. Smith held numerous consultations with Secretary Meyer and Inspector General Uhler, but he worked virtually alone on the report, aided only by his son, who indexed the voluminous testimony and endlessly cross-checked different themes as told from various points of view.

The senator once again became mindful of state politics and the fact that it was an election year. Still confident of his own position, he nevertheless worried that British criticism of himself and his state might have damaged the political prospects of fellow Michigan Republicans. He sent copies of the *Titanic* testimony to his friend Governor Osborn along with this note:

> Dear Old Chase—
>
> I am sending you the Titanic testimony. . . . I want you to know that the "fool" questions were born in simple heads and not at any time in the record. I interrogated every witness personally and looked after every detail—the whole burden fell on me and it has been honestly and vigorously performed—and I hope is no discredit to my friends. Always yours . . .

On May 20, Smith's report was approved by the subcommittee members with only one correction. Smith had chastised the White Star office in New York for sending out several telegrams assuring the *Titanic*'s safety after they had received word she had foundered. Franklin had conducted a rigorous search through the office records and concluded that the telegrams were an accident perpetrated by an unknown underling. Smith rewrote the passage in less harsh terms, and the subcommittee approved the report. On May 23, Senate Report Number 806, "The Investigation into the Loss of Steamship *Titanic*," was read and adopted by the full Committee on Commerce.

The next day, May 24, Smith tried to write a speech that would be delivered to the Senate along with the report, but for some reason could not concentrate on the task. Something was missing—he didn't know what. By then, the senator had begun reading the newspapers again and discovered that the *Olympic* was in dock in New York. He promptly cajoled Rear Admiral Richard M. Watt, chief constructor of the U.S. Navy, into accompanying him on yet another mission to New York.

The next day, May 25, the senator, the admiral, and a navy stenographer arrived in New York and went aboard the *Olympic.* Their visit was an utter surprise to Captain "Pappy" Haddock, who immediately called up IMM. P.A.S. Franklin said he would be right down, but that in the meantime Haddock should comply with anything Smith wanted.

Smith was immensely pleased by the sight of all the additional lifeboats IMM had now placed aboard the *Titanic*'s sister ship—she now carried forty-three boats—and asked the captain if it would be possible to lower one of them. Haddock was perfectly agreeable and called up six men who began removing the tarpaulin and swinging the boat out. When the gunnel of the boat was level with the rail, Smith stepped forward and, turning on every ounce of his charm, asked the captain if it would be too much bother to fill the boat with sixty-five of the ship's crew before lowering away. Haddock was taken aback, but mustered the requisite crew, who jumped in the boat. Smith stepped back from the rail, his pocketwatch and a memorandum book in hand. The crewmen fit snugly but securely in the boat, which was neatly dropped into the water. The entire operation had taken only eighteen minutes. Amazing, what a trained and experienced boat crew could accomplish!

Haddock mentioned that one of his firemen had also served aboard the *Titanic* that night, and Smith expressed immediate interest in interviewing him. Haddock was about to call the stoker on deck, but Smith explained that he would much rather go down and see the man in the fireroom. The captain called for an escort, and Chief Engineer Fleming appeared on deck. Haddock gave the senator and the admiral several large pieces of white cloth, explaining, "You'll need these to wipe the dirt from your faces."

In what the *New York Journal* called "one of the strangest official trips ever made by a U.S. Senator," Fleming escorted Smith, Watt, and the stenographer down a winding staircase into the belly of the ship, where they met Fireman Frederick Barrett in an atmosphere billowing with coal dust. Barrett showed them through the *Olympic*'s compartment Number 6, a duplicate of where he'd been the night of April 14. Smith was instantly arrested by the sight of the watertight door on compartment Number 6 and asked Barrett if it could be lowered without disturbing the ship. The fireman released the trigger manually, and Smith studied the steel door as it geared down, notch by notch.

Barrett next showed Smith the red and white lights that signaled instructions from the bridge. Until the collision that night, Barrett explained, the white light had indicated full speed ahead. The fireman also related that on Sunday the fourteenth three additional boilers had been lit for the first time, so more boilers were functioning than at any time previous. Smith's old question had finally been answered. Although, as Ismay contended, the *Titanic* had not realized her maximum speed as she entered the ice region, she had nevertheless steamed faster than ever before in her brief lifetime.

Smith now returned to Washington satisfied. Owing to the senator's frugality, the entire investigation had cost only $2,385 (in contrast to the British inquiry, which would cost $87,500). Assessing his own work in an interview in the *New York World*, Smith confessed:

> I am no sailor and don't pretend to have any nautical knowledge. . . . But just the same, I think it will be acknowledged that not a single detail it was possible to learn—important or otherwise—escaped the attention of the committee, and I am personally convinced that all the information it was humanly possible to obtain concerning the *Titanic* on this side of the Atlantic lies in that typewritten record of the committee's proceedings. If I asked questions that seemed absurd to sailors, it did no harm. Everybody isn't a sailor, and lots of people who have never been to sea want to know all about the loss of the *Titanic*, even down to the inconsequential details that marine experts scoff at. And I *know* we got the truth.

The *Titanic* disaster now dropped from the first page of the nation's newspapers. In Los Angeles, Clarence Darrow was on trial for jury bribing. In Milwaukee, Harry Houdini was thrilling audiences with his spellbinding feats. In New Jersey, Taft and Roosevelt were battling for the primary. The fight for Ohio (the President's home state) had been particularly ugly. Although Taft lost his own state to the Colonel, he was now fighting back with no holds barred. In fact, he was beginning to enjoy fighting Teddy as much as he had once appreciated his "friendship." To his Aunt Delia, Taft wrote: "I have a sense of wrong in the attitude of Theodore Roosevelt toward me which I doubt if I can ever get over. The fact is that I do not think I ought ever to get over it!" In New Jersey, the President was revealing even more of Teddy's secret deals with the trusts and emphasizing that George Perkins of the House of Morgan (and IMM) was the major financier of Roosevelt's ongoing campaign.

In Michigan, residents were winding down from the month-long vicarious odyssey their senator had led them through. The *Muskegon News-Chronicle* wryly observed: "Once more editors are turning their attention to the fight between Roosevelt and Taft. Once more the President of the United States has a chance at the first page in rivalry with Michigan's senior senator."

On Sunday, May 26, Smith arrived back in the capital from his visit to the *Olympic.* Late in the afternoon, while trying to cross to the Treasury Department, he found his way blocked by a circus parade. As usual, William Alden was in a hurry. He cut into the parade, hoping to get all the way through it, but instead found himself locked in and marching to the beat of the band. Squeezing in between the elephants and equestrians, he asked someone on horseback, "Is there some way I can get by this? What *is* this anyway?"

The equestrian replied, "Why, this is Barnum and Bailey's World-Defying Circus. Hey, aren't you William Alden Smith?"

The senator flashed a smile and nodded, still looking intently for a point of exit.

"Senator," piped the equestrian, "you sure did us all a favor with that *Titanic* investigation." To the flanks alongside and behind him, the horseman shouted, "Hold up so Senator Smith can get through!"

A space opened, and William Alden slipped out, waving his thanks to the man on horseback. Once again, he began briskly pacing to the Treasury Department. He had but one day remaining in which to write a speech that would summarize for the world the disaster of the century.

PART THREE

Sea Change

One cannot "avoid strange thoughts as to the destiny of the very material that expressed all this wealth and luxury—the silver plate, the beautiful china, the hot-house flowers, the Jacobean panellings, the Louis XV suites, the tapestries, the brocades, the rare polished woods and inlays, the clothes from Paris, the diamonds and the gold—all within the space of an hour or two converted into an indescribable mess and mush of lumps and fibres under the stupendous pressure at the ocean bed. . . . And strange it is to think that among the many lovely works of man crushed out of recognition by that mighty two-mile pressure, the only practically indestructible things are the diamonds, the last expression in material of human wealth; and that they will lie there for ever, valuable no more, beautiful no more, harmful no more."

—FILSON YOUNG

18

"A New Birth of Vigilance"

On Tuesday morning, May 18, 1912, the chamber of the United States Senate was filled to overflowing. Nearly every senator was in his seat and the galleries almost dangerously overcrowded. The occasion was a unique address by Senator Smith of Michigan on the causes of the greatest marine disaster in history. The event had been well publicized. In the Senate's printed agenda, announcement of Smith's forthcoming speech had been mysteriously rendered in boldface type, a novel distinction that drew an immediate objection from the senior senator from Massachusetts. "If we begin to print *headlines* for each speech," bristled Henry Cabot Lodge, "it will extend the notices on the calendar almost indefinitely!" For once agreeing with his Senate adversary, William Alden had explained that he wasn't responsible for the format of the announcement and agreed that the practice should be discontinued. The incident had nevertheless caused considerable gossip in the capital, further boosting anticipation of the event.

The excitement of the crowd now gathered in the

chamber was matched by the cursing of Vice-President "Sunny" Jim Sherman in private conference with the Senate sergeants-at-arms. The session had already been opened and Senator Smith couldn't be found anywhere. The pageboys had been sent to comb the Senate Office Building for him, but there wasn't a trace. In the course of the delay, Progressives shrewdly introduced debate on a bill that would limit the daily service of U.S. government laborers to eight hours a day. The Old Guard quickly parried and an outright battle seemed imminent.

"I suggest the absence of a quorum," piped "Pitchfork Ben" Tillman. "That will consume some time."

At 11:00 A.M., after restricting debate to pending bills of a pedestrian nature, the Vice-President had just announced morning business closed when William Alden Smith bounded through the chamber doors, an enormous sheaf of papers under his arm. The senator had come directly from home where he had been up all night putting the finishing touches on the Commerce Committee's formal report on the *Titanic* investigation. Running out of time in which to write his scheduled speech, he had come prepared with only an outline, a few prose passages, and quotations jotted down from the testimony. Dropping the formal report into the hands of Commerce Chairman Knute Nelson, to whom he muttered something inaudible, William Alden dashed to his own desk, clamped his pince-nez on his nose, and addressed the Senate.

> Mr. President, I had expected to send to the Clerk's desk this morning the unanimous report of the Committee on Commerce. For the purpose of verifying some figures it will be delayed a few moments. I shall not detain the Senate, but will proceed with my address.

> Mr. President, my associates and myself return the commission handed to us on the eighteenth day of April last, directing an immediate inquiry into "the causes leading up to the destruction of the steamship *Titanic* . . ." Mindful of the responsibility of our office, we desire the Senate to know that in the execution of its command we have been guided solely by the public interest and a desire to meet the expectations of our associates without bias, prejudice, sensationalism, or slander of the living or dead. That duty, we believed, would be best performed by an exact ascertainment of the *true state of affairs.*

Expecting one of William Alden's famous "stampedes," news reporters were surprised to hear him speaking with such "deliberation and moderation of phraseology." Smith had correctly deduced that the facts of the disaster were sufficiently eloquent. After recounting the dramatic arrival of the *Carpathia* with the survivors of the disaster, Smith jumped backward in time to the building of the "practically unsinkable" *Titanic.*

> From the builders' hands, she was plunged straightaway to her fate—and christening salvos acclaimed at once her birth and death. Builders of renown had launched her on the billows with confident assurance of her strength, while every port rang with praise for their achievement. Shipbuilding to them was both a science and a religion; parent ships and sister ships had easily withstood the waves, while the mark of their hammer was all that was needed to give assurance of the high quality of the work. In the construction of the *Titanic,* no limit of cost circumscribed their endeavor, and when this vessel took its place at the head of the line every modern improve-

> ment in shipbuilding was supposed to have been realized. So confident were they that both owner and builder were eager to go upon the trial trip.
>
> No sufficient tests were made of boilers or bulkheads or gearing or equipment, and no lifesaving or signal devices were reviewed. Officers and crew were strangers to one another (and passengers to both); neither was familiar with the vessel or its implements or tools. No drill or station practice or helpful discipline disturbed the tranquility of that voyage; and when the crisis came, a state of *absolute unpreparedness* stupefied both passengers and crew. And in their despair, the ship went down carrying as needless a sacrifice of noble women and brave men as ever clustered about the Judgment Seat in any single moment of passing time.
>
> We shall leave to the honest judgment of England its painstaking chastisement of the British Board of Trade, to whose laxity of regulation and hasty inspection the world is largely indebted for this awful fatality. Of contributing causes there were very many. In the face of warning signals, speed was increased; and messages of danger seemed to stimulate her to action rather than persuade her to fear.

The senator reviewed the ice warnings sent to the *Titanic* by the *Baltic*, *Amerika*, and *Californian*, and documented a fact the surviving senior officers of the *Titanic* had adroitly downplayed—that ice is a well-known hazard to navigation. He then moved toward the culpability of the *Titanic*'s late commander. The "heroism" of Captain E.J. had been praised from nearly every American and British pulpit, and introducing the inescapable fact of the captain's negligence was going to be a matter of the utmost delicacy. William Alden approached the task by adopting the sepulchral rhetoric of the clergy.

> Captain Smith knew the sea, and his clear eye and steady hand had often guided his ship through dangerous paths. For forty years storms sought in vain to vex him or menace his craft. But once before in all his honorable career was his pride humbled or his vessel maimed [the *Olympic*'s collision with the S.S. *Hawke*]. Each new advancing type of ship built by his company was handed over to him as a reward for faithful services and as an evidence of confidence in his skill. Strong of limb, intent of purpose, pure in character, dauntless as a sailor should be, he walked the deck of this majestic structure as master of her keel.
>
> Titanic though she was, his *indifference to danger* was one of the *direct and contributing causes* of this unnecessary tragedy—while his own willingness to die was the expiating evidence of his fitness to live. Those of us who knew him well, not in anger but in sorrow, file one specific charge against him: *overconfidence* and neglect to heed the oft-repeated warnings of his friends.

Many in the audience recalled the well-publicized-words of E.J.'s last interview: "I have never been in any accident of any sort worth speaking about. . . . I never saw a wreck and never have been wrecked, nor was I ever in any predicament that threatened to end in disaster of any sort."

> The mystery of his indifference to danger, when other and less pretentious vessels doubled their lookout or stopped their engines, finds no reasonable hy-

> pothesis in conjecture or speculation. Science in shipbuilding was supposed to have attained perfection and to have spoken her last word. Mastery of the ocean had at last been achieved. And overconfidence seems to have dulled the faculties usually so alert. With the atmosphere literally charged with warning signals and wireless messages registering their last appeal, the stokers in the engine room fed their fires with fresh fuel, registering in that dangerous place her *fastest speed.*

Since Ismay had refuted this last point, the senator recounted his recent trip to the engine room of the *Olympic*, where Fireman Fred Barrett had affirmed that at no other time on the *Titanic*'s maiden voyage had so many boilers been lit. Continuing, William Alden drew a comparison between the captain's disregard of wirelessed warnings and the officers' blasé response to the warnings of nature. The sudden plunge in temperature as the liner approached the region of ice had been dismissed by senior officers, even though, as William Alden noted, sailors of the Grand Banks consider the thermometer "almost as necessary to their safety as the compass." The importance of this precaution had quite recently been sustained by Rear Admiral Robert E. Peary in an article in the *Army and Navy Journal.*

The senator then discussed the collision and Officer Murdoch's error at the helm.

> At that moment the ice, resistless as steel, stole upon her and struck her in a vital spot, while the last command of the officer of the watch in his effort to avert disaster, distracted by the sudden appearance of extreme danger, sharply turned aside the prow—the part best prepared to resist collision—exposing the temple to the blow. At the turn of the bilge, the

> steel encasement yielded to a glancing blow so slight that the impact was not felt in many parts of the ship. . . . [Many] of the passengers and crew did not even know of the collision until tardily advised of the danger by anxious friends, and *even then* official statements were clothed in such confident assurances of safety as to arouse no fear. The awful force of the impact was well known to the master and builder, Mr. Andrews, who from the first must have known the ship was doomed and never uttered an encouraging sign to one another. Neither ever adjusted a life belt to himself. The builder, whose heart must have broken when he realized he had not prepared that ship to resist a blow so dangerous, seemed to have been quite willing to go down with the ship.
>
> There is evidence to show that no final warning was given by any officer. . . . No general alarm was given, no ship's officers formally assembled, no orderly routine was attempted or organized system of safety begun. Haphazard, they rushed by one another on staircase and in hallway, while men of self-control gathered here and there about the decks, helplessly staring at one another or giving encouragement to those less courageous than themselves.

Avoiding technicalities, Senator Smith briefly explained that although the ship had been constructed to withstand flooding in any two adjacent compartments, the damage from the iceberg was such that, in the forward section, "five compartments filled almost instantly." The ship was thereby pulled down by the bow, the water in these compartments spilling over into those aft and culminating in the *Titanic*'s nosedive.

> I then reached a conclusion which in my opinion accounts for the small proportion of steerage passen-

> gers who were saved. The occupants of the forward steerage were the first of the passengers to realize the danger—one or two witnesses said they stepped out of their berths into water probably an inch or two inches deep. Those in the forward steerage knew directly of the impact and of the presence of water which came up from the lower part of the ship into the mail room and the forward steerage. Those steerage passengers went on deck and, as fast as they were able, took places in the lifeboats. While the after steerage, more than an eighth of a mile away, was by the operation of the added weight [the flooding forward] raised out of the water . . . so that *these* steerage passengers got their first warning of real danger as the angle of the deck became very great. I feel that the small number of steerage survivors was thus due to the fact that they got *no definite warning* before the ship was really doomed—when most of the lifeboats had departed.

The senator strongly condemned the manner in which the lifeboats were loaded and manned.

> The *Titanic*'s boats were only partially loaded and in all instances unprovided with compasses and only three of them had lamps. They were manned so badly that, in the absence of prompt relief, they would have fallen easy victims to the advancing ice floe, nearly thirty miles in width and rising sixteen feet above the surface of the water. Their danger would have been as great as if they had remained on the deck of the broken hull. And if the sea had risen, these toy targets with over seven hundred exhausted people would have been helplessly tossed about upon the waves without food or water. . . . The lifeboats were filled *so indifferently* and lowered *so*

> *quickly* that, according to the uncontradicted evidence, nearly five hundred people were needlessly sacrificed to want of orderly discipline in loading the few that were provided. . . . And yet it is said by some well-meaning persons that the best discipline prevailed. If this is discipline, what would have been disorder?

The crowd in the Senate chamber murmured in agreement.

> Some of the [crew] men, to whom had been intrusted the care of passengers, never reported to their official stations, and quickly deserted the ship with a recklessness and indifference to the responsibilities of their positions as culpable and amazing as it is impossible to believe. And some of these men say that they "laid by" in their partially filled lifeboats and listened to the cries of distress "until the noise quieted down" and surveyed from a safe distance the unselfish men and women and faithful fellow officers and seamen, whose heroism lightens up this tragedy and recalls the noblest traditions of the sea.

At this juncture, Smith turned to an issue with which he was now virtually obsessed—the wireless. After lavishing praise on the two "ill-paid" operators, Phillips and Bride, he launched an exhaustive criticism of the policies of the Marconi Company. He condemned the laissez-faire status of the wireless and concluded with an emotional appeal for the international regulation of radio.

> When the world weeps together over a common loss, when nature moves in the same direction in all spheres, why should not the nations clear the sea of

> its conflicting idioms and wisely regulate this new servant of humanity? To that end, wages must be increased in proportion to the responsibility assumed, and service to be useful must be made continuous *night and day.* While this new profession must rid itself of the spirit of venality to which, in my opinion, the world is indebted for a systematic reign of silence concerning the details of this disaster.

After reviewing the evidence for this last charge, Smith introduced a subject of striking interest, since, outside Boston, the matter had received scant attention in the press.

> It is not a pleasant duty to criticize the conduct or comment upon the shortcomings of others, but the plain truth should be told. Captain Lord of the steamship *Californian*, sailing from London to Boston, who stopped his ship in the same vicinity where the *Titanic* is supposed to have met with the accident, passed two large icebergs at 6:30 P.M. Sunday evening, April 14. At 7:15 he "passed one large iceberg and two more in sight to the southward." Because of ice, he stopped his ship for the night in latitude 42° 5′ North, longitude 50° 7′ West. And at 10:50 ship's time (and 9:10 New York time), he sent a wireless message to the *Titanic*, telling them he was "stopped and surrounded by ice." The *Titanic* operator brusquely replied to "shut up," that he was "busy." Captain Lord stated that "from the position we stopped in to the position in which the *Titanic* is supposed to have hit the iceberg was nineteen and a half miles . . ." I am of the opinion it was much nearer than the captain is willing to admit, and I base my judgment upon the scientific investigation of the Hydrographic Office of our government.

The senator offered point-by-point quotations from the *Californian* testimony emphasizing Captain Lord's admitted awareness of how dangerous the North Atlantic was that particular evening and the sightings of rockets by his ship. Smith noted that Lord doubted the *Californian*'s ability to see the *Titanic*'s Morse lamp, but was "not quite so doubtful about being unable to see rockets" from that distance.

> Why did the *Californian* display its Morse signal lamp from the moment of the collision continuously for nearly two hours if they saw nothing? And the signals which were visible to Mr. Gill at 12:30 and afterwards—and which were also seen by the captain and officer of the watch—should have *excited more solicitude* than what was displayed by the officers of that vessel. And the failure of Captain Lord to arouse the wireless operator on his ship . . . places a tremendous responsibility upon this officer from which it will be very difficult for him to escape. Had he been as vigilant in the movement of his vessel as he was active in displaying his own signal lamp, there is a very strong possibility that every human life that was sacrificed through this disaster could have been saved. The dictates of humanity should have prompted vigilance under such conditions.
>
> . . . I am well aware from the testimony of the captain of the *Californian* that he deluded himself with the idea that there was a ship between the *Titanic* and the *Californian*, but there was no ship seen there at daybreak and no intervening rockets were seen by anyone on the *Titanic*—although they were looking longingly for such a sign—and only saw the white light of the *Californian*, which was flashed the moment the ship struck and taken down when the vessel sank. A ship . . . could not have gone west

> without passing the *Californian* on the north or the *Titanic* on the south. That ice floe held but two ships—the *Titanic* and the *Californian.*

Smith cited Britain's endorsement of Article 2 of the Brussels Convention, which obligated masters to render assistance to vessels in distress, and drew the following conclusion.

> The conduct of the captain of the *Californian* calls for drastic action by the government of England and by the owners of that vessel, who were the same owners as those of the ill-fated ship.
>
> Contrast, if you will, the conduct of the captain of the *Carpathia* in this emergency and imagine what must be the consolation of that thoughtful and sympathetic mariner—who rescued the shipwrecked and left the people of the world his debtor—as his ship sailed for distant seas a few days ago. By his utter self-effacement and his own indifference to peril, by his promptness and his knightly sympathy, he rendered a great service to humanity. He should be made to realize the debt of gratitude his nation owes to him; while the Book of Good Deeds, which has so often been familiar with his unaffected valor, should henceforth carry the name of Captain Rostron to the remotest period of time. . . . It falls to the lot of few men to perform a service so unselfish. And the American Congress can honor itself no more by any single act than by writing into its laws the gratitude we feel toward this modest and kindly man.

Smith was now prepping his colleagues for a joint resolution lying on his desk requesting the Senate to grant Captain Rostron the Congressional Medal of Honor, but it wasn't time yet. Shifting his papers, Smith found his notes on J. Bruce Ismay whom the United States had already pilloried in its eagerness to place blame for the disaster. William Alden refused to hold Ismay equally responsible with the captain. The senator had looked searchingly for evidence that Ismay had pressured the captain to keep up speed so as to make a "good passage," but could find nothing. Both Captains Rostron and Sealby had refuted the possibility of such a thing happening; and even if it had happened, the captain was still to blame. Instead, the senator praised Ismay's sense of urgency and care in helping to load the lifeboats and argued that the White Star chairman's culpability was tangential at best.

> I think the presence of Mr. Ismay and Mr. Andrews stimulated the ship to greater speed than it would have made under ordinary conditions, although I cannot fairly ascribe to either of them any instructions to this effect. The very *presence* of the owner and builder unconsciously stimulates endeavor; and the restraint of organized society is absolutely necessary to safety.

It was now time to instill a legislative mood in the U.S. Senate.

> The calamity through which we have just passed has left traces of sorrow everywhere. Hearts have been broken and deep anguish unexpressed. Art will typify with master hand its lavish contribution to the sea. . . . Hills will be cleft in search of marble white enough to symbolize these heroic deeds and, where kinship is the only tie that binds the lowly to the humble home bereft of son or mother or father, little groups of kinsfolk will recount around the kitchen fire the traits of human sympathy in those who went

> down with this ship. These are choice pictures in the treasure house of the affections. But even these will some time fade.
>
> The sea is the place *permanently* to honor our dead. This should be the occasion for a *new birth of vigilance.* And future generations must accord to this event a crowning motive for better things.

For William Alden Smith, "better things" meant more practical laws. He listed changes that were vitally needed in marine legislation—all of which were included in a new bill he would soon be introducing. As a newcomer to the field of marine law, he told exactly what he thought of present statutes. In his opinion, they weren't just ineffective; they were actively hindering the development of American seapower and discouraging Americans from entering the merchant service.

> Americans *must* reenlist in this service; they must become the soldiers of the sea. And whether on lookout, on deck, or at the wheel; whether able or common seamen, they should be better paid for their labor and more highly honored in their calling. Their rights must be respected and their work carefully performed. Harsh and severe restraining statutes must be repealed, and a new dignity given this important field of labor.

The senator now moved toward the finale. Newsmen noted that "for more than two hours he had held the floor with a narrative the like of which for pathos and tragedy had never before been heard in the United States Senate." The correspondent for *Leslie's Weekly* (forerunner to *Life*) observed: "Now and then again from the packed visitors' galleries was heard a muffled sob—possibly from a survivor or relative of a loved one who never returned from the ill-fated voyage." Senator Smith was himself beginning to be affected by his own narrative and by the audible sorrow in the galleries. Tears were visible in his eyes, but he continued speaking in a moderate tone and evenly paced tempo.

> In our imagination, we can see again the proud ship instinct with life and energy, with active figures again swarming upon her decks—musicians, teachers, artists, and authors; soldiers and sailors and men of large affairs; brave men and noble women of every land. We can see the unpretentious and the lowly progenitors of the great and strong turning their back upon the Old World, where endurance is to them no longer a virtue, and looking hopefully to the New. At the very moment of their greatest joy, the ship suddenly reels, mutilated and groaning. With splendid courage the musicians fill the last moments with sympathetic melody. The ship wearily gives up the unequal battle. Only a vestige remains of the men and women that but a moment before quickened her spacious apartments with human hopes and passions, sorrows and joys. Upon that broken hull new vows were taken, new fealty expressed, old love renewed. And those who had been devoted in friendship and companions in life went proudly and defiantly on the last life pilgrimage together.
>
> In such a heritage, we must feel ourselves *more intimately related to the sea than ever before.* And henceforth it will send back to us on its rising tide the cheering salutations—from those we have lost.

After a poignant pause, in which the sobbing from the galleries mingled with the clearing of throats from the Senate floor, Smith played his hand: three new pieces of legislation. The first, a joint resolution calling for the coining of a one-thousand-dollar medal to be presented to Captain Arthur Henry Rostron by the President of the United States. Smith took deft advantage of the emotional uniformity of his colleagues.

> Mr. President, this recognition is so highly deserved, the valor shown by this officer is so marked and worthy of emulation, I am going to ask the senators to give unanimous consent for immediate consideration and that this joint resolution be put on its passage without a reference to committee.

Whereupon Rostron's medal was granted by acclamation.

Smith then introduced Senate Bill Number 6976 (later known as the Smith Bill), which radically altered the existing statutes of marine legislation. His final joint resolution called for the creation of a maritime commission to investigate the laws and regulations for the construction and equipment of all oceangoing vessels. These last two bills were referred to the Committee on Commerce, whose chairman now brought to the desk the "Investigation into the Loss of the Steamship *Titanic.*"

Smith's formal report on the disaster filled ten columns of the Congressional Record. Hardly a detail had been overlooked. The wireless warnings, the cancellation of boat drill, the absence of binoculars in the crow's nest, the loading of the lifeboats, the rockets, the *Californian,* every ironic circumstance of this unbelievable catastrophe—it was all there. Specterlike, the ghost of the *Titanic* disaster, which had faded from the front pages of the newspapers, again loomed to the forefront of international concerns.

19

The American Inquiry and the Law

"On the whole, Senator Smith will probably not strike most people as being an unkind man, but without doubt he is a man that we describe in England as an ass." So spoke Britain's *Saturday Review* in response to William Alden's speech and report on the causes of the *Titanic* disaster. Other British appraisals of the senator's findings were less than generous. In an editorial entitled "Bombastes," the *Daily Express* observed that "the grotesque oration of Senator Smith" deprived his reported findings "of much value. That extraordinary mass of grandiloquent bosh is probably without a parallel in the history of parliaments." The *Daily Mail*, which had popularized Smith's supposed gaffe about watertight compartments, called his speech "a violent, unreasonable diatribe, in which the senator betrays once more the amazing ignorance that prompted him to ask during the inquiry whether watertight compartments were intended as a refuge for passengers."

The editors of *Blackwoods* magazine offered the best articulated condemnation, in which criticism of Smith was generalized into unflattering observations on the American character:

> Wherever there is a democracy you will find the triumph of shoddy eloquence. . . . And if America had done nothing more than produce Senator Smith she need not fear the competitions of any rival. . . .
>
> The wreck of the *Titanic* was Senator Smith's opportunity. This eminent politician concluded the tragedy with a satiric drama of his own. He introduced, into a solemn occasion, the comedy of ignorance. He deemed himself competent to discover the cause of a disaster at sea, though he seemed to think that a watertight compartment was a refuge into which drowning men might creep for safety, and though he demanded anxiously what was an iceberg and whence it came. But the undesigned touches of farce which this landsman imparted into a solemn discussion are insignificant beside the oration which he delivered to his delighted countrymen. To describe this oration adequately is impossible. We bow before it in respectful humbleness. The fact that it was listened to with some show of gravity makes the whole American people an accomplice in its magnificent absurdity. . . . Senator Smith's oration suggests that there is something in the American character which suffers no change. In spite of ceaseless immigration, the Land of the Free remains faithful to its primitive love of rhetoric. . . . The blood of God's own country suffers a weekly admixture. And while the type of this confused race, rejecting all European peculiarities, tends year by year to approximate to the type of the North-American Indian, its demagogues preserve inviolate the old provincial tub-thumping, beloved by countless generations of stern-faced Puritans.

For the most part, British editors paid little attention to Smith's *specific* findings; the essence of their criticism was that he talked too funny for his findings to be taken seriously.

But there were a few choice items of praise in the British press as well. The *London Economist* concluded: "It is right that the whole truth should be known, and every reflecting person should be grateful to the American Senate for its prompt and searching inquiry." The *London Daily News* retreated considerably from its original position and said: "Senator Smith had no need to apologize for his committee. The Senatorial inquirers got the witnesses when they were available, when the facts were too fresh in their memory for art or delusion to color them, and the questions put by the committee were, on the whole, a model of rigorous investigation. . . . Some, at least, of its conclusions are irresistible, and they are very disturbing."

Alfred Stead, the first British journalist to have come out in the senator's defense, argued in the *Review of Reviews:* "There has been so much cheap and uncalled for abuse of Senator Smith in the columns of the less responsible papers of this country that we feel it our duty to assure Mr. Smith and the Senate of the United States, as well as the American nation generally, that the British public and the officers of the British mercantile marine are grateful for their remarkable and conscientious effort to get at the truth of these things and to hasten the day when modern regulations shall make ocean travel more humanly safe." Stead sent William Alden a copy of his editorial along with this note:

> Whatever the yellow papers here may have said about your speech, there is no doubt that the general public are very grateful to you. I was talking the other day to Viscount Esher, who, as you know, is a

> friend of the King and a member of the Imperial Defense Committee, and he spoke most warmly of the good work which you had done. Besides which many officers of the British mercantile marine look upon you as their potential saviour.

Although it is unknown to what extent the *officers* of the British merchant marine felt the way Stead averred, it is a fact that the senator received scores of complimentary letters from England's common sailors who claimed that the depth of his inquiry and his arraignment of the Board of Trade would have been impossible in Great Britain.

In the United States, response to Smith's findings was a sigh of relief. Calling his Senate oration one of "fiery eloquence," the liberal *New York World* called the investigative report "a grave indictment of the methods employed in ocean traffic where the lives of thousands of human beings are daily involved." From coast to coast, the Hearst papers were unanimous in praise; Hearst himself sent the senator a letter expressing his "very deep and sincere admiration for your humane and vigorously patriotic American attitude in regard to the *Titanic* investigation." Addressing British criticism of Smith, the *Washington Evening Star* editorialized: "There may be a fundamental difference between the English and the American sense of propriety in the matter of public expression, but the people of this country have no complaint to make of the manner in which the chairman of the committee laid its findings before his colleagues. . . . He has shown a thoroughness which does credit to him as an investigator, and in his handling of witnesses and in his final summing up of conclusions he has manifested a temperate and dispassionate spirit that commands admiration."

The Michigan press was forgivably jubilant. Among the more temperate summations was that of the *Detroit News:* "The speech was by far the best and most statesmanlike Senator Smith ever delivered in Congress, and it plainly made a good impression." The *Battle Creek Enquirer* declared: "If this investigation—painstaking and thorough as it was—makes unlikely a similar disaster, as is likely, Senator Smith will have won a place in the country's history that will make him proof against the shafts of either ridicule or envy. Michigan should be elated that, through Senator Smith, she had so large a part in clearing up the causes of this gigantic disaster."

Rather surprising was the fact that even William Alden's enemies felt congratulations in order. The *Springfield Republican* regretted the "unnecessary rhetoric" in the senator's speech, but felt that it was "a useful summing up of the results of his inquiry. . . . The promptness with which the committee acted, its ability to obtain the testimony of those concerned as soon as they landed—these things alone made the inquiry thoroughly worthwhile." *The New York Times*, having fully recovered from the exploratory surgery the senator had performed on its ties with Marconi, editorialized:

> Probably never was there a marine catastrophe whose causes lay more completely within the landsman's comprehension than the *Titanic*'s. If the disaster had been of another sort, Senator Smith's lack of special qualifications in knowledge of maritime affairs might have been important. As the matter stands, he has the right to say that it was a case where promptness, energy, and good faith in inquiry were important. The qualities the case called for he has shown, and his critics are put upon the defensive

> by a report which is all the more crushing because of its lack of vindictive spirit or language.

In fact, some of Smith's critics were astonished at the objectivity of his formal report. Both the *London Times* and *Engineering News* believed it "fair to assume" that the moderation in Smith's report was "due to the other members of the committee," which was not the case. Smith wrote the report alone, the other members of the investigative team striking a mere sentence from the finished draft. William Alden knew the difference between oratory and investigative reporting, and the conclusions of his *Titanic* report are entirely consistent with other examples of his draftsmanship.

As far as the specific conclusions of the report were concerned, nearly every American editor was in agreement with them. Many regretted with the *Cleveland Plain Dealer* "that the memory of gallant Captain Smith of the *Titanic* must be darkened by knowledge of the absolute foolhardiness of his conduct during the closing hours of his life." Yet such was "the irresistible logic of the situation." The *New York Press* and *New York Tribune* and the *Philadelphia Press* concurred with this judgment and further approved the senator's refusal to divide the captain's responsibility with Mr. Ismay. Although many papers noted that the condemnation of Captain Lord of the *Californian* was "harsh and severe," a majority agreed with *The New York Times* and *Springfield Republican* that it was "no more so than the evidence warrants."

Few editors, however, cared to address the exposed myth of Anglo-American heroism during the disaster—the much touted "grace under pressure" of the English-speaking race. Smith's report suggested that, in actuality, the conduct of the *Titanic*'s seamen and passengers alike had been heroic only when ignorant of the seriousness of the danger and organized only when most self-serving. His recounting of the lifeboats' refusal to aid the struggling victims was particularly grim. Only the feisty *New York Gaelic-American* dared say that Smith's report "certainly offers no balm to Anglo-Saxon pride. All those racial qualities which have been assumed to distinguish the Anglo-Saxon from the emotional races of Southern Europe and the heathen breeds were wanting in that tragic test among the ice floes of the North Atlantic."

Although William Alden appreciated the compliments his controversial methods had ultimately achieved, he was personally unable to rest until the legislation he had drawn became law. After examining the terms of the Smith Bill, maritime experts were stunned at how "very sweeping" its provisions were. The senator actually intended to run the North Atlantic passenger service with the stringency of a railroad! Moreover, his bill virtually prohibited any American or foreign vessel from entering or clearing a U.S. port unless its statutes were observed.

The first section of the Smith Bill addressed Morgan's IMM and any comparable trust that toyed with the idea of buying the North Atlantic passenger service. The new requirements demanded that all corporations (with headquarters at home or abroad) engaged in the transportation of passengers from American ports file with the U.S. Commissioner of Corporations a copy of its charter and a sworn affidavit giving the particulars of its assets and liabilities and the amount of authorized capital stock and amount outstanding. No trust in violation of the Sherman Act could enter the American passenger trade without risk of exposure, nor could a bona fide company operate without risk of suit should it fail to live up to the terms of the new rules. A special clause provided the legislative muscle for withholding certificates of inspection and otherwise penalizing companies for failing to comply with the new standards.

Section Five of the bill was enormously comprehensive, encompassing everything from the construction of oceangoing vessels to the specifics of its lifesaving equipment. Looking over this section agape, the editors of the *Marine Review* concluded: "That Senator Smith did not draw the bill is obvious, as it contains a great deal of technical knowledge with which he could not be expected to be acquainted." True, the senator had spent innumerable hours in consultation with George Uhler, Secretary Myer, and other experts from the Department of the Navy, but he had drawn the bill nonetheless.

As to the construction of future passenger liners, the Smith Bill required longitudinal bulkheads as well as transverse ones (the *Titanic* had had only transverse bulkheads). It ordered increased pump facilities for the discharge of water from the hold. It demanded enough lifesaving equipment—belts, floats, and drags—for everyone aboard. Also, two searchlights would be required on every liner. (Searchlights were standard equipment on naval dreadnoughts and had been included in the bill at the urging of Secretary Myer and committee member George Perkins, who, after three days of the hearings, declared that the testimony had convinced him "of the absolute necessity of legislation requiring all ships to carry searchlights." The searchlight provision failed to achieve the endorsement of marine experts and was eventually dropped.)

The section on lifeboats was a veritable mirror image of the *Titanic* disaster, and the facts first brought to light by Fifth Officer Harold Lowe can be retraced in its specific clauses. The Smith Bill demanded that lifeboats be constructed to government standards (no more collapsibles!). Ships would be required to carry "lifeboats of an aggregate capacity computed in cubic feet equal to ten times the total number of her crew, plus the total number of passengers stated in her certificate." A team of four crewmen would be required to be skilled in the handling of lifeboats and assigned to *each* boat carried. Every lifeboat would be "lowered into the water at least twice in each month and the crew drilled in handling and rowing it; and at least once in six months all the lifeboats on such vessel shall [at the same time] participate in the drill and the fact of every such drill and practice shall be noted in the vessel's log." Finally, before any vessel sailed from any port in the United States, *a place in one of the ship's lifeboats would be assigned to each passenger and member of the crew.* (The number of the boat designated for each passenger would eventually be printed right on his ticket.) The assigned boat and the shortest route to it would further be stated in a notice posted in every passenger and seaman's room or over his berth.

William Alden's obsession with the wireless resulted in the following provisions: (1) that no vessel carrying fifty passengers or more be permitted to clear U.S. ports without a wireless set with a minimum range of 100 miles; (2) that an auxiliary power supply for shipboard wireless be provided and certified to operate until the wireless room itself was under water or otherwise destroyed; (3) that direct means of communication be provided between the wireless room and the bridge, so that operators may at all times communicate directly with those in command of the ship (the senator had fumed over the *Titanic* operator's unwillingness to leave his post to deliver critical last-minute warnings to the officer of the watch); (4) that two or more wireless operators provide continuous service day and night (a consequence of the *Californian*'s ignorant proximity); and (5) that any master willfully failing to enforce these stipulations at sea be heavily penalized.

Finally, in order to clarify a matter for future *Californians*, the Smith Bill stated: "Any person who shall discharge or permit the discharge of any rocket or candle from any vessel on the high seas or within the jurisdiction of the United States for any purpose other than a signal of distress shall be guilty of a misdemeanor punishable by law as like offenses are now punishable."

Professional response to the Smith Bill was mixed. On the positive side, the *Marine Review* declared that "whatever the British papers may say about it, the inquiry will bear much fruit of value to ocean travelers in the future." The *Scientific American* claimed that the Smith Bill "commends itself to the serious consideration of the owners and builders of oceangoing steamships and the general traveling public." On the other hand, a few technical journals disliked the stringency of the bill as much as they abhorred the fact that it had been written by a landsman. The *Shipbuilder* took umbrage at Smith's proposed regulation over Mr. Marconi's wonderful apparatus. "Considering that without the aid of wireless telegraphy it is probable no lives would have been saved at all, any adverse criticism of the wireless arrangements" seemed to the *Shipbuilder* "altogether out of place." The same journal deemed William Alden's demand for two shipboard operators providing continuous wireless service "quite unreasonable."

Professional antagonism, surprising from a present-day perspective, grew particularly heated over Smith's demand for enough lifeboats for all aboard, which some experts regarded "an ill-considered concession to public hysteria." The *London Morning Post* argued: "People need not be afraid of going into a ship because there are not lifeboats for all on board. They have been doing it all their lives without knowing it, and whether there are lifeboats or not, they would run risks of being drowned if the ship went down." In a more logical vein, the *Shipbuilder* maintained that while a moderate increase in the number of boats "is certainly desirable," it "does not by any means assure the safe removal of all passengers from the ship." *Engineering News* agreed, saying: "Properly speaking, the lifeboat is not a 'safety' appliance. It affords only a chance of saving life after all other hope has failed, but it is a chance at best and not seldom it proves a hopeless chance." Ironically, these same arguments had been advanced in 1854 when the steamship *Arctic* went down, a majority of her passengers losing their lives because there hadn't been enough boats. In that year the editors of *Nautical Magazine* had begged Congress for an act guaranteeing "that the number of boats shall be regulated by the number of souls on board," but experts had talked Congress out of it. In fifty-eight years, the lesson had been learned. Enough lifeboats would be provided for all.

Senator Smith moved swiftly for quick passage of his bill. He had finished the work of the committee with particular haste in the hope of getting as many of the new provisions as possible passed before Congress adjourned. He ultimately succeeded in getting the provision on lifeboats and continuous shipboard wireless service passed before the second session of the Sixty-second Congress was over. Working together, Senators Smith and Bourne further managed to tie to the shipboard wireless law a bill passed by the House for the federal regulation of all wireless in the United States. Henceforth, all radio operators would have to be licensed by the government and adhere to standards of broadcasting set and overseen by a special bureau under the Department of Commerce—a forerunner to the present-day FCC.

Two other pieces of legislation passed by the Sixty-second Congress were related to the *Titanic* disaster. The North Atlantic passenger-ship lanes were moved sixty miles to the south for the summer route (January 15–August 14) when threat of ice was maximal. This revision added several hours to the trip, but no one seems to have objected. Also, the Panama Canal Act was passed with a special rider giving the President discretionary authority to provide subsidies to American shipping engaged in both coastal and international trade. The spotlight the disaster had thrown on weaknesses in Britain's Board of Trade also had illuminated the fact that the American merchant marine had all but desiccated after the dissolution of the ill-fated Collins Line in 1858. Previous attempts to resuscitate American shipping with government subsidies had been defeated by Progressives who had merely seen government payoffs to big business in such proposals. In the wake of the *Titanic* disaster, however, Progressives suddenly realized that subsidies would indirectly promote the safety of the American traveling public as well, and passage of the act with its subsidy rider gave a much needed jolt toward the reawakening of the American merchant marine.

The Smith-Martine Resolution calling for "an international agreement to secure the protection of sea-traffic" passed the Senate on April 20, 1912, and went immediately to the President. It is worth noting that the ongoing inquiry into the loss of the *Titanic* played a key role in gaining Taft's endorsement of the resolution. The President had initially felt an international treaty unnecessary, the disaster alone being sufficient to move nations to include enough lifeboats on ships. Alluding to facts then being brought out in the Senate inquiry, however, Commerce Secretary Charles Nagel wrote to the President:

> . . . I take it that provision for more lifeboats will be made without coercion from us. It appears to me that the real danger lies in a broader field involving navigation, crews and officers, and that, therefore, no effective and comprehensive measure can be adopted without the cooperation of the more important countries owning merchant marine.

The President granted the point and approved the resolution.

The International Conference for the Safety of Life at Sea convened in London on November 12, 1913, and concluded on January 20, 1914. It was the first such convention in modern maritime history and would be successively reconvened throughout the twentieth century. The American delegates to the convention included Senator Burton and George Uhler, who urged an international adoption of a number of provisions from the Smith Bill. Consequently, the lifeboats-for-all measure was adopted as well as others; for example:

> When ice is reported on or near his course, the master of every vessel is bound to proceed at night at a moderate speed or to alter his course, so as to go well clear of the danger zone.

And:

> The convention prohibits, in the future, the use of the international distress signals for any other purpose than as distress signals. This rule will prevent any vessel hesitating to respond to what is apparently an international distress signal on the supposition that it was intended for another purpose, as was the case with the master of the *Californian* at the time of the loss of the *Titanic*.

The rules adopted by the conference for shipboard wireless, however, were below the United States's new standards, a consequence of successful lobbying by the British Marconi Company. On the matter of continuous service by two operators, the convention permitted certain cargo steamers to substitute for the second operator "a member of the crew" who was "competent to receive and understand distress calls or other unusual calls indicating danger." The convention concurred, however, with the U.S. provisions for wireless aboard every ship, for increasing the standard power of existing sets, and for an auxiliary power source. In all, five special committees met and generated better standards for the construction of vessels, the relay of meteorological information (such as icebergs), radiotelegraphy, lifesaving appliances and fire protection, and safety certification.

Perhaps the most significant achievement of the conference was its creation of an international derelict-destruction and ice patrol service: two vessels that would patrol the steamship lanes for ice and report all hazards to ships. Responsibility for the new service was offered to the United States, and the President authorized a portion of the Revenue Cutter Service to mount the task on February 17, 1914. The financing of the operation remained an international matter, the cost allocated on the basis of the tonnage of ships each country operated:

Great Britain	30%
France, Germany, USA (each)	15
Belgium, Italy, Netherlands (each)	4
Norway	3
Austria-Hungary, Canada, Denmark, Russia, Sweden (each)	2

Within a year, this service officially became the U.S. Coast Guard, whose duties, in addition to patrolling the lanes for ice, include enforcing maritime treaties and laws, maintaining seaborne weather-observation stations, and generally safeguarding navigation on the high seas. Every April 15, the U.S. Coast Guard continues to drop a wreath over 41°46′N., 50°14′W.—the grave of the fabulous ship whose epoch had instigated its service.

The Senate swiftly ratified the international treaty, adding a clause from the Smith Bill that gave the United States the right to impose the higher standards of safety now demanded of its own vessels upon foreign ships using American ports. Unfortunately, many of the statutes of the 1914 convention did not go into immediate effect on an international basis due to the outbreak of the European war. The treaty was revised, however, and put into worldwide effect at a postwar reconvening of the conference.

Between the actions of the Sixty-second Congress and the Senate's ratification of the International Conference treaty, several provisions of the Smith Bill were left outstanding—most important of these, the standards for lifeboat drills and the training of seamen assigned to boats. William Alden continued to fight strenuously for passage of these provisions, eventually managing to link them to another bill he favored, sponsored by Robert LaFollette, which extended the Thirteenth Amendment to American seamen.

Previous statutes had permitted iron contracts that, under threat of criminal prosecution, had bound American sailors to shipping companies and discouraged Americans from shipping with American firms. (At this time, nearly 80 percent of the seamen in the American merchant marine were foreign mercenaries, predominantly ill-paid and poorly trained Orientals.) LaFollette's bill abrogated binding, one-year contracts and permitted American sailors to quit ships as soon as their cargo was unloaded. It further required that three-fourths of the crews of American ships speak English—not merely to protect American seamen from foreign competition, but to assure a crew "with sufficient knowledge of the language of the officers to be able to understand their orders." The bill relieved American sailors of criminal prosecution for violating shipping contracts and limited their service to eight hours a day.

The first version of LaFollette's bill was vetoed by President Taft in 1913. In combination with Smith's provisions for trained boatmen and other standards of passenger safety, however, the bill grew tighter and more potent. The idea of a bill benefiting the rights of both sailors *and* passengers especially appealed to Smith. To the senators favoring sailors' interests, Smith proclaimed: "I want to see this bill so framed . . . that the personnel of the vessels of the ocean and of the lakes may rise to that standard of efficiency which will *guarantee* to those who travel upon the sea, and to those who work in that calling, the greatest safety from the ordinary perils of the sea that it is possible for us to attain." To those representing the shipping industry, he roared: "Unless the calling of the sailor can be dignified and put upon a basis which will encourage efficiency and devotion to that calling, we shall not have American sailors!" To those unmoved by rhetoric, both Smith and LaFollette threatened filibusters against appropriation bills until the seamen's bill passed on March 4, 1915. The new law was the culmination of William Alden's appeal in his *Titanic* speech for Americans to reenlist in the merchant marine: "Their rights must be respected and their work carefully performed; harsh restraining statutes must be repealed, and a new dignity given this important field of labor." The Seamen's Act of 1915 has been called by one authority "the most important law concerning the conditions of sea employment ever passed by Congress." In effect, it heralded the rebirth of American seapower in the twentieth century.

The British investigation into the loss of the *Titanic* had been ordered April 22, 1912, three days after the American hearings had begun in New York, and was well under way by the time Smith reported his findings to the Senate. The appointment of Lord Mersey to head the investigation had, for the most part, met with England's approval. The *London Nation* and others, however, recalled with apprehension that Mersey had been

> a member of the Jameson raid committee [of the Boer War]. We should have been glad if every gentleman who sat on that body had been passed over for any service touching upon the investigation of a public scandal. The Jameson committee was perhaps the greatest exploit in hushing up which this country ever achieved.

Senator Smith, who owing to the Dutch sector of his Grand Rapids constituency had been pro-Boer, was very familiar with Mersey's role in the Jameson Raid cover-up—precisely why he had refused the suggestion of colleagues such as Lodge to suspend the Senate inquiry and let England take over the investigation in midstream.

At the conclusion of the American hearings, the *Washington Herald* had speculated on the effect of the Senate inquiry on the British investigation, noting:

> Lord Mersey, well known from the days of his justiceship, is not the man to acquit the British Board of Trade, thus declaring that the *Titanic* was sailed admirably, unless he can disprove the charges laid by

> Senator William Alden Smith and his committee upon evidence cited. Were he to do so, it would incite travelers who could consult their own convenience to patronize any line except a British, because of the apparent desire of the British government to be an accomplice in manslaughter by bad seamanship.

While it is difficult to say exactly how much the American inquiry forced Mersey to conduct a thorough investigation, an estimate is afforded in a look at each of the most famous cases Mersey tried before and after the *Titanic* investigation: the Jameson Raid and *Lusitania* investigations—both of them official government "whitewashes." When the British investigators were finished with the *Titanic*, however, *International Marine Engineering* compared their report with Senator Smith's, noting: "While the report from the British inquiry is by far the longer document . . . it contains little information that would contradict or add materially to the facts brought out in the American investigation." Critics of Smith such as *Engineering News* were frankly surprised that, "contrary to the general expectation, the two reports are essentially the same in effect."

Lacking the pressure of time limits and controversy, the British *Titanic* hearings were better organized than the American version and more expertly conducted. There were other differences. In such time as had lapsed since the disaster, the testifying officers were able to treat a number of critical points—in the words of the *London Daily News*—with "art" and "delusion." The British investigators paid far less attention to the human facets of the disaster and focused more exclusively on nautical and navigational matters. How the *Titanic* was damaged and subsequently flooded was covered in considerable detail by an impressive panel of marine authorities, including members of the Board of Trade whose "laxity of regulation and hasty inspection" Senator Smith had held largely accountable for the disaster. In many instances, expert testimony was given more weight by the British team than eyewitness accounts. No steerage survivors were called to testify. The role of the *Californian* was examined in depth and Captain Lord severely censured. In his final conclusions, however, Lord Mersey was far more generous to the *Titanic's* captain and the Board of Trade than William Alden had been. Considering that the British panel declined to level blame for the disaster—a right the American Senate did not possess—a contemporary critic has called the British report "a vague, contradictory and a revolting example of official whitewash."

Yet it is a curious paradox that history has tended to discount the American inquiry and pronounce the British investigation the superior of the two. Much of this is due to a scholarly overreliance on British source materials. It is also due to a vogue earlier in the century for preferring style to substance. But it is predominantly due to the curious romanticism that began suffusing the disaster shortly before the official reports were in.

Fibers of the rose-colored veil that fell over the catastrophe had been spun in the American newspapers as soon as the survivors had disembarked from the *Carpathia.* But these individual fibers seem to have been woven into an enduring fabric by the British press in response to nationally embarrassing bits of testimony wired over from the Senate hearings. George Bernard Shaw, an eyewitness to the romantic transformation of the disaster, began questioning his own sanity:

> Why is it that the effect of a sensational catastrophe on a modern nation is to cast it into transports, not of weeping, not of prayer, not of sympathy with the be-

> reaved nor of congratulation of the rescued, not of poetic expression of soul purified by pity and terror, but of wild defiance of inexorable fate and of undeniable fact by an explosion of outrageous, romantic lying? . . . What is the use of all this ghastly, blasphemous, inhuman, braggartly lying? Here is a calamity which might well make the proudest man humble and the wildest joker serious. It makes us vainglorious, insolent, mendacious. The effect on me was one of profound disgust, almost of national dishonor. Am I mad?

Shaw was most incensed by the "lies" (embraced by Americans as well) elevating Captain E.J. to the stature of Lord Nelson; and those contrasting the "heroism" of Anglo-Americans "with the hypothetic dastardliness" of "lascars or Italians."

Great Dreams die with great difficulty, and it is understandable that the English-speaking people of 1912 preferred accounts of the disaster consistent with their hopes to the cold harsh facts of Smith's report. No one really appreciated hearing about the need for "a new birth of vigilance." Consequently, in spite of Smith's report, the *Titanic*'s officers became heroes, the passengers (particularly first-class male passengers) became stoic self-sacrificers, and E.J. a martyred saint who went down with his ship, saying, "Be British, boys, be British!" Captain Lord of the *Californian* is, depending on one's bias, either Everyman or Pantaloon. Poor J. Bruce Ismay, in spite of having his conduct cleared at two different investigations, remains the villain of the piece, while—after the stirring sentiment of "Nearer, My God, to Thee"—William Alden Smith comes on at the end of the show to deliver the satirical epilogue and provide comic relief. It is hardly a wonder that earnest historians of the disaster have been unable to extricate themselves completely from this grotesque amalgam of nineteenth-century melodrama and eighteenth-century farce.

Ismay and William Alden seem to have suffered the most (Captain Lord at least has his defenders); each was especially suited as a scapegoat for the American and British character respectively. Ismay remains locked in the mold of a bad baronet who drove his lackey, the captain, to high speed. Senator Smith, however, is inconsistently portrayed as both a fiendishly clever politician and a dimwitted dolt. He is attributed with asking all kinds of stupid questions he never asked and with stupid questons Lord Mersey *did* ask. He is accused of mounting a farcical inquiry that lost the favor of his countrymen—a contention swiftly disposed of by existing evidence. Even accredited historians have examined the repetitiveness of Smith's questioning during the *Titanic* hearings and concluded, without regard for context, that he suffered from an "incredible ignorance" of all nautical matters. The senator's technique of protracted detail in interrogation and methodical repetition, however, may be seen elsewhere in matters in which he was expert. It was simply his method of choice for dealing with hostile witnesses and one aptly suited to the *Titanic* inquiry's witnesses, most of whom were British citizens. As Michigan Minuteman Ed O'Donnell recounted:

> The senator was confronted by the task of finding out the exact truth from a multitude of unwilling witnesses. I have listened to many lawyers extracting information from reluctant witnesses in many courtrooms, but never have I seen it done with as much skill and tact as displayed by the senator.

The "tact" was a matter of necessity. Any outright bullying of the witnesses, to which Lord Mersey resorted (and which was the subject of a satire by G.K. Chesterton), would have heightened the British-American antagonism to an execrable degree; and the inquiry simply could not have tolerated further opposition. Arthur Vandenberg, Smith's protégé who was with the senator in Washington during the final days of the hearings, related that the senator was faced "with opposition of such stupendous size that no one can appreciate it who does not know the inside history of what effort was put forth to put out his searchlight."

William Alden Smith lived long enough to read articles critical of the controversy his investigation had stirred up in Great Britain. To such criticism, he would simply mention the legislation it had achieved and also point to a stack of complimentary letters he had received from Britain's "little people," particularly a letter that had surprised and especially pleased him—a resolution from the Amalgamated Society of Railway Servants of Great Britain.

> We congratulate Senator William Alden Smith on the courageous manner in which he conducted the searching inquiry into the deplorable loss of the *Titanic.*

In a note accompanying this resolution, John Phipps, the secretary of the society, wrote: "In brushing aside all red tape, you created a precedent which will benefit humanity."

It *was* a precedent—especially for the United States Senate. In less than a year, the Senate began conducting investigations on factory working conditions, canning-factory hours and wages, the "money trust," the cost of living, and oyster-bed pollution. Eventually, there would be Watergate. The *Titanic* inquiry had singlehandedly bent an instrument, constitutionally intended for the sole purpose of obtaining data useful to legislation, into a public forum by which the rise of an inequitable power could be stayed and a wound in national solidarity healed. Irrespective of the tremendous legislation it launched (which is William Alden Smith's true monument), it had demonstrated to the trusts—and to any agency or individual usurping power—that a formidable vehicle existed for mobilizing the power of public opinion. All that was required was an event of major significance and a leader of uncommon independence, integrity, and foolhardy gutsiness.

At the present writing, the prevailing historical verdict on the Senate's *Titanic* inquiry has gone no further than the judgment of Second Officer Charles Lightoller, who pronounced it "nothing but a complete farce, wherein all the traditions and customs of the sea were continuously and persistently flouted." Indeed they were. Among the traditions flouted was the habit of driving full speed into known ice-floe areas. Among the customs was that of sailing with an insufficient number of lifeboats. The *Titanic* not only embodied a lofty dream; its presumptuous innocence was akin to a fairy tale. And it had taken a "fool" to look into the floating palace and declare that the emperor had no clothes.

20

End of a Dream

The law of the sea wasn't the only thing changed in the wake of the *Titanic*. In spite of the barrier of romanticism erected against the humiliating facts of the disaster, society was nevertheless affected. In the United States, two civil-rights movements were immediately and most tangibly affected by the disaster and deserve special attention.

In 1912, American feminists had courage, a visible target, and—most importantly—a complete philosophy of female emancipation. Whatever women gained from male protection, they argued, was lost in social enfranchisement and integrity. It was a bold and valid view, but enthusiasm for it began to waver as soon as survivor lists appeared in the newspapers. The policy of "women and children first" aboard the R.M.S. *Titanic* highlighted a problem that feminists had not previously considered: Full equality means equal risk of life with men in times of adversity; and endorsement of *both* female emancipation and the *Titanic*'s lifesaving policy entailed a major inconsistency.

True to their integrity (though harmful to their cause), radical suffragettes promptly denounced the *Titanic's* lifesaving policy. Dr. Anna Shaw of Boston was probably the first American woman to denounce it publicly. In England, it was Millicent Murby who, in a speech to the Cambridge University Fabian Society, warned women that they "must consider very carefully whether it is worthwhile to let men assume the entire burden of physical sacrifice in times of danger." If this became widely endorsed, argued Ms. Murby, "it will be difficult to get men to relinquish their heroic ideals."

Less militant suffragettes tried instead to isolate the points making for the inconsistency. Maud Nathan of New York declared it "preposterous . . . to confuse the issue of equal suffrage with the problems of the best methods to insure safety in times of panic, and the immemorial usage of seeking to protect the weak and helpless ahead of the strong." Men wouldn't permit a division of the dilemma, however. Clark McAdams, columnist for the *St. Louis Post-Dispatch,* ruffled and crowed:

"Votes for women!"
Was the cry,
Reaching upward
To the sky.
Crashing glass,
And flashing eye—
"Votes for women!"
Was the cry.

"Boats for women!"
Was the cry.
When the brave
Were come to die.

When the end
Was drawing nigh—
"Boats for women!"
Was the cry.

Women, too, were unable to bifurcate the problem. Mrs. John Martin of the League for the Civic Education of Women noted with concern: "We are willing to let men die for us, but not vote for us." Annie Nathan Meyer, founder of Barnard College, set an example followed by many others in returning her pledge card for a forthcoming public demonstration by suffragettes.

In the midst of this, a rally by antisuffragettes resulted in a campaign for a monument to be built to "the everlasting memory of male chivalry." The fund would be raised exclusively by women—no donations from men. Only a dollar from each would be subscribed, assuring the memorial's standing for a plurality of American women. Two weeks after the disaster, on April 28, the President's wife gave the first dollar toward the memorial and solicited futher donations by appealing to the thrifty-mindedness of American housewives. "I am grateful to do this in gratitude to the chivalry of American manhood," said Nellie Taft, "and I am sure that every woman will feel that the smallness of the contribution will enable her to do the same."

Over 25,000 women sent in dollars. The resulting monument, sculpted by Gertrude Vanderbilt Whitney, was unveiled in Washington, D.C. and can still be seen across from East Potomac Park. It consists of an eighteen-foot classic statue of a half-clad male, his arms outstretched in the form of a cross. This stunning figure is posed on a thirty-foot pedestal on which is engraved homage "to the brave men" of the *Titanic* "who gave their lives that women and children might be saved."

The inscription also records that the monument was "erected by the women of America."

The endorsement of the *Titanic*'s lifesaving policy by a plurality of American women proved to an uncertain nation that male chivalry wasn't quite as passé as supposed. Newspapers rejoiced. And, in spite of the strides suffragettes had made in offering social reasons for the durability of male chivalry, racial explanations were revived. Henry Moy Fot, special agent for the Chinese Merchants' Association, announced that Chinese sailors would have saved the men and children, leaving the women to drown. Whereupon thinking people ascribed male chivalry to Anglo-Saxon genetics. (It was eventually determined to be a property of "northern blood"—something shared "by Kelts, Gauls, and Teutons.")

On May 4, 1912, the suffragettes' demonstration took place on Fifth Avenue in New York, led by women on horseback. Although a first of its kind, even its leaders expressed disappointment. Many potential demonstrators had agreed with Annie Meyer that after "the superb unselfishness and heroism of the men on the *Titanic*," the march was "untimely and pathetically unwise." Out of an anticipated 16,000 women, only 8,000 showed up to take an active part. As Lida Stokes Adams of Philadelphia ruefully noted: "Women passengers of the *Titanic* lost one of the greatest chances ever presented to aid the cause of suffrage when they did not assert themselves and prove they are as courageous as men."

Antisuffragettes took prompt issue with Ms. Adams. It was not the case that women aboard the *Titanic* lacked courage; rather, their courage was to be defined differently from that of men. Janet Barry spelled out the "true" definition of women's courage in an article published in the *New York Evening Telegram:*

> What measure of courage is this that can see the sacrifice of their own for the safety of women and children they may not even know? It is the courage of woman seeing her dear one standing on the sinking deck while her maid huddles in terror at her side. It is the heroism of the woman who would rather see that dear one dead than dishonored.

"Better Death than Dishonor"—was the motto of manhood at the apex of the Age of Romance; and, in 1912, given timely resuscitation by American females.

Although women received the vote in 1920, the more critical issues of woman's independence voiced by the radical suffragettes became submerged in the course of almost continuous male sacrifice during the twentieth-century wars. It seems significant that these older issues did not resurface until the 1960s, when war itself was questioned. At that time, male chivalry was rechristened chauvinism and ascribed to predominantly male motivations. What the *Titanic* disaster revealed is that, when it came to the issue of men bearing the burden of physical risk, male chivalry—or chauvinism—was endorsed equally by the sexes. The issue still provides knotty problems for feminists today.

Although the thrust of women's emancipation was blunted by the disaster, the consciousness of American blacks was raised by it. In 1912, nearly fifty years had passed since the Emancipation Proclamation, but Afro-Americans still lived in a fear-haunted limbo between slavery and freedom. Jim Crow laws guaranteed rampant segregation, and attempts in Congress to outlaw lynching were defeated by Southern determination and Northern apathy.

Given their skein of problems, one wonders what possible significance the loss of the *Titanic* would have held for blacks. The black intelligentsia, in fact, ignored it, a majority of its newspapers failing even to mention the catastrophe. In the ghettoes, however, black response to the disaster was one of enthusiasm—cautious enthusiasm, certainly, but as heartfelt as the burden of their oppression. Just as black heavyweight Jack Johnson had recently trounced the "Great White Hope" in the person of Jim Jeffries, so had inexorable fate sent the white man's "practically unsinkable" ship to the bottom of the sea. Symbolically, the millionaires' lily-white liner was Jeffries on a colossal scale: The Anglo-American Dream had gone down far more dramatically than the Great White Hope, revealing the myth of white superiority and its fallible epicenter, technology, in the most blatant and embarrassing way imaginable.

Blacks found particular satisfaction in the irony of the disaster. Jim Crow laws had guaranteed that no black person would be among those aboard White Star's acme of floating luxury and technological achievement. The consequences were celebrated by Leadbelly in, musically speaking, the best song inspired by the disaster:

> Jack Johnson wanted to get on boa'd;
> Captain Smith hollered, "I ain' haulin' no coal."
> Cryin', "Fare thee, *Titanic*, fare thee well!"
>
> . . .
>
> Black man oughta shout for joy,
> Never lost a girl or either a boy,
> Cryin', "Fare thee, *Titanic*, fare thee well!"

Black interest in the disaster led to other folk songs and one poem—a milestone in black underground literature known as the "*Titanic* Toast." This long narrative poem with dialogue tells the story of Shine, a black stoker aboard the ill-fated ship. When the iceberg is struck, the Toast tells us:

Up jumped Shine from the deck below,
Says, "Captain, captain, you don't know
There's forty feet of water on the boiler room floor."

But E.J. remains confident in the invulnerability of his ship, replying:

"Never mind, Shine, you go on back,
I got forty-eight pumps to keep the water back."

Shine, convinced that the white folks are all crazy, jumps overboard and "begins to swim." When the dire situation is realized on board, a bevy of wealthy and attractive white ladies (social status to black males in 1912) offer Shine money and sexual favors if he will take them with him. Shine refuses, telling one:

"Miss, I know you is pretty and that's quite true,
But there's women on shore can make a ass out a
you."

Shine keeps swimming, eventually reaching New York, and is safe and quite drunk when news of the *Titanic*'s foundering comes ashore.

There are at least fifteen variants of the "*Titanic* Toast" in print and many more uncollected. Carl Sandburg claimed that one version was popular among segregated black soldiers during World War I. Another version toured the South in a minstrel show of the 1920s. Others were sold in the form of broadsides. The "Toast" is still retrievable from blacks to whom it was passed in oral tradition and is currently a subject of interest to scholars of folklore. Bruce Jackson, an authority on the "*Titanic* Toast," observed that its significance is found in Shine's accomplishing his adventures against a foil of whites. Its rejection of white bribes and status symbols is, moreover, unique in the toast literature. Since most blacks in 1912 were seeking emancipation through pleasing and imitating the white man, the "*Titanic* Toast" represents a turning point in black consciousness: Not in the emulation of white values but in their rejection does the Afro-American realize himself. As such, the "*Titanic* Toast" marks a seminal stage in black pride and is a portent of the true course of black freedom in the twentieth century.

Elsewhere in society the effects of the *Titanic* disaster were more subtle. Having been accused of "mass murder," Wall Street moguls soon discovered that comforting homilies and promises would no longer spare the arcane practices of the trusts from public scrutiny and censure. Political chieftains wrestled with a heightened conflict between rhetoric and reality and were eventually forced to choose between representing the plutocracy or the populace. Literature became preoccupied with the themes of lost innocence and, as in Dreiser's *The Titan*, the despair of upward struggle. Theologians did their best to hold onto the Dream insofar as it affected the social gospel, but their efforts disintegrated into a babel of conflicting religious interpretations of the disaster.

There could be no doubt that things had changed, that something had passed by; but it would take many years to know what and how much. In retrospect, we can see that with the foundering of the *Titanic* an era passed that had been spawned by the Second Industrial Revolution—an age of stolid complacency and effulgent materialism. Gone was the national stability that had been maintained by a rigid structure of social caste. Gone was the optimism and smug self-assurance that had been sustained by a dream that technology would materialize heaven on earth. Technology would not restore Eden. Instead, the trials and tribulations of mankind would always be. It was bitter fruit, this loss of innocence, this painful reacquaintance with human limitations. And as Anglo-Americans grappled with it, certainty gave way to doubt; optimism hardened into vigilance.

Whether fortunately or not, the meaning of the disaster would not have to be pondered to its fullest, for the intervention of war spared the English-speaking world from a complete integration of the *Titanic*. In May 1912, the *London Economist* had envisioned the worst: "Imagine the horrors of the *Titanic* multiplied a hundredfold, intensified by the passion of hatred and the suffering of the wounded, and we may achieve a dim picture of the 'inevitable' naval war on which so many armchair Chathams and live-on-shore Nelsons are daily speculating so cheerfully." Three years later, the *Lusitania* went down—another British ship carrying Americans. The rage that had barely been contained over the *Titanic* erupted with a vengeance. This time it was no "Act of God," but an act of "godless Huns," and Britain and America forgot their differences as they rallied against a common enemy. They also forgot the *Titanic*.

Consequently, the meaning of the disaster has been bequeathed to the latter half of the century, where we are far enough to gain a perspective on it, yet close enough to see its relevance to the world of today. Present-day efforts at divining the meaning of the *Titanic* take three different approaches: an obsessive concern with the disaster's mundane mysteries; a romantic glorification of the *Titanic*'s hyperbole; and a near-religious appreciation of her mystique.

The mundane mystery of the *Titanic* will always be: What *really* caused the disaster? Experienced seamen maintain that it was a plain case of negligent navigation, particularly on the part of Captain Edward J. Smith. It was E.J. who neglected to pay sufficient heed to numerous ice warnings, who neglected to reduce the speed of the ship, who neglected to post extra lookouts in the eyes of the ship, and who neglected to inform his officers of the gravity of the situation before they loaded the lifeboats. His was the negligence of following his own experience. There was also the responsibility of the officer of the watch, William M. Murdoch, who, seeing the iceberg virtually upon him, went "against the book" in reversing the engines *and* shifting the helm. His was the negligence of following his own instincts. Negligence arising from such simple misjudgment is paltry gratification indeed, and we have therefore sought evidence of more sinister motives. While scapegoating J. Bruce Ismay may have satisfied American needs for magnitude and definiteness of treachery, it has done so at the expense of credulity.

The inescapable fact is that the *Titanic* duly mirrored her culture. Growth in the size of things had exceeded the rate of accompanying changes in law—a problem Louis Brandeis would call "the curse of bigness"—and the *Titanic* was a fatal manifestation of this problem. Her builders had never proclaimed her "unsinkable," rather it was the work of enthusiastic technical journals and newspapermen who merely acknowledged what the traveling public already believed—or at least wanted to hear. Even E.J.'s remarkable indifference to danger was little more than the complacency of his era. "We are all to blame for the wreck of the *Titanic,*" *Harper's Weekly* boldly stated, "not Captain Smith alone—gallant man—not her owners only, but the dominating spirit of our time, to which each of us contributes his quota of impatience."

In short, what *really* caused the loss of the *Titanic* were the unrecognized weaknesses of her day—hype, haste, and hauteur—all of which are familiar facets of Western civilization today. In 1912, however, self-responsibility for the disaster was painful to see, difficult to grasp, and impossible to accept. It still is. That's where the *Titanic*'s romance comes in.

Bernard Shaw thought he would go mad before understanding the reasons for the "outrageous, romantic lying" inspired by the disaster, but we've since acquired sufficient distance to appreciate them. One must first bear in mind that romantic transformations of the *Titanic* were unavoidable. It was, and still is, impossible to imagine the largest moving object in the world suddenly swallowed by the black abyss and remain dispassionate. It was impossible to be objective about a cruise transformed from Paradise to Chaos in less than three hours. These are more often the elements of fiction than fact. And as Jay Robert Nash has noted, "The sinking of the *Titanic* was the kind of tragedy and drama seldom found even in the best of fiction." Romance over the *Titanic* was therefore inevitable; and its overflow into countless novels, poems, films, and even a "*Titanic* game" has provided a useful medium by which people have been able to approach this monumental disaster.

There is a more crucial reason for the *Titanic*'s romance, however. Anyone who examines the transformations that occur in the *Titanic*'s legends will see simplification and certainty: Her characters become cardboard cutouts, her mistakes the result of determined perfidy, her epoch that of Paradise Lost. Here, complexity is reduced to manageable proportions, but here too responsibility is skirted. In reducing the mistakes of the calamity to the evil of a few, society absolves itself of all culpability. In glorifying her epoch as Paradise Lost, we overlook the means by which that "paradise" was attained.

The pleasures of the Gilded Age existed for the very few. They rested top heavy on a social structure ready to crumble. Luxury and excess were justified on assumptions of limitlessness, both in fuel and in human suffering. This wasn't fulfillment, but the *illusion* of fulfillment wrought by the oppression of the lower echelons of society whose labor materialized it. Nostalgic glorifications of this Age of Security and Splendor automatically condone its grave social injustices; and responsibility for these conditions has yet to be owned completely by Anglo-Americans in the late twentieth century. Although the organization of society is beginning to look more equitable, what we have truly managed to redress is only the tip of the iceberg.

So much for the *Titanic*'s mystery and romance. Between the mystery of the unknowable and the certainty of romance lies her mystique. When the Dream ended in a nightmare, the material world lost its credibility and, for a moment in passing time, myth became reality. The *Titanic*'s mystique is therefore a poetic realm, in which her maiden voyage expresses the blind justice of Greek Tragedy and the allegorical warning of the medieval morality play. Here, the *Titanic* is an eternal symbol: She was, is, and will be. She was the Titans' struggle against Jove, the Babylonians' ziggurat to heaven. She was Lucifer's fall from Grace, the "Night Sea-crossing" of the medieval alchemists, and the moment of truth realized too late by the tragic hero whose aspirations led him fatally beyond his limitations. She is not mere history, but a parable to the effect that the mighty of each age must fall. In a word, she is Hubris.

Almost immediately after the disaster, the *Nation* declared: "Although we sometimes pride ourselves upon a higher moral enlightenment in the interpretation of human affairs than was possessed by an ancient people, it may well be questioned whether the Greek genius was not more equal than ours to a relevant understanding of those tragedies which 'stagger humanity' by their magnitude and unexpectedness. To them, at least, this fearful catastrophe, with all its apparently fortuitous happenings, would have seemed a plain manifestation of Hubris." Indeed, every tragically ironic circumstance would have been held to contribute to the rebuke of overweening pride. For the *Titanic* was the incarnation of man's arrogance in equating size with security; his pride in intellectual (apart from spiritual) mastery; his blindness to the consequences of wasteful extravagance; and his superstitious faith in materialism and technology. What is really alarming, however, is how much these pitfalls still typify the Western—especially the English-speaking—world of today in the Age of Anxiety. As long as this self-same Hubris is with us, the *Titanic* will continue to be not just a haunting memory of the recurrent past but a portent of things to come: a Western apocalypse, perhaps, wherein the world, as Western man has known and shaped it, is undermined from within, not overcome from without; and ends not in holocaust but with a quiet slip into oblivion.

Feuilleton

COLLAPSIBLE "A." the *Titanic*'s most imperiled lifeboat, which Officer Lowe was sure would sink within minutes after he rescued its near-frozen survivors, was discovered miraculously afloat by White Star's *Oceanic* on May 13, 1912. It had drifted for nearly a month at a rate of seven and three-quarters miles per day, still containing three abandoned corpses: a sailor, a fireman, and a first-class gentleman in evening clothes. The passengers of the *Oceanic* lined the rails in awe as crewmen rowed over to "A," sewed up the bodies in canvas for burial at sea, and then capsized the collapsible. The ghoulish incident later inspired one of Rod Serling's best teleplays, "Lone Survivor."

MRS. ALLEN O. BECKER AND HER THREE CHILDREN eventually reached the Midwest where they were later joined by Reverend Becker who, fortunately, had not accompanied them on the *Titanic*. Mrs. Becker died in 1961, Marion in 1944, and Richard in 1975. Ruth attended college, married, and taught elementary school for eighteen years. She now lives in retirement in California.

MR. AND MRS. DICKINSON BISHOP returned to their home town in Michigan, where local jealousy spawned the rumor that it had been Mr. Bishop who had dressed in women's clothes to get into a lifeboat. The Bishops' marriage suffered from the gossip, and they were eventually divorced. Mrs. Bishop died on the same day her ex-husband remarried. Mr. Bishop died in 1961.

JOSEPH G. BOXHALL, the *Titanic*'s fourth officer, stayed with the White Star Line and during the 1930s was the first officer of Cunard-White Star's *Aquitania*. He eventually attained the rank of commander, RNR. It was Boxhall who had determined the *Titanic*'s final position. Years later, in order to support their contention that the *Californian* had been farther from the *Titanic* than that determined, Lordites challenged Boxhall's position, but he adamantly maintained its accuracy. Commander Boxhall died on April 25, 1967, at the age of eighty-three. At his request, his cremated remains were scattered at sea over the position he had defended throughout his later life: Lat. 41°46′ N., Long. 50°14′ W.

THE CARPATHIA served in World War I. On July 17, 1918, she was hit by three torpedoes and foundered about 170 miles from Bishop's Rock.

FREDERICK FLEET, the *Titanic*'s lookout, was coldly ostracized by the surviving senior officers for revealing the absence of binoculars in the *Titanic*'s crow's nest. He spent the next twenty-four years at sea until the depression forced him to take a job in the shipyards of Harland and Wolff. Upon retirement, Fleet sold newspapers on the streetcorners of his native Southampton. On January 10, 1965, two weeks after his wife's death, Fleet hanged himself from a clothes post in the garden of his home. He was seventy-six years old.

MRS. FRANK GOLDSMITH AND FRANK JR.—through the personal attention of the Salvation Army and the financial assistance of various New York charities—were able to reach their relatives in Detroit. Mrs. Goldsmith eventually remarried and died in 1955 while a passenger on a train. Frank J. W. Goldsmith worked for the Air Force and is now retired and lives with his wife in Ohio.

INTERNATIONAL MERCANTILE MARINE (IMM) had never floated well, even before the disaster. Insurance companies and other underwriters had held its bonds, which sold in the United States for far less than replacement value of the property. The giant amalgam had planned to charge off $3,500,000 for 1911 and, with the advent of the "monster ships," raise its surplus account by a million. The fate of the *Titanic* ruined these prospects. With a net loss above all insurance of over $2 million, the disaster set back the surplus to a deficit, and the IMM settled into a slow but steady decline.

P.A.S. Franklin was appointed president of IMM in 1916. For a while, World War I kept the corporation afloat, but thereafter it reached such desperate financial straits that it was forced to put up all its foreign-flag holdings for auction. A European syndicate, headed by Harland and Wolff's Lord Pirrie, offered £27,000,000 for IMM's foreign holdings. The deal was quickly accepted by IMM, but was overturned by President Woodrow Wilson for "reasons of state."

In 1927, the Coolidge administration permitted IMM to sell to British interests the share capital of the White Star Line, which was purchased by the Royal Mail

Steam Packet Company. With its major holdings gone, IMM eventually dissolved. Of all J.P. Morgan's financial ventures, IMM was the one conspicuous failure.

J. BRUCE ISMAY, upon his arrival in England, was immediately called to testify at the British *Titanic* inquiry, where he underwent a grueling examination at the hands of Clement Edwards, who argued that it had been Ismay's "duty" to have gone down with the ship. Concurrently, some of the British press began echoing America's scurrilous attacks on Ismay's character. Although Ismay very much wanted to defend himself publicly, he was dissuaded from doing so by the directors of the White Star Line, who maintained that it wouldn't be good for business. Ismay had given notice of his resignation to the directors of IMM a month before the disaster. In October 1912, he wrote to them expressing his desire to retain at least his chairmanship of the White Star Line. He was summarily refused and, accordingly, gave up both the presidency of IMM and the chairmanship of White Star on June 30, 1913.

Determined to keep himself out of the public eye, Ismay seldom again entered the Liverpool offices of the company his father had founded. He did retain his membership on the boards of various corporations and contributed £10,000 toward the creation of the Mercantile Marine Widows' Fund, an organization compensating wives of British sailors lost at sea. (The fund retroactively helped widows of the *Titanic* disaster.) Thereafter, Ismay retired to a lodge at Costelloe in County Galway, Ireland, and was seldom heard from again. In 1936, owing to diabetic complications, Ismay suffered the amputation of his right leg. Returning to England, he died at the age of seventy-four on October 17, 1937. His wife was often heard to remark, "The *Titanic* disaster almost ruined our lives."

CHARLES H. LIGHTOLLER, the *Titanic*'s second officer, was principal witness and defender of White Star at the British inquiry and at a civil suit that followed. After serving his country in World War I, he returned to the White Star Line until his retirement. Having defended the former chairman of the line, Lightoller suffered by association with Ismay, and the directors of White Star never gave him his own command.

During World War II, Commander Lightoller distinguished himself by taking, with his son, the family's sixty-foot yacht to Dunkirk and rescuing 130 men. The yacht was incredibly crowded and completely unarmed. Bombed and machine-gunned all the way back to Ramsgate, it arrived safely in England only by virtue of Lightoller's superior skill and seamanship. Lightoller died on December 8, 1952, at the age of seventy-eight.

CAPTAIN STANLEY LORD, of the *Californian*, suffered the stigma of a British master who had refused to go to a vessel in distress. Although his certificate was neither revoked or suspended, the owners of the Leyland Line requested his resignation. Lord appealed to the Board of Trade and the Mercantile Marine Service Association to reopen his case, but both declined. Lord abandoned his efforts at the outbreak of World War I. In 1913, he was given a command in the Nitrate Producers' Steam Ship Company Ltd., which he served for the next fourteen years. Due to poor health, he retired from the sea in 1927.

In the 1950s, a renaissance of interest in the *Titanic* brought Lord's role in the tragedy to the forefront again, and he renewed his efforts to have the Board of Trade reopen the "*Californian* incident." This time, the Mercantile Marine Service Association took up his fight and petitioned the Board of Trade, which again refused to hear the case. Captain Lord died on January 25, 1962, at the age of eighty-four. Although a great many people defend his innocence, the preponderance of professional opinion supports the 1912 verdicts of the American and British inquiries.

HAROLD G. LOWE, the *Titanic's* fifth officer, served in the British navy during World War I, attaining the rank of commander. He then returned to his native Deganwy, Wales, where he took an active part in local government. At the outbreak of World War II, he offered his home as a sector post and, even in poor health, carried out his duties conscientiously. Commander Lowe died at the age of sixty-one in May 1944. His remains underwent both a civil funeral and Masonic rites. Although Lowe rarely spoke of the role he played in the *Titanic* disaster, his friends and neighbors grasped the essence of it when they eulogized him as "a man who made up his mind what his duty was and did it regardless of personal consequences."

J.P. MORGAN had cancelled his passage aboard the *Titanic* and was thereby spared the fates of Astor, Widener, Guggenheim, and the other millionaires. Throughout the crisis triggered by the disaster, Morgan's whereabouts were uncertain. An enterprising reporter finally found him isolated in his French château and was granted a brief interview. Asked about the financial loss of the *Titanic*, Morgan replied, "Oh, someone pays, but there is no such thing as money losses in existence. Think of the lives that have been mowed down and of the terrible deaths."

Following the sensation of the Senate's *Titanic* inquiry, a House investigation of the "money trust" (the Pujo committee) gained in momentum and public interest. Morgan was called as chief witness before this committee and was made the prime target of criticism for the top-heavy concentration of economic power in the nation's leading corporations. According to his physician, Dr. M. Allen Starr, Morgan never recovered from the effects of this investigation and died at the age of seventy-six in Rome on March 31, 1913. At the time of his death, his net worth was calculated at $100 million—not nearly as much as everyone had imagined.

THE OLYMPIC was taken back to Harland and Wolff after the disaster and rebuilt at the cost of £250,000. Her double bottom was extended up the sides and her bulkheads raised. After rebuilding, she was able to withstand flooding in six compartments, rendering her impervious to the damage that had sunk the *Titanic*. She returned to service in 1913 and, as the *Titanic*'s sister ship, enjoyed much favor by enthusiastic tourists who vicariously relived aspects of the disaster on her decks: "Isn't this the boat that Ismay left in?" "Isn't this where Mrs. Straus remained with her husband?"

During World War I, the *Olympic* became a troop transport. In May 1918, she was attacked by a U-103. Surprisingly, she turned around, rammed, and sank the U-boat and was promptly dubbed "Old Reliable," a name that stuck. In 1919, she became the first large Atlantic liner to become oil fired.

On May 16, 1934, the *Olympic* accidentally collided with and sank the Nantucket lightship in a dense fog off the New England coast. All seven of the lightship's crew were lost, and the U.S. government sued the White Star Line. Shortly thereafter, the *Olympic* was removed from service. In September 1935, she was sold to the wreckers and broken up. (Parts of her fittings may be found today in London pubs.) Her lifetime was in striking contrast to that of her more elegant sister ship, and one of her commanders called her "the finest ship in my estimation that has ever been built or ever will be."

THEODORE ROOSEVELT was denied the nomination of his party in 1912. Disgruntled Republicans immediately formed the Bull Moose party and made Teddy their standard bearer. Roosevelt's candidacy split the Republican vote, and the Democratic candidate, Woodrow Wilson, easily won the election. TR very early supported America's entrance in World War I and endlessly criticized Wilson's "timidity" in getting the nation involved. When war was finally declared, TR became a ruthless critic of conscientious objectors and "disloyal" German-Americans. After the war, he became a key force in opposition to America's joining the League of Nations. Roosevelt died unexpectedly of a blood clot on January 6, 1919; he was sixty years old. Had he lived longer, he surely would have received the GOP nomination in 1920 and won the election.

CAPTAIN ARTHUR ROSTRON found his star in the ascendant after his heroic rescue of the *Titanic*'s survivors—an adventure he called "the most drastic and memorable night of my career." In 1915 he was given command of Cunard's *Mauretania,* a position he retained until 1926 and during which the "Maurey" established some of her speed records. From 1928–31, he commanded the *Berengaria* and served as commodore of the Cunard fleet. He retired in 1931, wrote his memoirs, and died on November 4, 1940.

WILLIAM ALDEN SMITH, as he had anticipated, easily won reelection to the Senate in 1912. From 1913 to 1919 he continued taking bold stands on behalf of fiscal conservatism and social liberalism. Notable for standing up for the rights of black Americans, he led the Senate in approving the Emancipation Proclamation Exposition, in fighting for the rights of black landowners in the

South, and in blocking a movement that would have barred black women from suffrage under the Nineteenth Amendment. He became ranking member of the Foreign Relations Committee, and was delegated chairman of a select committee to investigate the causes of revolutions in Mexico. One of the unexpected outcomes of his study was his indictment of the corruptive effects on Latin America of United States Dollar Diplomacy, which he pronounced "only for the benefit of Wall Street."

Smith became a vigorous opponent of America's entry into World War I and a bitter critic of Wilson's prewar foreign policy, particularly as it affected Germany. He declared Wilson's partisanship with Britain "obvious" and his neutrality "a sham," and argued that sooner or later Germany would be forced to retaliate, whereupon war would be inevitable. Although Smith intended to run for the Republican nomination for the Presidency in 1916, the nation was growing more conservative and a new hero had arisen in his home state—Henry Ford. When Ford won Michigan's nomination as "favorite son," Smith decided to retire from public life. One of his last projects in the Senate was an investigation of the effects of "lobbying," which he claimed had the potential for undermining the democratic process in American government.

Smith retired from politics in 1919 and returned to Grand Rapids, where he looked forward to going into business with his son, who had just returned from the war. A month after his retirement, Smith suffered a tragic shock when Will Jr., his only child, died of pneumonia contacted during his service as an aviator. The senator was never the same again, growing increasingly isolated and conservative. He continued in business alone, active in the *Grand Rapids Herald* and the Grand

Rapids Savings Bank. He also became a director of the Celotex Company, a concern making insulation board from the refuse of sugar cane.

On October 11, 1932, at the age of seventy-three, William Alden Smith died of a heart attack after making an impassioned speech requesting a second chance for Herbert Hoover. Upon his death, one reporter evaluated his career, saying that Smith had brought to the U.S. Senate "a new type of aggressive honesty and devotion to principle, which was more characteristic of the west than of any other section of the country." Another reporter remembered him as "the friendliest man in Michigan." Today, his name is barely recalled in the state whose faults and virtues he exemplified and whose interests he served so well.

William Howard Taft left the White House in 1913, more pleased at TR's defeat than saddened at his own. For eight years Taft served as professor of constitutional law at Yale University and president of the American Bar Association. In 1921, he was appointed Chief Justice of the United States Supreme Court, a position he had always wanted and for which he was ideally suited. In his later years, he cheerily observed, "I don't remember that I ever was President." He died at the age of seventy-two on March 8, 1930; and along with John F. Kennedy is the only President buried in Arlington National Cemetery.

The Titanic rests on the bottom of the North Atlantic, somewhere in the region of 41°46′N.,50°14′W. Oceanographers have determined that she sank at the rate of twelve miles per hour, that her superstructure was shattered by the impact of hitting bottom, and that she most likely lies on her side. She reposes at a depth of 2,000 fathoms, where the pressure is two tons to the square inch. This would have crushed any air-filled, nonporous receptacles like tissue paper; while eggs, with their porous shells, would have withstood the pressure and still be edible, though salty, today. The salinity at the depth where she lies is less than that of surface water, but she still would have rusted considerably. No plant life would have attacked her, but animals would have ravaged much of her wooden components, which also would have been compressed somewhat by time and the tremendous pressure. Her astounding headstand before she foundered would have rendered her internal fixtures an unholy mass of twisted metal and unrecognizable debris. She lies today, as Filson Young speculated in 1912, not like a "great seagoing town," but as the "ruins of the material of which the town and ship were made."

Ever since Merritt and Chapman were consulted by the Astor, Widener, and Guggenheim families in 1912, there have been numerous schemes—using everything from Ping-Pong balls to helium balloons—to raise the *Titanic*. The most ambitious plan came in 1968 from a firm called *Titanic* Salvage Ltd. The architect of the project was an Englishman, Doug Woolley, who bought up all the salvage claims on the ship and who proposed raising her from her two-mile abyss by means of containers attachable to the hull that would electrolyze seawater into hydrogen. Woolley maintained that "the technical know-how" for raising the *Titanic* existed in fragments all over the world; all that was necessary was for someone to bring the pieces of technology together "like a jigsaw." Woolley was unable to subscribe the $300 million necessary even to consider the venture.

In 1977, *Science* magazine reported a new endeavor, a project not to raise the ship but merely to locate and photograph it. *Science* related that Big Events, a California-based organization, was consulting the Woods Hole Oceanographic Institute of Massachusetts.

Robert Ballard, head of Woods Hole's diving expeditions, admitted that the proposal was receiving serious consideration. "Eighty percent of the technology for finding the *Titanic* exists somewhere," Ballard said. "We'd be interested in integrating it."

Since then, the project has acquired an international appeal, and a major thrust to the venture has come from the National Geographic Society and a consortium of European television broadcasters headed by the BBC. The project directors intend to lower an array of advanced undersea cameras from a surface ship. Film tests have already been made in the vicinity of the wreck, and a spokesman for the National Geographic Society reports "fine visibility." It is possible that we could see the first photographs of the wreck of the *Titanic* by 1980.

CARR VAN ANDA, managing editor of *The New York Times*, lived long enough to see the *Times* become the world's leading newspaper—an achievement due in no small way to his ingenious enterprise in reporting the *Titanic* story. Owing to ill health, Van Anda left the *Times* in 1925, but continued in a consulting capacity and retained the title of managing editor until his retirement in 1932.

An amateur Egyptologist, Van Anda created a sensation when he translated the hieroglyphics of King Tut's tomb from photographs of the inner chambers sent over from the Carnarvon expedition. He also did much to popularize Einstein's theory of relativity by lucidly explaining it to the layman. In his last years, Van Anda was preoccupied with theories on the origin of the solar system. He died in New York on January 28, 1945.

THE WHITE STAR LINE, having been returned to British interests in 1927, had expected to resume competition with its old rival, Cunard. In early 1934, however, Chancellor of the Exchequer Neville Chamberlain informed Parliament that, owing to world depression (particularly in the United States), both shipping companies were in serious financial difficulty. The British government offered to advance the two companies a sum of £9,500,000, providing they merge into a single organization. This they did, with Cunard holding 62 percent of the shares and White Star 38 percent. For thirteen years, Cunard-White Star Ltd. flew double house-flags from the masts of their ships. In 1947, Cunard bought the balance of White Star's shares and liquidated most of its shipping and material holdings. By January 1, 1950, the White Star Line—celebrated for its creation of the fabulous *Titanic*—had ceased to exist.

Bibliography

PRIMARY SOURCES

ROOSEVELT, THEODORE

1. Library of Congress, Manuscript Division; Washington, D.C.: *The Presidential Papers of Theodore Roosevelt*
2. William Clements Library, University of Michigan; Ann Arbor, Michigan: *Theodore Roosevelt Papers*

SMITH, WILLIAM ALDEN

1. Archives and Historical Collections, Michigan State University; East Lansing, Michigan: *William Carpenter Collection, Ransom E. Olds Collection*
2. Clarke Historical Library, Central Michigan University; Mount Pleasant, Michigan: *William Alden Smith's Washington Guestbook*

3. Grand Rapids Public Museum; Grand Rapids, Michigan: *Clippings in Regard to Hon. William Alden Smith* (letters and clippings, 1913–15)
4. Michigan Historical Collections, Bentley Historical Library, University of Michigan; Ann Arbor, Michigan: *Junius Beal Collection, George Booth Collection, Marshall Cook Collection, Chase Osborn Collection* (Box 33), *John T. Rich Collection.*
5. Michigan Room, Grand Rapids Public Library; Grand Rapids, Michigan: *William Alden Smith Letters,* Volumes 1–4, *William Alden Smith Scrapbooks* (letters, clippings, memoranda), Volumes 1–8
6. William Clements Library, University of Michigan; Ann Arbor, Michigan: *Russell Alger Papers*

TAFT, WILLIAM HOWARD

Library of Congress, Manuscript Division: Washington D.C.: *The Presidential Papers of William Howard Taft*

TITANIC, ROYAL MAIL STEAMSHIP

1. Library of Congress, Manuscript Division; Washington, D.C.: *Taft Papers:* Case File #3175 ("Titanic"), Case File #303 (Archie Butt)
2. Sterling Memorial Library, Yale University; New Haven, Connecticut: *Francis G. Newlands Collection*
3. Titanic Historical Society, Inc.; Indian Orchard, Massachusetts: *THS Archives:* Letters and memoranda regarding Joseph Boxhall,

Frederick Fleet, Mrs. Sylvia Lightoller, and Harold G. Lowe

Remember the Titanic: Tape-recorded transcript of the tenth anniversary of the Titanic Enthusiasts of America, including interviews with survivors

4. Unpublished Manuscripts:
Blanchard, Ruth M. "The Titanic Disaster," 1977. Courtesy of the author.
Goldsmith, Frank J.W. "Honor Him," n.d. Courtesy of the author.
Wennerstrom, August E. "The Titanic," Promptbook for a Speech, n.d. Courtesy of the author's descendants.

DOCUMENTS

Great Britain, *Parliamentary Debates* (Commons), 5th ser., 37–42, 15 April–25 October 1912.

U.S. Congress, House, *Free and Efficient Seamen,* 62d Cong., 2d sess., 2 May 1912 and 22 May 1912, H. Rept. 645, pts. 1 and 2 (#6131), 21 pp.

U.S. Congress, House, *Inspection of Steam Vessels,* 62d Cong., 2d sess., 4 May 1912, H. Rept. 657 (#6131), 8 pp.

U.S. Congress, House, *Regulation of Radio Communication,* 62d Cong., 2d sess., 20 April 1912, H. Rept. 582 (#6131), 21 pp.

U.S. Congress, House, *Routes for Trans-Atlantic Steamships,* 62d Cong., 2d sess., 20 April 1912, H. Rept. 580 (#6131), 4 pp.

U.S. Congress, House and Senate, Congressional Record, 54th–63rd Cong., 1896–1915, 28–52.

U.S. Congress, Senate, Congressional Record, 62d Cong., 2d sess., 1912, 48, pts. 5–12.

U.S. Congress, Senate, *Hearings of a Subcommittee of the Senate Commerce Committee pursuant to S. Res. 283, to Investigate the Causes leading to the Wreck of the White Star liner 'Titanic,'* 62d Cong., 2d sess., 1912, S. Doc. 726 (#6167), 1163 pp.

U.S. Congress, Senate, *International Conference on Safety of Life at Sea*, 63rd Cong., 2d sess., 1914, S. Doc, 463 (#6594), 142 pp.

U.S. Congress, Senate, *Loss of the Steamship 'Titanic': Report of a Formal Investigation . . . as conducted by the British Government, Presented by Mr. Smith*, 62d Cong., 2d sess., 20 August 1912, S. Doc. 933 (#6179), 88 pp.

U.S. Congress, Senate, *Report of the Senate Committee on commerce pursuant to S. Res. 283, Directing the Committee to Investigate the Causes of the Sinking of the 'Titanic,' with speeches by William Alden Smith and Isidor Rayner*, 62d Cong., 2d sess., 28 May 1912, S. Rept. 806 (#6127), 92 pp.

U.S. Congress, Senate, *Safety of Life at Sea: Analysis and Explanatory Notes of the London Convention on Safety of Life at Sea in relation to the American Merchant Marine, Prepared by Andrew Furuseth*, 63rd Cong., 2d sess., 1 May 1914, S. Doc. 476 (#6594), 16 pp.

U.S. Congress, Senate, *Speech in the Senate on May 28, 1912 presented by Mr. Guggenheim*, 62d Cong., 2d sess., 15 June 1912, S. Doc. 850 (#6178), 39 pp.

U.S. Navy Department, "Report of the Hydrographer." In *Annual Reports of the Navy Department*, Appendix 3, pp. 193–208. Washington, D.C.: Government Printing Office, 1913.

TECHNICAL JOURNALS

"Belfast." *The Shipbuilder* (April 1912): 244–45.
"The British and the American *Titanic* Investigations." *Engineering News* 68 (15 August 1912): 308.
"*Carpathia's* Crew Honored." *Power* 35 (11 June 1912): 855–56.
"Did the *Titanic* Sink to the Bottom?" *Scientific American* 106 (27 April 1912): 374.
"The Disaster to the *Titanic.*" *Electrical World* 59 (27 April 1912): 879–80.
"Electrical Lifts on the *Olympic* and *Titanic.*" *The Engineer* 109 (24 June 1910): 640.
"Final Reports of *Titanic* Inquiries in America and England." *International Marine Engineering* 17 (September 1912): 372–76.
"Foundering of the *Titanic.*" *International Marine Engineering* 17 (May 1912): 198–200.
"Harland and Wolff's Works at Belfast." *Engineering* 94 (5 July 1912): 3–12, Continued (12 July 1912): 38–50.
"Helical Gears for Steering Apparatus of the New White Star Liners." *The Engineer* 110 (21 October 1910): 445.
"High Speed through the Ice Fields." *Scientific American* 171 (6 July 1912): 2.
"Icebergs and their Location in Navigation," A Review of Studies by Dr. Howard T. Barnes, McGill University. *Engineering* 93 (7 June 1912): 774–75.
"The Launch of the *Titanic,*" *The Engineer* 111 (2 June 1911): 575.
"Launch of *Titanic.*" *International Marine Engineering* 16 (July 1911): 281–83.
"The Lessons of the *Titanic* Disaster." *Engineering* 93 (26 April 1912): 566–67.

"Loss of the Steamship *Titanic*." *Marine Review* 42 (May 1912): 156–160.

"Monster Ships." *Engineering News* 65 (12 January 1911): 47.

"The *Olympic* and the *Titanic*—Two Giant Ocean Steamships." *Scientific American*, Supplement #1850 (17 June 1911): 380–83.

"The *Olympic* and *Titanic*." *The Engineer* 111 (3 March 1911): 209–15.

"*Olympic* and *Titanic*." *The Shipbuilder* 6, Special Number (Midsummer 1911).

"*Olympic* and *Titanic*. Ocean Giants." *Power* 34 (11 July 1911): 44–47.

"The Senate Committee's Report on the *Titanic*" and "Shortcomings of Wireless at Sea." *Scientific American* 106 (8 July 1912): 510.

"Ship Construction Bill." *Marine Review* 42 (June 1912): 202–3.

"The *Titanic* Investigation Report." *Engineering Magazine* 43 (August 1912): 767–69.

"The *Titanic* Inquiry." *Engineering* 93 (14 June 1912): 802–6, Continued (21 June 1912): 847–50.

"*Titanic*'s Rescued Firemen." *Power* 35 (30 April 1912): 642.

"The White Star Line." *The Engineer* 109, Supplement (24 June 1910).

"The White Star Liner *Olympic*." *Engineering* 90 (21 October 1910): 564–72, Continued (4 November 1910): 620–21, Continued (18 November 1910): 693–95.

"The White Star Liner *Titanic*." *Engineering* 91 (26 May 1911): 678–81.

"White Star Liners *Olympic* and *Titanic*." *The Engineer* 109 (4 March 1910): 231.

"The Wreck of the *Titanic*: Its Effect on Transatlantic

Steamship Routes." *Engineering News* 67 (25 April 1912): 805–6.

NEWSPAPERS

Ann Arbor Daily Times News
Atlanta Constitution
Baltimore Sun
Battle Creek Enquirer
Benton Harbor (MI.) *News-Palladium*
Boston American
Boston Globe
Boston Post
Chicago Daily News
Chicago Evening Post
Chicago Record-Herald
Chicago Tribune
Cleveland Plain Dealer
Des Moines Register and Leader
Detroit Free Press
Detroit News
Detroit Times
Dowagiac (MI.) *Daily News*
Edinburgh Review
Flint (MI.) *Daily Journal*
Grand Rapids Evening Press
Grand Rapids Herald
Grand Rapids News
Jackson (MI.) *Daily Citizen*
Kalamazoo Telegraph-Press
Kansas City Star
Lansing State Journal
London Daily Express
London Daily Mail
London Globe
London Morning Post

London Standard
London Times
Los Angeles Tribune
Miami Herald
Milwaukee Journal
Muskegon (MI.) *News-Chronicle*
New York American
New York Evening Mail
New York Evening Post
New York Evening Telegram
New York Gaelic-American
New York Herald
New York Irish World and American Industrial Liberator
New York Journal
New York Press
New York Sun
The New York Times
New York Tribune
New York World
Philadephia North American
Philadelphia Press
Pittsburgh Gazette-Times
Portland Oregonian
St. Louis Post-Dispatch
San Francisco Examiner
Sault Ste. Marie Evening News
Seattle Daily Times
South Bend Tribune
Springfield Republican
Toronto Globe
The Wall Street Journal
Washington Evening Star
Washington Herald
Washington Post
Worcester Evening Gazette

SELECTED SECONDARY SOURCES

AMERICAN POLITICS

Anderson, Donald F. *William Howard Taft: A Conservative's Conception of the Presidency.* Ithaca, New York: Cornell University Press, 1973.

Bolles, Blair. *Tyrant from Illinois: Uncle Joe Cannon's Experiment with Personal Power.* New York: W.W. Norton, 1951.

Bowers, Claude G. *Beveridge and the Progressive Era.* New York: Literary Guild, 1932.

Brandeis, Louis D. *The Curse of Bigness.* Edited by Osmond K. Fraenkel and Clarence M. Lewis. Port Washington, New York: Kennikat Press, 1965.

Butt, Archibald. *The Letters of Archie Butt.* Edited by Lawrence F. Abbott. Garden City, New York: Doubleday Page & Co., 1924.

———. *Taft and Roosevelt: The Intimate Letters of Archie Butt.* 2 vols. Garden City, New York: Doubleday, Doran & Co., 1930.

Campbell, John P. "Taft, Roosevelt, and the Arbitration Treaty of 1911." *Journal of American History* 53 (September 1966): 279–97.

Coletta, Paolo E. *The Presidency of William Howard Taft.* Lawrence, Kansas: University Press of Kansas, 1973

Crissey, Forrest. *Theodore E. Burton.* New York: World Publishing Co., 1956.

Cullom, Shelby M. *Fifty Years of Public Service.* Chicago: A.C. McClurg & Co., 1911.

Darling, Arthur B., ed. *The Public Papers of Francis G. Newlands.* 2 vols. Boston: Houghton Mifflin, 1932.

Fisher, H.A.L. *James Bryce.* 2 vols. New York: Macmillan Co., 1927.

Gaynor, William J. *Mayor Gaynor's Letters and*

Speeches. New York: Greaves Publishing Co., 1913.

Hechler, Kenneth W. *Insurgency: Personalities and Politics of the Taft Era.* New York: Russell & Russell, 1964.

Heindel, Richard H. *The American Impact on Great Britain.* Philadelphia: Univeristy of Pennsylvania Press, 1940.

Ions, Edmund. *James Bryce and American Diplomacy, 1870–1922.* London: Macmillan, 1968.

Jaffray, Elizabeth. *Secrets of the White House.* New York: Cosmopolitan Book Corp., 1927.

Kelly, Frank K. *The Fight for the White House: The Story of 1912.* New York: Thomas Y. Crowell, 1961.

Phillips, David Graham. "The Treason of the Senate." *Cosmopolitan Magazine* 40 (March 1906). Stanford, California: Academic Reprints, n.d.

Wiebe, Robert H. *The Search for Order: 1877–1920.* New York: Hill and Wang, 1967.

MARITIME HISTORY AND LAW

Albion, Robert G. *Five Centuries of Famous Ships.* New York: McGraw-Hill, 1978.

Anderson, Roy, *White Star.* Prescot, Lancashire: T. Stephenson & Sons, 1964.

Armstrong, Warren, *Atlantic Highway.* New York: John Day, 1961.

Babcock, F. Lawrence. *Spanning the Atlantic.* New York: Alfred A. Knopf, 1931.

Barnaby, K.C. *Some Ship Disasters and their Causes.* New York: A.S. Barnes & Co., 1970.

Bisset, James. *Tramps and Ladies.* New York: Criterion Books. 1959.

Bowditch, Nathaniel. *American Practical Navigator.*

Washington, D.C.: Government Printing Office, n.d.

Brinnin, John Malcolm. *The Sway of the Grand Saloon.* New York: Delacorte Press, 1971.

Brown, Alexander Crosby. *Women and Children Last: The Loss of the Steamship Arctic.* New York: G.P. Putnam, 1961.

Chatterton, E. Kemble. *The Mercantile Marine.* Boston: Little, Brown & Co., 1923.

Dugan, James. *The Great Iron Ship.* London: Hamish Hamilton, 1953.

Floherty, John T. *White Terror: Adventures with the Ice Patrol.* Philadelphia: J.B. Lippincott, 1947.

Gibbs, C.R. Vernon. *Passenger Liners of the Western Ocean.* London: Staples Press, 1952.

Hoehing, A.A. *Great Ship Disasters.* Chicago: Cowles Book Co., 1971.

Hohman, Elmo P. *History of American Merchant Seamen.* Hamden, Ct.: Shoe String Press, 1956.

Knight, Austin M. *Modern Seamanship.* New York: D. Van Nostrand Co., 1910.

McFee, William. *The Law of the Sea.* Philadelphia: J. B. Lippincott Co., 1950.

Maxtone-Graham, John. *The Only Way to Cross.* New York: Macmillan, 1972.

Mielke, Otto. *Disaster at Sea.* New York: Fleet Publishing Corp., 1958.

Newell, Gordon. *Ocean Liners of the Twentieth Century.* Seattle: Superior Publishing Co., 1963.

Phillips-Birt, Douglas. *A History of Seamanship.* London: George Allen & Unwin Ltd., 1971.

Reiff, Henry. *The United States and the Treaty Law of the Sea.* Minneapolis: University of Minnesota Press, 1959.

Rideing, William H. "Safety on the Atlantic." In *Ocean Steamships,* pp. 185–216. New York:

Charles Scribner's Sons, 1891. [See "The Region of Ice," 197–203.]
Zeis, P. M. *American Shipping Policy.* Princeton: Princeton University Press, 1938.

THE MEDIA

Baker, W.J. *A History of the Marconi Company.* London: Methuen & Co., 1970.
Berger, Meyer. *The Story of the New York Times.* New York: Simon and Schuster, 1951.
Codding, George A. *The International Telecommunication Union.* Leiden: E.J. Brill, 1952.
Fine, Barnett. *A Giant of the Press: Carr Van Anda.* Oakland, Ca.: Acme Books, 1968.
Greene, Laurence, *America Goes to Press.* London: George G. Harrap, 1936.
Lyons, Louis M. *Newspaper Story.* Cambridge, Mass.: Belknap Press, 1971.
Sarnoff, David, as told to Mary Margaret McBride. "Radio." *Saturday Evening Post,* 7 August 1926.
Weeks, Edward, *The Open Heart.* Boston: Little, Brown & Co., 1955.

PERSONALITIES

Dunlap, Orrin. *Marconi: The Man and his Wireless.* New York: Macmillan, 1937.
Garraty, John A. *Right-hand Man: The Life of George W. Perkins.* New York: Harper & Bros., 1960.
Hovey, Carl. *The Life Story of J. Pierpont Morgan.* London: William Heinemann, 1912.
Howe, Mark A.D. *George von Lengerke Meyer: His Life and Public Services.* New York: Dodd, Mead & Co., 1919.
Lyons, Eugene. *David Sarnoff.* New York: Harper & Row, 1966.

Manners, William. *TR and Will.* New York: Harcourt, Brace, & World, 1969.

Marconi, Degna. *My Father, Marconi.* New York: McGraw-Hill, 1962.

Satterlee, Herbert. *J. Pierpont Morgan: An Intimate Portrait.* New York: Macmillan, 1940.

WILLIAM ALDEN SMITH

———. *The Nomination of a Senator.* Grand Rapids: Bender & Brewer, 1907.

———. "Notes from the Capital: William Alden Smith." *The Nation,* 11 May 1916, pp. 513–14.

———. "Senator William Alden Smith." *The Independent,* 1909, pp. 133–34.

———. "William Alden Smith." In *A History of the Republican Party.* vol. 2, pp. 360–62. Detroit: William Livingstone, 1900.

Dunn, Arthur W. "From Newsboy to Congress." *Leslie's Weekly,* 28 June 1906, p. 622.

Goss, Dwight. "William Alden Smith." In *A History of Grand Rapids,* pp. 801–2. Chicago: C.F. Cooper, 1906.

Graves, John Temple. "From Newsboy to the Senate." *Cosmopolitan,* October 1914, pp. 631–33.

Moore, Charles. "William Alden Smith." In *A History of Michigan.* vol. 4, pp. 1978–80. Chicago: Lewis Publishing Co., 1915.

Reed, George I., ed. "William Alden Smith." In *Bench and Bar of Michigan,* pp. 171–73. Chicago: Century Publishing Co., 1897.

Sarasohn, Stephen B., and Sarasohn, Vera H. *Political Party Patterns in Michigan.* Detroit: Wayne State University Press, 1957.

Smith, Beverly. "Grand Rapids Boy Makes Good." *American Magazine,* January 1938, p. 23.

Sparks, Frank M. "William Alden Smith." In *Men Who Have Made Michigan*, edited by E.G. Pipp, pp. 8–9. Detroit: Pipp's Magazine, 1928.

Thompson, Charles W. "The Stampedes of William Alden Smith." In *Party Leaders of the Time*, pp. 205–13. New York: G.W. Dillingham Co., 1906.

Vandenberg, Arthur. "What One Man Thinks of William Alden Smith." Pamphlet reproduced from the Detroit *Saturday Night* and printed under the Auspices of the Lincoln Club and the Young Men's Republican Club of Grand Rapids, 1912.

Warner, Robert M. "Chase S. Osborn and the Progressive Movement." Ph.D. dissertation, University of Michigan, 1957.

SOCIETY

Abrahams, Roger D. *Deep Down in the Jungle*. Chicago: Aldine, 1970.

Adams, Henry. *The Letters of Henry Adams (1892–1918)*. Edited by Worthington C. Ford. Boston: Houghton Mifflin Co., 1938.

Aptheker, Herbert, ed. *The Correspondence of W. E. B. DuBois.* vol. 1. Amherst: University of Massachusetts Press, 1973.

Churchill Winston S. *The World Crisis.* New York: Charles Scribner's Sons, 1949.

Des Pres, Terrence. "Survivors and the Will to Bear Witness." *Social Research* 40 (1973): 668–90.

Dreiser, Theodore. *A Traveller at Forty.* New York: The Century Co., [1913] 1920.

Festinger, Leon; Riecker, Henry W.; and Schacter, Stanley. *When Prophecy Fails.* Minneapolis: University of Minnesota Press, 1956.

Gelman, Woody, and Jackson, Barbara. *Disaster Illustrated.* New York: Harmony Books, 1976.

Gilmore, Al-Tony. *Bad Nigger! The National Impact of Jack Johnson.* Port Washington, New York: Kennikat Press, 1975.

Grosser, George H.; Greenblatt, Milton; and Wechsler, Henry, eds. *The Threat of Impending Disaster—Contributions to the Psychology of Stress.* Cambridge: M.I.T. Press, 1964.

Hubbard, Elbert. "A New Religion." *Cosmopolitan,* June 1912, pp. 2–3.

Jackson, Holbrook. *The Eighteen-Nineties.* New York: Capricorn Books, [1913] 1966.

Kartman, Ben, and Brown, Leonard, eds. *Disaster!* New York: Pellegrine & Cudahy, 1948.

Lomax, John, and Lomax, Alan. *Negro Folk-songs as Sung by Leadbelly.* New York: Macmillan, 1936.

May, Henry F. *The End of American Innocence.* New York: Alfred A. Knopf, 1959.

Nash, Jay Robert. *Darkest Hours.* Chicago: Nelson-Hall, 1976.

Rabkin, L.Y. "Survivor Themes in the Supervision of Psychotherapy." *American Journal of Psychotherapy* 30 (1976): 593–600.

Sorokin, Pitirim A. *Man and Society in Calamity.* New York: E.P. Dutton, 1942.

Valentine, Alan. *1913: America Between Two Worlds.* New York: Macmillan, 1962.

Wolfenstein, Martha. *Disaster: A Psychological Essay.* Glencoe, Illinois: The Free Press, 1957.

R.M.S. TITANIC

———. "The Lesson of the Lifeboats." *Outlook,* 27 April 1912, pp. 884–86.

———. "The Monster Ship." *The Economist.* Reprinted in *Living Age,* 18 May 1912, pp. 444–47.

———. "*Titanic*'s Gus 'The Cat' Cohen Lives On." *Titanic Commutator* (Official Journal of the Titanic Historical Society), Fall 1978, 11 pp.

Baarslag, Karl. *SOS to the Rescue.* New York: Oxford University Press, 1935.

Baldwin, Hanson W. "R.M.S. *Titanic,*" *Harper's,* January 1934, pp. 170–79.

Beesley, Lawrence. *The Loss of the SS Titanic.* Boston: Houghton Mifflin, 1912.

Bellairs, Carlyon. "The *Titanic* Diaster." *Contemporary Review,* 1912, pp. 788–97.

Biles, J.H. "The Loss of the *Titanic.*" *The Engineer* 113 (19 April 1912): 409–10.

Candee, Helen Churchill. "Sealed Orders." *Colliers,* 4 May 1912, pp. 10 ff.

Carmichael, Colin. "Was *Titanic* 'Unsafe at Any Speed'?" *Steamboat Bill* (Official Journal of the Steamship Historical Society of America), Spring 1972, pp. 5–9.

Carrothers, John C. "Lord of the *Californian.*" *United States Naval Institute Proceedings* 94 (March 1968): 58–71. [See commentary by Carroll E.B. Peeke, John P. Eaton, and Roy C. Smith. (June 1968): 109–11; and by Walter Lord. (August 1968): 112–14.]

———. "The *Titanic* Disaster." *United States Naval Institute Proceedings* 88 (April 1962): 57–69.

Coit, Stanton. "The Rescued—By an Eye-witness on the *Carpathia.*" *Outlook,* 27 April 1912, pp. 894–95.

Collyer, Charlotte, "How I was Saved from the *Titanic.*" *Semi-Monthly Magazine* (Washington *Post*), 26 May 1912, pp. 3–4 ff.

Conrad, Joseph. "Some Aspects of the Admirable Inquiry." *The English Review* II (1912): 581–95.

———. "Some Reflexions, Seamanlike and Otherwise, on the Loss of the *Titanic." The English Review* II (1912): 304–15.

Culliton, Barbara J. "Woods Hole Mulls *Titanic* Expedition." *Science* 197 (26 August 1977): 848–49.

Dodge, Washington. *The Loss of the Titanic.* Riverside, Ct.: 7 C's Press, [1912].

Dudley, Brian A. "The Construction of *Titanic." Steamboat Bill,* Spring 1972, pp. 10 ff.

Duff Gordon, Lady Cosmo. "I was Saved from the *Titanic." Coronet,* June 1951, pp. 94–97.

Everett, Marshall, ed. *Wreck and Sinking of the Titanic.* L.H. Walter, 1912.

Fowler, Gene. "The Unsinkable Mrs. Brown." *Coronet,* October 1949, pp. 116–21.

Gracie, Archibald. "Out of the Wreck." *Outlook,* 27 April 1912, pp. 895–97.

———. *The Truth About the Titanic.* New York: M. Kennerley, 1913.

Greenspan, Bud. "Deaf to Disaster." *Coronet,* May 1953, p. 31.

Griffin, Henry F. "Sixteen Boats and a Quiet Sea." *Outlook,* 27 April 1912, 898–905.

Heinl, Robert D. "How Shall We Further Safeguard Ocean Travel?" *Leslie's Weekly,* 4 July 1912, p. 752.

Hobson, Richmond P. "Sea-borne Traffic and the *Titanic* Disaster." *Engineering Magazine* 43 (June 1912): 329–40.

Hudson, Derek. "SOS *Titanic."* In *Saturday Book,* edited by John Hadfield, pp. 73–80. London: Macmillan, 1952.

Jackson, Bruce. "The *Titanic* Toast." In *Veins of Humor,* edited by Harry Levin, pp. 205–23. Cambridge: Harvard University Press, 1972.

Kamuda, Edward S. "Reflections of a Disaster." *Titanic Commutator,* April 1974, 4 pp.

Kennedy, C., and Prentice, S., eds. "A Night Still Remembered: Checking in with a Last Survivor." *MacCleans Magazine,* 23 January 1978, pp. 38–39.

Lightoller, Charles H. "Testimonies from the Field." *Christian Science Journal,* October 1912, 2 pp.

———. *Titanic and Other Ships.* London: Ivor Nicholson and Watson, 1935.

Lord, Walter. "Maiden Voyage." *American Heritage,* December 1955, pp. 46–53 ff.

———. *A Night to Remember.* New York: Holt, Rinehard & Winston, 1955.

Marcus, Geoffrey. *The Maiden Voyage.* New York: Viking Press, 1969.

Marshall, Logan. *Sinking of the Titanic and Great Sea Disasters.* Philadelphia: John C. Winston Co., 1912.

Meyer, George von L. "Safety at Sea." *North American Review* 195 (1912): 744–47.

Mizner, Wilson. "You're Dead" (fiction). In *Stories for Men,* edited by Charles Grayson. New York: Garden City Publishing Co., 1938.

Mowbray, Jay H. *Sinking of the Titanic.* Harrisburg, Pa: The Minter Co., 1912.

Neil, Henry. *Wreck and Sinking of the Titanic.* Chicago: Homewood Press, 1912.

Nevinson, H.W. "On the Ocean Wave" (fiction). In *In the Dark Backward,* pp. 243–53. New York: Harcourt & Brace, 1934.

Oldham, Wilton J. *The Ismay Line.* Liverpool: The Journal of Commerce, 1961.

Padfield, Peter. *The Titanic and the Californian.* New York: John Day Co., 1965.

Prechtl, Robert. *Titanic* (fiction). New York: E.P. Dutton & Co., 1940.

Root, E. Merrill. *Of Perilous Seas* (poetry). Francestown, N.H.: Golden Quill Press, 1964.

Rostron, Arthur H. "The Rescue of the 'Titanic' Survivors." *Scribners Monthly*, March 1913, pp. 354–64.

Russell, Thomas H. *Sinking of the Titanic.* Chicago: Homewood Press, 1912.

Thayer, John B. *The Sinking of the S.S. Titanic.* Riverside, Ct.: 7 C's Press, [1940] 1974.

Warchol, Clara B. "Mrs. Chris Christensen, She Survived the *Titanic* Horror." *Titanic Commutator*, December 1976, p. 25.

Weeks, Jack. "*Titanic.*" *Holiday*, June 1953, pp. 91–94.

Winocour, Jack, ed. *The Story of the Titanic as told by its Survivors.* New York: Dover Publications, Inc., 1960.

Wood, W.J. "Construction of the *Titanic.*" *The Marine Review* 42 (May 1912): 160–62.

Young, Filson. "God and Titan." *Saturday Review* (London), 20 April 1912, p. 490.

———. "A Sea Birth." *Saturday Review* (London), 27 April 1912, pp. 520–21.

Index